FENVELDAS

EMPTY IDEAS

A Critique of Analytic Philosophy

Peter Unger

OXFORD

UNIVERSITY PRESS

OXFORD
UNIVERSITY PRESS

Oxford University Press is a department of the University of Oxford. It furthers
the University's objective of excellence in research, scholarship, and education
by publishing worldwide. Oxford is a registered trade mark of Oxford University
Press in the UK and certain other countries.

Published in the United States of America by Oxford University Press
198 Madison Avenue, New York, NY 10016, United States of America.

First issued as an Oxford University Press paperback, 2017

Library of Congress Cataloging-in-Publication Data
Unger, Peter K.
Empty ideas : a critique of analytic philosophy / Peter Unger.
pages cm
ISBN 978-0-19-933081-2 (hardback : alk. paper); 978-0-19-069601-6 (paperback : alk. paper)
1. Reality.   2. Substance (Philosophy)   3. Matter—Philosophy.
4. Analysis (Philosophy)   I. Title.
BD331.U49   2014
110—dc23   2013042262

For three younger Ungers,

My son, Andrew, my daughter-in-law, Nishi, and, by
far the youngest, their son, Cole, my grandson

CONTENTS

ACKNOWLEDGMENTS

Eight years in the writing, various earlier versions of the present work each had a different number of chapters, as well as differing in other ways. This makes it impossible to thank people in a perfectly accurately way, and hard to do so in even a pretty accurate way. But, I shall try to do the latter, lesser thing, even if I misrepresent, to some degree, the help others have given me.

Years ago, several people commented most helpfully on much of what has become chapters 1 and 2 of this book, saliently including John Carroll, Don Garrett, Alan Sidelle, and David Chalmers. I now gratefully thank them.

During the summer of 2012, three young philosophers read through chapters 1 through 8 of the book, providing me with much helpful input. For that, I am happy to thank Katie Elliot, Dan Greco, and Yu Guo.

Kit Fine read through a nearly complete version of chapter 6, wherein I discuss his work, and gave me his thoughts on that chapter's main matters. My thanks go to Kit.

The last chapter was added during the first half of 2013 and has been read by only two people, other than me, of course: An expert on philosophy of science generally, and philosophy of physics, in particular, one was my colleague Tim Maudlin. An expert in neither field, and more like most readers, the other was our student Yu Guo. For his expert advice and sound judgment, I thank Tim. For his care with details and his sound judgment, I thank Yu.

Giovanni Merlo read chapters 1 and 3, providing me with comments important for changing the first chapter, and with reassuring comments on chapter 3. Mike Raven commented helpfully on the penultimate draft of chapter 1, guiding my polishing of that introductory chapter. I happily thank both of them.

The three people to whom I am most greatly indebted for their wise help on this project are these three: David Chalmers, who commented trenchantly on more than half the material now in chapters 1 through 8, getting me to make key changes in important places; Yu Guo, who read both all of the penultimate 8-chapter version of the book in 2012 and, in 2013, all of the present and final 9-chapter version; and an anonymous reader for the Oxford University Press, who seems to agree with virtually all of the book's many negative claims and, quite wisely, had me delete from this work almost all of the positive suggestions made in the penultimate version, leaving hardly anything positive in this published version of *Empty Ideas*. I am especially grateful to these three people.

New York   P.K.U.
October 2013

1

HOW EMPTY IS MAINSTREAM PHILOSOPHY?

During the middle of the twentieth century, perhaps until 1970, mainstream philosophers generally agreed that, by contrast with the natural sciences, intellectually responsible philosophy should offer no substantial thoughts about the general nature of concrete reality. This was conspicuously so during the heyday of "ordinary language philosophy" - though the period in question began well before that and it continued for quite a while after. As many mainstream philosophers now would agree, those times may be most aptly called *the bad old days*.

In the bad old days, as I will boringly relate, it was widely thought that, unlike scientists, proper philosophers shouldn't bother considering substantial ideas about concrete reality, except for those found in our fund of common sense and those concerning how certain people use certain words, or something similarly parochial. For example, none should seriously consider the thought that many of our concrete world's individuals are material particles and many others are immaterial souls or, equally, the negation of that idea.[1]

---

1. There were a few exceptions to this, but, then, only few. Perhaps the most salient of these was the materialistic claim that sensations are brain processes—at least some sort of physical processes—advanced and defended by U. T. Place, in his "Is Consciousness a Brain Process?" *British Journal of Psychology*, Volume 47, 1956, pages 44–50, and by J. J. C. Smart, in his "Sensations and Brain Processes," *Philosophical Review*, Volume 68, 1958, pages 141–56.

Putting aside any worries about what a so-called process might be, the heart of their writing is just old-fashioned materialism, whatever the details of the then-new garb that Place and Smart saw as fit clothing for their materialism. To most mainstream philosophers at the time, these materialist

Many much earlier philosophers, of course, endorsed substantial views regarding the nature of concrete reality. Or, at least to all appearances, that certainly seems so. For example, Descartes held that concrete reality comprises exactly two basic sorts of entities, some of which are always spatially extended and never thinking—the material bodies—and others of which are always thinking and never spatially extended—the immaterial souls. In advocating this dualistic view of concrete reality, Descartes endorsed a position that conflicted with other substantial views concerning the nature of reality, as with the materialism upheld by Hobbes, according to which concrete reality comprises only one basic sort of entity, material entities. In contrast with them, most mid-twentieth century philosophers endorsed nothing concerning concrete reality even nearly as robustly substantial.

Far from being bothered by this contrast, most leading mid-century academic philosophers, who were, broadly speaking, just so many analytic philosophers, took it as a point in favor of their quite limited activity that it avoided making any grand claims as to concrete reality's general nature, structure, or character. Rather than making any such terribly ambitious and sweeping claims, they were more than content to place on offer just so many thoughts as to how it is that we ordinary speakers and thinkers use those words we most ordinarily and effectively employ and, relatedly, to make proposals about those concepts that, with our use of these words, we employed in our discussions and in our discursive thinking. For example, such a painstaking philosopher might offer an idea, quite surely a correct idea, to this quite limited effect: While someone may be correct in saying "I *believe* that there's a table before me" *whether or not there is* a table before her, she will be correct in saying "I *perceive* that there's a table before me" *only if there actually is* a table before her. And, as may then be observed, that is because when saying the first thing our speaker employs a relevantly less demanding concept, the concept of believing that something is the case, while, when saying the second, she employs a more demanding concept, the concept of perceiving that something is the case.

Because they were primarily concerned with our ordinary usage of words, and with the ordinary concepts we employed with these words, and because this was quite clear to them, it was pretty easy for these philosophers to communicate to outsiders what it was on which they focused their attention, so that the outsiders understood, well enough, the central concerns of the philosophers. As well, it was easy for them to communicate, quite well, what they took to be central examples of progress they made on these quite limited questions. In the bargain, it was easy to understand why almost all outsiders weren't much

---

writings were regarded as not just quite crude philosophical essays, but, worse than that, as being overly worldly and dangerously adventurous, by contrast with "more purely conceptual philosophy".

interested in the questions the philosophers strove to investigate, or in the progress they may have made in their inquiries. And, it was easy to see why the outsiders thought that their philosophical contemporaries, or many of them, should redirect their focus, and they should try to address, concerning the concrete world we all inhabit, some far larger questions.

Since about 1970, among mainstream philosophers things have changed a little bit, I think, in respect to the matters that I've been discussing. For example, nowadays it's fine for philosophers to endorse materialism, while denying, most conspicuously, that any of us is ever an immaterial soul. But, of course, materialism is nothing new. (And, in recent years, there have been precious few novel attempts to argue for that old view, maybe none of them very convincing or impressively illuminating.[2]) Comporting with that, within the core of analytic philosophy—within *mainstream philosophy*—things have changed *only a little bit*.

At least at first blush, that thought will seem wildly inaccurate to most engaged in recent and current mainstream philosophy. As well, it will appear to them to be a very radical idea. But, as I suspect, by the end of this book, quite a few of its readers will find my appraisal to be a rather accurate assessment; indeed, many may find it strange that they ever thought otherwise.

At all events, it must be admitted that, for the last several decades, many mainstream philosophers have taken themselves to be concerned with matters far more general, and far deeper, than just so many questions concerning our usage of words, and regarding the concepts we deploy, often with that linguistic usage of ours. To be sure, just as in the bad old days, nowadays terribly few outsiders are much interested in the activity of, or in the putative progress of, leading mainstream philosophers. But, unlike then, recently and currently hardly anyone ever bothers (even to try) to say why this is so. As indicated, I will be, with this book, an exception to that general truth. And, trying to avoid mere side-issues, my explanation will be, in its central thrust, about as straightforward as possible: Despite some contrary appearances, it remains true that, when they're involved with issues that aren't just so many parochial matters, the questions most exercising mainstream philosophers are questions that turn, quite entirely, upon whether or not certain conceptual connections hold, or certain semantic relations obtain, between certain words, or certain concepts, and certain other words, or concepts.

---

2. Few contemporary materialists bother to argue for the view, spending their efforts, instead, on arguments against the opposition, mostly against mind-body dualism. But some do. For example, see David Papineau, *Thinking about Consciousness*, Oxford University Press, 2004, chapter 1 and, especially, the book's Appendix, "The History of the Completeness of Physics". Reasons for finding such (precious few) arguments unconvincing may be found in, for example, David J. Chalmers, "Consciousness and Its Place in Nature," Stephen P. Stich and Ted A. Warfield, eds., *The Blackwell Guide to the Philosophy of Mind*, Blackwell, 2003.

As already indicated implicitly, but as I will now make more explicit, my target is meant to be somewhat limited. I do not mean to say much about what's been going on lately in absolutely every area of terribly respectable philosophical activity. To help you appreciate the range of my argumentation, I say that it's aimed at what's recently and currently regarded as *analytic philosophy's core*. Certainly metaphysics, and also the most general and metaphysical-seeming parts of, or aspects, of philosophy of mind, philosophy of language, and epistemology. By contrast, my argumentation *won't* concern anything that's deeply normative, or fully evaluative, or anything of the ilk. Most certainly, I won't seek to address any claims that are obviously, or explicitly, or paradigmatically of any such sorts or kinds. So, even while I think that precious little of any *substance* has been offered regarding normative epistemological matters, in any philosophically important sense of that italicized term, *my arguments won't be aimed at showing that to be so*. In line with that, my work *won't concern any ethical or moral philosophical offering*, though there, too, I think that hardly any substantial idea has lately been placed on offer. So, it is certainly true that, even as concerns just recent philosophy, my work will be limited in its scope or compass. Still and all, I'll be addressing plenty of recent philosophy, including the prestigious core of the field. In short, I'll be addressing a very great deal of recent and current *mainstream philosophy*.

Though I may well be deceived as regards this present paragraph's topic, I have come to think that I might be most helpful to my readers by endeavoring to supply my informal suggestion with a conceptual framework of its own. This will require me to introduce a bit of terminology, and to advance quite a few ideas couched in those new terms. When all is said and done, all of that may well be jettisoned. Though not absolutely sure of it, of course, it is my informal suggestion in which I have most confidence here. That said, I will try to build a bridge, however contrived, from where most of my readers now find themselves to the thought that there is not much more to recent and current mainstream philosophy than there was to be found in the philosophy of fifty or sixty years ago.

1. Most Recent Mainstream Proposals Are *Concretely Empty* Ideas

In the heyday of ordinary language philosophy, as I've said, it was agreed that mere philosophers should steer clear of views about the nature of concrete reality. But then, what may such constrained philosophers place on offer? Toward quickly beginning to answer that, it's useful to confront examples of what was, even in the bad old days, clearly acceptable philosophical fare.

Very near the very beginning of this book, we all but directly confronted two contrasting cases of just such acceptable fare. That happened when we did directly confront precisely this:

While someone may be correct in saying "I *believe* that there's a table before me" *whether or not there is* a table before her, she will be correct in saying "I *perceive* that there's a table before me" *only if there actually is* a table before her.

Correlative with the starting clause of that sentence, its "while"-clause, there is this thought, proposition, or idea: Someone may believe there's a table before her whether or not there is a table before her. And, correlative with the sentence's closing clause, there is this very different thought, idea, or proposition, more striking to mid-century mainstreamers: Someone may perceive there's a table before her only if there actually is a table before her. Paralleling this thought so centrally involving perceiving, numerous examples are found with numerous other thoughts, each relevantly resembling it not only superficially, but also deeply, or, at least, as deeply as this sort of stuff ever goes. For example, there is this thought, not centrally involving perceiving, but centrally involving, instead, remembering: Someone will remember that he went to college only if he actually went to college. In addition to examples like these, which closely resemble each other even most superficially, there are many related examples, which do not resemble them, or each other, so very superficially.

Easy to grasp, here's one of them: Someone will *perceive a cat nearby her* only if there actually *is a cat nearby her.* Also easy to grasp, here's another: Someone will *remember his old college days* only if he actually *went to college.* (If a person didn't go to college, then, no matter how much he learned through his experience, he won't remember his old college days.[3])

Now moving a bit further afield, here's still another example. Taking it that you're a normal human being, living a normal life, we suppose you sometimes feel pain. But, there's this limit on the pain you feel. It will always be *only your own pain you'll feel, never anyone else's pain.*[4]

When using the term "concrete" as it usually occurs in philosophical discourse, it's quite correct, I suppose, to say that people are *concrete individuals.* That supposed, we allow that our three illustrative ideas are thoughts *about* concrete individuals, in a perfectly ordinary sense of "about". In the bargain, even as every thought about any concrete individual is a thought about *concrete reality,* in the senses of the terms usually used in philosophy, so each of our illustrative ideas will be a thought *about* concrete reality. But, that means little. What means

---

3. Nowadays, mainstream philosophers will find these illustrative examples to be quite boring propositions. But, even nowadays, they appear quite interesting, it seems, to some academically influential nonphilosophers. See Stephen Pinker's *The Stuff of Thought,* Viking, 2007.

4. As you're not me, you won't ever feel my pain. To express your empathy *obliquely,* we may *say* you do. But, speaking straightforwardly, not obliquely, we say only that you don't.

more is this: None *delineates a way for* concrete reality to be which *differs from other ways for* it to be.[5]

As I expect, you'll have gotten the hang of what I'm after. So, you'll have a fair grasp of what's meant when saying that none of our three illustrative ideas is a *concretely substantial* thought. Rather, each is *concretely insubstantial*. That's some helpful terminology. Let me introduce a bit more terminology. To begin, I observe that, as a concretely *insubstantial* thought *doesn't* delineate any ways for concreta to be from any other such ways, such a thought is *empty of import for, or as regards to, concrete reality*. So, as we may then say, a concretely insubstantial idea will be a *concretely empty idea*.

Silly mistakes of formulation placed to the side, you may take what's just above, and what's just next to occur, as relevantly fundamental for this book's exposition: (With a pair of possible exceptions that hardly ever need consideration) what the previous paragraph provides may define what I mean by saying that a thought, proposition, or idea is *concretely substantial* and, on the other side, it may define what I mean by saying that a thought is *concretely empty*.[6] Of course, what I've just written is little more than an attempt to give the reader a grasp of some new terminology. But, for many the terminology may prove pretty useful, with the grasp just provided being a pretty good start toward grasping this book's central thrust.

---

5. Not that it makes any difference for this essay's main contentions, but when I speak of a way for concrete reality to be, I mean what many philosophers would call an *intrinsic* way. Correlatively, I mean a way for concrete reality *just itself* to be, quite apart from how any concreta might, or might not, ever be related to any nonconcreta—if there should be anything that's not concrete.

In what's just above, I said my attending to only intrinsic ways wouldn't make any difference for my essay's main claims. What was that? Well, the gist of it is this: Any idea that differentiates between some ways for concrete reality to be as it is *intrinsically*, or *just by itself*, and any other such purely intrinsic ways, will differentiate, just as well, between some ways for concrete reality to be *all things considered*, or *without the qualification*, and, on the other side, other such all-encompassing ways. And, the converse will also be true.

6. Here is the first possible exception, expressed in two complementary ways: There is no concrete reality; there are no concrete items at all. And, perfectly paired with it, here is the second possible exception, which is, of course, simply the negation of the previously recorded possibly exceptional thought: There is at least some concrete reality; there is at least one concrete item. Granting that we have even a moderately decent idea of what it is for some item to be a concrete item, or a *concretum*, it is perfectly obvious and certain that the first of these thoughts is true, or correct, and that the second is untrue, or incorrect. That is one reason, of course, that these correlative possible exceptions will receive, in this work, hardly any attention or mention. Another reason, far more important for practical purposes, is that any very readable exposition will make mention of that peculiar pair of propositions, or even just one of the ideas, at most only very rarely. So, in almost everything to follow, when giving any articulation to the idea of what it is for a thought to be concretely substantial, I will say, simply, that the thought *delineates a way for* concrete reality to be which *differs from other ways for* it to be. And, similarly, when giving a bit of articulation to the idea of what it is for a thought to be a concretely empty idea, I will say, simply, that the idea *doesn't provide any such delineation*.

With that said, let me proceed to provide a bit more help, by presenting another example of a concretely empty proposition.

Directly concerning matter more than mind, here's a fourth illustrative example: A rock that's wholly composed of some matter won't continue to exist if, all at once, all its matter ceases to exist. (Now, perhaps some of a rock's matter might cease to exist, and yet the rock will continue to exist. And, in a gradual and overlapping way, perhaps all the rock's present matter may cease to exist and, with other matter gradually replacing all that's lost, the very same rock may continue to exist, eventually composed of entirely new matter. But, if *all* a rock's matter *suddenly* ceases, the rock itself *won't continue to* exist.)

Unlike the four thoughts just used as illustrative examples of concretely empty ideas, there are, of course, very *many other ideas, each of which is a concretely substantial thought.* Assuming our ordinary common concepts are satisfiable, it is pretty certain this is one:

Each of very many people remembers that he or she went to college.

On that same assumption, another will be the negation of the commonsense idea just displayed.[7]

The displayed commonsense thought differentiates among, or between, alternative ways for concrete reality to be. As we might say, the thought *favors* all the ways in which each of many folks remembers that she went to college and it *disfavors* the ways in which that *doesn't* obtain.

With many empty ideas, it's obvious that the thoughts are insubstantial. With many others, things aren't so obvious. Often, this happens with wholly correct ideas.

As I suppose, these next two thoughts *are correct* ideas, though *that's not obvious*:

Someone can't be happy that she went to college unless she knows she went to college.

7. Unless otherwise indicated, throughout the present work I assume our ordinary concepts, e.g., the concept of a person, the concept of a rock, the concept of a table, the concept of thinking, and the concept of remembering, are all *semantically satisfiable* concepts. In that respect, they're utterly unlike, say, the idea of a perfectly round perfect square, and, say, the idea of an expression that's not true of itself. In early writing, all done over a quarter-century ago, I argued that, with few exceptions, these concepts are semantically *unsatisfiable*. (For the details of that, see my paper "Why There Are No People," *Midwest Studies in Philosophy*, IV [1979]: 177–222, an essay reprinted in my *Philosophical Papers, Volume 2*, Oxford University Press, 2006, on pages 53–109. A brief exposition of the paper's main ideas is given in "Appendix: Beyond Discriminative Vagueness, Safe from Nihilistic Sorites," which is the brief appendix to chapter 7 of my *All the Power in the World*, Oxford University Press, 2006. In this book, that appendix appears on pages 465–69.) As I see it, all those "nihilistic" arguments turn on certain *concretely empty* ideas. Here, I assume them to be *incorrect* empty thoughts.

Someone can't assert that she went to college without representing herself as knowing she went to college.[8]

Though it's *unobvious* that the ideas are *correct*, it's *pretty obvious* that they're *concretely empty*.

In the recent philosophical literature, we find many cases where it's *unobvious both* whether a thought that's on offer is correct *and also whether the offered thought is concretely substantial*.

One of the most widespread and influential of these cases concerns the offering of ideas to the effect that people can think about various concrete substances, like water, wood, or gold, only if the people have had a suitable causal history, however appropriately complex and indirect, involving the substances their thought concerns. Most prominent here are thoughts flowing from various versions of Hilary Putnam's Twin Earth examples, and other far-fetched examples flowing from Putnam and his admirers.[9] For a salient instance of such companion offerings, think of Donald Davidson's example of his Swampman, and Davidson's claim that, as he has no apt history, Swampman can't, really, even think (about anything) at all.[10] In chapter 3, I will argue that, first, and less importantly, all these offerings are incorrect ideas, even if their incorrectness may be quite unobvious. Secondly, and more importantly for our present work, I will there argue that they all represent just so many concretely empty ideas, and not any new philosophical thoughts that are concretely substantial, however unobvious this may be.

Another terribly widespread and influential case concerns certain ordinary individuals, as with ordinary tables and chairs, and the origins of these entities. Most prominent here is an example featured in Saul Kripke's enormously influential *Naming and Necessity*. Concerning a certain quite typical wooden table, Kripke there famously offers a thought to just this effect: It is absolutely essential to anything's being that very table that the concrete candidate in question first have been made of some certain wood, much as that table itself was first constituted, and not be, for example, first composed of just so much ice from the Thames.[11] As we may usefully say, Kripke offers the thought

8. See my first book, *Ignorance*, Oxford University Press, 1975. The first of the two displayed sentences, the one "about happiness," finds a home there starting on, or about, page 171. The second sentence, "about asserting," finds a home that starts on, or about, page 252.

9. Putnam's Twin Earth cases most famously appear in his enormously prominent paper, "The Meaning of 'Meaning,'." As well as elsewhere, this essay appears in Putnam's *Mind, Language and Reality: Philosophical Papers, Volume XX*, Cambridge University Press, 1975, on pages 215–71. Putnam most famously moves from semantic matters, like reference, to mental matters, like a thinker's thoughts, in his *Reason, Truth and History*, Cambridge University Press, 1981.

10. Davidson famously discusses his Swampman in "Knowing One's Own Mind," *Proceedings and Addresses of the American Philosophical Association* (1987), pages 441–58; that is reprinted as Essay 2 in Davidson's *Subjective, Intersubjective, Objective*, Oxford University Press, 2001.

11. See Saul Kripke, *Naming and Necessity*, Harvard University Press, 1980. The body of that short book is a virtually unchanged version of a very long paper of Kripke's named the same as the

that, for the likes of such ordinary things as tables, the objects have *origination conditions* that, in certain ways, are *at least fairly strict origination conditions*. In chapter 4, I will argue that, first, and less importantly, these Kripkean offerings are, more likely than not, incorrect ideas, even if their incorrectness may be quite unobvious. (Even so, and most fair to Kripke, it might well be that, somewhere in the neighborhood of what he actually offers, there is a correct idea.) Secondly, and more important for our present work, I'll argue that these Kripkean thoughts are also just so many concretely empty ideas.

Correlative with the idea of an ordinary thing's origination conditions, there is the philosophically more familiar idea of such a thing's *persistence conditions*. For one example here, many have noticed that a ship composed of ever so many planks may persist, at least under certain conditions, throughout certain gradual replacements of its planks—so that this ordinary material thing comes to be composed, by the end of this process, of matter entirely different from that which composed it at the start. For another, it appears that some bronze may compose, at once, both a bronze sculpture and a terribly nicely shaped piece of bronze. While the nice piece can survive radical "shapewise" alteration to, say, the shape of a certain rectangular solid, not so for the sculpture. Even such a brilliant philosopher as Kit Fine thinks that there is a deep truth here, crying out for explanation, some of which, at least, he's in the business of providing. By contrast, in chapter 5 I argue that all of these thoughts about persistence are concretely empty ideas. And, as I'll explain, *that's due to their being analytically empty* ideas.

When one considers Kripke, both a brilliant thinker and one of the two most influential philosophers of my generation, one often considers David Lewis, another brilliant thinker and the other of the generation's two most influential philosophers. As may be quite unobvious to quite a few mainstreamers, almost all of Lewis's philosophical offerings are, on my way of dividing matters, *concretely empty ideas*, and not any substantial philosophical thoughts. To some extent, this will be confirmed by our work in chapter 6, where we discuss, among other things, when it is that there may be certain things, rightly regarded as parts, that together compose other things, rightly taken as composed of just those parts. As I'll be arguing there, all those issues are just so many concretely empty issues.

To a greater extent, our work in chapter 7 will confirm the thought that ever so many Lewisian offerings are just so many empty offerings.[12] Still and all,

---

book. That is his "Naming and Necessity" in D. Davidson and G. Harman (eds.), *Semantics of Natural Language* (Dordrecht, Holland: D. Reidel, 1972), pages 254–355.

12. I won't try to canvass Lewis's dauntingly large and systematic corpus. For the most part, I'll confine our exploration of this thinker to some salient sections of his masterwork, *On the Plurality of Worlds*, Blackwell, 1986, though, when apt, I'll notice other work by Lewis.

and by contrast to that, the idea for which Lewis is most notoriously famous, namely, the thought that—as I will put it—there is a plurality of mutually absolutely isolated concrete worlds, well, that's a concretely substantial proposition. At least near enough, that may be the only truly novel concretely substantial philosophical thought that Lewis ever placed on offer.[13]

As I was just saying, it may very well be that Lewis offered only just one truly novel concretely substantial idea, far more comprehensive than any merely parochial proposition. If so, then, as best I can tell, that puts him one up on the other mainstreamers just lately mentioned, one up on Putnam, Davidson, Kripke, and Fine. And it puts him one up on (at least almost) all other very prominent mainstreamers of the last half-century or more. Though I mean to support this charge in the book, right now it is far more tantalizing than compelling. So, I'll soon present some far less tantalizing fare, a fairly fully articulated dialectic that, by steps, proceeds to engage in some pretty paradigmatic mainstream metaphysical ideas, quite fashionable to argue over during the last several decades.

2. A Working Idea of *Concrete Reality*

In this short section, I'll set the stage for the dialectic just promised. Without further ado, I begin this very modest preparatory work.

Pretty roughly, you may think of *concrete* reality as comprising all those individuals, and only those, as are ever in time or, perhaps, in space-time. This will presumably include any material individual that there may be, or any physical individual, whether basic or not, and whether simple or not. And it will include, presumably, any immaterial individual that there may be, whether basic or not, and whether simple or not. So, just as a (physical) electron may count as some of concrete reality, at least presuming there's at least one such electron, so a (nonphysical) soul may also count as some of concrete reality, at least presuming there's at least one such soul. By contrast, even if many may exist, no *abstract* entities exist in time, or in space-time. Presumably, the natural numbers, as usually understood, are abstracta and, presumably, they don't exist in time, or space-time.

Perhaps more importantly, concrete reality may comprise all those individuals, and only those, that are each propensitied, or powered, or disposed in any way, whether with respect to themselves or whether with respect to other concreta, actual or merely possible. So, for its being propensitied to repel any

---

13. Or, at the very least, there is a novel concretely substantial philosophical idea at the heart of this astonishing offering, and it is this that may be the only such thought Lewis ever offered. This parenthetical qualification, a pretty minor one, will be discussed in an appendix to chapter 6.

other electron, actual or possible, a given electron will count as a concrete entity. Indeed, even if it's just probabilistically disposed to continue to exist, for at least the next nanosecond, any given electron will be, just on that account, a concrete entity. By contrast, no number is disposed to do anything at all, not even to continue to exist. Again, numbers aren't concreta.

In this section, I'm trying to provide you with a modestly helpful idea of *concrete* reality. As is well known, it's extremely difficult, maybe impossible, to define *concrete* in terms that are, at once, both more basic and more familiar.[14]

To be sure, as philosophers use the (technical) terms "concrete" and "abstract", they're *mutually exclusive* terms: Whatever is concrete isn't abstract, and whatever is abstract isn't concrete. And, as most philosophers use the terms, they're to be *jointly exhaustive* of absolutely all reality: Whatever is real is either concrete or else it's abstract.[15] At any rate, "concrete" and "nonconcrete" are certainly just so jointly exhaustive. And, as I'll be using "abstract" in this synonymous way, on my usage "abstract" and "concrete" will be jointly exhaustive.

As the book progresses, you'll come to know, well enough, what I mean by *concrete reality* and, by extension, what's meant when saying that a thought is a concretely empty idea.

3. Observing the Concretely Empty in Some Recent Mainstream Philosophy

Having just set the stage for it, in this section I'll present the promised dialectic. Toward that end, I'll proceed in three steps: First, I'll sketch a make-believe philosophical debate. Second, I'll sketch a closely related *quasi-philosophical* debate. Third, and again closely related, I'll sketch a debate that mainstream philosophers have found very engaging. Unless my writing is very ineffectual, it should strike you that there's a deep similarity among the three disputes.

First, our make-believe debate has two thinkers agreeing that, in a certain spatial region and at a certain time, there are six perfectly fundamental physical concreta. As agreed, they are arranged hexagonally. Now, one of our thinkers holds that, in addition to the six particles, there's a certain further thing in the region, namely, a hexagonal *arrangement*. Perhaps, she may be a quite commonsensical

14. To appreciate just how very difficult this is, see Gideon Rosen, "Abstract Objects," *The Stanford Encyclopedia of Philosophy (Spring 2012 Edition)*, Edward N. Zalta (ed.), URL = <http://plato.stanford.edu/archives/spr2012/entries/abstract-objects/>. As well, see the section "Concreteness" in *On the Plurality of Worlds*, Blackwell, pages 81–86, even if Lewis may overstate the trouble.

15. Most, I think, but almost certainly not all. For a nice discussion of how various philosophers have drawn a distinction between what is abstract and what is concrete, see Amie L. Thomasson, *Fiction and Metaphysics*, Cambridge University Press, 1999, especially pages 126–27. Thomasson there argues that, on some traditional ways of formulating such a distinction, the abstract and the concrete are not jointly exhaustive of absolutely all reality.

thinker. Her opponent, apparently an *ontologically stricter* thinker, holds that, then and there, all that exists are the six particles. Let me amplify.

One of the parties to our dispute, apparently a quite commonsensical person, endorses this nicely named and neatly displayed idea:

> HEXAGONAL ARRANGEMENTS: If there are, at a certain time in a cer-
> tain spatial region, six particles arranged hexagonally, there will be, then and
> there, a hexagonal *arrangement* (of the particles).

But, then, who would deny that? Well, usually it will be someone who doesn't know English well, or at least someone who prefers or pretends to ignore any such knowledge. That is obviously just so very boring. At least a tiny bit less boring may be this: Once in a great while HEXAGONAL ARRANGE-MENTS may be denied by someone who fancies himself an *ontologically strict* thinker. This peculiar person takes it that endorsing HEXAGONAL AR-RANGEMENTS commits one to upholding the existence of (massless) ar-rangements. And this person would prefer either to deny their existence or, at least, to suspend judgment on the matter. (The things arranged have mass, but not any arrangement of such things.) Now, if he is even the least bit prolix, he may place on offer this opposing idea:

> NO HEXAGONAL ARRANGEMENTS: Even if there are, at a certain
> time in a certain spatial region, six particles arranged hexagonally, there (still)
> won't be, then and there, any hexagonal *arrangement* (of the particles).

Barring a poor choice of words, both HEXAGONAL ARRANGEMENTS and NO HEXAGONAL ARRANGEMENTS fail to delineate any way for concrete reality to be, differentiating it from others. Here the same, both are empty ideas.

Unlike what we've just observed, the next debate won't be so very easily grasped by folks unfamiliar with analytic philosophy. But, a brief discussion may, I think, greatly help them.

Second, and at all events, next there's our quasi-philosophical dispute. As before, both parties agree on quite a lot: First, in a certain spatial region and at a certain time, there are enormously many elementary particles. And, second, these particles are arranged *tablewise*. What's this? Don't worry. To be sure, "tablewise" is something of a barbarism. But, for some philosophers, the barbarism may hold interest. Anyway, when agreeing on how it is that our particles are arranged, it's mostly these following points on which these de-baters agree: The aforesaid particles are related to each other in a way that, then and there, is as conducive as can be for the constitution of a table by just those very particles. (Given the propensities of the basic particles, and other physical factors, this will mean a certain mutual cohesiveness for our particles, and other "nice physical features", too.) Being so related will include even such unobvious things as the fact that the aforesaid particles are *tellingly separate from other particles,* as well as any other concreta most relevant to having them be disqualified as table-constituents. Perhaps, each particle is nearer all the others than any is to any other particle, or to any other would-be disqualifier.

Well, then, given all their shared common ground, what's debated by our quasi-philosophical disputants? No surprise, here our story goes like this: On one side of this second dispute, there's a quite commonsensical thinker. She holds that, in our considered spatial region at our contemplated time, there is, *in addition to* the particles arranged tablewise, a tablewise *arrangement* (of the particles).[16] As before, her opponent is, apparently, an *ontologically stricter* thinker. He holds that, in our region and at our time, all that really exists are the enormously many particles themselves (arranged tablewise).

The quasi-philosophical debate concerns only a concretely empty issue. One party accepts an empty idea relevantly paralleling HEXAGONAL ARRANGEMENTS:

TABLEWISE ARRANGEMENTS: If there are, at a certain time in a certain spatial region, very many particles arranged tablewise, there will be, then and there, a tablewise *arrangement* (of particles).

Her opponent denies that, and he accepts this, instead:

NO TABLEWISE ARRANGEMENTS: Even if there are, at a certain time in a certain spatial region, very many particles arranged tablewise, there (still) won't be, then and there, any tablewise *arrangement* (of particles).

The dispute between these two parties will be just as empty a debate as that observed just before.

Third, and finally, there's a debate that's been quite salient during the last few decades of mainstream philosophy. In this third debate, the two parties

---

16. For extraordinary clarity, I'll make a remark best confined here to a mere note. Tables are one kind of putative concrete item and, not to be confused with them, tablewise arrangements are quite another, a point I'll bother to notice in the body of the book's sixth chapter. Just so, as just might possibly be true, for all I know, whenever there are very many basic particles arranged tablewise, there'll be tablewise arrangements of basic particles, at least one such, and there'll be tables composed of such particles, at least one such. But, none of the tablewise arrangements will be any table and none of the tables will be any tablewise arrangement of particles. But, of course and quite certainly, for the present discussion, such niceties don't matter at all.

agree on just what was agreed by the disputants in the quasi-philosophical debate. With no difference as regards agreement, what's newly debated here?

On one side, there's a commonsensical thinker. She holds that, in our considered space at our contemplated time, there *exists a table*, and *not only* many particles arranged tablewise.[17] (Typically, she might say that the particles in focus serve to *compose* the table in question, which ordinary thing thus may well be called a *composite* table. But, as concerns the crux of the current discussion, she needn't say anything more.) Predictably, her opponent holds that, in our region and at our time, all that really exists are the enormously many particles themselves (arranged tablewise). (The thought of a composite table, he might say, is "an ontologically profligate idea fostered by a certain way of talking". Or, he might say nothing further at all.[18])

The third dispute is also a concretely empty debate. One party accepts some such thought as:

17. A nice example of this, which justifies my use of the feminine pronoun, is Lynne Rudder Baker, *The Metaphysics of Everyday Life*, Cambridge University Press, 2007.

18. Several recent deniers of tables see no serious troubles with having there be lots of much simpler things arranged tablewise. Perhaps the most salient of them is Peter van Inwagen, as in his *Material Beings*, Cornell University Press, 1990, especially on page 109 ff. Another is Trenton Merricks, as in his *Objects and Persons*, Oxford University Press, 2001, as on page 2 ff. Still another is Cian Dorr, as in his *The Simplicity of Everything*, 2002, which is his Princeton University Ph.D. dissertation.

(When I was in the business of denying tables, by contrast, I was just as much in the business of denying, in effect, that any things could ever be arranged tablewise. For me then, just as "table" was impossible to satisfy, governed as it was by conflicting conditions of application, so, also, "tablewise" was unsatisfiable, governed as *it* was by conflicting conditions. Regarding that, there are several old papers of mine, with the most directly relevant being, perhaps, "Why There Are No People," cited in note 6 of this present chapter.)

Until *Material Beings* made a pretty big splash, around 1995 or so, claims to the effect that there aren't really any tables or other (inanimate) ordinary things were considered unworthy of much attention by most mainstream philosophers. Now things are very different.

Among those championing tables and other ordinary objects, much of the credit should go, I think, to Eli Hirsch. See, for one example, his (2002) paper "Against Revisionary Ontology," *Philosophical Topics* 30 (1): 103–27. Quite recently, an entire book has been published much of whose point has been to provide arguments to the effect that tables do indeed exist, as do many other ordinary objects, like rocks. See Amie L. Thomasson, *Ordinary Objects*, Oxford University Press, 2007. Yet more recently, all this has seemed sufficiently important, to so many mainstreamers, that there is now a lengthy entry in the *SEP*, at this point the reference work most widely used by mainstreamers. See, Daniel Z. Korman, "Ordinary Objects," *The Stanford Encyclopedia of Philosophy (Winter 2012 Edition)*, Edward N. Zalta (ed.), URL = <http://plato.stanford.edu/archives/win2012/entries/ordinary-objects/>. At or near its end, this lengthy entry has an immense bibliography, in which there are listed all the works mentioned earlier in this note, save Dorr's dissertation, and my own paper here cited. Happily, the author with the most listings, fully fourteen, is Hirsch, a greatly underappreciated philosopher, though all this book's main charges may be brought against almost everything he has said. Peculiarly, what may well be his very most interesting work, his *Dividing Reality*, Oxford University Press, 1993, is left off the list. Also peculiar, while the paper of mine referenced in this note isn't found there, five works of mine are on the long list.

COMPOSITE TABLES: If there are, at a certain time in a certain spatial region, very many particles arranged tablewise, there is, then and there, a composite *table*.[19]

Rejecting COMPOSITE TABLES, the other party accepts some such opposite thought as:

NO COMPOSITE TABLES: Even if there are, at a certain time in a certain spatial region, very many particles arranged tablewise, there (still) won't be, then and there, any composite *table*.

With neither thought delineating any way for concrete reality to be, both are empty ideas.[20]

19. The friend of COMPOSITE TABLES, it should be stressed, doesn't think that any of his many tables has any special emergent powers, or holistic propensities, whatever any such things as those might ever be. Rather, all the (intrinsic) powers of a table will be just so many fully physically derivative (intrinsic) powers, physically deriving from the basic physical dispositions of its basic constituents, along with what are the physical relations among relevant basic concreta.

20. Most readers need not concern themselves with this lengthy note, but some may profit from it quite greatly, perhaps especially those familiar with a fair bit of my much earlier work. At all events, for them, and for others, too, I'll now aim to clarify my present aims and my take on how they might be largely met both most relevantly and quite successfully.

As I should be the first to admit, it may well be that, either wholly or in largest measure, the position I've been developing here may find no adequate expression in English, or in any other ordinary language. How might that be? Already obliquely indicated, one "possibility" is that, even as almost all ordinary terms are vague discriminative terms, perhaps all such terms are inconsistent terms. Just perhaps, with respect to any of these terms, the thought that it's ever satisfied, or ever applies to anything, may be inconsistent. Closer to what will now concern us, I'll briefly indicate another "nugatory possibility".

Almost always, or in almost all contexts, this following sentence should be taken to express a concretely substantial idea:

There (is at least one concrete world in which there) are at least fifty (concrete) tables.

But, in some high-minded contexts, perhaps, things may be taken quite differently, with the thought then in focus regarded, most aptly, as deeply infected with utterly empty issues. In what follows, I'll briefly sketch an extreme example of how that may occur.

First, it's at least arguable that this following thought is concretely empty: Anything that's a (concrete) *table* is a (concrete) *individual*. And, in the wake of that, there are empty ideas to be confronted that, rightly or wrongly, challenge the existence of all concrete individuals. Here is one of them: Even if there should be a very great deal of concrete stuff, there will never be—there can't ever be—any concrete individuals. In particular, even if there should be much material stuff that's distributed tablewise, there still won't be any (concrete) individuals and, for that reason, there'll never be even so much as a single (concrete) table. Of course, material reality played no crucial role there: Even if there should be much *immaterial* stuff, or *immaterial substance*, patterned tabularly, there still won't be any (concrete) individuals or (concrete) tables.

The sort of concern just considered, and aptly treated, is by no means a completely isolated misplaced worry. As I should think, a quick treatment of just one more example will make that point quite fully. Let's observe that now.

Almost always, or in almost all contexts, this following sentence also should be taken to express a concretely substantial idea, even if a thought that is very boring:

4. Our Central Distinction and Three That Have Been Philosophically Salient

For those thoroughly schooled in the ways of mainstream philosophy, I should say something about how our newly drawn distinction, between the concretely empty and the concretely substantial, compares with three philosophically highly salient distinctions, both insofar as the latter are usually conceived and also insofar as they might be more usefully conceived.

First, there's the distinction between thoughts that are *necessary*—necessarily true, when true at all—and thoughts that are (merely) *contingent*—even if true, not so much as necessarily true. (Of the three old dichotomies, it's this one that most nearly lines up with our new distinction.)

When prominent philosophers try to articulate what is meant to go on with this distinction, they usually say something like this: A *necessary* truth will hold true in, or for, or at, *all possible worlds*, whereas a *contingent* truth will hold true in, or for, or at, *some possible worlds*—including the actual world—but *not* in all. But, excepting David Lewis, no prominent author gives us a satisfying idea as to what sort of items are these possible worlds of which they speak. Or, at least, so it seems to me.[21] What's worse, they say nothing helpful in grasping

---

In our actual world, some people like to spend a lot of time at the beach.

Taking it that the semantic conditions of mental verbs like "like" are somehow very demanding, various mainstream materialist philosophers have denied that, at least in our actual world, anyone ever likes anything at all. But, of course, these so-called "eliminative materialists" are no more materialistic, in how they take concrete reality to be, from materialists who sound less radical and, so, sound more commonsensical. As concerns how things are with concrete reality, even just as regards our actual world, there is no concretely substantial dispute among these materialist philosophers, between the so-called eliminativists and the conceptually more relaxed physicalist thinkers, except if it's just a quite superficial dispute, regarding just some perfectly parochial propositions. In the present work, we will avoid all such empty or parochial questions, or at least we'll bracket them, seeking to focus on more serious philosophical issues, always assuming of course, that there are such more serious issues.

Though nowadays there seems very little interest in the shallow and arid topic, in the latter half of the 20th century quite a lot was written advocating eliminative materialism, as well as quite a lot "defending common sense" against the charges of the eliminativists. For an overview of much of that big boring business, see Ramsey, William, "Eliminative Materialism," *The Stanford Encyclopedia of Philosophy (Fall 2012 Edition)*, Edward N. Zalta (ed.), URL = <http://plato.stanford.edu/archives/fall2012/entries/materialism-eliminative/>.

What's just been sketched may mean, I suspect, that a certain deficiency will attach to almost everything attempted in this book. (But, of course, the same will apply to (almost) any other book written in any earthly natural language.) As the upcoming chapters will confirm, the suspected deficiency won't make our exploratory endeavor a completely pointless exercise. So, even if there really should be the trouble just suggested, it wouldn't be any *stultifying* problem, no more than what would befall us should vague discriminative terms all be inconsistent terms.

21. Toward letting the reader make her own informed judgment, at this point I should like to refer to the entry on the topic, possible worlds, in the currently most used, and most useful, reference work in philosophy, the *Stanford Encyclopedia of Philosophy*. Unfortunately, however, while there is meant to be an entry for that, none is actually available. Towards noting what frustration may

what's what with respect to what certainly appear to be different ways for all concrete reality to be.

Let me amplify, availing myself of what I take to be a happy heuristic: Consider two candidate pairs of concrete spherical balls, one being or containing just the white balls Bill and Bob, and the other being or containing just the black balls Barbara and Beth, neither or them being white. Now, let us stipulate, first, that Bill and Bob are spatially related to each other and, second, that Barbara and Beth are spatially related to each other, and, third, that neither Bill nor Bob is spatially related to Beth or Barbara (and, of course, conversely). Then, with our new distinction in mind, we may entertain, at least, these four different ways for concrete reality to be: First, both pairs of balls may exist, with the white balls inhabiting a certain possible world, and, perforce, with the black balls inhabiting only another possible world, these two worlds related only as regards qualitative difference and qualitative similarity. Second, only Bill and Bob may exist, in which case, all concrete reality may well be smaller than on our first supposition, and less variegated, as well, perhaps with there not being any black concreta. Third, only Beth and Barbara may exist, in which case, all concrete reality may well be, again, smaller than on our first supposition, and less variegated, as well, but this time with there being, perhaps, no white concreta at all. Fourth, and last, none of our contemplated balls may exist, in which case concrete reality may well be quite small, perhaps containing neither any white concreta nor any black concreta.[22]

After all is said and done, it will be a contingent matter which of the foregoing suppositions obtains. Or, perhaps better, it will be a contingent question which one of some perfectly parallel but not merely suppositional thoughts obtains. With our new distinction in hand, we may understand all this reasonably well, I think, even if far from perfectly well. But, of course, as everything in play is a contingent issue, we cannot get any help here from the traditional distinction between necessary thoughts and contingent ideas (at least glossed in terms of possible worlds and, most likely, I think, glossed in any sensible way whatsoever). Again, and by contrast with that, with our new distinction we may happily regard each of the thoughts, that are here most relevant, as delineating a way for all concrete reality to be that differs from other ways for concrete reality to be.

await us there, one might well see these two available entries. First, see Takashi Yagisawa, "Possible Objects," *The Stanford Encyclopedia of Philosophy (Winter 2009 Edition)*, Edward N. Zalta (ed.), URL = <http://plato.stanford.edu/archives/win2009/entries/possible-objects/>. Next, and as may boggle your mind, see Francesco Berto, "Impossible Worlds," *The Stanford Encyclopedia of Philosophy (Winter 2012 Edition)*, Edward N. Zalta (ed.), URL = <http://plato.stanford.edu/archives/win2012/entries/impossible-worlds/>.

22. Going just by ordinary intuition, most will have simply assumed that all four of our balls are spatially related to each other. But, as Lewis brilliantly suggested, that may a groundless assumption and, at least apparently, even an incorrect idea.

Before passing on to notice two other old distinctions, let me make a final point about the distinction between the necessary and the contingent. For this, we may grant that, or we may pretend that, even in traditional terms, the hoary distinction may be adequate to serve, as it should do, quite comprehensively.[23] And, with this pretense in place, I'll do nothing more than remark on what's to fall on just one side of the distinction, namely, on the side of the (putative) necessary propositions. Look, insofar as (many of) these propositions hold true in, or for, or at, all possible worlds—that is, insofar as (many of) them hold true *no matter how everything is with concrete reality*—well, just because *that's* so, then it must *also be that* the truth of such necessary propositions—the truth of those that are true—well, it's all *irrelevant to (any question of) how anything is with concrete reality*. Now, as seems quite certain to me, that simple thought has been entertained by hardly anyone at all — just perhaps, even by nobody except for me and, in my tiny wake, those few whom I may have caused to do that. But, then, whenever this thought should be entertained, at all clearly or fully, then, straightaway, it becomes perfectly obvious to anyone, who then does so entertain the idea, that the thought is completely correct. (At the same time, I fear, it is very hard for people to hold fast to this obvious point, so utterly easy is it for them to fall into older ways of consideration, wherein all that's salient about necessary truths is something like how comprehensive the thoughts are, or how deeply secure they must be.) With that said, I've said quite enough, for present purposes, about the first of our three old distinctions.

We next turn to consider an old distinction—whatever it may amount to—between *a priori thoughts* and *empirical propositions*, the latter also called *a posteriori propositions*. Even as it appears, no useful understanding of this epistemological dichotomy will have anything much to do with our new distinction. Using our newly introduced material about spatial balls, we may have that aptly appear to us with great clarity. For that, we may begin by stipulating that, in one or another empirical way, we (have come to) know that there are many balls spatially related to many other balls, with each of those balls spatially related to each of us, or to our bodies. So far, everything is just fine. But, then, how is anything empirical to help anyone to decide in favor of the thought that there are *not some still other balls none of which is spatially related to any of our "empirically established" balls* and, to boot, none of which is externally related, in any way, either to those established balls, or to any of us? Given our question's happy formulation, any proposal must be hopeless. Equally, how is anything empirical to help decide *oppositely*? Again, any proposal must be hopeless. But, if this old epistemological dichotomy divides matters much as does the distinction between the concretely

---

23. Or, perhaps better, we may provide new definitions, and relevantly more comprehensive definitions, for our contrast terms: A proposition is *contingent* if, and only if, (the answer to the question of) whether the proposition is true *depends on how things are with concrete reality*. And, a proposition is *necessary* if, and only if, (the answer to the question of) whether the proposition is true *does not depend on, but rather it has nothing to do with, how anything ever is with concrete reality*.

substantial and the concretely empty, then the empirical should align well with the substantial. Evidently, that doesn't happen.

Reflection on certain time-honored ideas serves only to confirm what pondering newer material yields quite clearly. Just so, a thesis of *subjective idealism*, (at least something like) a Berkeleian idea, delineates a certain way for concrete reality to be from certain other ways, saliently from any way that a materialist thesis would favor, with the former favoring ways where every concrete item is mental and none material, and with the latter delineating things quite differently. As history has made amply evident, there's no way for any empirical considerations to favor either of these contenders at the expense of the other. Owing to that, the logical positivists, and the logical empiricists, wanted nothing to do with any such metaphysical theses, whether mentalistic or whether materialistic. As with most, I disagree with any such limiting view.[24] At any event, the old epistemic distinction has little to do with the distinction between the concretely substantial and the concretely empty.

Finally, for this section, I'll briefly consider the distinction between thoughts that are analytic and thoughts that are synthetic.[25] Well, if the third and last of our three old distinctions is to line up well with the new one I've been making, then the analytic should exhaust, and it should be exhausted by, the concretely empty, even while the synthetic should exhaust, and it should be exhausted by, the concretely substantial. But, with the possible exception of some very simple mathematical thoughts, as with, perhaps, the proposition that one plus one equals two, it is at least contentious that (all of, or most of) the propositions of pure mathematics—mathematics just all by itself—are analytic propositions, as is also likely for any other complex system of thoughts most directly concerning abstract items (if any such there be). So, it is most doubtful that this third distinction is even coextensive with our newly introduced dichotomy, much less that the two amount to the same.

At least for the meanwhile, that's enough to show that we may do well to deploy most saliently our distinction between the concretely substantial and the concretely empty.

Having said that, all of this section's main points have now been made. Before closing the section, I'd like to say a bit about how, for purposes of a happily simple and brief exposition, I will be using certain traditional terms in a nonstandard sense or way.

24. Still speaking just for myself, I'll also say this: Though not absolutely certain of it, I'm pretty sure that there is no distinction between the a priori and the empirical that can be important to any fundamental philosophical thinking (at least on any understanding of those terms remotely like any I've ever encountered).

25. If it really denotes anything at all, then, familiar to philosophical sophisticates, the label "the distinction between the a priori and the empirical" denotes a family of distinctions, some having nothing or little to do with some of the others. Similarly, if it really denotes anything at all, then, as is also familiar, the label "the distinction between the analytic and the synthetic" also denotes just some such motely. But, for the present discussion, none of that is very important.

It will be convenient to speak not only of analytically correct ideas as being analytically empty, but also to say the same of analytically *incorrect* ideas, as with the thought that people remember the future. What's more, it will be useful for me to say that about many offered thoughts that, while actually incorrect, were proposed as deep philosophical truths. To be apt, that may require us to construe the offered thoughts as best expressed with an appropriate "must" or an apt "can't". For example, that's how I will construe the thought that, for someone to think about an individual external to herself, or external to her mind, she *must* have a certain sort of rich history, relevantly involving the external object in question.

What's yet more, there's this still further liberality about my use of "analytic" and cognate terms: Contrary to the externalist thoughts just noted, my belief is that it *isn't* impossible for someone to think about an external object if she lacks a suitably rich history (or even any history at all). Supposing that I'm right, we may then say that the thought that such a history *is* required will be *an analytically incorrect idea* and, as such, it will be an *analytic idea*. In any case, nothing of substance will be lost through my writing in that way, and it will improve my exposition.

5. The Concretely Empty, the Analytically Empty and Mainstream Philosophy

Except when it's trafficked in quite parochial thoughts, mainstream philosophy has, in recent decades, offered hardly anything by way of novel concretely substantial ideas. Or so I'll be arguing throughout most of the present work. Does this mean that, *assessed by the standards historically dominant for philosophy*, mainstream philosophy currently is, and it recently has been, quite *deficient*? Yes; of course it does. I'll amplify.

Suppose that, as many believe, all of reality comprises not only all concrete reality, but, beyond that, abstract reality, as well. And, suppose that, far from comprising just something scant or marginal, abstract reality comprises a great deal of reality. Finally for now, suppose that, although it says little or nothing about *concrete* reality, pure mathematics offers us a *great deal about abstract* reality, at least many of which offerings are absolutely necessary truths. Now, given these assumptions, which many have found plausible, it may be that mathematics offers us *many* ideas, indeed, many *correct* ideas, each of which is, in at least *one* importantly apt sense of "substantial", a *substantial thought about abstract reality*, And, hence, it may be that, about all reality, mathematics offers a lot that's *substantial*, in an important sense of the term.

Well, even if all its offerings should be concretely empty ideas, mightn't mainstream philosophy be quite like pure mathematics, offering us *many* ideas, even many *correct* thoughts, concerning abstract reality, each a strictly necessary truth about what may be a vast realm of reality? And, in that case, mightn't mainstream philosophy be perfectly adequate philosophy, not in the least bit deficient, not even when assessed by typically dominant standards?

The previous paragraph comprises two questions. The answers to those questions are, respectively, "No" and "No". Let's start by seeing why there's a negative answer to the second and last question: (Supposing it offers many strictly necessary truths about a vast realm of abstract reality), mightn't mainstream philosophy be perfectly adequate philosophy?

In many ways, philosophy differs from mathematics. In line with that, there's this: Throughout most of its history, philosophy has aspired to offer substantial thoughts about concrete reality, whatever it may have said concerning abstracta. And, perhaps with fair frequency, it may well have succeeded in this, and not just by offering quite parochial ideas. So, it has generally been supposed, at least, from ancient times right up through the present. Happily enough, I will continue to suppose it.

Thus, as very many believe, philosophy has offered us various sorts of concretely substantial idealism, and various sorts of concretely substantial materialism, and various sorts of concretely substantial dualism, to take just one philosophically central way of slicing a big concrete cake. Now, it must be admitted, of course, that many who have offered such apparently concretely substantial and impressively general thoughts are philosophers who have been concerned, as well, to offer ideas not concerned with concreta, but, rather, concerned with abstract matters. And, it may well be that they have been at least as successful in offering apt ideas of the latter sort, as in offering impressively general thoughts that are concretely substantial ideas.

But, of course, that can't cast even the slightest doubt on whether it's proper for philosophy to offer substantial ideas about concrete reality, including many that are nothing even remotely like just some perfectly parochial propositions. So, *even if* recent mainstream philosophy should offer many important thoughts about abstract reality, it may *still be terribly deficient philosophy*, at least as compared with much philosophy saliently offered in earlier eras (or, at the very least, as compared with what has been so widely and plausibly presumed for a good deal of earlier philosophy). Quite *unlike with pure mathematics*, it may be important for *philosophy* to offer quite a few substantial ideas concerning *concrete* reality—and many of them not just perfectly parochial propositions. So, if this mainstream philosophy offers little or nothing substantial about concrete reality, beyond what's quite parochial, then this recent philosophy has been terribly deficient— not by the standards historically dominant for, and to, mathematics, of course, but by the standards historically dominant for, and to, philosophy itself.

In a central way, the previous paragraph has been very generous to recent mainstream philosophy. As it had us suppose, many of the propositions that philosophy has offered, which are quite characteristic of this discipline, are perfectly on a par with those properly provided by (only) pure mathematics. But, now, let us try to be more realistic, even if that means being less generous. So, now we should notice this: Even though purely mathematical ideas are concretely empty thoughts, at least in my specified sense of "concretely empty", the reason for their being so empty has, so far as any of us can tell, little or nothing to do with *analyticity*, in any of what may be several senses of the term saliently employed by one or another prominent analytic philosopher. Indeed, at least as appears, *most mathematical thoughts* are synthetic ideas, *not any analytic thoughts* at all. Consider the fairly simple (and uninteresting) arithmetical thought that *twelve is the sum of seven and five* (let alone any of the very many far more complex and intellectually striking mathematical propositions). Far from its presumed truth being due mostly to what are just verbal, or grammatical, or linguistic, or semantic considerations, things appear to be very different from that in almost all of mathematics. So, as it certainly appears, there's a gulf between that (synthetic) thought and, on the other side, the (analytic) thought that, for someone to perceive a cat near her, there must actually be a cat near her.

This book will suggest that, with hardly any exceptions, the ideas of mainstream philosophy have been, when not just so many perfectly parochial propositions, then just so many analytically empty ideas. Oftentimes the analytically empty ideas offered are, if true, some *conceptual* truths. This may well happen with the analytic thought that if someone perceives a table nearby him, then, as must needs be, there is a table nearby him. For, as seems intuitive, that thought may hold true owing to a certain feature of the concept of one's perceiving something nearby oneself. Of course, it also happens with thoughts that, unlike those heavily involving perceiving, directly concern only some matters very far from any interest to mainstream philosophers. For example, it happens, quite as well, with the thought that if someone is a husband, then, as must needs be, there is another person to whom that first one is married. By contrast with those two *conceptually analytic* thoughts, it doesn't happen, it seems, with the analytic thought that if someone is a regular smoker of cigarettes, then that person smokes cigarettes regularly. Nor does it happen with the thought that when someone writes a book, then, as must needs be, a book is written by someone. Assuming them to be correct, and giving them an apt label, these latter two thoughts are just some *grammatically analytic* ideas, or some *syntactically analytic* thoughts, by contrast with ideas conceptually analytic.

As may become fairly clear, it is not very often that mainstream philosophers offer analytic thoughts aren't conceptual thoughts, thoughts that don't even purport to be conceptual truths. But, throughout most of this book, I won't bother to notice that point. Rather, when noting a typical mainstream offering, it will be enough to observe that the thought placed on offer is an analytic idea, without bothering to say that it's a conceptually analytic idea.

Nowadays, I'm happy to say, the vast majority of mainstream philosophers agree that there is, at least, *some* conception of analyticity that is not only sound enough, but of some philosophical utility, as well, however modest may be that utility. Perhaps somewhat unfortunately, or perhaps just all so predictably, different writers fasten on different conceptions, even if most might not differ all that much from most others.[26] In this book, it will become pretty clear which thoughts are, on the conception I favor, paradigmatically analytic ideas.

As indicated, I offer this following (vaguely expressed) diagnosis of why mainstream philosophy is quite deficient philosophy, when assessed by the standards dominantly deemed proper for the subject, throughout virtually all of its very long history. First, and foremost, there is the central idea of the book: Except when being parochial thoughts, as with the differences between how we use "believe" and how we use "perceive", the ideas offered in this philosophy are, almost without exception, concretely empty ideas. Second, and less centrally, there is this vaguely expressed hypothesis regarding all those concretely empty offerings. Unlike propositions of pure mathematics, the concretely empty ideas of analytic philosophy are analytically empty ideas. But, now, this following point cannot be overemphasized. Even if I am wrong about the second part of my diagnosis—and the ideas of analytic philosophy differ from those of mathematics for a reason left untouched by anything I say—that is a relatively minor error. The main point of the work will stand: Except when being parochial thoughts, the ideas offered by analytic philosophers are, almost without exception, concretely empty ideas, making or meaning no difference, at all, for how anything ever is with concrete reality. Just so, it's mainly for that reason that, in its mainstream core, analytic philosophy has been pretty deficient philosophy, when assessed by the standards usually deemed most apt for assessing philosophy.[27]

26. In the SEP, the entry most directly relevant here is: Georges Rey, "The Analytic/Synthetic Distinction," *The Stanford Encyclopedia of Philosophy (Summer 2012 Edition)*, Edward N. Zalta, ed., URL = <http://plato.stanford.edu/archives/sum2012/entries/analytic-synthetic/>. Most recently, the philosopher giving most attention to this somewhat technical topic is, perhaps, Gillian Russell. For a short, challenging treatment of the topic, see her paper "The Analytic/Synthetic Distinction," *Philosophy Compass*, 2/5 (2007) 712–29. For a longer, more positive treatment see her book *Truth in Virtue of Meaning: A Defence of the Analytic/Synthetic Distinction*, Oxford University Press, 2008. For an even more recent defense of this distinction, see relevant sections of David Chalmers, *Constructing the World*, Oxford University Press, 2012.

27. Though this chapter's last note may be gratuitous, it is far worse for philosophical writing to be unclear than for it to be redundant. So, even if it means I must be something of a bore, in this chapter's last note I try to close in a way that has things be crystal clear.

With that said, I'll now say this: Even while I greatly doubt that any recent philosophy has achieved more than recent mainstream philosophy has attained, I won't bother to argue that point in this book. Quite in line with that, and as I said near the outset, my argumentation *won't* concern anything that's deeply normative, or fully evaluative, or anything of the ilk. Or, at the least, I won't try to address claims that are obviously, or explicitly, or paradigmatically of any such forms or sorts. (Along with many others, I greatly doubt that, excepting, perhaps, those of them as may be just so

Here and now, that will be far from apparent to most readers or, at least, to most who are professional philosophers. Indeed, to most of them, it may now even seem quite implausible. But, as I trust, once the whole of this book has been read, and not just its first chapter, most will find its central thrust to be more than just pretty plausible. As I suspect, they may find my message to be, at least in largest measure, so utterly unsurprising as may have it appear perfectly humdrum, perhaps even somewhat disappointingly boring.

---

many analytically empty ideas, any purely evaluative or deeply normative claim is any truth at all. But, here, that thought, considered by many to be controversial, is hardly the main point.

Rather, what's crucial here is this quite plain and uncontroversial idea. If there should be any purely evaluative or normative truths (beyond such analytically empty ideas as, say, the thought that doing something good is better than doing something bad) then none of them is a thought whose truth ever makes any difference for how things are with concrete reality. Of that, I think, we can be all but absolutely certain. But, in this book's pages, that's just overkill, perhaps no better than just some easily achieved bullying.) Even while avoiding such relatively marginal philosophical topics, what I'll be taking on board, in this book, looks to be, quite certainly, a very great deal of academically prestigious and philosophically influential material, quite aptly called nothing less than *mainstream philosophy*.

2

PROMISING EXAMPLES OF CONCRETELY SUBSTANTIAL PHILOSOPHY

As I've been saying, when it's not been downright parochial, recent and current philosophy are heavily pervaded with concretely empty ideas and, what's more, the emptiness of those thoughts is due to their analyticity. But, for a philosophy that aims to be highly relevant to concrete matters and issues, is there really any alternative?

It's very doubtful, I think, that we'll find anything much when looking for synthetic strictly necessary truths, which truths are supposed to govern, somehow or other, any and all concrete reality. That said, in this chapter I'll look for some *characteristically philosophical thoughts*, none of them just a parochial proposition, but, still, each of them a *concretely substantial idea*.

1. Some Pretty Promising Examples of Concretely Substantial Philosophy

For the better part of a century, and with no end in sight, and to a far greater degree than is usually realized, ours is an age when philosophers have been enormously concerned with conceptual connections, with linguistic issues, and with little that's far more widely worldly. To be sure, in much philosophically prominent writing, many more worldly substantial thoughts also have been espoused.

But, for the most part, these concretely substantial thoughts have been just so many *commonsense* ideas. Among them is the thought that many people each remembers that he, or she, went to college. Also, among them is the thought that there are many tables, each spatially separate and distant from many other tables. And, as for the rest, most are just the denials of commonsense ideas.

As should be clear, none of those ideas will be aptly called a *characteristically philosophical* idea. So, to encounter much *concretely substantial philosophy*, we must look beyond not only questions concerning the languages and concepts we earthlings employ, but also beyond our fund of commonsense thought, as well.

Looking far beyond that, during much of its history philosophy comprised all sorts of concretely substantial offerings, many of them characteristically philosophical propositions. Or, at the least, an apt contemporary take on much old philosophy might see the subject that way. Even by my lights, it may very well be that most olden philosophers who offered grand concretely substantial thoughts *also offered concretely empty* ideas, just perhaps even almost all of those long dead thinkers.[1] So, I certainly don't say that an old thinker's favorite

---

1. Since ancient times, philosophers have put forth various ideas as to what to make of the case known as The Ship of Theseus, wherein a wooden ship's planks, for example, are each replaced, serially and in a very gradual process, by terribly similar wooden planks. Is the resulting ship the original ship, or is it not the original ship? As should already seem quite clear, and as will become yet clearer as our explorations advance, this is an analytically empty issue.

In the early modern era, Thomas Hobbes exercised himself of just such a question. Not being an historian of philosophy, I'll give you a report from my colleague Don Garrett, a leading authority on the early modern period. As to the question of whether Hobbes labored over this question, Garrett reports:

Yes, he did this in *De Corpore* II.11.7. For reference purposes, the standard edition is *The English Works of Thomas Hobbes of Malmesbury*, William Molesworth, ed. London: John Bohn 1839, Volume 1. The discussion occurs on pages 135–138.

As to the positions Hobbes considers on the matter, and the view of them he labors toward, Garrett has this to tell us about Hobbes:

He notes that philosophers have disputed about identity over time, some placing it in sameness of matter, some in sameness of form, and some in 'aggregate of accidents.' He proposes his own version of the ship of Theseus as a counterexample to the sufficiency of sameness of form:

For if, for example, that ship of Theseus, concerning the difference whereof made by continual reparation in taking out the old planks and putting in the new, the sophisters of Athens were wont to dispute, were, after all the planks were changed, the same numerical ship it were at the beginning; and if some man had kept the old planks as they were taken out, and by afterwards putting them together in the same order, had again made a ship of them, this without doubt, had also been the same numerical ship with that which was in the beginning; and so there would have been two ships numerically the same, which is absurd.

His own view is that no one of the three theories will account for everything we say, since "we must consider by what name anything is called, when we inquire concerning the *identity* of it."

So if the word "ship'" is "'given for the matter only,'" the ship composed the original pieces is "'the same ship'" (and was even when those parts were disassembled.) If the word is given for form ""'proceeding from the same beginning of motion,'"" then the ship

philosophical thoughts were all concretely substantial ideas. But, in many cases, an aptly charitable reading will have them proposing quite a few concretely substantial ideas or, at the least, it may use their proposals as templates for quite a few such substantial thoughts. Though *there may be serious doubts* about it, that suggestion is a pretty plausible one and, at the least, it might greatly help the presentation of our exploration. Let me amplify.

For starters, I'll focus on three mutually exclusive sorts of metaphysical position, already adumbrated, each resonating with a lot that's been in traditional philosophy. Though they're hard to articulate helpfully, which may indicate serious problems with them, with each it at least appears that we can grasp the thought quite well:

> *Entity Materialism*: There's at least one concrete entity. Any concrete entity is a purely material entity; that is, it's fully physical. (So, if there are any minds or souls, then each will be something material.)
>
> *Entity Idealism*: There's at least one concrete entity. Any concrete entity is a purely mental immaterial entity; none is at all material, or physical.
>
> *Entity Dualism*: There are at least two distinct concrete entities. Any concrete entity is of either one or another of two radically different kinds. Some concrete entities are purely material, or fully physical; none of them is mental. Other concreta, each a mind, or a soul, are wholly and purely mental individuals; none is at all material, or physical.

As I trust, you'll easily see each to be in strict conflict with the two others, with the conflicts concerning concretely substantial questions. At least on my way of taking things, these three apparently substantial ideas are nothing new: Thomas Hobbes was a materialist and, in important ways, he was at least a lot like our Entity Materialist. By the same token, Rene Descartes was at least a lot like our Entity Dualist, as was John Locke. And, in important ways, George Berkeley was at least a lot like our Entity Idealist.

In several cases, my contemporary take on a metaphysical position is rather different, in certain ways, from how the metaphysical view was understood by famous historical proponents of the view. As I understand the three thoughts just placed in display, each certainly appears to be, and each most likely actually

---

composed of replacement pieces is the same ship. He adds that if you use the term for '"same matter figured"' as a ship, then it is the same as long as all the matter remains so configured, and '"partly the same and partly not the same"' if some but not all of the matter is replaced. This seems, actually, pretty close to your view that it is not a substantive issue but just a question of how to talk.

It is gratifying to learn that, after exercising himself over such a question, much as I myself have done, this canonical figure arrives at the idea that, at bottom, so far as anything happily general concerning concrete reality may be concerned, there is precious little substance, or nothing, to be found in the issue, much as I myself eventually concluded.

is, a concretely substantial idea that favors a certain way for concrete reality to be, as against conflicting ways for it to be. Apparently, in some cases, that's not (even very much like) the understanding of a noted view's noted historical advocate(s).

Just so, as I understand him, the actual, historical Hobbes held that the only sensible statements claiming existence were statements concerning material bodies, immediately ruling out the possibility of there being concretely substantial thoughts as to the existence of immaterial souls. On that interpretation of his writing, Hobbes held a very radical view and, perhaps, a very radically confused view. For, on that interpretation, Hobbes's materialism would amount to nothing more than the statement that something concrete exists (rather than there being nothing concrete at all).[2] (Perhaps worth noting, the statement that at least one concretum exists is a concretely substantial claim, even if not at all materialist.) More usefully, we may count Hobbes an Entity Materialist, or we may contrive just such a descendant from him.

On the other side, it seems that Berkeley held that our notion of matter was hopelessly defective. For some such reason, words like "material entity" couldn't apply to any reality. But, even as it's useful to treat Hobbes charitably, so it's also useful to do that with Berkeley. When that's done, we may count Berkeley an Entity Idealist, or we may contrive just such a descendant for *him*. At least for now, that's enough about such canonical philosophers.[3]

But, then we must ask, or at least we should ask: What is it for something to be *material*? Relatedly, but in terms currently more widely used in philosophy, we also ask: What is it for something to be *physical*? Well, perhaps one thing required is that anything material should be spatially located, or be spatiotemporally located. Even if so, that won't help much. And, it is extremely difficult, perhaps even impossible, to do much more. For all I can tell, with the philosophically relevant senses of the terms, there's hardly anything we ever mean when

2. Of course, if Hobbes—or anyone else, for that matter—thought that these two propositions amounted to the very same thing, he'd be radically confused. But, of course, the presence of some radical confusion may detract little from a thinker's philosophical contribution.

3. Nowadays, almost all respectable philosophers embrace Entity Materialism, while hardly any accept Entity Dualism, much less the likes of an extremely unfashionable Entity Idealism. But, at all events, regarding concretely substantial philosophy, there's nothing here that's very novel. So, for philosophically fresh substantial offerings, we must look elsewhere, quite beyond Entity Materialism's neighborhood.

I've offered arguments for four forms of Entity Dualist View, each an Interactionist Dualism, with material bodies affecting immaterial souls, and with souls affecting bodies. Mostly, this occurs in long stretches of *All the Power in the World*, Oxford University Press, 2006. Some of the Interactionist Dualisms I've promoted are, I think, quite novel positions, even if others may differ little, if at all, from Descartes' view. At any rate, all four are characteristically philosophical views that are concretely substantial positions. Well, in this big neighborhood, that's what I've *argued*, and I *would still argue*. Though I've been arguing all that, I have little idea, really, about what to *believe* on these large metaphysical matters. And, so, I'm agnostic, regarding them all.

saying that something is material, or physical. This is a main reason for my saying, so very guardedly, no more than this: Our three highlighted metaphysical views, our displayed materialism and dualism and idealism, *at least may* be concretely substantial ideas.

On the other side of the presently salient issue, we ask: What is it for an entity, or a being, to be *mental*? Well, perhaps one thing required is that a mental being should have a power to think, or to experience. Even if so, that will help only a little. And, perhaps nothing will help a lot more. Now, my sense is that our grasp of what it is for something to be mental, in a philosophically central sense of that term, is not quite as terribly inchoate, diffuse, and murky as our poor grasp of what it is for something to be material, in a philosophically central sense of *that* term. Still, for all I can tell, it *may just possibly* be that there's nothing of philosophical moment we ever mean when saying that something is mental. So, that's another reason, quite slight, for my saying, cautiously, our three thoughts *may* be concretely substantial ideas.

Using traditional thought as a guide, we may do somewhat better, I think, in displaying some views, correlative with the foregoing trio, that are almost certainly concretely substantial, even if many philosophers may, nowadays, consider them incorrect. Following Descartes, we may consider just such concrete entities as are spatially extended entities. Almost certainly, there *are some* ways for concrete reality to be on which it comprises spatially extended concreta (even if none obtains). Even if we should find it hard to think that we have a very clear grasp of what it is for something to be material, or to be physical, that's not so for the question of what it is for something to be spatially extended.

For good measure, and again following Descartes, we may take "conscious" as our contrast term for "spatially extended", even as for Descartes, I trust, anything mental was conscious.

Employing these Cartesian suggestions, we may now display this trio of concretely substantial views, each logically conflicting with the others:

Entity Spatial-Extentionism: There's at least one concrete entity. Any concrete entity is a spatially extended entity. (So, if there are any minds or souls, then each will be spatially extended.)

Entity Idealism that Precludes Spatial Extension: There's at least one concrete entity. Any concrete entity is a purely conscious entity; none is spatially extended. (So if there are any rocks, each will be something purely conscious, even while, perhaps despite appearances, none will be spatially extended.)

Neo-Cartesian Entity Dualism: There are at least two distinct concrete entities. Any concrete entity is of either one or another of two radically different kinds. Some concrete entities are spatially extended; none of them is conscious. Other concreta, each a mind, or a soul, are wholly and purely conscious individuals; none is spatially extended.

Being so closely and nicely related to our previously displayed threesome, this newly displayed trio leads us to realize, with no great leap of the intellect, that various further such threesomes may also be displayed, even with each, very likely, being less vulnerable than its predecessors to any charge of comprising only ideas that all fail to be concretely substantial.

At all events, we may see that, with any of these trios of views, the situation is this: If any of its three salient thoughts should be true, then, even logically, that will preclude any of the others from being true. So, for example, there is this quite correct utterly empty idea: If Entity Materialism is true, or correct, then Entity Dualism and Entity Idealism are untrue, or incorrect.

That empty idea is very uninteresting. Other empty thoughts may be more interesting. And, some may be, as well, characteristically philosophical thoughts.

Let's try to consider a concretely empty idea that, nonetheless, is a philosophical idea. To set the stage for doing that, I'll bring up a couple of substantial ideas. Each has long figured in philosophical debate. Rather rough, here's a brief formulation of the first of the two:

> *All Too Full Determinism*: As regards any event in which any of us is involved, like your thinking about baseball an hour ago, it was fully determined, by events occurring at times long before any of us existed, that the event would occur and, so, from those early times onward, it was inevitable that your thinking about baseball should occur an hour ago.

This Determinism is, I suggest, a characteristically philosophical thesis, maybe about as much as are the Materialism, the Idealism, and the Dualism just considered.

By contrast with All Too Full Determinism, the second concretely substantial idea is just a commonsensical idea, nothing peculiarly philosophical:

> *Real Choice in Thinking*: From time to time, at least, many of us choose what to think about, from among actually available options for her own thoughtful activity.

As far as I can tell, just about all normal human adults believe this. In their philosophical writing many philosophers uphold it, many others deny it, and most don't address the matter.

Contrasting with that Determinism and that Real Choice idea, there's this empty idea:

> *Real Choice Incompatibilism*: *If* many of us *do* choose what to think about, from among actually available options for her own thoughtful activity, *then* it's *not* true that, as regards any event in which any of us is involved, it was fully determined, by events occurring at times long before any of us existed, that

the event would occur and, so, from those early times onward, it was inevitable that the event should occur.

Though figuring in philosophical discussion for centuries, this Incompatibilism *doesn't* differentiate any way for concrete reality to be from any other way. Though it's concretely empty, philosophers do, and should, seriously consider this Incompatibilism.[4]

Finally, and now turning away from interesting empty thoughts, I'll close this section by considering what may well be another substantial philosophical claim:

> *The (Causal) Closure of the Physical*: Insofar as it's brought about by anything at all—and it's not just some wholly random happening, any wholly physical event, or any physical process, is brought about only by just something that's itself physical—whether some physical events, or some physical processes, or some other physical whatnots. Just signaled by the latest occurrence of "only," the wholly physical whatnot, or item, is *never* brought about by any *nonphysical* whatnot, or item.

Nearly all mainstreamers accept this thought of The (Causal) Closure. As I understand him, Descartes denied it. Truth to tell, I deny it as well; indeed, I even endorse its denial. Of course, the negative thought I endorse is also a concretely substantial idea.

2. The Substantial Scientiphicalism of Mainstream Philosophy

As we do well to suppose, if only for reasons exploratory and expository, there are many old philosophical thoughts that are concretely substantial ideas. It's

---

4. My distinct impression is that the vast majority of mainstream philosophers accept Real Choice in Thinking or, in short, Real Choice. What of the other two thoughts just displayed?

Well, until several decades ago, very many philosophers were quite willing to allow that All Too Full Determinism might well be true. No surprise, they didn't want that to be any great threat to Real Choice. After all, Real Choice is quite central to commonsense thinking. So, they denied Real Choice Incompatibilism, and they accepted *Real Choice Compatibilism*.

With modern physics having greatly pervaded our common culture, many philosophers are confident that All Too Full Determinism *isn't* true. With that being so, many very recent and current advocates of Real Choice in Thinking may accept *Real Choice Incompatibilism*: Even as they believe the Determinist thesis to be clearly false, they may believe that it presents no credible threat to Real Choice. Of course, in this *other* bargain, they may well deny *its* opposing empty claim. Thus, they may deny Real Choice Compatibilism. Full disclosure: I'm an *advocate of Real Choice* who *accepts* Real Choice *Incompatibilism*.

harder to propose new ones. Recent decades have seen precious little of it and, in this section, I'll do nothing to change that.

Rather, here I'll try to articulate, if only quite roughly and very partially, some concretely substantial thoughts that, during the last third of the twentieth century, came to enjoy something like the status of orthodoxy among most prominent mainstream philosophers. And, at least for the most part, they continue to enjoy this status. Some of the thoughts are materialistic ideas; others are closely allied with the physicalist thoughts. No surprise, the allied thoughts are less ambitious than the fully materialist ideas with which they are to comport. At all events, we may recognize all of these thoughts, from the most ambitious through the least, as being parts of, or features of, a pretty familiar worldview, a view aptly called *Scientiphicalism*.

Thus, many now accept various theses about how anything not material will wholly *supervene on* something that is material. Widely accepted, here's one of them: Whenever one concrete individual should be exactly like another in *all physical* regards, both intrinsic and relational, too, the two will be exactly alike in *absolutely all* regards, intrinsic and relational.

There is little in the Scientiphical worldview, maybe nothing at all, that is accepted only by professional philosophers. Quite the contrary is true: At least implicitly, even back in the 1950s, when only a schoolboy, I accepted it, or at least most of it. And, even if none of us could give much voice to the ideas, so did many of my young friends, most of them, like myself, then unquestioning atheists. But, then, what is this (worldview I've called) *Scientiphicalism*?

Let me rehearse a rough sketch of the worldview's core:

First, insofar as it's determined by anything at all, and it isn't merely random, the spatial distribution of all the world's matter at a time (including what wholly composes all the world's physically composite entities) is determined by the distribution of the matter at earlier times—and maybe some other earlier material factors, not well covered by the label "the distribution of matter at earlier times". (We understand this, I suppose, so that it allows there to be, but it doesn't require there to be, a time before which there isn't any matter.) This determination proceeds according to the world's basic natural laws, which are its basic physical laws.

Second, owing to the variety in these material distributions, at certain times, like right now, much matter composes complex physical structures or systems, many of which are stars, for example, and some of which are, say, planets. Salient among the systematic physical complexes, and relatively rare in our physically vast world, are those that are alive. Yet more salient, and also still rarer, are the highly complex living physical entities that are feeling and thinking beings.

Third, on the Scientiphical Metaphysic all living human people are highly complex physical entities, each with many physical parts, but no other substantial parts. These people include me myself and, so far as I can tell, everyone with whom I'll ever communicate any of my thoughts or experience; each of us is a physical entity *ultimately wholly constituted* of just so many basic physically simple things, like quarks, maybe, or maybe like superstrings. (On a Nonstandard Version of the Scientiphical Metaphysic, there aren't any absolutely basic entities; rather, there's an infinite sequence of "more and more basic physical constituents". As I suspect, a Nonstandard Scientiphical Metaphysic cannot be sustained. Whether or not that's so, it won't do anything toward having us be entities with important mental powers, including the power to really choose....) Just so, and at all events, none of us ever has any constituents except all those that are fully and wholly physical entities.

Fourth, all our powers and propensities are physically derivative dispositions, whether they're "deterministic" dispositions, or whether they're (merely) "probabilistic" propensities, or whether, just perhaps, they're best covered only by some still quite different labeling, whatever any such better labeling should be.[5]

As I hope and expect all that's so terribly credible as to be quite boring.

Pretty soon, I'll articulate, however partially, some further tenets of Scientiphicalism, showing each to be a concretely substantial proposition. As a prelude to that, I'll offer some concretely empty comments that may help us grasp the substantial tenets that I'll be articulating.

Let's start by focusing on a presumably simple and basic physical entity; let's say it's a certain electron. Well, our electron is propensitied to attract any basic physical thing that's electrically charged oppositely from how it's charged. It will have this propensity even if there never are, in the concrete world inhabited by our considered electron, any entities electrically charged oppositely. In such a circumstance, our electron will still have its noted electrical power, all right; it just won't ever have any chance to manifest the power. (As some say, its power is "directed at" whatever, in its world, might be charged positively—*even if there never is*, in its world, anything that's so charged.[6])

In a properly general way, this is how things stand propensitively, not only with simple and basic physical concreta, but also with any such complex and

---

5. In *All the Power in the World*, the passage rehearsed is on pages 324–25. Unless otherwise indicated, when discussing Scientiphicalism now, I *won't* discuss the Nonstandard Scientiphical Metaphysic. Nothing of moment will turn on that; and it will allow for a simpler, more reader-friendly presentation.

6. For an early discussion of such (supposed) directedness, see C. B. Martin and K. Pfeifer "Intentionality and the Non-Psychological," *Philosophy and Phenomenological Research*, 1986, Volume 46, pages 531–54. Subsequent discussions, developing matters along much the same lines include George Molnar's *Powers: A Study in Metaphysics*, Oxford University Press, 2003, especially Chapter 3, and my *All the Power in the World*, especially Chapter 5. No surprise, both in the noted paper and the noted chapters, almost everything offered is concretely empty. Still, much of it may be, I think, both correct and usefully clarifying.

derivative things as there may be. For example, consider a refrigerator that's propensitied to cool items, like pieces of cheese, whose temperature is between 41 degrees Fahrenheit and an extremely high temperature. The fridge will have this propensity *whether or not there ever are* any apt items for it to interact with in an appropriately cooling way. Of course, for the complex fridge to *manifest* its power to cool things placed inside it, the refrigerator will need some such items, each of which will be, or would be, an apt reciprocal interaction partner for our powerfully cooling refrigerator. Unlike the *interactions* that they serve to promote, which are all *relational* affairs, the reciprocal power of any such partner will be intrinsic to the partner, just as our fridge's power is intrinsic to it. Of course, a particular's propensities may be *described in relational terms*. But, for clarity's sake, it's best to focus on what's basically something nonrelational here, however that may be described. Then nobody will be confused by, for example, words like these: Only a refrigerator that's *already cooled* a container of milk has *the real power to recool* a container of milk. Even if it's an old fridge's perfect physical duplicate, a just newly made fridge can't have the *power to recool* anything. That's true. But, if we focus on thoughts like that, we may neglect other truths. And, without them, we can't articulate, at all well, our accepted Scientiphicalism.

Focusing properly, we may say how it is that a complex physical concretum's propensities physically derive from just these three things: They derive, first, from *how it is that the complex's basic components each are propensitied* and, second, from *how its basic components are physically related to each other* within the physical complex they all serve to constitute—and, less saliently but still third, from *how nicely freestanding they are from still other concreta.* Central to Scientiphicalism, *that philosophical thought is a concretely substantial idea.*

Our Scientiphicalism has the world comprise only a fairly few basic kinds of basic individual. And, correlatively, our Scientiphicalism will have the world's stuff be matter of only a fairly few basic material kinds. The few basic kinds of material stuff will be *mutually exclusive for* the world's matter. And, they'll be *jointly exhaustive of* all its matter. So, while there just might be, say, a basic kind of stuff that's electronish matter and a distinct basic kind of stuff that's, say, quarkish matter, there won't be basic stuff of all these following kinds, along with very many more: brass, butter, copper, plastic, cloth, jam, Styrofoam, porcelain, flesh, pulp, bone, Formica, and oak. Rather, any brass that there is will be only a physically derivative sort of stuff; basically, the brass will be just some electronish stuff, say, aptly intermingled with some quarkish stuff—or, at the least, something much like that. The same holds for butter and for bone.

As we've noted repeatedly, our Scientiphicalism has it that the powers of a *nonbasic individual,* a copper wire, for example, will be physically derivative propensities. Similarly, our Scientiphicalism also has it that the powers of *nonbasic stuff* are physically derivative: Just as the power of a certain copper wire to conduct electricity is a physically derivative propensity, so also is the electrical-conductive power of the wire's copper.

On our Scientiphical Metaphysic, that's just how things are: Just as there aren't many quadrillions of utterly different perfectly basic individuals, each with its own distinctively irreducible and irreducibly distinctive powers, there aren't, either, quadrillions of utterly different basic (kinds of) stuffs, each with *its* distinctively irreducible and irreducibly distinctive powers.

Here's more of our Scientiphicalism: It's perfectly possible for *any* physical complex to have a perfect physical duplicate, with each of the two precisely similar complexes spatially quite separate and distant from the other. A very obvious way for that to happen is along "particulate" lines: In each of two spatially separate regions, there are very many particles of exactly three basic kinds. And, in each region, there's exactly the same number of particles, of any given kind, as there are in the other region. For example, each region has exactly 2.3457×10^{26} electrons, and each has exactly 3.71965×10^{26} up-quarks, and each has exactly 3.71965×10^{26} down-quarks. And, in each region, all the particles are physically related to each other in just the same way as occurs in the other region.

As Scientiphicalism has it, *any* complex individual is perfectly duplicable. Even if some complexes are more than merely physical, that will be so. True or not, the thought's substantial.

According to our Scientiphical Metaphysic, what "underwrites" the ubiquitous possibility of precise duplication? Now, by themselves, the *Core* tenets of Scientiphicalism, sketched above, can't do the wanted underwriting. But, in addition to those Core Scientiphical thoughts, many mainstream philosophers accept other metaphysical ideas, thoughts taken to comport well with the Core of the View. They accept *Extended Scientiphicalism*, not just Scientiphicalism's Core.

As I'll suggest, the wanted underwriting may be done with the aid of an Extended Scientiphical idea that goes something like this: Even with respect to the very most basic physical individuals, all of an entity's powers with respect to anything other than itself are *generalistically-directed* physical propensities, each directed with respect to certain *general features of whatever other* entities there may be. For example, our electron will be propensitied to repel any other entity that has certain electronish characteristics, as with whatever we label "negative electric charge". Our electron won't be propensitied, for this repelling, with *only certain of the* other generally electronish particles, while *not* disposed to repel others, also negatively charged. It's a concretely substantial thought, I stress, that all of an entity's dispositions with respect to other things are generalistically-directed powers.

In the brief sketch of Scientiphicalism provided so far, many matters are nowhere near fully specific. With these many matters, each of many quite various fuller specifications will itself be a distinctively different concretely substantial idea. For example, here's one such specification, only fairly full: Every perfectly physical complex entity will have, as its basic constituents, a plurality of metaphysically simple or partless physical particles, with each such particle spatially separated from all others by perfectly empty space. On a very different specification, also only fairly full, things will be like this: (What are casually taken to be) basic physical particles are all (mere) perturbations in a (heterogeneous) physical field.

For decades, Extended Scientiphicalism has been accepted, if only implicitly, by most prominent mainstream philosophers. That's greatly constrained what they've produced or proposed. So, compliance with Scientiphicalism will constrain how we understand their work.

3. Memory, History and Emptiness

Rightly placing aside any and all skeptical worries—as they're irrelevant, here and now—it may be said that I fondly remember my college experiences. As it's only an everyday remark about Peter Unger, that's certainly not any impressively sweeping statement. To the contrary, so perfectly personal and provincial is that expression of my reminiscence that there's little temptation, indeed, to confuse it with any characteristically philosophical statement, whether the prototypical piece of philosophy be a concretely substantial statement or whether it be an empty proposition. Yet, when we're thinking along a certain fashionable line of thought, my innocent little reminiscence may have us confront ideas currently considered quintessentially philosophical. This may happen even when the confronted ideas are just so many obvious truths and, in the bargain, they're boring bits of philosophy. Now, I'll start to make good on that.

Much as many recent philosophers have done, especially many of the Scientiphically inclined among us, we may consider a person who's quite separate and distinct from me, but (Scientiphically supposing that I'm at least largely physical) who's precisely like I am, in every physical way, respect, or regard. Without needing to go in for wonderfully symmetrical worlds, we may do this very readily, when all the physical ways we're considering are just those that are commonly taken, by recent philosophers, to be nonrelational respects or regards. Or, putting a more positive spin on things, we may readily do this when we consider just those physical regards or respects that are all *qualitative* respects or regards—ways that are each wholly *intrinsic* to, or wholly *internal* to, the person under consideration.

Almost all contemporary philosophers are very comfortable with this supposition concerning physical duplication. Indeed, most are just as comfortable with the more ambitious thought that, whenever there should be a person who's (intrinsically) physically perfectly similar to me, that man will be, in *absolutely all qualitative* respects, exactly the same as I am. As our Scientiphicalism certainly allows, this may happen in a way that, in all relevant regards, is quite random, as with some lightning rearranging many of the elementary particles composing a stone.

Going along with this, we'll suppose there to be a "physical duplicate" of me. He might be two inches away from me, or three miles, or four light-years. As we'll suppose, this will be someone who, right now, is precisely similar to how I am, right now, in absolutely all purely qualitative or intrinsic respects. Now, even supposing that this duplicate person should be just as well endowed as I am, with lots of real mental power, can my duplicate fondly *remember my* old college experiences? No; he cannot.

Quite correct, that's also concretely empty. By considering an aptly symmetrical universe, we may have that be perfectly clear: In parallel with our planet's development, and that of our solar system, and so on, there developed, far away but simultaneously, a precisely similar planet, in a precisely similar solar system, and so on. Each inhabitant of our planet has a precise total duplicate on the other planet and, of course, vice versa. In this symmetric example, the duplicates are not only qualitatively or intrinsically the same, but they'll also be *relationally*, or *extrinsically*, just the same. Just so, in every last detail, your life developed precisely in parallel with the life of your intergalactic twin, just as his life developed in perfect parallel with yours. Still, your twin remembers *only his* own college experiences, not any of yours.

With certain duplicates not so grandly symmetric, we come to appreciate the emptiness of further thoughts concerning the philosophically prominent topic of memory and the past. So, consider a duplicate just one nanosecond old. At least according to Scientiphicalism, this person won't be *only* a precise *physical* duplicate. For example, there's this: To just exactly the degree and in just the same way you're talented musically, he will be musically talented.

As we've already observed, this person won't remember any of your old college experiences. That's old hat. So, looking for something new to try on, let's ask this further question: Will such a "newly arrived" duplicate remember *anyone's* old college experiences? Well, if he's to remember anyone's college experiences, it had better be *his own* college experiences that this duplicate remembers. On that much, we're already agreed. Well, *can* he remember *his own* college experiences? No; of course not. Being such a newly arrived person, this duplicate *never had* any college experiences. So, there *aren't* any such experiences of his *for him* to remember. So, he can't remember any college experiences. Quite correct, that's also *empty*.

We ask: Why can't your new duplicate remember any experiences? We may answer: It's because he lacks an appropriate *history*. No doubt, that's also both correct and empty.

Here's another matter concerning memory; perhaps more subtle: Suppose you know a great deal of chemistry. Then, it may occur to an extra-terrestrial super-scientist to make someone who knows a lot of chemistry, in this almost automatic way: He'll make an atom-for-atom duplicate of you. Presumably, even upon arrival the new man will be, *in all nonrelational respects,* just like you were so very recently. Does the newcomer *remember that,* when oxygen and hydrogen atoms combine, each oxygen atom combines with two hydrogen atoms?

As it's anything but accidental that the duplicate is right about the chemical matter, a pretty plausible case can be made for an affirmative answer to this question. But, as well, a pretty fair case can be made for a negative answer. And, what's more, a pretty good case can be made for the thought that there's *no determinate answer* here, *either* way. But, whatever else may be going on with it, does the question concern any concretely substantial issue? I think not.

Apparently, there's little need to support my negative view, even as it appears pretty obvious that nothing concretely substantial is really at issue. But, even if it involves overkill, we do well to examine a certain bit of apparently supportive reasoning, gaining clarity by doing that.

Let's suppose our question gets a negative answer: The duplicate *doesn't* really remember any chemical facts, not really and truly. All right, now let's suppose that, after your duplicate is constructed, you yourself are locked up for awhile, so that you can't perform any experiments, or do very much calculation. Indeed, you can't do much of anything at all: Literally, your hands are tied. At least for that reason, during this next year you'll be prevented from doing any serious chemistry. No longer thinking about you, we now consider two other people. One of these is just a mediocre chemist, one Joe Blogs. And, the other person is your precise duplicate, just so newly existing. Now, even as you're one of the world's leading chemists, the new duplicate has a very great ability to do chemistry. Well, over this next month, both of these people, Joe Blogs and your new duplicate, are quite free to work at chemistry. And, that they both do. Now, whom do we think will discover more about how things are chemically, Joe Blogs or your qualitatively identical duplicate?

As most are wont to believe, and as our widely shared Scientiphicalism certainly implies, your duplicate may be expected to achieve more, in this area of empirical scientific discovery, than will be accomplished by old Joe Blogs. For one salient point to that effect, there's this: Even right from the get-go, your duplicate will do more penetrating chemistry than Blogs will. And, as we're supposing, the duplicate will do this in *spite* of the fact that, at the month's start, he doesn't remember any of the facts of chemistry! Well, evidently, in *such* an event, really *remembering* those facts isn't all that important for making chemical discoveries. That is, whatever difference there is between really remembering chemical facts and, on the other hand, what's going on with your duplicate, well, *that* isn't important for doing productive work in experimental chemistry.

Or, so we should do well to conclude, on the supposition that your new duplicate won't remember, at the start of the month, any of the facts of chemistry.

Given our agreement about your duplicate's *impoverished history*, but *also*
given our *Scientiphical* agreement, the question of whether the newly arrived
duplicate *remembers* chemical facts won't be any concretely *substantial* issue. And,
even without supposing Scientiphicalism holds true, we may be pretty sure this
question's concretely empty.

To some very astute sophisticates, it will occur to ask whether, right from the
start, your duplicate can *think about* chemical substances, like water, and like gold.
They will realize that if the answer is "No", as most mainstreamers believe, then
being able to think about chemical substances isn't important to doing penetrating chemistry. So, toward critiquing mainstream philosophy, this section
made several points. In the next chapter, we'll pursue them.

4. Various *Specifications of* Scientiphicalism and Various *Departures from* Scientiphicalism

At this point in our discussion, it may be most useful, I imagine, to switch from
mostly considering empty ideas to mostly considering substantial propositions.
Right now, that might be especially true I imagine, if some of the substantial
thoughts we'll consider are novel philosophical thoughts, at least pretty novel
ones. Without our going terribly far afield, so far that the present section will
lack any (even apparently) close connections with the section just finished, how
might we do that?

Well, my sketch of our shared Scientiphicalism was very far from being
fully specific. So, to contemplate some substantial philosophical thoughts, including some pretty novel ones, one thing to try is this: Forsaking great gener-
ality, we may consider various forms, each fairly specific, and some incompatible
with some others, that Scientiphicalism may take.

Here are just four examples of that, each being a further specification of
what's involved in there being, at different times, in our actual world, different
distributions of matter: First, at least during one greatly long Eon, all our
world's matter may comprise just so many distinct particles in an infinitely vast
void. Second, at least during one Eon, nothing much like that obtains; instead,
all our world's matter may comprise a single infinitely vast and highly heterogeneous material field, without even so much as a single hole anywhere, not
even the tiniest little void. Third, at least during one Eon, all our world's matter
may comprise a single infinitely vast and highly heterogeneous material field,
all right, but, instead of it being any spatially exhaustive material field, it's a
field with very many holes in it, with ever so many perfect voids, each completely and perfectly surrounded by (some of) the material field. Fourth, at least

during one Eon, our world's matter may comprise a vast variety of heterogeneous material fields, with each overlapping all the others, or even with each
fully coalescing with all others, even while each field is perfectly permeable,
everywhere, by all the other fields.

Even while *one* way for us to consider a variety of interestingly conflicting
substantial philosophical thoughts is to contemplate various ways in which our
Scientiphicalism may be more fully *specified*, quite *another* way, terribly different
from that, is to articulate various substantial thoughts each of which is *inconsistent with* Scientiphicalism.

In articulating substantial ideas that contravene Scientiphicalism, many
diverse paths may be pursued, many strikingly different from many others.

Along a pretty interesting path, we may articulate *certain substantially conflicting forms of Entity Dualism*. As you'll remember, on this concretely substantial
idea all concrete entities fall into one or the other of two radically different
kinds. Some are material things, none of which is mental. The others are mental
entities, none of which is material. For instructive illustration, we may suppose
that I'm *exactly one* of the immaterial mental individuals and, perfectly distinct
from me, you're *another* immaterial mental entity.

In relatively *nonspecific* terms, that's Entity Dualism for you. But, then, how
might we encounter some *more specific* sorts of this Dualism? Following philosophy's history, we may consider various possibilities concerning how the
world's immaterial souls, or some of them, might dynamically *interact with* the
world's material bodies, or with some of them.

On the most commonsensical of these positions, *Dualistic Interactionism*, my
soul—or, maybe better, the soul that's me—*directly interacts* with just my body,
and never with a body that's quite separate and distinct from mine, such as your
body, or the body that I call, aptly enough, "my computer keyboard". And, for
your part, your soul—or, maybe better, the soul that's you—*directly interacts* with
just your body.

Insofar as my soul interacts with someone else's body, not mine, then, that
will be only a very *indirect* interaction, or transaction—with my soul *first interact-
ing with* my body, which body *then interacts* with various other material things:
Usually, my body will then most directly interact with only something other
than someone else's body, as with, say, (the particles constituting) the air that's
between us, as we converse in the same room. Occasionally, my body may quite
directly interact with yours, of course. This will happen if, say, we shake hands,
all perfectly in the flesh, with neither of us wearing gloves, and so on.

Whenever I interact with another immaterial being, the interaction will be
indirect. Take ordinary face-to-face oral conversation, for example. Here, my
soul may directly interact with (a certain brainy part of) my body, which then
interacts with more of my body, so that my lips, throat, and tongue move appropriately for the production of speech; then there's the interaction between

my speaking body and the intervening air; then there's that between the air and your ears,...and, finally, there's the dynamic interaction between (a certain brainy part of) your body and your immaterial soul (which soul might be you, yourself). Much the same happens when I purposefully and consciously punch you in the nose, so that you'll feel pain. And, it occurs when I tell you something that makes you happy.

On this Dualistic Metaphysic, there are interactions, between certain immaterial minds and certain material bodies, of two quite different main sorts: Some interactions occur wherein a certain mind affects a certain body. And, less disturbing, perhaps, to many Scientiphicalists, there occur many wherein a body affects a mind. As Descartes did, I favor such an Interactionist Dualism.

Our Interactionist Dualism *conflicts dramatically* with Scientiphicalism. Just so, thoughts central to this Interactionist Dualism are concretely substantial philosophical ideas.

As opposed to Dualistic Interactionism, various other forms of Entity Dualism have also been advanced. Even if none of them may find any very salient friends nowadays, in times gone by, quite a few had prominent advocates. At all events, each of these other forms of Entity Dualism is far less commonsensical than Interactionism. Briefly, let's consider one of them, *Entity Dualistic Epiphenomenalism:* On this Epiphenomenalism, bodies dynamically affect minds. In this respect, there's no difference between this Dualistic Epiphenomenalism and our Dualistic Interactionism. But, in another respect, there's a great difference: On Interactionism, minds dynamically affect bodies. But, on Epiphenomenalism *that never happens.* Indeed, on Epiphenomenalist Dualism, each mind *is propensitied not* to affect anything material.[7]

As it may appear to our human mind's eye, so to say, there'll be no difference between a concrete world with Interactionism holding and a correlative concrete world where Epiphenomenalism holds. As we might say, there'll be no

---

7. We need to say *propensitied not to* affect bodies here, rather than *not propensitied to* affect bodies. Otherwise, we allow it to be a wonderfully happy accident that no soul ever affects a body, not even just by chance. As I take it, our noted Epiphenomenalism should have at least this much bite to it. At all events, the Entity Dualistic Epiphenomalism sketched differs, at least in form, from that discussed in the philosophical literature. While ours is a view about concrete individuals, other Epiphenomenalisms concerned items of other sorts: events, processes, states, or properties. As best I can tell, there's precious little substantial difference, if any, between our Entity Epiphenomenalism and the commonly found forms.

For a nonhistorian (like me), a useful way to trace the history of epiphenomenalism is found in Victor Caston's "Epiphenomenalisms, Ancient and Modern," The *Philosophical Review*, Vol. 106, No. 3 (July 1997), pages 309–63. Placing aside ancient themes, the paper's long note 4 is especially helpful. It may well be that a clear statement of anything like a contemporary form of the view didn't occur until fairly late in the 19th century, with Thomas Huxley, perhaps with some others. Apparently, the term itself was introduced by William James, when arguing against Huxley's view. Anyway, I claim no notable novelty for our Entity Epiphenomenalism.

humanly *surveyable* difference.[8] But, even so, there'll be a concretely substantial difference between these two worlds. At least pretty well, we may grasp this difference, barely employing the experiential aspect of our understanding, but heavily employing its intellectual aspect.[9]

Even as any sort of Entity Dualism is a view that differs substantially from any Entity Materialism, and from any Entity Idealism, so, certain fairly specific forms of Entity Dualism will substantially differ from other fairly specific forms. Thinking about concreta just in terms of these few categories, we may see quite a variety of substantially different ways for concrete reality to be. Several of these will, no doubt, now occur to readers quite familiar with much traditional philosophical writing. Rather than specifying any of them now, or any of their close cousins, I'll focus on Interactionist Dualism and, with that in focus, I'll look to propose some more novel concretely substantial ideas, at least somewhat more novel.

5. Interactionist Entity Dualism and the Problem of Causal Pairings

In this section, I'll discuss what may appear to be a very serious problem for Interactionist Dualism. Quite aptly, John Foster has called it "the problem of causal pairings".[10] In a medium-sized nutshell, here's how that runs.

When a pin is stuck in my body, that causes certain electrical impulses to occur in my body, with the upshot that there are certain alterations made in (the part of my body that's) my brain. Alternatively, when a pin is stuck in your body (and not in mine) *that* causes certain electrical impulses to occur in your body (and not mine), with the upshot that there are certain alterations made in your brain, even while there don't then occur such changes in my brain. Why does there occur, in the two cases, the two very different alterations, one a change just in a certain single human body, including just its brain, and the other in just a certain other human body, and brain?

Part of the story is this: In the one case, a certain pin made spatial contact with, and then spatial penetration into, just the first body, but not the second. And, in the other case, there obtained quite the reverse spatial relations—with a pin spatially near the second body, and not near the first, making spatial contact, and so on, with just the second body. So, at least in large measure, a

---

8. In *All the Power in the World*, I try to give *surveyable* a sense where it would serve to good philosophical effect. I begin that attempt on page 129.

9. At length, I discuss these matters of understanding in *All the Power in the World*. But, perhaps most useful to most readers, is the discussion of them in my "Reply to James Van Cleve," part of a book symposium on that work in *Philosophy and Phenomenological Research*, March, 2010.

10. See John Foster, *The Immaterial Self*, Routledge, 1991, pages 163–71.

difference in the spatial relations, between the penetrating pins and the pene-trated bodies, will account for the differences in the causal upshots: In each case, an intruding pin will distinctively affect just the human body with which it is intimately related spatially. It will have no (distinctive) effect on human bodies not very close to, or ever in contact with, the pin.

Apt spatial relations will allow certain spatially located objects, as with particular sharp pins, for example, to affect certain other spatially located ob-jects, spatially related to the first objects, as with particular human bodies and their brains. But, nothing like that is available for allowing certain spatially lo-cated objects, like the pins, or the brains, for that matter, to affect any objects not spatially located anywhere and, thus, not spatially related to our spatially located objects. Thus, it's at least mysterious, and maybe it's even impossible, that any human body, or any human brain, should ever affect any immaterial soul—a mental entity that, on our strict (Cartesian) Entity Dualism, *isn't spa-tially located anywhere* and, as such, isn't spatially related, at all, to any human brain, or any human body. At least as it appears, there may be a serious problem for our Interactionist Dualism.

How might this Dualism deal with this apparent problem? There are two main options.[11]

11. There's a less radical form of Entity Dualism also to be considered. On (what at least may be) Locke's Entity Dualism, though souls aren't spatially extended, they're spatially located, each at a spatially extentionless point. As I see it, the problem of causal pairings may also arise for this Lockean view. For nothing precludes two souls from being located at the very same spatial point, even throughout the existence of each soul. And, in such a circumstance, how is it that just one of the souls should dynamically interact with just a certain spatial body, even while the other should so interact just with a separate spatial body.

Though I'm not an historian of philosophy, my colleague Don Garrett is a leading authority on the work of leading thinkers of the "early modern" period. For those skeptical of what I just attributed to Locke, here is his reading of that thinker's view of souls:

Locke says that spirits/souls have location at *Essay*, II.xxiii.19–20:

19. There is no reason why it should be thought strange, that I make mobility belong to spirit: For having no other idea of motion, but change of distance with other beings that are considered as at rest; and finding, that spirits, as well as bodies, cannot operate but where they are, and that spirits do operate at several times in several places; I cannot but attribute change of place to all finite spirits; (for of the infinite spirit I speak not here.) For my soul being a real being, as well as my body, is certainly as capable of changing distance with any other body, or being, as body itself; and so is capable of motion. And if a mathematician can consider a certain distance, or a change of that distance between two points, one may certainly conceive a distance, and a change of distance between two spirits: And so conceive their motion, their approach or removal, one from another.

20. Every one finds in himself that his soul can think, will, and operate on his body in the place where that is; but cannot operate on a body, or in a place an hundred miles distant from it. Nobody can imagine that his soul can think, or move a body at Oxford, whilst he is at London; and cannot but know, that, being united to his body, it constantly changes place all the whole journey between Oxford and London, as the coach or horse does that carries him, and I think may be said to be truly all that while in motion: Or if

First, there's this (almost) universally neglected option: Contrary to what we've been implicitly assuming for our two cases, each a case with a pin penetrating a human body, it needn't be that each case's salient objects are, in their qualitative characters, so to say, relevantly like those in the other case. As we might alternatively assume, these cases occur in a world where, rather than there being only a few basic sorts of (nonindividual) substance, or stuff, or whatnot, there are enormously many different sorts of that—with these differences each being just about as impressively effectual as you please. So, it may be that the first-mentioned human body is entirely made of a certain sort of material—I'll call it *firstium*—whereas the second-mentioned human body is entirely made of a very different sort of physical material—which I'll call *secondium*. Perhaps, both pins may be made of the same material substance, presumably a physical material of a still different sort; I'll have them be composed entirely of *pinium*.

Along with that, we may have one of our immaterial souls be propensitied to interact dynamically with a body composed of firstium—no matter where that firstium object should be spatially located—while this soul is propensitied *not* to interact dynamically with any physical thing that's composed of secondium—no matter where that secondium object should be spatially located, nor with any material thing composed of any still other sort of physical stuff, like pinium, for example. And, conversely, we may have our other immaterial soul be propensitied in a quite opposite way: This second soul is propensitied to interact dynamically with a body composed of *secondium*—no matter where that secondium object should be spatially located—while this same second soul is propensitied *not* to interact dynamically with any physical thing that's composed of *firstium*—no matter where that firstium object should be spatially located.

Finally, we may make these suppositions: Just as there's only one body ever composed of firstium, there'll only ever be one soul that's propensitied for dynamical interaction with any firstium body. And, just as there's only one body

---

that will not be allowed to afford us a clear idea enough of its motion, its being separated from the body in death, I think, will; for to consider it as going out of the body, or leaving it, and yet to have no idea of its motion, seems to me impossible.

Locke says that spirits/souls have location at...*Essay*...II.xxiii.19–20.
Several dozen times Locke's refers to "thinking immaterial spirits". Immateriality for Locke entails unextendedness, as confirmed by *Essay* 3.3.6:

And he who will give himself leave to consider freely, and look into the dark and intricate part of each hypothesis, will scarce find his reason able to determine him fixedly for or against the soul's materiality. Since on which side soever he views it, either as an unextended substance, or as a thinking extended matter; the difficulty to conceive either will, whilst either alone is in his thoughts, still drive him to the contrary side.

Well, that's about as good as it gets, I think, as far as a reliable reading of Locke goes. (A standard edition of Locke's essay is: John Locke, *An Essay Concerning Human Understanding*, P. H. Nidditch (ed.), Oxford University Press, 1975.)

composed of *trillionium*, there'll only be one soul that's propensitied for dynamical interaction with any trillionium body.

On this first option, each human body is, literally, a qualitatively unique individual (at least as far as its own world is concerned). So, here, there won't be any precise physical duplicates.

Now, in one way, on this first option we depart very radically from the assumptions of our Scientiphical Metaphysic. On Scientiphicalism, each physical thing might be composed of the same basic sort of stuff as is every other physical body. And, at the least, there are only a few sorts of basic sorts of physical stuff ever involved in the composition of physical objects.

In another way, this option is the same as Scientiphicalism. On both, every propensity is a generalistic power. Each propensity is with respect to *any* (other) individual with certain *general* features; none is directed at just certain (other) particulars (whatever their general features).

Of course, I don't expect you to believe that there are any concrete worlds so very many of whose individual inhabitants are all as qualitatively so very different from ever so many of the others. But, I do think you've successfully conceived just such worlds as those. Closing our discussion of the Dualist's first option, we notice that it is, or it presents, a pretty novel philosophical thought that's a concretely substantial idea.

With the second main option, our Interactionist Dualist again proposes thoughts that go against, or depart from, our noted Scientiphicalism. Being conservative about kinds of stuff, this time our Dualist holds that, at least typically, a soul has *individualistically-directed* powers.

Typically, an immaterial soul will be propensitied for *dynamical* interaction with just *one human body*. (Or, so it will be on a *reasonably conservative* resolution of our problem, departing modestly from Scientiphicalism and commonsense.) Each soul will be propensitied, on this assumption, *not* to interact *dynamically with any other* human body, or any physical thing not part of its body. And, a human body is propensitied for *dynamical* interaction with just *one soul*.

In contemplating individualistically directed powers, we've been involved with philosophical thoughts that are clearly concretely substantial ideas. And, just as with the Scientiphical tenets they contravene, they're characteristically philosophical ideas. Unlike those tenets, however, few prominent mainstream philosophers will accept these thoughts about powers. As well, and unlike the substantial Scientiphical thoughts they accept, these thoughts are pretty novel ideas.

Neither bothering to specify our widely shared Scientiphicalism nor bothering to depart from that worldview, a lot later in the book we'll confront some other novel concretely substantial philosophical ideas, I say that now only to make it clear that the reader *shouldn't* think that, with what this section's featured, we've even come close to being exhaustive in that regard.

6. Exploring Philosophical Thoughts that May Be Analytically Empty Ideas

For recent mainstream philosophy, what's been observed in the just previous three sections, and even highlighted there, is quite exceptional. By contrast with that, what's generally happened, for many years by now, is this: Except when providing utterly parochial propositions, prominent mainstream philosophers have offered little more than just so many concretely empty ideas, thoughts whose vacuity is rooted in their analyticity. And, with scarcely any exceptions, the little more comprises only just so very many perfectly parochial ideas, none far deeper than, or far less superficial than this pretty petty proposition: Speakers of ordinary English use the terms "pain" and "skin" so very differently that, while one of them may correctly say "I feel my skin and her skin, too", nobody will ever correctly say "I feel my pain and her pain, too".

Now, it would be folly, of course, to attempt to show that in one fell swoop. So, instead, I'll discuss what's been saliently offered in some large parts of mainstream philosophy's analytical core, providing telling case studies. Once she's considered the studies I'll be presenting, the reader will be well placed to make sound inferences as to what's been offered elsewhere in the core of mainstream analytic philosophy.

3

THINKERS AND WHAT
THEY CAN THINK ABOUT

Empty Issues and Individualistic Powers

Shortly after 1970, Hillary Putnam proposed certain apparently exhilarating ideas, perhaps partly prompted by Saul Kripke's slightly earlier work. A few years later, a few other mainstream philosophers extended Putnam's heady ideas. A few years later still, Putnam proposed yet further extensions.[1] Flowing from this cluster of offerings, there developed a new orthodoxy about when it

---

1. For Kripke, the locus classicus is: Saul Kripke, *Naming and Necessity*, Harvard University Press, 1980. The body of that short book is a virtually unchanged version of a very long paper of Kripke's named the same as the book. That is, his "Naming and Necessity" in D. Davidson and G. Harman (eds.), *Semantics of Natural Language* (Dordrecht, Holland: D. Reidel, 1972), pages 254–355.

For Putnam, the single most salient locus classicus is: Hilary Putnam, "The Meaning of 'Meaning,'" appearing in his *Mind, Language and Reality: Philosophical Papers, Volume 2* Cambridge University Press, 1975, pages 215–71. Putnam's first published discussion of his Twin Earth examples may well occur in his "Meaning and Reference," *Journal of Philosophy*, Vol. 70, No. 19 (November 8, 1973), pages 699–711, where the main examples are mainly presented at pages 700–704. To that paper's title there is appended a note whose last sentence is this one:

> A very much expanded version of this paper will appear in volume 7 or 8 of *Minnesota Studies in Philosophy of Science* (edited by Keith Gunderson), under the title "The Meaning of 'Meaning'".

Published in the same year as the classic paper's "reprinting" in the volume of Putnam's papers I've cited, the year 1975, the bibliographic reference for that expansion is: "The Meaning of 'Meaning.'" *Language, Mind and Knowledge: Minnesota Studies in the Philosophy of Science*, vol. 7, ed. Keith Gunderson, Minneapolis: University of Minnesota Press, 1975, pages, 131–93.

For Putnam, the second most salient locus classicus is his book *Reason, Truth and History*, Cambridge University Press, 1981.

is that people are able to *think about* various concrete objects, and concrete stuffs, especially those "external to" each person in question.

What is this orthodoxy? According to the orthodox line, if you're to refer to *water*, or even think about *water*, there must be some suitable causal connection, or at least an apt quasi-causal relation, between you, on the one hand, and some water. (Perhaps you yourself never had any direct apt connection with water. Well, then you must be aptly connected with water in an apt indirect causal way. For example, that may happen should your grandpa have *normally and truthfully told you that*, many years ago, a wandering friend of his drank water, which episode that drinker normally and truthfully related to grandpa.) Moving from a stuff (like water) to an individual, the orthodoxy has it that, for you to think about *Plymouth Rock*, there must obtain, between you and *that rock*, some apt (quasi-) causal relation.

As is widely agreed among mainstream philosophers, these ideas about real reference and well-targeted thinking amounted to a philosophical discovery both deeply illuminating and happily substantial. With this new discovery, there was disclosed something much more robust than any empty truth. As it's thought, that discovery was far more substantial than, say, the idea that your perceiving a dog near you requires that there be, currently or recently, a dog there.

In this chapter, I'll argue that the widespread impression is a false impression. Whatever may have been discovered, it won't be any concretely substantial truth. At best or at most, it will be just a very unobviously correct concretely empty idea.

After providing that criticism, I'll try to articulate concretely substantial thoughts that may be readily offered with *sentences* much the same as those Putnam and company employed. How could I be at all successful here? No surprise, really, the answer's this: While I'll use the same sentences, I'll use them in a happily very different way.

Now, I *won't* say that the concretely substantial thoughts I'm placing on offer are correct ideas. Though it seems very unlikely to me, perhaps these substantial ideas held true in some of our own world's long-past vast Eons, each comprising billions of years. More far-fetched, but possibly less unlikely, these substantial ideas, or some very like them, may hold true in some concrete worlds other than our actual world.

In this chapter, the substantial philosophical thought I'll advance most saliently will be the idea that someone may be *individualistically propensitied* with respect to various individuals, and also various stuffs, each "external" to her. Akin to it, I'll also offer a concretely substantial idea about how thinkers may be propensitied to think about things of just certain real kinds.

Now, except in very far-fetched cases, the situation is this: Whenever an individual is so individualistically propensitied, there will be an historical aspect to the matter; in short, its propensity will be *historically based*. What are these very far-fetched cases? Well, at least for the most part, the far-fetched cases are those where entities just randomly come to acquire propensities just with respect to one another, and not with respect to any other entities. Yet more radically, there are the cases where entities randomly come to exist, each propensitied with respect to the others. In these cases, we may have the clearest examples of individualistic propensities that are not also *time-sensitive* propensities. (In the next chapter, there'll be a protracted, often positive discussion of time-sensitive propensities.)

As I was saying, except in very far-fetched cases, whenever an individual is individualistically propensitied, there's an historical aspect to the matter; its propensity will be *historically based*. But, as the main thrust of Putnam's cited work has been toward making certain sorts of *externalism* orthodox, as with externalism about "semantic content" and externalism about "mental content," in this chapter, I won't focus on such temporal matters.[2]

1. Language, Thought and History

You believe quite a lot about your own history, or about how things have been with you. For example, you may believe that you went to college.

Unlike how things are with correlative *memory* matters, with such matters of mere *belief* even your newly arrived duplicate will be in pretty good shape—apart from the fact that far more of his beliefs will be incorrect. Or, at least when we're taking our shared Scientiphicalism as given, that certainly seems so.

In recent decades, some philosophers have questioned this appearance. And, in questioning it, *perhaps they've meant* to make some concretely *substantial* claims, claims that *aren't* analytically empty. So it is that their words have been often understood, both by the authors themselves and by many of their readers.

As adumbrated at this chapter's start, some salient cases of that occur in the writing of Hilary Putnam. But, as I've already written quite a bit about remembering, I'll start with a well-known passage from Donald Davidson's writing:

> Suppose lightning strikes a dead tree in a swamp I am standing nearby. My body is reduced to its elements, while entirely by coincidence (and out of different molecules), the tree is turned into my physical replica. My replica, Swampman, moves exactly as I did: according to its nature, it departs the swamp, encounters and seems to recognize my friends, and appears to return their greetings in English. It moves into my house and seems to write articles on radical interpretation. No one can tell the difference.

---

2. That limitation on this chapter's focus need be no cause for concern. Indeed, in the next chapter, where I discuss *time-sensitive* powers, I'll give just such temporal matters their full due. This division in presentation should help foster both accessibility and clarity.

But, there *is* a difference. My replica can't recognize my friends; it can't *recognize* anything, since it never cognized anything in the first place. It can't know my friends' names (though of course it seems to), it can't remember my house. It can't mean what I do by the word 'house', for example, since the sound 'house' Swampman makes was not learned in a context that would give it the right meaning—or any meaning at all. Indeed, I don't see how my replica can be said to mean anything by the sounds it makes, nor to have any thoughts.[3]

As is apparent, one idea Davidson's there offering is this: (quantum-mechanical considerations aside) Swampman's then-current bodily behavior will be precisely similar to what Davidson's would have been, had there not been the lightning. So, as much as for you and me, for Davidson (the concept of) *how it currently is with someone purely behaviorally* has no real requirement to the effect that she have a certain sort of history, or that she even have existed, at all. As well, Davidson's used his words to express an idea to the effect that how it is experientially for Swampman, at the then-current time, will be just the same as how it would have been for Davidson, had he not been destroyed by the lightning: So, for him as much as for us, *how it currently is with someone purely experientially* also has no real requirement to the effect that she must have a certain sort of history, or that she even have existed at all.

Regarding how things are for Swampman purely experientially, this interpretation appears both most plausible and most charitable. Just so, we should take it that Davidson's claims about Swampman aren't meant to hold *only* for external observers; as well, they're to hold for Swampman himself. Even from Swampman's own perspective, there's no discriminable difference between Swampman's apparently thoughtful activity and what Davidson takes to be

---

3. Donald Davidson, "Knowing One's Own Mind," *Proceedings and Addresses of the American Philosophical Association* (1987), 441–58. The address is reprinted as Essay 2 in Davidson's *Subjective, Intersubjective, Objective*, Oxford University Press, 2001, pages 15–38. In this reprinting, the quoted sentences appear on page 19.

As Davidson observes, Swampman is just a minor variant on examples offered by others. As I'll now observe, the others range from, at least, Bertrand Russell, in the 1920s, to Peter Unger, in the 1960s. Stimulated by fundamentalist ideas from the Christian thinker Philip Henry Gosse, in *The Analysis of Mind*, G. Allen & Unwin, 1921, on pages 159–60, Russell writes these famous sentences:

> There is no logical impossibility in the hypothesis that the world sprang into being five minutes ago, exactly as it then was, with a population that "remembered" a wholly unreal past. There is no logically necessary connection between events at different times; therefore nothing that is happening now or will happen in the future can disprove the hypothesis that the world began five minutes ago.

Following far back in Russell's great wake, and while assuming that something at least a lot like materialism should be correct, in my first published philosophy paper I trafficked heavily in thoughts about pretty suddenly arrived duplicates of normally grown human people. See my ironically titled essay, "On Experience and The Development of the Understanding," *American Philosophical Quarterly*, 3 (1966): 48–56.

something very different from that. But, at all events, and however any of that should be, for our discussion none of this much matters.

Especially with all that being so, but even in any case, Davidson's most salient offering here *isn't* true. (Though it's true that, initially, Swampman *won't recall* anything—not even, say, facts of chemistry) it *isn't true* that he won't think anything, or believe anything.

Why do I deny what Davidson's saliently proposed? Well, suppose that, just before the story's lightning annihilated him, Davidson felt quite thirsty, and he very much wanted to drink something very drinkable, to quench his thirst. Then, the lightning strikes and, apparently feeling much the same thirsty way, Swampman proceeds, without further ado, to go where there's plenty of very drinkable stuff available—to what is, in fact, a nearby water tap, one that was well-known to Davidson. Swampman turns the tap; he drinks some of the water that rushes out; he quenches his thirst; and he feels quite satisfied. Myself, I'd happily describe Swampman, in those circumstances, in quite simple terms: He wanted to drink some water. And he believed that, by going in a certain direction, he'd soon encounter a useful water faucet. Due to the desire and the beliefs, Swampman went to the tap and drank his fill.

But, for our present discussion, observing Davidson's error is hardly the main point. Rather, what's central is an idea that might be well put in these words: Even supposing that everything Davidson says about Swampman is entirely correct, still, what he's offered us *isn't* anything that's *concretely substantial*. What Davidson's offered us about when it is that someone can believe, and want, and mean things, it all perfectly parallels empty ideas about when it is that someone can remember things. Let me amplify.

By contrast with Davidson's proposals, consider thoughts sincerely offered to his teacher by one of Peter van Inwagen's smartest undergraduate students. Here's van Inwagen, writing about that student of his, while also writing about Plato, and Descartes, too:

> Recall the "duplicating machine".... If you place any physical object inside one of the chambers and press the big red button, a perfect physical duplicate of the object appears in the other chamber.

> Let us put Alfred into one of the chambers of the duplicating machine and press the button. What do we find in the other chamber? A very intelligent Muslim student of mine once assured me that what one would find would be a dead human body—since the duplicating machine would not reproduce Alfred's soul, which was the principle of life. This dead body, at the instant of its appearance, would be standing just as Alfred stood, and on its face would be an expression just like the expression on Alfred's face. Even in that first instant, however, the body would not be alive, and, having appeared, it would immediately collapse and lie unmoving, its face the blank mask of a corpse.... I think

Plato would have agreed with my student. Descartes, however, would not have agreed. Descartes would have contended that a *living* human body would have appeared in the other chamber. But, Descartes would have said, this body would have immediately crumbled to the floor. It would then lie there breathing and perhaps drooling, and, if you force-fed it, it would digest the food and in time produce excreta. But, it would not *do* anything much. And this, of course, would be because there was no mind or soul or person in interaction with it.[4]

For van Inwagen's student, whom I'll call *Ali*, the way that Alfred's duplicate came into being will mean a *real deficit* on the part of that merely physical duplicate, a truly *substantial difference* from anyone who should have entered the machine. And, so, too, for Plato and Descartes, at least van Inwagen's Plato and Descartes.

By contrast with Davidson, when Ali contends that Alfred's physical duplicate won't be able to think, the thought he advances *is a concretely substantial* idea. Now, to express his thought, Ali might well have used some such sentence as "No duplicating machine can ever produce a being that, from the moment of its production onward, is able to think about things". And, to express his very different ideas, Davidson might well have used just that same sentence. But, then, their *uses* of it will differ markedly. Using it in a *certain* way, Ali employs the sentence to express, and even to assert, a *concretely substantial* idea. Using it in a *very different* way, Davidson employs it to express, and even to assert, an *empty* idea.

Now, in offering his ideas about Swampman's initial mental abilities, or lack thereof, Davidson was, I think we may say, *presupposing* quite a few substantial propositions, even if the thoughts actually offered were all just so many analytically empty ideas. How's that? Well, as I charitably read his passages, I take them as offered against a certain background of presupposed propositions, including several Scientiphical suppositions. As Davidson tacitly knew, they were accepted not just by him, but also by his intended audience, as well. (Unless we do that, we won't think, along with Davidson, that right away Swampman will emit just such *bodily behavior* as should be done by a certain ordinarily developed man, by Davidson, of course. We certainly won't know what to make of his "No one can tell the difference".) As in much subsequent discussion, we sensibly take mainstreamers merely to presuppose Scientiphicalism.

Quite beyond what's merely presupposed for his noted example, what's Davidson proposing, really, as to what's going on in his Swampman scenario? Whatever it really may be, exactly, it *certainly appears* to perfectly parallel, as concerns what's concretely empty and what's not, this perfectly vacuous old friend of ours: the thought that a person can't remember her old college days unless she really went to college.

---

4. Peter van Inwagen, *Metaphysics*, Second Edition, Westview Press, 2002, pages 198–99.

Toward rebutting this strong appearance, a devotee of Davidson's might reply, perhaps, that Swampman, at the very outset, *won't be as mentally powerful* as I seem to be saying. As she might suggest, Swampman, at first, *won't have the power* to think about anything. But, what can such a reply amount to? Isn't *it also* just a conceptual point? After all, and more certainly, Swampman, at the very outset, *won't have the power* to remember any experiences he's had (because, at the very outset, he *hasn't had* any experiences). But, to propose any *such* points about powers, whether the proposed powers concern thinking, or whether remembering, or whether cooling, or whether recooling, well, it's just to propose some analytically empty ideas.

With an eye toward upcoming sections, it's now helpful to consider a couple of chemical inquirers. One of the two is our old friend Joe Blogs, a pedestrian chemist. As Joe's chemical inquiries are the furthest thing from groundbreaking, so, unsurprisingly, such pleasure as he enjoys, for undertaking his investigative labor, is also quite modest. That's enough about Blogs.

Now, quite as happened with Davidson's Swampman, the *other* of our two guys will be someone who's created quite randomly, perhaps in another swamp. Not terribly much like any philosopher, our own newly arrived fellow will be, instead, the precise physical duplicate of one Sir Ian Beaker, (whom we may suppose to be) one of the planet's leading chemists. (At the same time, as we're also supposing, perhaps quite materialistically, the lightning will put an end to Sir Ian.) Memorably enough, I'll call this newly arrived duplicate "Swampchemist". And I'll suppose that, even as Sir Ian was long disposed to take great pleasure in making chemical discoveries, Swampchemist is also just so disposed, right from the moment he first exists.

Unproblematically, Joe Blogs is replete with correct beliefs as to chemical matters. And, of course, he's well able to think about many chemical matters. Though I doubt it, just maybe it's true that, at the start, Sir Ian's duplicate has no beliefs about chemical matters. And, just maybe it's correct to say that, right at the start, he's unable to think about any such matters.

Still and all, over this next month, the first month of this duplicate's existence, who will contribute more to chemistry—Joe Blogs or the newly arrived duplicate of Ian Beaker? Unless something quite miraculous happens, it will be the newly existent person. (Or, at the very least, the duplicate will *shmontribute* far more to chemistry than Blogs. Henceforth, I usually won't bother with explicit concessions.)

Denying the case's Scientiphical presuppositions, others would disagree. Our Ali, for instance, would expect Swampchemist to be DOA. And, maybe Plato would also expect that. There's a concretely substantial difference between that Platonic-Islamic position and, on the other side, the Scientiphicalism favored by recent and current mainstream philosophers. And, as for Descartes— at least, van Inwagen's Descartes—well, he'd have still other expectations for

our so-called Swampchemist: While he'd expect this precise physical duplicate
to be alive, even so, he'd expect no more new science from this living being than
he'd expect from a living mouse.[5]

Over the ages, various thinkers have variously disagreed with Scientiphicalism. Reflecting that is this: If Ali should say "Your Swampchemist won't
be able to think about anything," he'll be offering a concretely substantial
idea, a thought that really conflicts with our substantial Scientiphicalism. But,
Davidson *won't* offer us anything so substantial with his use of that sentence.
Though *they may use the same sentence*, the substantial *thought* expressed by the student will be *very different* from the empty *thought* expressed by the mainstream
philosopher.

On the page where he introduces his Swampman, Davidson has a note
where he says:

> I should emphasize that I am not suggesting that an object accidentally or
> artificially created could not think; the Swampman simply needs time in
> which to acquire a causal history that would make sense of the claim that he
> is speaking of, remembering, identifying, or thinking of items in the world.[6]

How much time may Swampman need for this? And, more importantly, during
this crucial period, what might happen to so greatly increase Swampman's real
mental powers?

On the first question, Davidson might suggest that only a little time will be
needed, no more than a single day's worth, for Swampman "to acquire all the
powers" requisite for him to be ordinarily proficient in English and, what's
more, to be extraordinarily proficient in chemistry. In such an event, it will be
no surprise for Davidson to expect, just as I do, that during his first month
Swampchemist will enjoy much more investigative success than Joe Blogs.
Though Swampman may start off at a disadvantage, which lasts for a day, he'll
outdo Blogs on each of the next thirty days, clearly doing more over the whole
month. But, what will happen in just the first day, or the first hour? Who'll be
better at doing chemistry then, and why?

5. As I'll bother to observe, if only in this note, the difference between the Cartesian view just
enunciated, where a living drooler will be produced by the lightning, and our Ali's view, where just
a nonliving corpse will be produced, well, that's a concretely substantial difference. And, in addition to those two concretely substantial thoughts, there's a third that's more in line with what the
historical Descartes should have expected for such a suddenly arrived purely material organic
being: It's able to behave in various ways conducive to its continuing to be alive—as with fleeing
from an oncoming lion—but it won't possess any properly mental powers, or properly rational
abilities, as with the ability to write philosophical articles—or even laundry lists. Anyway even as
there's a substantial difference between the three substantial views here noted, each substantially
differs from what our shared substantial Scientiphicalism will predict for such a suddenly productive happening.

6. Davidson, "Knowing One's Own Mind," page 19.

Continuing to suppose Scientiphicalism to hold, I say it will be Swampchemist. But, what can Davidson say? Gripped by Scientiphicalism, Davidson should expect Swampchemist to proceed more productively than Joe, at least a *bit* more, right from the moment of his sudden arrival. As far as relevant mental proficiency goes, there's *never any* catching up for Swampchemist to do. Even if, at the start, Swampchemist *won't be properly described* as someone who *thinks* about things, and he should be described only as, say, someone who *shminks* about things, or he shminks shmabout things, he won't be at any disadvantage.[7] With that being so, what's apparently central here is a question that's analytically empty.

As may well occur to some, much of what goes on with successful scientific discovery and theorizing may depend more on physical intuition, or on scientific intuition, than it depends on anything like propositional thinking, or on any ability to think discursively or formulaically, much as may happen in the purely mathematical case, where an investigator's mathematical intuition may be, in many matters explored, the ability most crucial to successful inquiry. In that respect, science and mathematics may be much like music and poetry, even if in the latter cases the aims are more purely creative, with no great goal being to make any discoveries. But, of course, on our shared Scientiphicalism all of these mental abilities, perhaps nested families of propensities, will be just so many more physically derivative powers. So, recognition of the more intuitive aspects of our productive mental lives will mean nothing for the issues this chapter most centrally concerns. A newly arrived Swampcomposer may be every bit as creative musically, for example, as ever was Bach or Beethoven, Ray Charles or James Brown.

Through much of our discussion, I've been making two perfectly separate points. The first is this: In offering the main thoughts they've recently provided, prominent philosophers typically offered us only just so many *incorrect* ideas. That's hardly this book's main message. Far more important to the book is this second point: In offering us their main philosophical thoughts, these philosophers provided just so many concretely empty ideas, even analytically empty.

2. Thinking about "The External World"

Perhaps more than any other twentieth century examples, Hilary Putnam's Twin Earth Cases have enormously influenced recent and current mainstream philosophy's analytic core. Of course, it's not simply the examples themselves

---

7. Perhaps it's arbitrary to represent the relevant semantic differences, in our discussions, as differences in the semantics of the one-word verbs in focus. Perhaps, as Crispin Wright has suggested to me, the differences should be more broadly spread. My use of "shminks shmabout", by contrast to the ordinary "thinks about" is a gesture in that direction. For all our main points, in any case, what's in focus, just now, are mere niceties, scarcely central issues.

that have been so influential. Rather, it's certain of his ideas about what the cases may show that, along with the cases themselves, have had this great influence. Anyhow, in the section succeeding this one, I'll begin to discuss the Twin Earth cases. Right here and now, I'll discuss Putnam's next most influential (treatment of) far-fetched cases, his discussion of "Brains in a vat," as presented in his book, *Reason, Truth and History*.[8]

For the longest time, philosophers have imagined brains in vats as a high-tech substitute for Descartes' time-honored deceptive demon, that is, as a device used to make vivid various sorts of epistemological skepticism. Typically, and as Putnam also supposes, this will be a brain that, from the very first moment of its existence, has been ensconced in a vat. The considered brain, as well as its containing vat, may have been constructed intentionally, perhaps by some philosophically obsessed super-scientists. Or, quite as well, the brain and its vat may have come into existence, all just like that, ever so accidentally. Perhaps this may have happened in much the manner of Swampman's origination. Or, perhaps it happened in a more radical way, as with the coming into existence of even the matter constituting the brain, and that composing its vat.

However it came to exist, exactly, we'll now consider an always-envatted brain that's physically just like the active healthy brain of one Professor Frederick Formula, a man who gets quite as much joy from his brilliantly fruitful scientific inquiry as did his good friend Sir Ian Beaker (before Beaker was killed by lightning). Much as Putnam does, we'll suppose that, just as there is a mentally able person "associated with" Professor Formula's brain—Professor Formula himself—so there's also such a person, mentally quite powerful, "associated with" the duplicate brain, the brain that's always been envatted.

Now, as will be agreed by all, Formula can think very well, indeed, especially about many matters of chemistry. This ability has been exercised in his making many chemical discoveries. Not so helpful in any of that fruitful scientific inquiry, but much more up Putnam's preferred alley, Formula can think about various "skeptical hypotheses", perhaps offered him by a philosophy professor he quite likes. For example, he can consider the question whether he is, as perhaps he always has been, a strangely stimulated envatted brain, perhaps from the very first moment of his existence, with no hands or feet, and with no eyes or ears. But, what should we say about his supposed precise intrinsic duplicate, entirely similar in all (present-moment) nonrelational respects? What should we say about our *Vatchemist*, so to label our envatted one?

(As stipulated, unlike Formula, Vatchemist has never perceived anything "external" to his mind. Still, both Formula and Vatchemist have enjoyed very varied and protracted experiencing. Recently and currently, each person's experiencing

8. Most saliently, this occurs in Putnam's, *Reason, Truth and History*, Cambridge University Press, 1981. Indeed, the title of the book's first chapter is "Brains in a vat".

is qualitatively just like the others. At the least, they've enjoyed terribly similar *shmexperiencing*.

Just above, I used a made-up term, "shmexperiencing". What was the point? Well, some may take the line that the term "experience" has implications concerning an agent's past history, much as do the terms "remember" and "recognize". And, some may take the line that the term has implication's concerning the agent's surroundings, much as does the expression "perceives a dog that's nearby". Along with that, they'll take a similar line with apparently purely experiential terms, as with the term "feel", when it's used in its purest and most experiential meaning.[9] Well, for folks who do that, my use of "shmexperiencing" allows us to be accommodating. Briefly, let me amplify.

Though I doubt it, let's grant that our entrenched verb "experience" properly applies only to subjects with rich past histories and impressive interactions with their surroundings. Even so, there'll be no such limitations on our newly introduced term. Whatever the semantics of "experience," with "shmexperience" it's *stipulated that* one who shmexperiences needn't even exist previously, much less need she have a certain sort of rich history. Nor is there any

---

9. In just the past decade or two, this peculiar position—that experiencing requires that the agent have a certain sort of history—has found quite a few adherents. Or, at the least, quite a few have thought to distinguish various sorts of experiencing; after making their distinctions, they've claimed that the philosophically most important sorts of experiencing require that the experiencer in question have a certain sort of history. Representative of a fair lot of this, and making references to almost all of it that's been salient, on my desk now is a fairly new book to that effect, Christopher Hill's *Consciousness*, Cambridge University Press, 2009.

Especially as Hill says quite a lot about Swampman, an example we've discussed, it will be useful to us to see how, even so terribly recently, the sorts of empty ideas this chapter addresses have been so entrenched in mainstream philosophy. Employing both terms found only or primarily in mainstream work, like "qualia'," and ordinary terms employed with technical senses, like "representation", here is a passage from the book's section 5.6, "Swampman":

> As described in the standard accounts, Swampman is a human-like creature who comes into existence accidentally.... Swampman has no capacity to represent things perceptually.....But still, he is amazingly similar to real human beings.....But if it is true that Swampman is aware of perceptual qualia, then all representationalist accounts of perceptual qualia must be wrong, including the one I have formulated above.

And, from that same section, here is a complementary passage:

> To summarize: Opponents of representationalist accounts of awareness of qualia often present Swampman as a kind of counterexample, claiming that he is aware of qualia but lacks the capacity to form and deploy representations. In responding to this view, I have allowed, in effect, that it would be reasonable to say that Swampman *possesses* qualia..., but I have maintained that there is no good reason to say that he is *aware of* qualia.... Further, I have urged that the fact that Swampman possesses qualia is of little philosophical significance.

Perhaps it's because I have little facility with such technical language, but I can't find any new concretely substantial philosophical ideas here. Nor does there seem to be any in the rest of the book, or in the many recent philosophical works to which it refers. But, perhaps, that's just appearance. If so, I'd be happy to learn the novel substantial philosophical ideas that, so far, have eluded me.

requirement that she be related, at present, to anything external to her, or even that there exist anything external to her. (Beyond that, the semantics of these two terms is precisely the same. Or, at the least, it's as nearly that as can possibly be.) Employing the newly stipulated term, we may say this: Right off the bat, Davidson's Swampman will shmexperience just like Davidson would have done, had the lightning not struck as it did. And, in our quasi-Putnamian circumstance, Vatchemist will shmexperience just like a normally developed chemist would do. But, let's return to consider what's, here and now, a more clearly central question.)

Can Vatchemist *think that* he *isn't* a brain in a vat? Or, perhaps in a moment of seemingly mad revelation, can he possibly *think that* he *is, and he always has been*, only such an envatted entity? Along somewhat the same long line, further questions may also be posed: Can our Vatchemist even so much as conceive of a mere concrete cube, or a spherical concretum?

Though I greatly doubt it, for all I really know, it just might be that all our "mental terms" are entirely relational terms, or very nearly that, packing no qualitative or intrinsic punch at all, or very nearly none. So, it may be that a typical mental term, like "thinks that", is on a footing with, say, our term "footprint", by contrast with our possibly more qualitatively involved companion terms, as with "normal human footprint" and "stereotypical equine footprint". Though something must be produced by a *foot*, if it is to be a *footprint*, perhaps it needn't be shaped in any given way, even if it can't be absolutely shapeless. And, perhaps, it need not be intrinsically qualitied in *any* one given way, as opposed to ever so many alternative ways. If that should be so, then my attempts to help out with such coined terms as *shmexperience* may be more misguided than helpful. But, even if so, that won't matter for the larger questions here at issue: Indeed, even if all our mental terms should be purely relational terms, that will serve only to reframe, or to reconceptualize, this chapter's most central concerns. The main dispute between Putnamians and their opponents, myself included, will still be just a debate that's just so very concretely empty, and analytically empty, to boot. That said, I'll proceed to say more about the nitty gritty of these empty issues.

Apparently, on Putnam's view, our Vatchemist can't do any of this. Putnam says: "Could we, if we were brains in a vat in this way, *say* or *think* that we were? I am going to argue that the answer is 'No, we couldn't.' "[10] After providing some argumentation, as promised, Putnam says: "I have now given the argument promised to show that the brains in a vat cannot think or say that they are brains in a vat".[11] About trees, he says: "In short, the brains in a vat are not thinking about real trees when they think 'there is a tree in front of me' "[12] Why? Putnam supplies this presumed explanation: "because there is nothing

10. Putnam, *Reason, Truth and History*, page 7.

11. Putnam, *Reason, Truth and History*, page 14.

12. Putnam, *Reason, Truth and History*, page 13.

by virtue of which their thought 'tree' represents actual trees".[13] Whether or not Putnam is right about Vatchemist, for our main topic another question is more important: Isn't his proposal concretely empty? We'll discuss that.

For clarity on this issue, Putnam himself takes a small step in the right direction. He says:

> The brains in a vat do not have sense organs, but they do have *provision* for sense organs; that is, there are afferent nerve endings, and these inputs figure in the 'program' of the brains in the vat just as they do in the program of our brains. The brains in a vat are *brains*; moreover they are *functioning* brains, and they function by the same rules as brains do in the actual world.[14]

Happily, that's a vivid cue for these remarks: As our Scientiphicalism allows, we may remove Vatchemist's brain from its vat and, with nary a hitch, we may then surgically insert it, quite perfectly, in a living brainless duplicate of the rest of Fred Formula's body, just newly arrived. In this way, we may ensure the continued existence of the previously isolated person. And, in the Scientiphical bargain, we may have our Vatchemist become someone who, in a far more full-blooded sense or way, is quite able, indeed, to interact tellingly with samples of chemical substances. Now quite thoroughly embodied, Vatchemist will be ready to embark on excellently fruitful scientific research, work worthy of our formidable friend Fred Formula.

Suppose that, for just a month, we make all chemistry facilities—even computers—entirely unavailable to Professor Formula. Happily enough, he enjoys a long sailing trip, on an enormously luxurious yacht. His mind is entirely occupied with enjoying sea breezes. Not even unconsciously does he think, to any great extent, about scientific matters. Now, with no interference from Formula, who's way out at sea, our Vatchemist will have the unfettered run of the whole place, so to say. He'll have full use of the fine labs, the excellent computing facilities, and all the rest, just as much so as each of a dozen normally grown chemical scientists, each of them just a so-so chemical scientist, none clearly more able than old Joe Blogs. Of all these people, whom do we expect, during the next month, to make the most far-reaching chemical discoveries? It's Vatchemist, of course. For, as we Scientiphically suppose, he'll be quite as successful as Formula himself would be.[15]

Against the appearances, suppose that Putnam is right about how Vatchemist will be at the month's start: At this early stage, we're supposing, Vatchemist isn't

---

13. Putnam, *Reason, Truth and History*, page 13 - right after the just previously cited words.

14. Putnam, *Reason, Truth and History*, page 12.

15. Even assuming that all the relevant mental abilities are probabilistic propensities, Vatchemist will be at least nearly as successful as Formula. And, with a little luck on Vatchemist's side, in the playing out of the presumed probabilistic propensities, he'll be a bit more successful.

able to think about chemical substances, and beakers, and computers, and so on. If that should be so, then we should have low expectations for Vatchemist, likely lower than those we have for any of the merely so-so chemists. But, we do not. Is Vatchemist supposed to go, from being such a limited thinker to being a brilliantly able scientist, all in the space of, say, fifteen minutes? That's incredibly implausible. So, against the supposition made at the paragraph's start, Putnam's wrong about Vatchemist: Apparently, Vatchemist *doesn't* start the month at any disadvantage, as regards what he can think about, or how well he can think about it.

Salient questions about Vatchemist are riddled with concrete emptiness. (The correct ideas, I've been urging, are just the positive empty ideas here, allowing him great ability.)

3. Earth, Twin Earth and History

For well over thirty years, and with no let-up in sight, Putnam's Twin Earth Cases have been enormously influential on the thinking of very many analytic philosophers. As everyone knows, they gave rise to various new forms of "externalism," at odds with more traditional "internalist" views. In turn, that gave rise to defenses of, even redefinitions of, the older views. With ensuing rounds of debate and discussion, there's now an enormous literature about all that.[16]

16. Only 21 years after "The Meaning of 'Meaning'" appeared, there appeared a collection of writings on the paper's main themes, with an Introduction to the collection by Putnam: *The Twin Earth Chronicles*, Andrew Pessin and Sanford Goldberg, eds., M. E. Sharpe, Armonk, New York, and London, England, 1996. Some of them (drawn from) papers and others drawn from books, most of the selections appearing there actually included the words "Twin Earth", including these following eight selections by quite prominent mainstream philosophers (as well as nine selections by not quite so prominent philosophers): John Searle, "From *Intentionality*: Are Meanings in the Head?," Tyler Burge, "Other Bodies," Daniel Dennett, "From 'Beyond Belief': Notional Attitudes," Jerry Fodor, "From *Psychosemantics*: Individualism and Supervenience," Frank Jackson and Philip Pettit, "Functionalism and Broad Content," Robert Stalnaker, "On What's in the Head," John McDowell, "Putnam on Mind and Meaning," Donald Davidson, "Knowing One's Own Mind". Including the two editors and Putnam himself, over twenty philosophers' work contributed to the volume, all of them males. To my only recently less than very clouded way of thinking, the concrete emptiness of all this work is *not explained by the gender* of the contributors. In the grand sweep of things, this may be quite a small point.

Even by that time, 1996, there had developed a huge literature around Putnam's Twin Earth cases, and, so, what's in *The Twin Earth Chronicles* is a very small sampling of what was available for the volumes editors to select for inclusion. Reaching further, on September 15, 2013, I did an advanced search with JSTOR, looking just for certain articles and reviews in the journals JSTOR lists as philosophy journals. I entered "twin earth", coming up with 1,941 items, comprising 1,571 articles and 261 reviews, and the remainder in other categories. Because of the lag in their "moving wall," that was, even then, a *very low count* for even just the journals so listed! What's more, when I added "Putnam" to my broad search, there appeared only (?!) 792 citations. This means that, without Putnam's name appearing anywhere, there was, even back then, and even with a very low

Nothing in all this huge production, on any side, is concretely substantial. Rather, even as all parties agree on what's (fairly) fundamental in the stimulating science-fictional scenarios, so their differences concern the range of terms, mainly mentalistic or pretty personal, fit for aptly describing the cases. Centrally, these empty issues parallel those already discussed.

Putnam most prominently presents his Twin Earth Cases in "The Meaning of 'Meaning'". That paper's section "Are meanings in the head?" starts like this:

> That psychological state does not determine extension will now be shown with the aid of a little science fiction. For the purpose of the following science-fiction examples, we shall suppose that somewhere in the galaxy there is a planet we shall call Twin Earth. Twin Earth is very much like Earth; in fact, people on Twin Earth even speak *English*. In fact, apart from the differences we shall specify in our science-fiction examples, the reader may suppose Twin Earth is *exactly* like Earth. He may even suppose he has a Doppelganger—an identical copy—on Twin Earth if he wishes, though my stories will not depend on this.[17]

But, as Putnam's scenario develops, it turns out that there *won't* be living complexes on Twin Earth even greatly like earthly tomato plants, much less like any earthly human animals:

> One of the peculiarities of Twin Earth is that the liquid called 'water' is not H_2O but a different liquid whose chemical formula is very long and complicated. I shall abbreviate this chemical formula simply as XYZ. I shall suppose that XYZ is indistinguishable from water at normal temperatures and pressures. In particular, it tastes like water and it quenches thirst like water. Also, I shall suppose that the oceans and lakes and seas of Twin Earth contain XYZ and not water, that it rains XYZ on Twin Earth and not water, etc.[18]

As there's no H_2O on Twin Earth, there's none in your so-called identical copy (or, if we're mind-body dualists, there'll be none in the body of your so-called identical

---

count, a *self-standing reference to twin earth* in fully 1,149 mainstream publications. Just so, "twin earth" has acquired pretty much the same status as the likes of "immanent universals".

For an up-to-date overview of a fair lot of much of this remarkably empty literature, see Joe Lau and Max Deutsch, "Externalism About Mental Content," *The Stanford Encyclopedia of Philosophy (Winter 2012 Edition)*, Edward N. Zalta (ed.), URL= <http://plato.stanford.edu/archives/win2012/entries/content-externalism/>. For an up-to-date overview of a fair lot of much of the rest of it, see Brown, Curtis, "Narrow Mental Content," *The Stanford Encyclopedia of Philosophy (Fall 2011 Edition)*, Edward N. Zalta (ed.), URL= <http://plato.stanford.edu/archives/fall2011/entries/content-narrow/>.

17. Hilary Putnam, "The Meaning of 'Meaning," appearing in his *Mind, Language and Reality: Philosophical Papers, Volume 2*, Cambridge University Press, 1975, page 223. The italics are Putnam's.

18. Putnam, "The Meaning of 'Meaning,'" page 223.

copy.) For this reason alone, it's absolutely impossible, of course, for you to have any precise physical duplicate on Twin Earth. Anyhow, even as ever so many others did, we may pass over this deficiency. (A small point: When he says "the oceans and lakes and seas of Twin Earth contain XYZ and not water, that it rains XYZ on Twin Earth and not water," Putnam loads the dice. Neutrally, he *should* have said that the oceans and lakes and seas of Twin Earth contain XYZ and not H_2O.)

At any rate, here's the thought that Putnam is advocating: Even if you and your Doppelganger should be intrinsically alike as can possibly be, still, when you normally use your word "water," you'll mean H_2O and, by contrast, when *he* standardly uses *his* (look-alike and sound-alike) word "water," your Doppelganger will mean XYZ. As well, you'll be referring to H_2O, and not to XYZ, whereas he'll be referring to XYZ, and not to H_2O.[19]

In "The Meaning of 'Meaning'" Putnam *doesn't* endorse this closely re-lated further idea: Even if you and your Doppelganger should be intrinsically as like as can be, the two of you will be very unlike as to what you believe it is that flows in the rivers on your planets, and as to what it is that you want to drink, especially when outdoors in the summer. In this early essay, Putnam *doesn't* say that you'll have *beliefs about* only H_2O, and not XYZ, and you'll have *desires for* only H_2O, and not XYZ (whereas quite the opposite holds true of, or for, your Doppelganger, as concerns what he, or she, will believe, and will desire). Indeed, in this paper, Putnam writes:

> We claim that it is possible for two speakers to be in exactly the *same* psycho-logical state (in the narrow sense), even though the extension of the term A in the idiolect of one is different from the extension of A in the idiolect of the other. Extension is *not* determined by psychological state.[20]

19. Most of the motivation for these claims, it seems clear to me, comes from "taking at face value" our off-the-cuff responses to obvious questions asked about the salient folks in the Twin Earth Cases, about the Earthians and, as well, about the (supposed) Twin Earthians. My off-the-cuff response, like Putnam's, is that it's just the Earthians who, with the word "water," are referring to water (that is, roughly, to H_2O)—and they're *not* referring to XYZ, while it's just the Twin Earth-ians who, with their homophonic "water," are referring to XYZ, and *they're not* referring to real water (that is, roughly, to H_2O.) But, unlike Putnam, and his many followers, I don't take these re-sponses to indicate anything of much philosophical moment—not even any philosophical salient utterly empty idea. Far better explanations of our responses can be given, than any ever offered by Putnam and company, though to do it here would take us very far away from any of our main topics, and even most of our secondary topics.

To some extent, I do such explaining in a couple of old publications, perhaps most directly in my paper "The Causal Theory of Reference," especially in section 7 of the paper, the section called "Twin Earth Revisited". Originally published in *Philosophical Studies*, as pages 1–45 of the journal's Volume 43, (1983), the essay is reprinted in Volume 1 of my *Philosophical Papers*, Oxford University Press, 2006, on pages 117–60. But, none of this business, about how best to explain our off-the-cuff responses to the cases, is relevant to the issues that are currently central.

20. "The Meaning of 'Meaning,'" page 222. In the passage cited, the italics are Putnam's, as also are the parentheses.

But, this happy conservatism about beliefs, desires and other so-called "intentional" psychological states was not to last long with our increasingly influential author.

Just a few years later and largely thanks to their contemplating Putnam's Twin Earth scenarios, several other philosophers did endorse this further idea, concerning who thinks what, the two most timely being, perhaps, Tyler Burge and Colin McGinn.[21] In his still slightly later writing, Putnam "goes externalist" on intentional psychological issues, as in his *Reason, Truth and History*, the book featuring his much-discussed envatted brains.[22]

In "The Meaning of 'Meaning,'" however, Putnam hasn't yet gone in for such psychological externalism. Partly for that reason, and wanting a considered earthling and his Twin Earth Doppelganger to be *psychologically alike*, Putnam greatly turns back the clock. In that way, there'll be no chance for chemical discoveries to introduce any asymmetries in belief between an early earthling and his Doppelganger. So, he has us consider this extension of his first example:

> Now let us roll the time back to about 1750. At that time chemistry was not developed either on Earth or Twin Earth. The typical Earthian speaker of English did not know water consisted of hydrogen and oxygen, and the typical Twin Earthian speaker of English did not know that 'water' consisted of *XYZ*. Let Oscar$_1$ be such a typical Earthian English speaker, and let Oscar$_2$ be his counterpart on Twin Earth. You may suppose that there is no belief that Oscar$_1$ had about water that Oscar$_2$ did not have about 'water.' [The foregoing sentence shows some of the noted favoritism.] If you like, you may even suppose that Oscar$_1$ and Oscar$_2$ were exact duplicates in appearance, feelings, thoughts, interior monologues, etc. Yet the extension of the term 'water' was just as much H$_2$O on Earth in 1750 as in 1950; and the extension of the term 'water' was just as much *XYZ* on Twin Earth in 1750 as in 1950. Oscar$_1$ and Oscar$_2$ understood the term 'water' differently in 1750 *although they were in the same psychological state*.[23]

Just so, in this essay Putnam has it that the considered agents are psychologically alike.

Given this (relevantly) complete psychological similarity, we shouldn't expect very much substance in Putnam's remarks about what people may mean, and about what they'll refer to, and so on. (By the use of a certain word of hers)

---

21. See Colin McGinn, "Charity, Interpretation, and Belief," *Journal of Philosophy*, Vol. 74 (1977): 521–35 and Tyler Burge, "Individualism and the Mental," *Midwest Studies in Philosophy*, IV (1979): 73–212.

22. Already given in this chapter's first note, I'll remind us of this book's publication details: Hilary Putnam, *Reason, Truth and History*, Cambridge University Press, 1981.

23. "The Meaning of 'Meaning,'" page 224. The italics are Putnam's.

someone will *mean* water, a certain substance, only if the person has had some causal, or quasi-causal, transactions with some water—with some of that very substance—no matter how indirect the transactions may be. Or so, at least, Putnam contends. As far as analytical emptiness goes, that's all on a par, I'll submit, with this: Someone will *perceive* some water nearby only if the person is now, or just recently has been, aptly related to some water near her. (This idea, about *perceiving*, is correct; by contrast, Putnam's ideas, about meaning and about referring, are incorrect.) For our *main* matter, the offered thoughts are on a par: Like the thought about perceiving, Putnam's ideas are *empty* ideas.

Along familiar lines, I'll present some arguments. First, I'll support the idea that you and your Doppelganger will be enormously alike as regards what you *believe about* the stuff that's in the lakes on earth, and about the stuff that's in the rivers on Twin Earth. (Then, I'll do something more important, in my view.) I directly proceed to provide the noted support.

Suppose that, along with an earthly Oscar, in 1750 there lived, on earth, one *Joseph Antoine Earthchemist*, who was then this planet's most talented chemical scientist, by far. For short we'll call him *J. A. Earthchemist* or, even, just *J. A.* This earthly J. A. was on the verge of discovering that earthly water is composed of hydrogen and oxygen. By contrast, *all the other* earthly scientists are very far from making such a momentous discovery.

On Twin Earth, the greatest chemist is, of course, a Doppelganger of the earthly J. A. We'll name him *Joseph Antoine Twinchemist*, often calling him *J. A. Twinchemist*. Now, for his part, this J. A. Twinchemist is on the verge of discovering that *twater*, the Twin earthly stuff that *he* calls 'water', is composed not of any hydrogen, or any oxygen, but of just three other chemical elements.[24] By contrast with J. A. Twinchemist, *all the other* Twin Earth scientists are very far from making such a momentous discovery.

In all their real mental powers, our two Joseph Antoines will be precisely similar, however we sensibly construe "mental powers". Not only as regards what behavior each is apt to produce (in any encountered environment) but also as concerns what experiencing each is apt to enjoy, each of our two chemists is, at our start, precisely similar to the other. Keeping that constant, we suppose each J. A. to switch places with the other, almost instantaneously. With this switch, Twinchemist will be here on earth, in 1750, before anyone's discovered the chemical composition of water, and Earthchemist will be on Twin Earth then, before anyone's discovered the chemical composition of *twater*, of what *they* call "water".

As to discovering the composition of what's called "water" on these planets, what do we expect? In this respect, will each J. A. be quite at a loss? No; he

---

24. For convenience, we may call *twater* the stuff (mostly) constituted of *XYZ*, as did many of Putnam's fellow mainstream philosophers.

won't. At least, that's what Putnam should think, along with other Scientiphically minded philosophers. But, let's suppose that, when first on earth, Twinchemist *can't be correctly* said to have *beliefs about* water. Then, having beliefs about water appears *irrelevant to being able* to discover water's composition.

4. The Banality of Successfully Investigating Unfamiliar Individuals

To many philosophers, the previous two sections will seem very interesting. Why so?

Well, on the one hand, it's widely held that, to think about water, one must have been, unlike Vatchemist and Twinchemist, richly involved in an environment rich with water, whereas those two men weren't thus involved. And, on the other hand, it also seems that, in order to be successful in inquiries concerning water, it should be quite especially helpful (to be able) to think about water: Without that, our inquirer would seem to be at a distinct disadvantage. But, as the two previous sections apparently made clear, neither Vatchemist nor Twinchemist will ever be, in fact, at any such serious disadvantage. Or, so it will be, at least, if our widely held Scientiphicalism should hold.

Anyway, we now face these three alternatives: First, and against the mainstream, it may be that Vatchemist and Twinchemist *are* able to think about water, and that's that. Or, second, it may be that, whether or not they're so able, being able to think about water *isn't* important even for successful inquiry into the nature of water, and *that's* that. Or, third, and ever so boldly, it may be that *both* hold true: not only are these two people so able, but, additionally, their being so able isn't important for their engaging in such successful inquiry.

What's really at stake here? There's just a question of whether certain putative conceptual truths really are just that, one a thought about thinking and environmental involvement, the other an idea about thinking and successful inquiry. Maybe both are, maybe only the first is; maybe it's only the second; and maybe neither is. Anyhow, these issues are all analytically empty.

How may we get a better perspective on all this? Well, along lines familiar from the literature, let's change the subject a bit. Now, the object of an agent's inquiry won't be any sort of stuff, or kind of things; rather it will be some particular individual. And, when we have two agents inquiring, each will investigate a (numerically) different individual. Let's proceed.

Suppose that, on earth, there's an amazingly effective super-spy. We'll call him *James Bond*, borrowing a name from the novelist Ian Fleming. Further, let's suppose that *our* Bond, no fictional character, is on the verge of unearthing the whereabouts of the West's most wanted miscreant, the notorious terrorist

Osama bin Laden. Left to run free, and left to his own devices, it will be no more than a day before this Bond will find the hiding bin Laden.[25]

For a first case, we may pretend that, always receiving the same stimulation as Bond himself, there's a brain precisely like Bond's brain; we'll call it (the brain of) *Vat Bond*. Now, we take James Bond's brain out of his head, and we put Vat Bond's brain in the cranium of that athletic de-brained body. That won't help bin Laden: Just as the original Bond would have daringly done, Vat Bond will soon unearth the terrorist.

As I'm happy to grant, even all this may be entirely true: At least when Vat Bond's brain was first in James Bond's cranium and, in that way, it was first in James Bond's body, this Vat Bond *wasn't thinking about bin Laden*, and was utterly *unable* to do so. At least to my mind, this is more plausible than the idea that he was unable to think about water. Still, beyond niceties concerning the proper names we employ, a pretty shallow (contingent) matter, what's concretely substantial here? Little or nothing, it surely seems. At all events, if it's true that Vat Bond can't think about Osama, then this will be another truth: To find bin Laden quickly and readily, it's not important to (be able to) *think about bin Laden*.

For the sake of completeness, let's turn from this vat business to discuss what I'll call *Identical Twin Earth*: This is a planet that, at least in every physical respect, is (at least nonrelationally) exactly like earth itself. Where there is water on earth, there is, in a correlative place on Identical Twin Earth, water just as well. And, if there's no XYZ on earth at all, then there won't be any, either, on Identical Twin Earth. More to present purposes, there's this that can be properly said: Where there's our Osama bin Laden in a compound in our Pakistan, there is, on Identical Twin Earth, a precisely similar terrorist, in a precisely similar compound in their (country of, as I'll call it) *Identical Twin Pakistan*. And, where our Bond is on the verge of discovering Osama, so their *Identical Twin Bond* is on the verge of discovering *Identical Twin Osama*. Now, we suppose that James Bond and Identical Twin Bond switch places. Owing to this, is either Bond at a loss now, less able to nab the noted terrorist that's pretty near him? No; given Scientiphicalism, neither Bond is at any disadvantage. Even if J. I. Twin Bond can't think about earth's Osama bin Laden, he'll soon find Osama. (J. I. T. Bond will be *wrong* in thinking the man he finds is the man he initially pursued. That doesn't matter.)

For those who've thought Putnam and company were onto something philosophically deep and dramatically worldly, things may be even much worse than I've so far allowed What I have in mind is this possibility: In this whole neighborhood, there may be so vast a mess that all the thoughts we've been

---

25. The first several drafts of this chapter were written well before bin Laden was found, and was killed, by U S Navy SEALS. I leave the passages in the present tense, and continue to pretend that SEALS are out of the picture.

considering fail to have any determinate truth-value: What's indicated by much of our ordinary talk, and by much of our nontechnical thought, will comport quite poorly with the much-discussed so-called "externalist" suggestions of Putnam's, and those of his many externalist followers. At the same time, it may be that there are other aspects of our ordinary talk that, oppositely, indicate that Putnam's ideas are correct thoughts regarding the semantics of the terms in question, both when the terms are standard proper names and perhaps also when the terms are certain common nouns. And, just perhaps, there is nothing in the language, or anywhere else, to decide between these opposing indications.

Let me say something about how some of our ordinary talk goes against the externalist line. First, here's a bit about our use of some proper names: Suppose James Identical Twin Bond believes that all terrorists, anywhere and everywhere, should be caught and, without any thought to their prosecution, they should be executed straightaway. Now, as it surely seems, this fellow has a hardliner belief about absolutely all terrorists. And, as it also then seems, our J. I. T. Bond has this extreme belief about, in particular, the very elusive and very earthly Osama bin Laden—as our earthly Osama is, certainly, included among absolutely all the terrorists. So, this denizen of the dramatically distant planet, Identical Twin Earth, believes that our earthly Osama should be caught and, without any thought to his prosecution, he should be executed straightaway. Even though our alien agent *hasn't* anything even remotely like any *acquaintance* with earth's Osama bin Laden, or any notable quasi-causal connection with the earthly terrorist, that seems to be so.[26]

Next, here's a bit about our use of some common nouns: Return to consider J. A. Twinchemist, Twin Earth's leading chemical scientist, by far, when that distant planet was just beginning to develop (its) modern chemistry. Among the things that this J. A. believed, there may be this hypothesis: All physical substances that are ever in a liquid state will, at some sufficiently higher temperature, transform to a gaseous state. As this is something that our distant J. A. believes about *all* physical liquefiable substances, so it is something that, in particular, he believes about twater (or XYZ) and, in particular, he also believes it about mercury, and also about alcohol, and also about (earthly) water (or H_2O). So, not only does J. A. Twinchemist believe that mercury will, at a suitably high temperature, transform into a vaporous form, he also believes that, when sufficiently heated, (liquid) *water* (or liquid H_2O) will, too.

As I was saying, there may well be nothing so much in this area as an unmanageable semantic mess. If that is so, then the main point here will be this idea: In all the mess, there's no philosophical thought, anywhere in this little neighborhood, that's a concretely substantial idea. And, if it is not so, then the

---

26. This little argument is a small variant of one proposed to me, and to others at NYU, by James Pryor. So, some arguments upcoming might be larger variants on his suggested reasoning.

main point here will be this related idea: However it is that the semantic and conceptual matters play out in this little neighborhood, there's no philosophical thought, anywhere in this neighborhood, that's a concretely substantial idea.

For the meanwhile, that's enough about the extraordinary paucity of novel philosophical thoughts that are concretely substantial ideas. Now, obliquely following the lead of Putnam's prominent passages, let's do a bit to remedy that sorry situation.

5. A Concretely Substantial Possibility: *Individualistically Directed Powers*

Before encountering the substantial thoughts just advertised, some stage setting will be useful. Here is some: The bare bones Scientiphicalism I sketched in chapter 1 is the core of a fuller view. As it's very nearly as widely held as the bare-bones core, we may well call the fuller view *Extended Scientiphicalism*. I don't expect I'll ever appreciate all of our Extended Scientiphicalism. Indeed, I'll be happy to appreciate, and to articulate, what's only a quite modest part of it.

Briefly and roughly, here's some of our Extended Scientiphicalism: Whenever one concrete particular is disposed to interact dynamically with others, the first concretum's disposition will be a *generalistic* power. For example, a proton is disposed to attract *not just* a certain particular concretum that has unit negative electric charge, or just certain ones among all such concreta. Rather, a proton's propensitied to attract any electron that ever there may be, assuming they'll all be similarly charged electrically.

But, then, is there any *coherent alternative* to this common assumption of ours? How should a proton—or any concrete particular, for that matter—be disposed to attract just a certain one of the electrons, just a certain one of the terribly tiny electronish particles each of which, in *all its general* features, or as regards *all its general* nonrelational properties, is just *like all the others*?[27] We needn't strive for credible options here; we may be content with *any coherent* alternative.

Well, let's suppose, then, that there are particles of a certain peculiar sort, I'll call them *centurons*, that divide in a certain characteristic way, providing that the conditions conducive for the nice division happily obtain, a supposition

---

27. A relational property of a given concretum entails that there should exist, at least at some time, some other concretum, to which the first is aptly related. Thus, my relational property of being a father entails the existence of another concretum—at least one such—to which I'm aptly related—so that I am the *father of* that other concretum. By contrast, my property of being a person is, I think, nonrelational. Like my property of being a person, all pure power properties are, I suggest, nonrelational properties. At any rate, please assume that for the present discussion. As I'll observe, what you'll be assuming here won't be any concretely substantial thought. Rather, it's an empty idea, though it may be one that, in our context, is helpful.

often satisfied. Further, among the many centurons in our own galaxy, in the case of a certain one of them, *Home-Mama*, as I'll call it, these conditions *do* obtain. So, now, Home-Mama divides in its characteristically centuronish way, that is, in just such a way that 99% of its matter comes to constitute a certain new particle, one *Home-Spinner*, and the other 1% comes to constitute another new particle, *Home-Spinnee*. Neither of them are centurons; rather, Home-Spinner is a particle of a certain other kind—it's a *ninetynineon*—and *Home-Spinnee* is a particle of a certain still other kind—it's a *oneon*. Now, as long as *these* two new particles are within a light-year of each other, Home-Spinner will spin Home-Spinnee and, so, Home-Spinnee will be spinning. But, should they become further apart than that, then Home-Spinner *won't* spin Home-Spinnee and, what's more, Home-Spinnee then *won't* spin.

When these two individuals are pretty near each other and, so, when there *is* the spinning, *why* does the spinning occur? Of course, part of the answer is that they're near each other. But, what's the rest of the story? Well, it *isn't* that Home-spinner is disposed to spin (just any) nearby oneons, and Home-Spinnee is disposed to be spun by (just any) nearby ninetynineon. No; as we're instructively supposing, it's not that, at all. Rather, what explains the noted spinning, we're supposing, is just this: Home-Spinner is propensitied to spin the *very individual* that is Home-Spinnee (whenever the two are close enough to each other). (For the case to be a nicely simple example, we'll suppose that it's *only* that very individual, Home-Spinnee, that Home-Spinner is thus propensitied to spin). Now, even as our tale features two main descendant characters, there's another side to the story. So, for its part, and reciprocally, Home-Spinnee is disposed to be spun by the *very object* that's Home-Spinner. (For the case to be nicely simple, we suppose that it's *only* by *that* very individual, Home-Spinner, that Home-Spinnee is so propensitied.) As we may say, Home-Spinner has an *individualistically directed* propensity, for spinning Home-Spinnee. And, reciprocally, Home-Spinnee has an *individualistically directed* propensity, for being spun by Home-Spinner. I complete this side of our story, well enough, by being a bit more explicit: Home-Spinner and Home-Spinnee are *so propensitied*, each with respect to only the other, that, when they should be more than a light-year apart, Home-Spinnee will *not spin*. So, that's the first side of our story.

Here's the other side: Among the centurons abounding in a *very distant* galaxy, a good 1000 light-years from our own, certain events occur in a perfect parallel with how the aforementioned events occurred here. So, way out there, with a certain very distant centuron, one Far-Mama, some similarly conducive conditions *also* obtain so that 99% of *its* matter then constitutes a certain new particle, one Far-Spinner, and the other 1% comes to constitute another new particle, a certain Far-Spinnee. Now, as long as *these* two new particles are within a light-year of each other, Far-Spinner will spin Far-Spinnee. But, should *they* become further apart than that, then Far-Spinner *won't* spin Far-Spinnee.

Of course, all that is due to how it is that the distant particles are propensitied. We will now bring together both sides.

Happily, our tale is set to end symmetrically: As we'll suppose, a great force has it that Home-Spinnee and Far-Spinnee suddenly switch places. Now, Home-Spinnee will be too distant from Home-Spinner to be spun by it, and Far-Spinnee will be too distant from Far-Spinner to be spun by *it*. So, neither Home-Spinnee nor Far-Spinnee will spin any longer.[28]

6. The Propensity to Acquire Individualistic Powers and Its Historical Manifestation

When Home-Mama fissioned, what happened to the *matter that constituted* Home-Mama? Even while Home-Mama divided, its constituting *matter similarly divided*. Quite suddenly, almost all the matter came to compose one new basic material particular, Home-Spinner, while the rest, just 1%, came to compose a spatially quite separate material individual, Home-Spinnee.

Now, in the specification of certain sorts of possible worlds, it may be laid down that this division should occur only quite randomly. But, now, we pass over that possibility.

Just so, we'll consider such other specifications as will have the emergence of Home-Spinner and Home-Spinnee be the manifestation of a certain propensity of Home-Mama (or of the matter constituting it) whether the propensity should be (simply) deterministic or whether it should be (merely) probabilistic. This will be a propensity, on the part of Home-Mama, for it to divide in just such a way that all its matter should persist, with most coming to compose a certain particle, and with the rest coming to compose a much smaller particle. What's more, the larger particle resulting from division will be individualistically powered with respect to (just) the smaller particle resulting, for the spinning of the smaller particle, even while the smaller will be individualistically propensitied, reciprocally, with respect to the larger resultant.

For the sake of simple exposition, and losing nothing crucial, we'll suppose that this propensity of Home-Mama's is a fully deterministic disposition, and not any merely probabilistic power. Then, upon the obtaining of conditions conducive to the propensity's manifestation, Home-Mama will divide, or it will fission, in the way we've indicated, so that there will emerge the noted pair of

28. In historically most seminal philosophy, as we saw in chapter 1, individualistic powers may play an important part: With the thought of a nonspatial soul that's propensitied for interaction with just a certain spatial body, there's a first substantial step to a coherent Cartesian Dualism. And, with the thought of a body that's reciprocally propensitied, for interaction with just that soul, there may be the rest of what's wanted for a happy Cartesian Dualism.

reciprocally partnered material particulars, Home-Spinner and Home-Spinnee, each propensitied in a way that's individualistically directed with respect *only to the other*. In time, optimal conditions obtain. Accordingly, Home-Mama fissions, and there comes into being the pair of partnered particles, Home-Spinner and Home-Spinnee, each individualistically propensitied, as indicated, with respect *only to the other*.

Finally, for now, and to complete our specifying tale most dramatically, we'll aptly assume that, in certain concrete realms, it's owing only to just such developmental sequences as those we've just supposed that any concretum will ever spin, let alone that any particle will ever be spun by any other particle. In these concrete realms, unless the right sort of temporal sequence first obtains, involving certain concreta, no concretum will ever spin at all.

In the case just discussed, the material concreta individualistically recipro-cally propensitied, as with Home-Spinner and Home-Spinnee, were produced in the same physical happening, a certain fissioning. And, each of the two individu-als was composed of matter coming from their common ancestor, Home-Mama. Owing to that, there's a certain intuitive intelligibility, it often seems, in the fact that they should be so nicely partnered propensitively, each individualistically propensitied with respect to the other. It was for this reason that, to introduce you to cases of individualistic propensity among material things, I chose to begin with that example. But, that said and done, please don't think that, in all such cases, matters will be so intuitively intelligible. So, without further ado, let's look at a less comfortable example.

Suppose that each electron has the propensity to acquire a certain power, for a certain dynamical interaction, with the first *strangeon*—a new and unusual sort of particle—to come within 1000 meters of it. (In the case of a tie, where there'll be no single first near-enough strangeon, no such power will be acquired.) We also suppose that each strangeon is propensitied to acquire an apt recip-rocal power, for dynamical interaction with the first *electron* to come within 1000 meters of *it*. So far, there haven't been any strangeons in our world. But, all of a sudden, now there are some, even very many of them.

Very specifically, let's consider a certain electron that we'll call *Ed*, and the first strangeon to come within a thousand meters of Ed, which we'll call *Steve*. When Ed and Steve are first within a thousand meters of each other, we're sup-posing, their noted propensities to acquire individualistic Powers will manifest like this: Ed will become disposed to have Steve revolve around it in a circular orbit, with a radius of a thousand meters and, reciprocally, Steve will become propensitied to circle around Ed, in just such an orbit. (For simplicity's sake, we suppose that no other strangeon, beyond Steve, ever becomes disposed to circle around Ed, and, Steve never becomes disposed to revolve around any other elec-tron, beyond Ed. As well, we suppose that all the dispositions discussed are deter-ministic dispositions, not probabilistic propensities.) Finally, we suppose that, for the manifestation of the powers just specified, conducive conditions obtain. So, then, Ed will come to have a certain power with respect only to Steve, and Steve will come to have a reciprocal disposition, directed only at Ed.

On top of that, we suppose this: Shortly thereafter, conducive conditions obtain for the manifestation of the individualistic powers just recently acquired by Steve. So, as must then happen, Steve will revolve around Ed, in the circular orbit specified for Steve's so doing.

Here are some complementary empty propositions, maybe also usefully clarifying: Suppose that Steve suddenly ceases to exist, and never again exists. Yet, Ed will continue to exist, quite unchanged in all its real dispositions. To be sure, Ed *won't* ever again have the *chance to manifest* its most salient individualistic propensity. Still and all, Ed *will continue to have the individualistic power* to have *Steve* revolve around it.

Along with the clarifying but empty thoughts we've been pondering, we may clearly contemplate some concretely substantial ideas. One such is that *there are*, in some concrete worlds, pairs of individuals that are propensitied individualistically for interactions in which a certain one of them revolves around the other, in a circular orbit with a radius of 1000 meters.[29]

29. Though it takes us away from the main points of this chapter, I will badly confuse very many readers, well do I know, unless I say these next few following things: *First*, each of many particles can be individualistically directed to each of many others, there then being very many pairs of individualistic reciprocal partners. For example, each of eight particles may be propensitied with respect to each of the others, individualistically, in such a way that they always form a cubical array, with the size of the array always oscillating between, say, a low of one cubic meter and a high of one thousand cubic meters. *Second*, in *certain* cases, that will happen even while it is *also true that, generalistically, too, the particles are so propensitied as to have such an oscillation occur.* With these cases there obtains, in addition to having the particles being so nicely individualistically propensitied with respect each other, the fact that each particle has a certain feature, the same for all eight, toward which all the other seven particles are generalistically directed, and in just such a way as to promote, or even to ensure, the aforesaid oscillation. *Third*, and finally here, there are cases where the noted oscillation can be promoted, and even ensured, where all that responsible for that is how things are generalistically with the eight particles, even as none of the particles is individualistically propensitied, in any presently relevant way, with respect to any of others.

Whichever one of those three sorts of scenario obtains, supposing that just one of them does, matters may seem the same to us, and they will do if we rely only on the experiential aspect of our understanding, only on our mind's eye, so to say. But, if we employ the intellective aspect of our understanding, instead, or as well, things may seem, to us, quite different, and rather richer. Thinking intellectively, as I say, we can discern that, in the previous paragraph, there were specified, quite well, three distinct sorts of nonrandom concrete scenario, each substantially different from the others.

In *All the Power in the World*, I discuss points like this at great length. For those interested in such points, it's probably enough to read just pages 248–53.

At this point, it may be that quite a few readers will still be rather confused, as to what is at stake when making points about concreta and their individualistic powers. But, as I feel sure, confusion won't be nearly as widespread as before, when no reader had the benefit of encountering this happy little digression. Anyhow, it's time to return to the chapter's more central themes.

7. A Concretely Substantial Possibility: Individualistically Directed *Mental* Powers

Our recent suppositions concerned only physical matters and *not any mental* matters at all. This was true for both the empty thoughts and for the substantial ideas. But, in parallel with that, we may contemplate various substantial statements concerning *mental* individuals (even if these mental individuals might also be, perhaps, certain physical entities).

Whether or not it ever happens in the actual world, we may imagine people who have generalistic propensities to acquire *individualistically directed mental powers* toward just some certain individuals. Just so, we may contemplate a person who, with respect to each (external) object she's clearly enough perceived, acquires a propensity to *think about the perceived object*, at least fairly effectively, by contrast with objects she's never perceived, which she cannot think about even nearly as effectively, and maybe not even ineffectively. With concrete objects she's never perceived, the would-be thinker typically draws a blank when, for instance, a more happily experienced person mentions the object, trying to get her to consider it. Or, things might go awry less dramatically, as I'll next relate, however vaguely it may be.

Suppose that, on a planet where things proceed pretty peculiarly, when someone perceived a certain deer, for example, she may be able to think much more clearly about the deer, and much more effectively, than she can think about any animal she's never perceived. Just so, although she can't make any plans to trap a deer that she herself has never perceived, she may be very able, indeed, to make excellent plans for trapping a certain absent deer she's already seen. By contrast, when trying to form a deer-trapping plan that's not aimed at some already-perceived deer, she makes a mess of things, in her quite futile attempt at some useful thinking.

In her perceptual interaction with the perceived deer, our agent acquired a certain power to think about that individual. And, of course, through its reciprocal perceptual interaction with our agent—through its being perceived by her—our deer acquired the reciprocal propensity, the propensity to be effectively considered by our peculiarly remarkable agent.

This may occur not just in a certain single distant galaxy, but, just as well, it may occur in each of several extremely distant galaxies—each terribly distant from both our own galaxy and also from each other. Each of these far-flung galaxies will have a planet whose most intelligent thinkers acquire *individualistically directed mental* powers, propensities like those just noted.

Now, let's suppose that a certain one of these planets, we'll call it *Distant Planet One*, is, as regards all its general features, precisely like another one of them, which we'll call *Distant Planet Two*. Suppose that, on Distant Planet One, a certain agent, *Distant Hunter One*, has just acquired the power to think, very effectively, about a certain particular deer, *Bambi One,* even while he can't think, at all well, about other deer. That is because Deer Hunter One has perceived Bambi One, but he hasn't perceived any other deer. Now, suppose that, on *Distant Planet Two,* there's a certain agent, *Distant Hunter Two,* who's precisely similar to Distant Hunter One *as regards all purely general features.* Symmetrically with Hunter One, Deer Hunter Two just acquired a correlative individualistically directed power, directed with respect to the only deer that he's perceived, *Bambi Two.* Just so, each Distant Hunter is able to think, at all well, about just the Bambi *he's* perceived; not any other Bambi (nor any other deer at all).

What will happen should Hunter One and Hunter Two suddenly be greatly shifted so that, suddenly, Hunter One is within trapping distance of only Bambi Two, not yet visible to him, and Hunter Two is within trapping distance of only Bambi One, not yet visible to *him?* In such a circumstance, Hunter One *won't* be well able to think about the Bambi that's near enough for him to trap soon. And, Hunter Two *won't* be well able to think about the Bambi that's near enough for *him* to trap soon.

This is utterly unlike what happened when our James Bond suddenly switched places with our James Identical Twin Bond. As both Bonds had only generalistically directed mental powers, each was well able to think about the Osama who suddenly came to be nearby him. Now, consider someone who, when describing *that* example, uses the words "James Identical Twin Bond can't think about Osama bin Laden, the terrorist so suddenly nearby him". Well, using the words as mainstream philosophers do, that person will be expressing a thought that's concretely empty (and, I'll submit, quite incorrect, to boot).

By contrast, consider someone who's describing our just lately presented example, featuring the two Deer Hunters and the two Bambis. When describing *this* case, someone may well use the words "Distant Hunter Two can't think about Bambi One, the deer just so suddenly nearby him". When using these saliently similar words in such a very different way, *this* person will be expressing a thought that's a concretely *substantial* idea (and, by hypothesis, quite correct, too.)

Somehow or other, when mainstream philosophers offer ideas as to when it is that someone can think about this or that, and when it is that she can't, they may have created the impression that they're offering importantly substantial claims, maybe quite as much so as with the claim about how our befuddled Deer Hunter Two is so unable to deal, thoughtfully, with our Bambi One. But, any such impression as that is an illusion. In truth, what's offered is on a par with the idea that, without attending college, you can't remember your old college days.

8. Generalistic Propensities to Acquire *Real-kind Directed* Mental Powers

Much as we may coherently suppose a thinker to acquire a propensity to think about only a certain individual, so we may also coherently suppose a thinker to acquire a propensity to think about only individuals of a certain *kind*—presumably a *kind some members of which* come to be aptly related to the thinker. And so it will be, too, with such various *non-individual* substances, or *stuffs*, which, along with portions of them, may come to be so aptly related.

In cases like these, it may not be quite correct to say that the thinker acquires a power that's individualistically directed. With little or nothing hanging on the question, we leave that open.

However any of that should be, at least something like this can be said: The power that's acquired will strongly resemble, in certain salient respects, certain individualistic mental powers. At all events, we might do well to call these strongly resembling mental powers, to be indicated in just a moment or two, *real-kind directed powers*.

In the actual world, a world we suppose to be Scientiphically well behaved, it may well be that there aren't any thinkers who ever possess any mental powers that are real-kind directed propensities. This was, of course, what we envisioned for our various examples of earth and Twin Earth. As was supposed for those cases, all concreta were propensitied only generalistically. (Indeed, they all comport well with all our Scientiphicalism's propositions.) Largely, that was why, as we agreed, the suddenly switched Twin Earthly Joseph Antoine would be the first person to discover that earth's water was composed of hydrogen and oxygen.

By contrast with all that, let's consider a radically different concrete world. In this newly considered world, we'll suppose there to be a certain planet, one *Counterpart Earth*, that's a lot like our actual earth is, except for some big business about some real-kind dispositions. So, *looking* much the same as Counterpart Earth does, which is, of course, much like *earth itself looks*, our new world will contain another new planet, *Counterpart Twin Earth*. In all the ways a reader will expect, and as regards all the planet's generalistic features, Counterpart Earth is just like earth. And, similarly, Counterpart Twin Earth is also just like Twin Earth. But, very saliently, there are certain differences between the two *pairs* of planets. Strikingly, there'll be differences in the acquisition of various mental powers. How's that? I'll begin here with earth.

Well, when someone on earth perceives some water, or he interacts with water in certain other apt ways, not only is that person well able to think about water but, quite equally, he's also well able to think about certain *other* substances; though they aren't deeply watery, or aqueous, perhaps, these other stuffs *seem to him* to be just like water is (when he's not performing some telling

chemical experiments, and so on). In line with this, and as you'll recall, earth's
J. A. was readily able to discover the chemical composition of twater, the stuff
he encountered on Twin Earth. Why? Well, to him, that stuff seemed just like
water. So, right off the bat, he could proceed with it, even as an inquirer into its
deeper nature, ever so effectively.

By contrast, when someone on *Counterpart* Earth perceives some water, he
doesn't acquire any such "widely reaching" ability. He doesn't gain any ability to
think about substances that look to him just as water looks, should the stuffs be
deeply different from water. Rather, what the Counterpart Earthian perceiver will
acquire is, as we're now supposing, the ability to think well about only stuff that's
of just the very same real-kind as what he perceived, that is, in fact, just some H_2O.
And, of course, happily correlative things take place on *Counterpart Twin* Earth.

When reasoning about Counterpart Earth and Counterpart Twin Earth,
we'll get very different results from those obtained before, when we reasoned
about relevantly similar scenarios involving earth and Twin Earth. Strikingly,
this will happen with scenarios before modern chemistry developed, simultaneously, on our Counterpart planets. Just so, consider a scenario starring *their* two
scientifically salient Joseph Antoines, back in the days of *their* 1750*s eras*. When
Counterpart Twin J. A. is switched to *Counterpart Earth*, he finds that he's *not* able to
think well, at all, about the stuff that looks just like the Counterpart Twin stuff
he's called "water". Even when all this J. A. does is *try to keep in mind* the newly
confronted stuff that looks like that, he fares poorly. Instead of succeeding in
that, he finds himself thinking about gold, on some occasions, and, on others,
wondering whether oak or maple is the harder material.

As this "peculiar" J. A. can't think well about Counterpart Earth's counterpart of twater, he *won't* soon discover that stuff's chemical composition. And,
should he take quite a while to acquire the relevant new real-kind directed
mental power, which may well be supposed, then, Counterpart Twin J. A. will
take far longer to discover anything much about water's chemical composition
than one of Counterpart Earth's far less talented chemists.

9. Wishful Blindness to Emptiness: Putnam's "Transcendental" Pronouncement

Apparently unable to realize the fact that so many of their offered ideas are just
so many empty ideas, mainstream philosophers have contrived obscure accounts of what they've done. An example of that occurs in Putnam's *Reason,
Truth and History*:

> Some philosophers, eager both to assert and minimize the claims of their
> profession at the same time (the typical state of mind of Anglo-American

philosophy in the twentieth century), would say: 'Sure. You have shown that some things that seem to be physical possibilities are really *conceptual* impossibilities. What's so surprising about that?'

Well, to be sure, my argument can be described as a 'conceptual' one. But to describe philosophical activity as the search for conceptual truths makes it all sound like *inquiry about the meaning of words*. And, that is not at all what we have been engaging in.

What we have been doing is considering the preconditions for thinking about, representing, referring to, etc. We have investigated these preconditions *not* by investigating the meanings of these words and phrases (as a linguist might, for example) but by *reasoning a priori*. Not in the old 'absolute' sense (since we don't claim that magical theories of reference are *a priori* wrong), but in the sense of inquiring into what is *reasonably* possible *assuming* certain general premises, or making certain very broad theoretical assumptions. Such a procedure is neither 'empirical' nor quite 'a priori', but has elements of both ways of investigating. In spite of the fallibility of my procedure, and its dependence upon assumptions which might be described as 'empirical' (e.g. the assumption that the mind has no access to external things or properties apart from that provided by the senses), my procedure has a close relation to what Kant called a 'transcendental' investigation; for it is an investigation, I repeat, of the *preconditions* of reference and hence of thought—preconditions built in to (sic) the nature of our minds themselves, though not (as Kant hoped) wholly independent of empirical assumptions.[30]

What decent sense can we make of this? I'll try to see what can be said.

First, there's this. Insofar as Putnam might make correct comments about referring, thinking, and representing, parallel remarks hold true for remembering, perceiving, and much else besides. So, perhaps very generously, let's agree that a *precondition* for *thinking* you went to college is that you be in some sort of quasi-causal nexus with (various things that themselves are....in a quasi-causal nexus with) at least one college. Then, in parallel, and more certainly, it will be a *precondition* for *remembering* you went to college that there was at least one college you attended. And, insofar as there's ever much relevance here in any of the quasi-causal stuff, whether it be for thinking or whether it be for remembering, a further *precondition* for your *remembering that*, one that's more robust and demanding, is that you be in some sort of quasi-causal nexus with (various things that themselves are....in a quasi- causal nexus with) at least one college. At any rate, whatever it may be that should fill Putnam's proposed preconditional bill for the thinking in question, it will

---

30. Putnam, *Reason, Truth and History*, pages 15–16. Evidently, the cited sentences serve just as well, or just as badly, as a reply to someone who wants to minimize the importance of what Putnam accomplished when he argued, correlatively, that a Twin Earthian can't refer to, and she can't think about, Earthly water. And, so it goes, quite generally.

find a perfectly parallel item that will fill a precisely parallel preconditional bill for a correlative remembering. Whatever fancy talk applies for the thinking case, it will be perfectly paralleled by fancy talk for the remembering case.[31]

Whatever in the way of a priori reasoning is needed for us to grasp the (probably incorrect) ideas about preconditions for certain sorts of thinking, and referring, and representing, it will all run perfectly parallel to whatever a priori reasoning is needed for us to grasp the (probably correct) ideas about preconditions for (certain sorts of) remembering. This will be so whatever it is, exactly, that these needs should ever be. Myself, I'm inclined to think that an investigation of certain linguistic and semantic considerations will be relevant to our having confidence in these claims. Just as much as it occurs with fruitful inquiry into thinking about things, that will happen with fruitful inquiry into remembering things. At all events, I can't see that there's anything, in any of this, that's *transcendental*, in any sense of that esoteric word. Trying to be more readily understood, I'll say I'd like to see more in the way of concretely substantial ideas, which thoughts are more than merely parochial ideas. In the next section, we'll try to do that.

10. Reading Modal Claims Substantially and Widening Our Philosophical Horizons

Salient claims endorsed by prominent mainstream philosophers are just some concretely empty ideas, even if, for quite some years, they've been treated as (at least something like) substantial discoveries. Now, shifting focus away from the empty thoughts the philosophers expressed, let's look at the *sentences* they used to make those unfortunately influential claims. While those philosophers used them in a certain way, the sentences can be used in very different ways, so that these same sentences express concretely substantial ideas, none of them merely parochial. Among the substantial thoughts, some concern individualistically propensitied concreta.

31. In the same neighborhood, we can go on and on. First, there's this to say: Whatever should be a precondition for someone's referring to something, say, to his mother-in-law's new hat, that will find a perfectly parallel precondition—and then some—in what may be truly said for someone's being happy about something, say, about his mother-in-law's new hat. In both cases, one thing that must hold true—a precondition for what's in focus, as Putnam might put it—is that the person should actually have a mother-in-law.

Second, there's this to observe: With the happy-about business, thought not the referring-to business, the agent must *know* that his mother-in-law has a new hat: If he's happy his mother-in-law's new hat isn't a fur hat, he must know that she has a new hat. Thus, with the happy-about stuff, there's a stronger precondition than with the referring-to stuff. And, come to mention it, so things go, too, with the difference between thinking and remembering: Only with remembering something to be so is there such a *knowledge precondition* in force, not with thinking something to be so. But, with the remarks in this note, I'm using an elephant gun to kill a mouse, and an ill mouse, at that. So, it's back to the text, and to the main line of business.

By itself, that's philosophically beneficial, at least to a quite minute degree. Might it be a benefit to *more* than such a terribly minute degree? For these four reasons, I think so.

First, we consider a very natural view of the relation between minds and bodies, though it's now an unfashionable philosophical position. Following Descartes—still the most influential Western writer on these topics—we consider an Interactionist Substantial Dualism, where your material body sometimes influences your immaterial soul (or the immaterial soul that's really you), and where your soul (or what's really you) sometimes influences your body. Now, if we think of all substantial individuals as propensitied only generalistically—not only material bodies, of course, but also immaterial souls, too—it may seem impossible that any given body should affect just a certain one particular soul. And, it may seem impossible, too, that any given soul should affect just a certain one particular body. At any rate, we'd like an attractive resolution of the problem of causal pairing, already observed in our second chapter. As also observed, perhaps the very most attractive will have it that a typical soul is individualistically propensitied with respect to just one body, and reciprocally for each of many bodies.

Second, physicists may one day discover that, in our present Eon, there are certain particles individualistically propensitied with respect to certain other particles. Indeed, for all I know, it may be that, in effect, they've already done this. (But, then, I am quite ignorant of modern physics. And, I haven't yet managed to gain any insight into whether our featured idea plays any role, or may well play some role, in basic science, pretty much as presently conceived.) But, at the least, natural scientists should be *open* to employing ideas as to individualistic powers.

Third, it may be that the actual world goes through very many terribly long time periods, or Eons, perhaps infinitely many.[32] Now, perhaps, our present Eon hasn't any concreta individualistically propensitied with respect to any others. But this may be a temporally provincial matter. Recall the scenario with strangeon Steve and electron Ed, propensitively paired individualistically so

---

32. For quite a few decades now, the preferred view of the cosmos, for most physical cosmologists, has it that the universe, or at least "our universe", first started about 15 Billion years ago, when there occurred a seminal Big Bang. What was there, in all concretely reality, before that fashionably posited physical event? Was there absolutely nothing at all? That boggles the mind, at least my mind. But, even for quite a while now, some leading cosmologists have held that any such Big Bang is not, really, such a very big deal. For example, see Sir Martin Rees, *Before the Beginning: Our Universe and Others*, Helix Books, 1997.

Pretty recently, even the very thought of the Big Bang has been seriously challenged by leading cosmologists, one at Princeton, and the other at Cambridge. See *Endless Universe: Beyond the Big Bang*, by Paul J. Steinhardt and Neil Turok, Doubleday, 2007.

Even according to various highly regarded physical cosmologists, then, there may be plenty of Eons, each lasting very, very many billions of years. As I've just been suggesting, though no more than suggesting, of course, in at least some of these Eons there may be concreta that are propensitied very variously, including many concreta that are individualistically propensitied with respect to many other concreta.

that Steve should orbit Ed. In an Eon ending many *trillions* of years before ours began, interactions like that, all manifesting individualistic powers, may have been the rule. For those who doubt that All Nature shows any "basic preference," here's an appealing speculation: In some Eons all interactions are generalistically powered, in others they're all individualistically powered, and in still others it's a mix of the two.

Fourth, consider a pluriverse that in some salient ways is like that proposed by David Lewis. But, *don't* think of this plethora of worlds as doing anything to diminish the ontological status of how it is that a world's basic individuals are propensitied. There's no reduction. Rather, how they're propensitied is fully on a par, ontologically, with how it is that they're (otherwise) qualitied. Paralleling the speculation concerning Eons, we may speculate about mutually isolated concrete worlds. Thus, beyond anything Lewis did, we may consider a deeply richer and greater plurality of worlds. In some worlds all interactions are generalistically powered, throughout all the world's Eons, in others they're all individualistically powered, and in still others it's one or another sort of mix of the two. And, various worlds may exhibit such differences in their Eons.

For at least those four reasons, our ideas as to these featured powers widen philosophical horizons, and even scientific horizons. So, our noticing them may be beneficial to more than a terribly minute degree. But, ignorant as I am of current science, I cannot see how noting them will be, any time soon, much more than just very modestly interesting.

To gain anything amounting to more than just that, along anything like the lines we've been pursuing, perhaps we must place on offer novel philosophical thoughts that are, not only nonparochial concretely substantial ideas, but that are, as well, at least some pretty plausible propositions, if not any quite credible ideas. At least apparently, that we *haven't* yet done.

Let me call everything in the present section before this very sentence our *Mantra*. Rather than frequently rehearsing it all over again, later in this work I shall, with some frequency, just refer you to our Mantra. Very occasionally, I may, in part, paraphrase the Mantra.

At all events, it is now high time that I bring this chapter to its end, however great the pessimism I was led to express, so near to the end. Right now, on a slightly brighter note, I will end the chapter with these next two sentences: Even in the face of our pessimism, it may be moderately interesting, at least, to explore some other mainstream offerings, all relevantly similar to those explored in this chapter, all of them thoughts that, to many, have seemed impressively deep ideas, even substantial discoveries about concrete reality. Having sent you that slightly bright signal, I directly proceed to explore some more of what's been most influential with, and most admired by, ever so many mainstream philosophers.

4

THE ORIGINS OF MATERIAL INDIVIDUALS

Empty Issues and Sequentialistic Powers

Perhaps more than any other philosopher, Saul Kripke may be responsible for the widespread impression that, quite unlike the bad old days, recent and current mainstream philosophy is replete with thoughts each far more worldly than one finds with any analytically empty ideas. Mostly, Kripke's great influence stems from his *Naming and Necessity*.[1]

1. Based on (edited) transcriptions of three lectures, the bulk of this short book was first published as a long paper, "Naming and Necessity," which appeared in G. Harman and D. Davidson (eds.) *The Semantics of Natural Language*, (Dordrecht, Holland: D. Reidel, 1972), on pages 254–355. The book itself, *Naming and Necessity*, came forth from the Harvard University Press in 1980. In these pages, it will be the 1980 book that I'll be citing.

For the record, it should be noted, I think, that many of the central ideas in the 1972 publication, the long paper "Naming and Necessity," were published yet a year earlier in Kripke's far shorter, standard-sized paper "Identity and Necessity" in *Identity and Individuation*, M. Munitz, ed., New York University Press, 1971, on pages 135–64. But, there's little or nothing in that piece that even appears to be a novel concretely substantial thought that's far from being just some quite parochial proposition. Or so it seems to me.

Finally, for this roundup of early Kripke productions, I'll take notice of the John Locke Lectures that he delivered at Oxford late in 1973. Nearly forty years after the oral presentation, and with some editing well beyond mere transcription, they came forth as written material, so to put things, with the appearance, pretty early in 2013, of a short book, namely, Kripke's, *Reference and Existence*, Oxford University Press, 2013. As with the paper "Identity and Necessity," there's little or nothing in this short book that even appears to be a novel concretely substantial thought and one far from being just some quite parochial proposition. Or, again, so it seems to me.

Just so, for seeking some novel nonparochial concretely substantial ideas from Kripke, during the period when he was most influential, we do quite well, I think, by focusing on just some of the 1980 book, essentially the same as the long paper from 1972.

As the first word of Kripke's title indicates—the word "Naming," of course—much of the book is focused on semantic matters. First, there's offered an account of proper names, like Aristotle, George Herman Ruth and Babe Ruth, on which the reference of these terms has little or nothing to do with whatever meaning (or Fregean sense) they have. As Kripke observes, in largest measure, this agrees with John Stuart Mill's ideas about proper names, as against the then dominant view stemming from Gottlob Frege and Bertrand Russell. Second, there's offered a complementary account of certain common nouns, as with "cat" and "dog", and "gold" and "water". These words are treated as "names for natural kinds" and, for Kripke, their reference also has little or nothing to do with any meaning they might have, at least as understood by Frege, by Russell, and by Mill, too.

But, of course, insofar as there are any concretely substantial thoughts offered in this discussion of semantical matters, whether by Mill, or by Frege, or by Russell, or, more recently, by Kripke, they're all pretty parochial propositions, as with how certain people, speakers of this or that earthly natural language, use certain expressions of the language they commonly employ. None are *philosophical* substantial thoughts, at least not in any ambitious sense of the term.

But, *Naming and Necessity* addresses more than just some linguistic and semantic matters. Far from it, and quite as Kripke meant it to do, the book makes certain claims about mind-independent concrete reality, as with claims about cats and dogs, tables and chairs, gold and water. Here Kripke offers what he takes to be *metaphysical* ideas, some of which are, as best I can tell, rather novel ideas (not just tentative nods toward dualism, as occur in certain parts of the work, or tentative nods toward materialism, as occur in certain other parts). Whether or not the novel thoughts are properly called "metaphysical" is, of course, a matter of little importance. On that very minor matter, my unconfident view is negative, as will emerge in what follows.

More important, I submit, is the question of whether the new nonparochial thoughts are concretely substantial ideas. On this more important matter, my pretty confident view is negative. In this chapter, I offer support for this negative view.[2]

---

2. To some extent, that's because much good deflationary work has already been done by Alan Sidelle and others (despite Sidelle's somewhat heavy-handed use of "convention"). The central thrust is already in Sidelle's early book, *Necessity, Essence, and Individuation*, Cornell University Press, 1989. Other helpful work is done in his early (1992) papers "Rigidity, Ontology and Semantic Structure," *Journal of Philosophy* 89 (8):410–30 and "Identity and the Identity-like," *Philosophical Topics* 20, 269–92. For recent developments of his general position, see his (2009) paper "Conventionalism and the Contingency of Conventions," *Noûs* 43 (2):224–41 and his (2010) paper "Modality and Objects," *Philosophical Quarterly* 60 (238):109–25.

To be sure, as with the philosophers he criticizes, mainly Kripke and Putnam, Sidelle's ideas are also concretely empty, except when they're parochial. But, as I see things, he's far more nearly correct than his opponents are, about pretty much all of the empty issues that exercise

1. The Origin of a Particular Wooden Table

In *Naming and Necessity*, Kripke offers many examples of thoughts which, though he says we (can) know them to be true *only empirically*, or only a posteriori, are perfectly *necessary* truths. In this terribly influential discussion, some of the most salient cases, perfectly central to Kripke's metaphysical remarks, concern the origins of certain concrete individuals. For those who hold with our Extended Scientiphicalism, as Kripke apparently did when presenting the examples, the cases will concern the origins of certain quite *complex physical* concrete individuals. Quite famously, he discussed the case of a certain wooden table, an example we'll discuss at length in this chapter, taking the table to have been composed, at moderately deep "levels of consideration", of very many molecules, which were composed, in turn, of yet more atoms, which were composed, in turn, of yet still more elementary particles, like quarks and electrons.

For those of us who want to spend much time and effort pondering questions concerning various (even just fairly) fundamental ways for concrete reality

---

both him and them. Despite some flaws, Sidelle's work is helpfully clarifying; most of it's vastly underappreciated.

Among other writers in something of the same vein, the most salient early critique is probably Nathan Salmon's Reference and Essence, Princeton University Press, 1981. Salmon's main thesis is this: There's no sound direct line of argument from Kripke's Millian view on names, or from his and Putnam's view on the semantics of certain common nouns, to any substantive metaphysical ideas. To get to anything like substantive "essentialist ideas," for example, there needs to be added at least one metaphysically quite rich premise. Even granting Salmon all he seeks, it will remain open, of course, whether, in their most widely cited philosophical writing, Kripke and Putnam offered novel substantive metaphysical thoughts, maybe even some correct ones. That may have occurred, for all Salmon argued, even if the new metaphysical ideas don't follow from the semantic offerings. So, I wish the book was yet more rather more deflationary, though I should record this belief here: Salmon's early effort contains lots of material that's both meticulously lucid and impressively ingenious. (Rather daunting even in its original form, a second edition of the book is yet more so: *Reference and Essence*, Prometheus Books, Amherst, New York, 2005.)

In some ways yet more impressive than Salmon's book are these two wonderful reviews of the book: First, see John Tienson's little gem in *The Journal of Symbolic Logic*, Vol. 49, No. 4 (Dec., 1984), pages. 1417–19. Then, see Paul Coppock's brilliant longer review in *The Journal of Philosophy*, Vol. 81, No. 5, (May, 1984), pages. 261–70.

For some fine recent work, see some of David Barnett's essays, as with his (2000) paper "Is Water Necessarily Identical to H2O?" *Philosophical Studies*, 98: 99–112 and his (2005) paper, "The Problem of Material Origins," *Noûs* 39:3: 529–40. In the first paper's first note, Barnett mentions eight earlier (than him) critics of Kripke's and Putnam's overlapping work, only two of whom are Sidelle and me. As best I can tell, all of us eight are, in these efforts, offering analytically empty ideas, except when we're offering pretty parochial ideas, which may also be said of Barnett's fine essays. (At all events, I blush to admit, that's certainly true of me.) Still and all, we're more nearly right about things, both the substantial quite parochial matters and the analytically empty issues, than are Putnam and Kripke. Or, so it seems to me.

Even as the previous chapter's work did something to support this last remark of mine, so the present chapter will do something more to that effect. None of this is a big deal, by my lights. But, still, it may be worth a little something.

to be, there's not much impetus to think long and hard about the likes of an ordinary table. While that's not deeply damning of Kripke, still, the comment should serve as a vivid cautionary signal: Even in advance of any detailed Scientiphically Respectable discussion of mere physical complexes, we should expect that, almost certainly, the discussion will offer precious little, indeed, by way of new concretely substantial thoughts that, far from being parochial, are characteristically philosophical ideas.

Central to Kripke's thoughts about the material origins of material complexes, there's his case of a certain wooden table, supposedly first made from a certain block of wood. In a few moments, we'll start to explore that. Before doing so, I'll say something about why, in these pages, that's the only example of Kripke's, concerning matters of material origins, that we'll seriously consider. Why? Well, in his book, Kripke presents two cases that, as he supposes, are both clearly of the sort just roughly characterized: one is the case of the wooden table and, just about as salient, the other is an example involving Queen Elizabeth II. Accordingly, I should say why I won't bother, in these pages, to seriously consider the case of Elizabeth II. In a note appended to this very sentence, I make sure to do that right now, happily avoiding several contentious suppositions, all irrelevant to the issues that, even going by Kripke's intentions, should be taken as those most central to his chosen topic.[3]

Helpfully passing over the contentious case of Elizabeth II, I move to focus attention on Kripke's case of a wooden table first made from a certain block of wood. As indicated, this example features only a quite ordinary piece of furniture, safely enough taken to be completely insensate, which Kripke indicated when uttering the words whose transcription follows:

3. When lecturing on matters of material origin, one part of Kripke's quite Scientiphical work concerns Queen Elizabeth II, the person herself, the fully sentient being, endowed with the power to think quite complexly, and to experience very variously. In his Scientiphical discussion of Elizabeth, Kripke considers whether that very woman, Elizabeth herself, could have developed from a different *fertilized egg* than the zygote that, as Kripke materialistically assumes, Elizabeth actually did develop from. In asking himself just that question, Kripke is presupposing that Elizabeth herself is a fully and purely material individual. Despite its having been favored by ever so many analytic philosophers over the last several decades, this is a very controversial presupposition.

Beyond concluding that Elizabeth II couldn't have developed from any zygote other than the one from which she actually did develop, Kripke also concludes that the old queen couldn't have been produced from a different sperm, and from a different egg, than just the very sperm and the very egg that, in fact, joined to form the zygote from which Elizabeth developed. As before, a fully materialist perspective is presupposed, no less questionable than just before.

Because Kripke's entire discussion of the queen rests on a controversial metaphysical thought about Elizabeth's basic nature, the discussion may well conflate matters that should always be kept quite separate and, in the bargain, what are clearly separate issues may well become quite confused. In the present work, I don't want to confuse matters by making, or by denying, any questionable metaphysical presuppositions. Accordingly, we'll ignore the contentious case of Elizabeth II. In so doing, we may gain clarity, and we'll lose nothing.

In the case of this table, we may not know what block of wood the table came from. Now, could *this table* have been made from a completely *different* block of wood, or even of water cleverly hardened into ice—water taken from the Thames River? We could conceivably discover that, contrary to what we now think, this table is indeed made of ice from the river. But let us suppose that it is not. Then, though we can imagine making a table out of another block of wood or even from ice, identical in appearance with this one, and though we could have put it in this very position in the room, it seems to me that this is *not* to imagine *this* table as made of wood or ice, but rather it is to imagine another table, *resembling* this one in all external details, made of another block of wood, or even of ice.[4]

If only for moments, suppose Kripke's claims about his indicated table are completely correct.[5] Let's further suppose that the table was *always wholly* made of just the wood that first formed it. So, as to the table's actual composition, matters are happily simple and boring. Maybe a bit less boring, there's this question a Kripkean would ask: Could this materially unchanging table first have been made not of wood, but of ice? Now, I ask: In that counterfactual question, is there anything concretely substantial that's at issue? As clearly as we can, let's explore the matter.

About material matters, Kripke's a Scientiphical thinker, quite as much as most other influential mainstreamers. So, a decent reading of his words has it that all the things and stuffs salient in his proffered example—a block of wood, a block of ice, a wooden table, and maybe more—well, they all should be understood in terms of our shared Scientiphical thinking. While that was presumed or presupposed by Kripke, he wasn't actually placing on offer, in any notably meaningful way, any such concretely substantial thoughts as our shared Scientiphicalism comprises. But, with what's Scientiphical aptly bracketed, is any concretely *substantial* thought suggested with Kripke's use of the words "*could* this table *have been* made from a completely different block of wood"? Here the same, is any offered with just such a use of the words "this table couldn't have been made from a completely different block of wood".

As I suspect, Kripke doesn't offer us any concretely substantial idea. Towards making clearer why I suspect that, I'll do several things.

---

4. *Naming and Necessity*, pages 113–14.

5. This supposition may be, in fact, a very generous assumption. For apparent counterexamples to various formulations of Kripke's thesis, to my mind apparently quite effective, see David Barnett, "The Problem of Material Origins," *Noûs* 39: 529–40 (2005). For another discussion that raises problems for Kripke, see Chapter 3, Section 3 of Christopher Hughes' *Kripke*, Oxford University Press, 2004, especially the material starting at the top of page 114. Later in this chapter, and along lines not very different from those mined by those authors, I (also) won't be so generous. But, that will be then, whereas this is now.

First I'll present an argument that's quite negative, indeed. As I believe, this argument will show, quite compellingly, that offerings like Kripke's have nothing to do with differentiating certain ways for concrete reality to be from other ways. Though the argument may be close to conclusive, it does nothing very positively instructive. So, to that end, I'll provide a protracted discussion of Kripke's table that, eventually, will lead us to ponder a few fairly novel philosophical thoughts, each a *concretely substantial* idea.

2. Some Thoughts about *Tables* and Some Thoughts about *Shmables*

Speaking with the vulgar, I'll now say something that, for present purposes, is quite clear enough and quite true enough, as well: Right before me here, in my dining area, there's a round wooden table. Beyond being made of wood, though it certainly is that, this table is, more specifically, made of *oak*, a certain kind of wood. As far as I can tell, not only is this table made of oak, and so made of wood, but, what's more, it *always was* made of oak, from the time it was originally constructed, or crafted, right up through the present moment. Heck, that had *better* be true; the piece was sold to us, years ago, as a genuine J & G Stickley, made by master craftsmen near the start of the twentieth century. At any rate, I'm going to suppose that much now, much as Kripke did for the table in the room where he was lecturing. For a reader-friendly exposition, I'll give my oak table a happily memorable name, *Toak*, a nice name for a *t*able always made of *oak*.

Now, following Kripke, let's assume that if a table *is first made* of wood, then, as a matter of the strictest necessity, that table *must have been first made* of wood, and it *couldn't possibly first* have been made of stuff that *wasn't wood*. Or, more cautiously, let's assume that then the table *couldn't have been first made of stuff none of which was wood*. As we've supposed, Toak couldn't possibly have been made of stuff that was all some *nonwooden metal*. If there had been, somehow or other, a terrible shortage of good wood a century ago, and the Stickleys made all their tables from fine nonwooden metal, then, as we've just supposed, Toak never would have existed. We will grant that, in such a merely hypothetical situation—in such a completely counter-factual circumstance—this much will be true, or it would be true: Even while I might well be confronting a fine metal table in my dining area, an item made by the Stickleys to have the look and the feel of an oak table, this costly Stickley piece wouldn't be Toak. Supposing all that to be so, what concretely substantial thoughts does it help us discern? Perhaps, a few very parochial ideas about which words, and which concepts, we happen to employ—or some among us, anyway. Beyond that, I'll say, there's nothing concretely substantial.

Why did I say that? There are several reasons. Right now, I'll relate just one, especially easy for readers to grasp quickly and clearly. This will involve us in a little contrivance; but this contrivance will be helpfully clarifying. So, let's prepare to contrive.

Continuing with all our generous suppositions, and putting matters in nicely fashionable terms, we may say that our usage of "table" runs something like this: Conventionally, our linguistic community has endowed this word with several meanings; but only one of the meanings is directly relevant to our present topic. In this most common and ordinary meaning of the term, it's to apply to certain pieces of furniture. (It's only in a quite different meaning that the word is used in, say, the expression "the periodic table of elements".) Conventionally, too, with this most ordinary meaning of the word, it's semantically most closely associated with just a certain particular concept, namely, *the concept of a table*. This is a concept for pieces of furniture of a certain sort, namely, the sort *tables*. To use a catchy fashionable phrase, our conventions for "table" have it that, with this word, we "latch onto" that concept of a table.

Now, for any entity to which this very concept properly applies, this concept of a table, the entity must have certain characteristic *persistence conditions:* First, the persistence conditions *aren't extremely lenient*: Suppose that, at a certain time, certain very numerous elementary particles wholly compose a certain copper table, Carl. But, then, all Carl's copper is pushed through an extruder and, out the other side, there gradually appears a very long and skinny copper wire. Then, though all of those particles will exist, and they'll still serve to form just so much copper, that very table, our Carl, *won't still* exist (leaving it open, here and now, whether at some still later time, Carl might exist again.) But, the persistence conditions for tables also *aren't extremely strict*: Fairly modest changes in Carl's shape will leave him be. Also, consider a wooden table, one Walter, made of very many small wooden slats; even each leg is composed of hundreds. And, suppose there's a changeover of the table's constituent slats (and thus of its matter) that's highly gradual, with only one slat replaced at a time; each removed slat is replaced by a precise duplicate of it, and the slat replaced is burned. By its end, none of the original matter is part of a table we're then confronting. Still, our original table exists.

Of course, all that's old hat. Indeed, even long before Kripke, it was already old hat. Doing well by the cited passage from that author, we may take him to have suggested, perhaps for the first time, an idea concerning certain conditions that are correlative with persistence conditions: For any entity to which the concept of a table properly applies, the entity must satisfy certain *origination conditions*, those required by that very concept. So, for instance, suppose that, at a certain time, a certain copper table first existed; it can be our Carl again, to keep things simple. At this time of its origin, certain very numerous elementary particles served to compose the table's copper and, in the bargain, they served to compose

Carl, too. Now, suppose that, *contrary to* fact, all those particles never served to compose any table at all; indeed, they're always scattered far and wide. Then, that very table, our Carl, never would have existed.

Charitably following Kripke's spirit, we've gone much further, and much deeper, in what should be (or should have been) his intended (empty) intellectual direction. For, what we've just supposed is this: None of the matter that first composed Carl, our considered table, ever served to compose any table at all. What we've concluded from that generous supposition is that, in *such a counterfactual* circumstance, Carl never would have existed. Quite plausibly, we've latched onto a correct thought here, even if it should be an analytically empty idea.

Well, on the supposition that our counterfactual thought about Carl is indeed correct, we've completed our preparation. (Supposing *otherwise* is to have Kripke be *wrong about absolutely everything in the neighborhood*, however empty the vicinity may be.) Well, then, so much for preparation, and now onto our contrivance.

Correlative with the word "table", I'll now introduce a new word, "shmable". Through my establishing the appropriate conventions for its doing so, with this new word we'll latch onto a concept that, in many respects, is quite the same as the concept of a table. But, in certain respects, the concept of a *shmable* is very different from that ordinary concept. As I stipulate, in these following two respects the concept of a shmable differs from the concept of a table.

First, as concerns its requisite *origination conditions*, the concept of a *shmable* is *rather more lax* than (what we've supposed for) the concept of a table: As concerns whether a certain shmable currently exists, let it be one Sam, it makes no difference what matter was doing what when Sam first existed. As long as there was enough matter nicely enough arranged, and providing that there's a nicely gradual transition from the shmable's originating matter to how things are right now with Sam materially, with *Sam now having just the matter that, in fact, it does now have*, Sam certainly will have existed at the beginning of the transition, just as certainly as it exists right now.

Second, as concerns its requisite *persistence conditions*, the concept of a *shmable* is *rather stricter* than (what we've supposed for) the concept of a table: Unlike a table, a shmable can lose only a tiny bit of the matter constituting the individual. When there's a very gradual changeover of the matter composing a shmable I'm confronting, then, after even just a certain small amount of that shmable's matter is lost, *that very shmable* will cease to exist (leaving it open, in this discussion, whether at some still much later time, the shmable might again exist.)

Just so, we do well to realize this: In any situation where someone confronts a table, as with me confronting my Toak, the person also confronts a shmable.

Just so, in the present instance, right when I'm confronting the table Toak, I'm also confronting a shmable, an enduring physical complex we may conveniently label *Shmoak*. The table and the shmable are both complex material individuals, each wholly coincident with the other. From the first moment of their existence right up through right now, that's how it is. Well then, while it may be true (as we're granting) that the *table* before us would never have existed had it not first been made of (at least) some of the matter that, in actual fact, first served to constitute it, that's *not* true of the *shmable* that, equally, we're also now confronting: So, suppose that the matter first constituting Toak never constituted anything even remotely like a table. Then, even if Toak never would have existed, *Shmoak still would have existed*.[6]

As regards concretely substantial questions and, on the coin's other side, just so many analytically empty issues, the thought about the table Toak is perfectly on a par with the thought about the shmable Shmoak. Neither being concretely substantial thoughts, both are, quite symmetrically and equally, just a couple of analytically empty ideas.

With just that reasoning, we may be quite confident that, in offering his ideas on the (alleged) necessity of certain material origins, Kripke's offered us just so much analytical emptiness. But confidence isn't everything. Perspective also matters. To that end, I provide the next section.

3. Origination Conditions, Persistence Conditions, and Boxing a Logical Compass

Right here and now, I'll introduce two more new terms, each as unfamiliar as "shmable" and, now coining a technical epithet, each as *inconvenient* as "shmable," too. On the whole, these new terms will be semantically similar to "table" and "shmable". As regards requisite origination and persistence conditions, however, they'll differ from "table" and "shmable," even as they also differ from each other.

In a certain way, as we observed or granted, "table" is pretty *strict* semantically. More specifically, it has pretty strict *origination conditions*. At the same time, but in a *different* way, "table" is pretty *lenient*; it has pretty lenient *persistence*

---

6. Whether there can be several individuals, each always wholly coincident with the others, spatially (or spatiotemporally) and materially is an issue much discussed in recent decades. It is, I'm quite sure, a concretely empty issue. In a later chapter, I'll discuss this issue and others nearby it. Mostly, I'll side with those who say "Yes", arguing that they're more successful at getting to the analytically correct ideas. Right now, nothing much hangs on any of that: Those opposing such coincidence can take my reasoning as a *reduction against tables*—for it's no good to think that, where I'm apparently indicating a table, a shmable, a strable and a lable, there's *only a table*, and not also the three others. It's all or none.

conditions. Now, where "table" is pretty strict, "shmable" is pretty lax, and vice versa. Well, then, with only a little attention to detail, we may realize this: In addition to those two concepts, there'll be two others, both inconvenient ideas that logically complement the first two most saliently. Together, all four concepts will fill out a complete schedule of the logical options presently in play, concerning origination conditions, on the one hand, and persistence conditions, on the other.

One of the two concepts, which we latch onto with the new word *strable*, will be a concept with *strict conditions of both* our currently considered kinds: Strables must satisfy pretty strict origination conditions and they also must satisfy pretty strict persistence conditions. The other further concept has *lenient conditions of both* our currently considered kinds. We'll latch onto this concept with the new word "lable," whose initial "l" matches those of "lax" and "lenient": Our newly noticed *lables* satisfy pretty lax origination conditions and they also satisfy pretty lenient persistence conditions.[7]

For quite a few readers, it may be helpfully handy to have all four terms properly placed, each relative to the others, via a very simple and visually vivid table. Arbitrarily, I'll have the vertical *columns* for this table representing the noted *persistence* conditions of the concepts—with one column for the ideas with strict p-conditions and with the other for the ideas with lax p-conditions. And, I'll have the horizontal *rows* representing the noted *origination* conditions—with one row for the ideas with strict o-conditions and with the other for the ideas with lax o-conditions. Finally, each of the four cells will contain the name for one of our four noted sorts of enduring entities. Just so, I'll *box the logical compass*, as it's said, with respect to this little conceptual neighborhood:

	Strict Persistence Condition	Lax Persistence Condition
Strict Origination Condition	Strables	Tables
Lax Origination Condition	Shmables	Lables

Of course, tables are no more realistic, or fundamental, than are strables, shmables or lables.[8]

---

7. Though "lable" is pronounced the same way as is the familiar word "label"—a word for an item involved in labeling—the spelling is notably different.

8. Some philosophers may think—heaven forefend—that a certain wooden table has a particular individual essence, whatever that should mean, which essence is tightly related to that table's origination conditions and/or its persistence conditions. Well then, they should also think that, right where that table is, and composed of the very same matter, there's *also* a material strable , as well, with *its* own particular individual essence. Not only is the individual essence of this strable numerically different from that of that table, they should think, but, what's more, it's even qualitatively

4. A Tenet of Scientiphicalism: Basic Individuals Have No "Memory-like" Propensity

Concerning the origins of complex material things, Kripke offers us only analytically empty thoughts, and no concretely substantial ideas. At some length, that's what I've argued. But, of course, all that argumentation was only just so much negative material. By contrast, so far this chapter's offered no concretely substantial philosophical ideas. But, following the previous chapter's lead, in some of this chapter's sections we may offer some such happily positive thoughts: Taking some sentences much like those that Kripke employed, we may use the sentences very differently. With our very different use, we may express concretely substantial philosophical thoughts, including some fairly novel ideas. In due course, that will be done.

One aim of this book, as you know, is to articulate not only our Core Scientiphicalism, but, as well, a fair amount of our Extended Scientiphicalism. In the previous chapter, we did some of that when noting that, on Scientiphicalism, all of an individual's other-directed propensities are generalistically directed powers. Here, I'll do some more, complementing what came before.

The upcoming discussion proceeds via a particulate vision of physical reality. But, that's not crucial. With a discussion proceeding via a fieldy vision, the same main points emerge.

For some happy specificity, let's suppose that all electrons are among the basic physical individuals, in the actual world, during its present Eon. And, let's suppose that, at least as regards their quite general intrinsic features, each electron is precisely similar to all the others. With all that supposed, let's consider a certain arbitrarily selected electron, which we'll call *Elliot*. Now, according to our widely shared Scientiphical View, all the real propensities that Elliot *ever* has are propensities that it will *always* have, for as long as Elliot should exist. So, if Elliot has a certain gravitational power, then, for as long as Elliot exists, it will have that power. In a word, however it is that our electron is propensitied, that will remain *constant*.

(In holding this to be so, it should be observed, our Scientiphicalism makes no discrimination between a basic physical thing's real propensities and *any other of their basic* properties, as with its intrinsic spatial properties, and as with its purely qualitative properties. So, suppose that Elliot now is spherical. Then, according to our Scientiphicalism, *that's constant*: Elliot always was spherical, whenever it existed, and it always will be spherical, for as long as it should exist. Still, here our focus will be on the Scientiphical idea of the constancy of propensity.)

different: Even as the *table's* essence is tightly tied to *that* object's *lax persistence* conditions, so the *strable's* individual essence is tightly tied to *this* object's *strict persistence* conditions. And, as they should also then think, there are *at least two other material objects* each spatially and materially coincident with both the table and the strable—each of these others having its own quite distinctive individual essence: There's also a shmable, right there then, and, what's more, there's also a lable, as well.

With that being so, Elliot's propensities will be unaffected by its serving to help constitute complex physical concreta—if any such there be, and if it should ever so serve. For example, if Elliot should become engaged in such electrical bonding as will have it help serve to constitute a certain water molecule, one Walter, that will mean nothing for how it is that Elliot's propensitied. Propensitively, Elliot will remain the same. Using a colorful phrase to make the Scientiphical idea a notably memorable thought, we may say this: As with any other basic physical thing, Eliot "has no memory". A little less colorfully, we might Scientiphically say that Eliot "has no memory-like propensities".

On our Scientiphicalism, basic physical concreta have no memory-like propensities.[9] (Less notable, for our present discussion, is this: On our Scientiphicalism, a basic concretum *won't have any memory-like purely qualitative* properties and it also *won't have any memory-like purely spatial properties.* Just so, and put less colorfully, on our shared Scientiphicalism, how it is intrinsically with any basic individual always remains the same.[10])

In our Scientiphical thinking, we make these assumptions of intrinsic constancy for (what we take to be) the basic physical individuals. And, partly for that reason, we make *aptly dovetailing* assumptions about physical complexes, which physically derivative entities we Scientiphically supposed to be wholly composed of basic physical individuals. Here's one of them: The powers of a complex physical thing derive from just two factors, one of them constant and the other variable. What's constant are the intrinsic powers of the basic physical entities wholly composing the complex in question. What's variable is how it is that the basic physical things may be physically related, even when serving

9. Complexes may have memorial powers, of course. Often, this happens when certain processes involving the complex lay down "memory traces", or otherwise appropriately alter how it is that the complex's (more) basic components are related. But, then, even as a complex may have a "suddenly arrived " duplicate, so the memorial power of a complex can always be precisely and effectively mimicked. That will be true even if, with the mimicking individual, it's *improper to call* the power a *memorial* power. At all events, with such nicely mimicking complexes, there's at least memory-*like* power. Not so with quarks and electrons—indeed, not so even with water molecules.

10. On this last point, our basic entity will always remain the same not only as regards all its generalistically directed propensities, but, as well, as regards any individualistically directed propensity that it should have. And, at least presumably, each will have *plenty* in the way of individualistically directed propensity, even if for no other reason than this fact, a reason that may be as widely unobvious, I fear, as it may be crucial to (explaining) the persistence of basic concrete particulars: Each basic physical individual will be propensitied individualistically with respect to *itself*, *whether or not* it's (also) individualistically propensitied with respect to *any other* individual. So, at least presumably, our electron, our Elliot, will be propensitied for (its own) continued existence, and for its continuing to be intrinsically propertied in just the way that it *is*, or it's *been*, intrinsically propertied. And, most saliently in this last regard, our Elliot will be *propensitied to continue to be propensitied in just the way it's been*—it's thus "having an aptly all-encompassing propensity for stable continuance". With such thoughts as just presented, we can provide a philosophical explanation, of sorts, for the intrinsic temporal constancy that, in our standard Scientiphical thinking, we implicitly presume to hold, for the likes of our Elliot.

to compose this or that complex. So, on our Extended Scientiphicalism, changes in the powers of a physical complex derive only from *changes in the physical relations* among its basic physical constituents.[11]

Now, according to these Scientiphical suppositions, it's easy enough for there to be many complex physical entities each of which is a precise duplicate of all the others. In particular, it's easy enough for there to be many physical complexes each precisely similar *propensitively*—that is, precisely similar just as far as their pure powers are concerned. This will be just as easy—a veritable piece of cake—as it is for there to be many physical complexes that are each *shaped* precisely the same as all the others. Indeed, it will be as simple as this: First, each of the candidates should contain precisely the same number of each sort of basic physical constituent: each should have the same number of up-quarks as does the other; each should have the same number of electrons, and so on. And, second, each of the physical complexes in question—the "candidate duplicates", so to say—should have its basic physical constituents be physically related to each other in just the same way as happens with all the other candidates.

These Scientiphical thoughts are concretely substantial ideas. Though this should be clear straightaway, it may be useful to amplify: Consider an electron that once served as a basic constituent of a wooden table. That won't affect it's being ever so apt, even right afterwards, for its serving to constitute something entirely different, say, a metal spoon in the next room. Likewise, an up-quark that once served toward constituting an ice cube will be precisely like, in regards to all its propensities, an up-quark that never served toward composing any such icy individual. As far as what it may contribute, at later times, toward constituting other physical complexes, our former-ice-cube-constituent up-quark will be quite the same as any other up-quark, including the very many that never did ice-cube-composing-duty. For example, in serving to constitute an automobile, say, or a piece of fried fish, each of these two up-quarks—both the one that served to compose an ice-cube and the one that never served to compose any ice at all—well, each will be propensitied to provide "just the same sort of service"

---

11. One consequence of these suppositions is that, on our Scientiphicalism, it's only certain physical complexes, and not any much more basic physical things, that have any memory-like powers. Typically, these powers, including powers of memory properly so-called, are acquired by the complexes when their basic components come to be physically related in certain suitable ways. This may happen, for example, when many of the basic concreta constituting your brain become so related that, as we say, "memory traces are laid down" in your brain. As our Scientiphicalism has it, when there is a nice arrangement of your particles to such an effect, you will have the *power to apparently remember*, at least, certain events, facts, objects, and people. And, when the nice arrangement arises owing to your being involved in certain temporally extensive causal processes that also aptly include those events, facts, objects, and people—processes that may satisfy the semantic requirements of "remember" and cognate terms—then you will have the power to actually *remember* those events, facts, objects, and people, sometimes having the power even to *recall* them. (*This* note, now closing, includes a mix of Scientiphical substantial thoughts and concretely empty ideas. As I trust, the latter are analytically correct.)

toward constituting the auto, or toward composing the piece of fish, as will the other. Neither up-quark will do the least bit more than the other, or do the least bit less, of course, in happily filling any constitutional role that may be "asked of it," whether it be "asked" by a truly constructive mindful agent or, perhaps much more commonly, whether it be "asked" just by "mother nature".

In more memorable language, I'll offer this quite central tenet of our Extended Scientiphical Metaphysic: Each basic physical individual, each electron, for example, will always be *perfectly interchangeable with* any other basic individual of *its same basic physical kind*, in this case, with any other electron. And, though no electron will be interchangeable with an up-quark, of course, and vice versa, none of that has any relevance, to the Scientiphical proposition just memorably offered. Rather, what's relevant, of course, is just this: Even as each electron is interchangeable with any other electron, so each up-quark is interchangeable with any up-quark.

Using some homey illustrative examples, I amplify: If a certain largely wooden piano has one of its electrons interchanged with an electron from a certain entirely brass trumpet, devoid of any wood at all, well, then, the powers of the piano won't be altered one bit—and, of course, neither will be those of the trumpet. In particular, and even as the piano will *still* be made *just* so largely of *wood*, the piano will still have precisely the same propensity toward the production of sounds—when played upon, and so on—as it did before the interchange—as *also* will be true of the still *entirely non-wooden* trumpet. The piano won't be disposed to sound a wee bit more trumpet-like than before; nor will the trumpet be disposed to produce sounds that are a wee bit more piano-like. And, this will be so even if, perhaps in sequence, many trillions of the piano's electrons should be interchanged with just as many trillions of electrons that, before the interchange, helped serve to compose the brass trumpet.

As I'm confident, this section's main points were quite fully accepted by Kripke, perhaps even more fully than I now accept them. And they were also accepted, of course, by almost all his most relevantly competent audience, mostly mainstream philosophers. *Given the acceptance of our shared Scientiphicalism*, what concretely substantial claim could Kripke have possibly been making, really, when he said, while indicating a certain table, that *this very table could not have been made of ice?* As I'm sure you're aware, the question's rhetorical.

5. How a Wooden Table Could Have First Been Made from a Hunk of Ice

When showing the emptiness of Kripke's ideas about the necessity of certain material origins, we made some extremely generous suppositions. In particular, we supposed that, with our considered table, Carl, none of its original matter ever served to constitute anything much at all, and certainly not any table. In that way, we had Kripke be somewhat near to latching onto an analytically correct thought, rather than only some clearly incorrect empty ideas. Now, let's be less generous. Just so, let's examine what he actually said.

Meaning to express a strictly necessary truth, what he said was this: If a certain table was actually first made from a certain block of wood, then it couldn't possibly have been first made of something very clearly other than that; in particular, and most certainly, it couldn't possibly have been first made of (a block of) *ice*. Is that really right? No; I don't think so.

Toward getting clear on how wildly incorrect is any idea even remotely like that, each of several routes will do very well. But, of course, I'd now like to take one that trades on our discussion in the just previous section. And, I'd like it to be a fun journey, too. With those aims in mind, I'll conduct some divinely focused thought-experiments, each tailored to feature tenets of our shared Scientiphicalism. (Divinely focused, I said, *not* divinely inspired.)

First, let's suppose that, a long time ago, an Almighty God wanted to construct the wooden table that, in his later lecture, Kripke indicated. Now, in our little experiment, God won't always take the course of least action. Rather, He'll place certain constraints on how He'll allow himself to operate. (Without any net, tennis wouldn't be much fun.) Just so, our God confines Himself to using already available basic physical concreta, in his construction of the wooden table.

More specifically, let's suppose that, at the time He wished to begin some super-fast table-construction, the world was in a Hyper Ice Age: Every electron anywhere, and every quark, too, was then serving to help constitute some ice. (Perhaps some were serving to compose certain hunks of ice, even while others were serving to constitute other icy hunks, many of the hunks quite distant from many of the others.) Now, we'll further suppose that He had it in mind to compose a wholly wooden table that, when it's first made, will be composed, most fundamentally, of just such-and-such particular quarks and just so-and-so specific electrons (even while it's then *not* composed of any *other* basic physical concreta).

In pursuing His self-given goal, would our God face a terrible difficulty? Of course, he wouldn't. Rather, even if He imposed upon Himself the aforesaid constraints, He'd be facing none at all. Indeed, even within the signaled Scientiphical constraints, there are many widely various ways for Him to have succeeded completely. Briefly, I'll mention just a few.

First, He could proceed by initially turning a biggish hunk of ice into a similarly biggish hunk of wood. (Quickly but gradually, He might rearrange one smallish area of the icy hunk's particles, so that they'd come to compose some wood, instead of any ice, and then He might rearrange an adjacent area, and so on—until the whole darned hunk of stuff didn't contain even a smidgeon of ice, and it was all just a biggish hunk of wood.) Only then, on this first way, would he use the produced wood to make just the table He wanted.

Second, and perhaps rather more radically, He could proceed like this: First, he'd decompose an icy hunk into many rather widely scattered quarks and electrons. After this radical decomposition, he'd bring together, into a very nicely wooden and tabular structure, the mutually quite isolated particles that He freed up for just such a constructive end.

Third, He could proceed quite *oppositely*, so to say, from how He did His work in the *first* of the (three) ways I'm indicating. Just so, He could proceed by first turning a hunk of ice into a table-shaped icy hunk, in effect at least, into an icy table. After effecting this merely "shapewise transformation," He could use the icy table he produced to make just the wooden table He originally wanted to be in Kripke's presence, at lecture-time, presumably always wanting to proceed in just this perversely refuting and roundabout way.

In some detail, how should he realize this third option? Well, even very readily, he might do that by rearranging the basic particulate constituents of the icy table He'd just recently produced, so that they came to form some wood, while always retaining their same overall shape, so happily tabular. Very readily, he could do this so that this wood—formed from the quarks and electrons of an *icy* table—would then be the wood of a (similarly shaped) *wooden* table. From a table first made of ice, He could produce in the targeted lecture room, and well before Kripke entered that hall, the wooden table our lecturer would observe and then indicate. (For this case to have "widespread intuitive appeal," He might do this both serially and also gradually.)

Even well within the confines allowed by our Scientiphical Metaphysic, each of these three ways is a perfectly allowable possibility, a perfectly possible way for our "somewhat self-challenging" God to produce an envisioned table— or to fabricate a table he intended to produce—from basic particles He selected for just that purpose. Whichever way our God chose to do His work, by time Kripke pointed at his then-indicated table, he'd be pointing at just the very same quarks and electrons, arranged in just the very same manner, before him right then and there. Call the bleeping thing "Tab". Even if our God took a work-route involving a "tabular hunk of ice", Kripke would be pointing at Tab, that very table. At least in my idiolect, that's fine.

Some won't like examples adverting to a Deity. Very well, just substitute Chance for God. Indeed, on some respectable versions of modern physics, where objective probabilities play out this way and that, all the routes I've been sketching, for quarks and electrons to be related over time, are *even physically* possible. So, suppose that Chance had it that, as was ever so likely all along, Kripke pointed at a wooden table first made of wood. Still, it was possible for Chance to have had things proceed differently: First, a hunk of ice, then an ice table, then a gradual changeover to a table composed of wood, no ice at all. Foregoing a God, we now say this: Even if just *Chance* had taken a route involving a "tabular hunk of ice", Kripke would have been pointing at Tab. At least in my idiolect, that's fine.

On these points, is Kripke's idiolect quite different from mine? Not so likely, I think. More likely, it seems, he simply didn't consider a sufficiently wide variety of scenarios. Had he done so, I imagine, he wouldn't have proffered the idea that a table made from a certain block of wood simply must have been first so composed. Rather, he'd have offered something more like what I generously placed on offer: If a table is first composed of certain matter, then, for anything to be that table, it must be first made of at least some of that matter. Of course, even this last might fail to be an analytically correct idea. But, by contrast with Kripke, it's at least a fair candidate.

6. Tood and Tice, a Table First Made of Wood and a Table First Made of Ice

In this book, I'm most interested in distinguishing between philosophically salient thoughts that are concretely substantial ideas and, by contrast, those that are merely empty ideas. Not so important, for our explorations, are questions of the sort central to the previous section, questions about which empty thoughts are correct ideas and, by contrast, which are not. With that in mind, here's something more to consider, certainly no very esoteric material.

In addition to the table Kripke had us consider, let's also consider another table. Still thinking in terms of our received Scientiphicalism, let's consider a table that originally *was* made entirely of ice, perhaps the proud production of a human ice sculptor. Maybe this other table will be only hypothetical; on the other hand, it's not very unlikely that one ice sculptor, at least, actually made at least one ice table. At any rate, in central respects, our considered table will be very like some actual tables, even as regards questions of origination and other historical matters.

To continue our discussion of Kripke's ideas, we'll suppose that our frozen table should seem, as regards all its surface appearances, terribly similar to some tables that are made of wood. (How this should come to pass I leave open. Could it be done by mixing some suitable dye in with the water, before the darkly colored water was frozen into a big block of ice, ready for the ice sculptor to shape tabularly? Very possibly, I suppose, but we needn't settle the question.) At any rate, and as I imagine, you might enjoy considering this scenario: For a table that's originally just 99.9% pure ice—much as (impure) water that's taken right out of a river is just 99.9% pure (or rather less so)—a realistic enough specification is quite easy, as I'm sure you know as well as I do: The ice sculptor may apply to his table, all over its surface, a very thin coat of opaque dye. (With a certain sort of dye, perhaps he could make it appear like a table made of "natural wood".) Quite certainly, by using just a simple opaque black dye, he could *easily* make it appear the same as a *wooden table that's painted black*.

And, with another sort of dye, of course, he could easily make it appear the same as a wood table that's painted *red*.

Now, let's consider a certain easily understood "Ship-of-Theseus-Style Scenario" for our happily contemplated *ice-table*. (Unlike our examples involving a self-challenging God, who confined himself to working only in Scientiphically Respectable ways, this upcoming Scientiphically Respectable case won't be any very far-fetched scenario.) Here is the case I have in mind: Kept nicely in a freezer room, our ice-table—we'll name it *Tice*—is frequently used as a table. Perhaps, while supporting some wooden carving boards, some butchers use it when cutting meat, perhaps warmly dressed butchers. After a certain period of such use, some of Tice's ice is replaced by a spatially congruent piece of wood, the replacing wood quickly fusing, quite well, with ice that *hasn't* (yet) been replaced. If need be, we'll use a smidgeon of fusing material, an apt glue, perhaps, that's neither ice nor wood, for such an interim step.

After a similar period passes, much the same happens again. After months go by, all Tice's ice gets replaced. Before us now, there's a table composed entirely of wood, without any ice at all (and without any glue). Well, if there ever are any tables at all, then *this table is Tice*.

Shortly after Tice is composed entirely of wood, it's taken from the freezer room and placed in a typically warm lecture hall. After several hours, Tice's temperature is the same as other items in the hall. When that happened, we suppose, Tice became a precise physical duplicate of Kripke's indicated wooden table, Tood, each only a few feet from the other. Thinking in our shared Scientiphical terms, we've imagined all that both very easily and very clearly.

As Tice and Tood are precise physical duplicates, each has precisely the same propensities as the other: Precisely as Tood should be expected to interact with any other object—as with its happily supporting a certain bowl, perhaps—just so will Tice interact with that very same other object, or with any object precisely similar to that one. Just as our always-wooden Tood will burn when near a hot flaming torch, so will our currently wooden Tice also burn then. No more than Tood would, Tice won't now melt into water. Tice and Tood have very different histories. Still, *at present, there's no concretely substantial difference between* the two complex concreta.

For the moment, and just for the sake of potentially instructive reasoning, let's generously agree with the Kripkean thought that Tood *could not have* been originally made of ice. On the other hand, of course, Tice *actually was* originally made of ice. And, so, at least in the way philosophers usually use the words, Tice certainly *could have* been originally made of ice. But, even if Tood could not have first been made of ice and Tice could well have been, what concretely substantial difference is there, now, between these two tables? As our Scientiphicalism directs us to answer, there's none. That being clear, I make a related point.

Suppose that, contrary to Kripke's claims, I make these following opposite claims, if only for the sake of a potentially instructive argument: Even as Tice could have been originally made of ice, so also, even if not so obviously, *Tood could have been* originally made of ice. While I'll then be disagreeing with Kripke, is our dispute concretely substantial? No; I don't think so.

At the level of our language, the disagreement amounts to little more than this: On the one side, I'll claim that, in line with English semantics, it's sometimes correct to say a table first made of wood could first have been made of ice. And, on the other, he'll claim that I've gotten the semantics wrong. Is there, really, much more at stake here? Again, I don't think so.

7. Using Modal Terms Substantially: The Case of Determinism

So far, I've been urging that, with his use of locutions involving ordinary modal phrases, like "could have" and "could not have," Kripke hasn't offered us any new characteristically philosophical concretely substantial ideas. But, as hardly needs argument, that's not the only way in which, quite in keeping with their ordinarily accepted meaning, we may properly use our common modal words. Here's a salient example of that.

Traditionally, many philosophers have advocated a strict thesis of *determinism*. And, what I think amounts to much the same, many have endorsed a strict thesis of *fatalism*, in one fairly familiar sense of that term. According to this traditional deterministic view, the actual world's situation is always this: *Whatever* actually does exist, or does obtain, and so on—those things always *had to* exist, or they *had* to obtain, and so on. Every blade of grass that does exist, it simply had to exist—just when it does, and just as it does, and so on. With regard to the shape of any given one of those blades, that blade always had to be shaped in just precisely the way that, at any given time, it actually was shaped.

This thesis of determinism is, I think, a substantial statement about concrete reality (as I believe, it's probably a substantial claim that's not true.) If this fatalism *is* true, then concrete reality will be a *certain* way. And, if it *isn't* true, which is also consistently conceivable, then reality *won't be that* way—rather, it will be some *other* way. As this determinism is a concretely substantial idea, it's a thought that conflicts with various other concretely substantial propositions. For example, it conflicts with the thought that, with some occurring events, their occurrence is, or it was, a perfectly random matter. And, it conflicts with the thought that the occurrence of some event—as with the decay of some radioactive substance—is the manifestation of a probabilistic propensity, of that substance, to decay.

Another point: Though this next thought has been denied by many intelligent philosophers, still and all, it is true that our concretely substantial strict determinism also conflicts with a concretely substantial thought that's much closer to home, so to say. Our common thought is that, at least from time to time, each of very many people really does choose, really choosing from fully available *genuine alternatives* for her thoughtful activity. (At least as far as this common thought has it, the situation will be this: On such an absolutely fatalistic view as our noted determinism, there'll *never be*, for anyone or anything, *any real alternatives at all*. And, so, there'll never be any that are ever actually available to anyone. And, so, there'll never be anyone who really chooses from among actually available alternatives for her activity.)

It matters little, for our present discussion, whether any actual philosophers ever upheld such an absolutely fatalistic deterministic proposition. Maybe, Leibniz did. And, perhaps more likely—I don't know—certain ancient philosophers may have upheld it, as with perhaps, the Megarian thinkers. But, as I just said, for our present discussion, that's no big deal.

To express a deterministic view with reference to any particular state of affairs, it is certainly quite natural for us to use locutions involving "could not have". So, for those expressing a deterministic view, it's perfectly natural to say that, whenever something is a particular way, then it *could not have been* any other way.

With this deterministic view in mind, it may be *substantially* claimed that, as a certain table was actually first made of wood, so that table *could not have* first been made of anything other than wood. But, of course, it *also* may be substantially claimed, quite as well, that, as this table was first made with a *light brown* top, it *could not have* first been made with a *jet-black* top.

As should seem quite compelling, there's a great difference between these deterministically oriented thoughts, each a concretely substantial idea, and the analytically empty thoughts that, while *very differently using the same modal words*, Kripke prominently placed on offer.

Besides the thesis of determinism, are there other *concretely substantial* philosophical thoughts that, with locutions like "must have been" and "could not have been," we may naturally place on offer? When recalling our discussion of certain entities propensitied individualistically with respect to other individuals, we should say "Yes". But, let's explore the matter.

8. Distinctive Material Objects and These Objects' Distinctive Matter

During this present Eon, at least, there's nothing all that special about any particular table, or about any particular rock, for that matter. The matter composing a particular table is, in all fundamental respects, quite like the matter composing any other table, and also quite the like matter composing any particular rock. Fundamentally, it's all little more than just so very many quarks and electrons, or whatever an even later Scientiphical physical story will say. That's an idea that helps ground this Scientiphical thought of ours: At least in principle, for any given table, there may be precise physical duplicates of the object, and the same for any given rock, and the same for any given acorn and oak, and human heart and human head.

Just so, concerning any of our Eon's ordinary complex material entities, there's nothing *deeply distinctive* about the complex individual and, relatedly, there's nothing *deeply distinctive* about the *matter constituting* the composite material particular: There's no table with a shape, for example, that can't be duplicated, at least in principle, no matter what merely technical difficulties may, in actual fact, stand in the way of that. And, similarly, there's no rock with any propensity, or power, that can't be duplicated—so that, existing simultaneously with it, and spatially quite separate from it, there'll be other rocks, each propensitied precisely the same.

The sentences I've just presented were used to make substantial claims, even if, perhaps, such obviously acceptable claims as are terribly boring. So, we should be able to express, with complementary sentences, many very different substantial claims, each conflicting with those boring claims, quite a few of which will be *UnScientiphical* ideas.

Here's a shot at that: We begin by considering the big bang that, according to physical cosmologists, initiated our current Eon, just (about) some fourteen billion years ago. Next, we consider this "conceivable possibility": There might have been, very much earlier than that, a much earlier big bang. And, this much earlier big bang might have produced two fundamentally very different sorts of matter, both of them visible to, and tangible to, the very much earlier people—all very much earlier than us, that is—who inhabited a certain planet, on whose surface there was matter of both of the very different sorts. Now, *almost* all of that produced matter may have been of a quite familiar sort—it may have been just like the ordinary matter of our present Eon. But, then, a little bit of the produced matter may have been of a very peculiarly different sort. So, among all the hunks of matter that were then around, there was just one hunk whose matter was some very *special* matter—*fundamentally* very different from any ordinary matter. As with the special matter wholly composing it, this hunk had the power to heal any afflicted man, woman, or child that *came in contact with that matter*, even if only very briefly, even if for only one one-thousandth of a second. Even very many ailing beasts could be so surely cured. To have a memorable term for this wonderfully special stuff, I'll call it *healthite*.

Throughout the early times of that great old Eon, all the healthite in the world was just the healthite first composing that one hunk, and then still composing that same single hunk of the wonderfully special material. Nicely comporting with that, we may usefully suppose this: If the original healthite hunk should be evenly cut in two, then all the healthite in the world would still be just the same quite limited quantity of stuff, with half of it now serving to compose one newly separate hunk of healthite and with the other half now serving to compose another. And, if it should be evenly cut into ten roughly equal pieces, there's still just the same amount of healthite, with about a tenth of the stuff composing a certain smallish but potent hunk, while another tenth composed another, and so on.

To be healed by (contact with) the healthite, ill people came to the hunk, from near and far, so as to make curative contact with the wonderful stuff. Of course, this presented something of a hardship for many of the ill pilgrims, as they had to come to the single hunk's location, on one of the planet's continents, from places on other continents. Most pilgrims needed to cross a vast ocean as part of their required journey. To reduce these hardships, and to make the precious healthite more widely available, it was decided that an able carver should cut the healthite hunk in such a way as to produce ten separate wands of healthite—each wand to be located at a place pretty distant from all the others, and *no very* great distance from *any* ill individual. As each continent would have at least one wand of healthite, nobody would have to cross an ocean, to make contact. For simplicity's sake, we suppose that each of the wands was precisely like each of the nine others. And, as far as its curative power was concerned, each was just like the original hunk, to boot. Now, if *more than ten* wands were made from that hunk, then *none of the newly composed (smaller) items would have enough healthite* to be curatively all that effective. Realizing that, and knowing others realized it, too, the carver made no more than ten wands.

Arbitrarily selected from among the wondrous ten, let's consider, right now, a certain one of these ten congruent wands, a wonderful wand that, alliteratively, we'll call *Wanda*. As is true of all the other wands, too, Wanda was originally composed of, and Wanda still is composed of, and only of, pure healthite. Even as all the world's healthite is just that which came from the original hunk, so it must be that all the healthite composing Wanda (from the first moment of its existence right until its last, when the next big bang occurred) is just some of, a certain tenth of, all the healthite from the single original healthite hunk. And so, too, with the nine other wands.

Suppose that, not knowing much about all this, a benevolent ignoramus wanted to make more wands, each as wonderfully curative as Wanda, but from much more ordinary, vastly more plentiful matter—since he didn't have any healthite available. At the start, the only wonderful wand our benevolent guy knows of is Wanda. Now, in an effort at setting him straight, someone may tell this guy how wonderfully different healthite is from any other matter, and how very rare healthite is, and how all the healthite serves to compose one or another of the world's ten wonderful wands, one of them being Wanda.

Let's be completely clear about this: All the healthite is used up in composing the wands; that's why no healthite is available for anything else. Taking healthite out of any of these wands would only worsen the situation. And, trying to make a wonderfully curative object out of anything other than healthite is only an exercise in futility.

To emphasize what's most relevant here, and to drive it home to the would-be wonder- wand -maker, we might well say this: Wanda *could not have been* made from anything but healthite. About equally, we might say that Wanda could not have been made from anything but (some of) the original hunk of healthite, from which hunk Wanda was, of course, first made.

As with almost all our other uses of "could not have" and kindred expressions, in making those statements about Wanda, I've set a context where certain things are fixed, that is, where we take it that *those* things *could not have* been different.

Return to consider our benevolent ignoramus, a guy who wanted to make, not from rare healthite, but from just so much far more ordinary matter, some wands as curatively wonderful as Wanda. As I said, we might usefully tell him that Wanda *couldn't have been* made from anything but healthite. And, as all the (world's, and Eon's) healthite is just the healthite first composing the one original healthite hunk, Wanda *couldn't have been* made from anything but (some of) that hunk. Now, in making those remarks to our benevolent ignoramus, I would be indicating that there's something special about the matter composing Wanda, by contrast with all the other matter then around.

Even quite fundamentally, *that's very* different from how things are in our present Eon. And, of course, that's *not* just because we don't have any such wonderfully curative physical objects here and now! In our actual circumstance, any simple physical individual, like an up-quark, perhaps, is precisely like each of terribly many other simples, each of them also up-quarks. So, in our actual circumstance, each curative sort of stuff, and as with aspirin, and each curative (complex) individual, as with a penicillin capsule, may be *precisely duplicated*, over and over and over. It's just a matter of, say, getting more and more elementary particles to be arranged aspirinwise, in the one case, or, in the other, arranged both penicillinwise and capsulewise. Indeed, here that's overkill: There are, in point of fact, very many arrangements of electrons and quarks, say, each sufficient for there being a happily curative capsule of penicillin. Here, no precise duplication is needed, or even anything terribly like that.

Return to the Kripkean thought that, if an ordinary table is first made from certain wood, or from a certain block of wood, then anything not first made of at least some of that wood, or from at least some of that block, wouldn't be that very table. As I've said, there's little reason to think that's correct and a lot for thinking it incorrect. But, let's *suppose* that (against the appearances) *it is correct*. If *that* should be so, *then* what should we think?

We should then think this: There's *still a world of difference* between (1) the thought that our wand Wanda couldn't first have been made out of any very different matter, disjoint from the rare healthite from which it was first formed, and (2) the thought that our table Tood couldn't first have been made out of any very different matter, disjoint from the ordinary wood from which *it* was first formed. Employing our terminology, we may mark the great difference by saying that (1) is a *concretely substantial* idea, whereas (2) is *concretely empty*. And, happily enough, I'll suggest, we may also say that (2) is analytically empty, with the source of its emptiness being its analyticity.

9. Sequentialistically Propensitied Concrete Particulars

In the just previous section, the issues discussed were some terribly far-fetched matters—where far-fetchedness is assessed relative to how (we take it that) things are in the actual world, in our current Eon. Indeed, it's fair to say, I think, that our extreme deviation from current concrete reality enabled our discussion to be a philosophically somewhat worthwhile endeavor. Still and all, as we know full well, there'll be quite a few left cold by discourse as deviating as that.

Partly toward helping them become more friendly to (what I regard as) aptly imaginative substantial metaphysics, and partly to notice more of the variety that may be found with such substantially imaginative philosophical thinking, in this present section I'll be discussing some ideas happily different from, though nicely related to, those featured in the previous section. This shouldn't get readers to be all that excited about what I'm doing in this chapter's latter half, but it might get them to go from being quite cold to being refreshingly cool.

To begin this nicely related discussion, I'll have us focus on frogs for a while. Now, whether it's tables we're thinking about, or whether it's frogs, in very many contexts we're not much concerned with any metaphysically basic substantial matters. Just so, in *ordinary* contexts, we *won't* be concerned to affirm our shared Scientiphical Metaphysic. For, in all these quite ordinary circumstances, it's not any metaphysical matters, really, with which we're concerned. Casually, even a staunch Scientiphicalist may aptly enough say this: For there to be a full-fledged frog, there must first be a tadpole, from which the frog develops.

In metaphysically serious contexts, rare beyond the philosophy room, our Scientiphicalist won't be so casual. Seriously, he may say this: "So far, there haven't been any suddenly arrived full-fledged frogs, leastways not in our solar system. But, the reasons for that are all pretty superficial. As far as *the nature of things* goes, there's no "must" about the matter. For example, as is perfectly possible, lightning may aptly rearrange a goodly assortment of particles that, just before the lightning struck, served to compose a twig. Then, with no need for any tadpole, there'll suddenly be a new full-fledged frog".

Some may suppose, wrongly I think, that such a directly arrived being *won't properly be called a frog*. Even if they should be right, it cuts no ice. For, as we'll then be Scientiphically thinking, it's perfectly possible for a *shmog* to be suddenly produced, where "shmog" applies both to naturally developed frogs and to suddenly arrived duplicates. In all *nonrelational* respects, at least, a suddenly produced shmog will be just like an ordinarily developed shmog.

As many readers may recall, our Scientiphicalism says this: Even as many a complex physical thing will be propensitied in quite a complicated way, still, the propensities of each will be just so many physically derivative powers. Spelling that out just a bit, all of a physical complex's powers will (physically) derive from these two, or three, factors: (1) how the complex's elementary constituents themselves are each (intrinsically) propensitied, and from (2) how these basic physical individuals are physically related, while they're constituting the complex in question, and, perhaps, from (3) some other current physical factors, as with how the complex's constituents are spatially related to other physical things, external to the complex.

Certain *Anti-Scientiphicalists* will disagree, saying this: In the case of many physical complexes (whether or not absolutely all) a fourth factor is also an irreducibly important aspect of the basis for the complex's powers. Relevantly independent of the other factors, this is (4) how the complex's constituting particles *were previously* related, at least with respect to each other, and, perhaps as well, with respect to other concreta, too. Unlike (1), (2) and (3), which allow that the potency of a particular's past may be entirely used up in, and by, its contribution to how things are quite currently, this fourth condition, (4), may be rightly regarded as *sequentially selective;* for short, it's *sequentialistic*. When someone proposes this sequentialistic (4), then she may say that there are basic spatial concreta with "memory-like" propensities. As she may continue, many of them serve to constitute more complex spatial concreta.

Due to the "memory-like" or sequentialistic propensities of our instructively presumed particles, it will be impossible for these basic concreta to constitute a frog without some of them, at least, having already served to constitute a tadpole, from which tadpole a full-fledged frog may then develop. What's more, if there's an Eon when all (a world's) matter is exhausted by such particles, it will be impossible for a frog to come into being (in that Eon of that world) without a frog's developing from a tadpole. In *such* an Eon, there really *can't be a Swampfrog*.

Confining Himself to working with only just such *sequentialistically propensitied* particles, even a God-like Arranger can't make a frog all of a sudden, or right off the bat. Rather, our God-like Arranger must *first* arrange lots of these particles in such a way that they constitute a *tadpole*—and not yet any full-fledged frog—*before* He arranges at least *some of those* particles (perhaps along with other particles) in the intended full-fledged frog way. Unless He does that, he won't succeed in producing (even anything much like) a frog, not even one lasting for just a few moments. By contrast, when He has those particles proceed through a suitable sequence, our Arranger will produce a frog, a full-fledged frog.

10. Wooden Tables, Ice, and Sequentialistically Propensitied Concrete Particulars

We've just engaged in an instructive exploration of some concretely substantial ideas very naturally expressed with such ordinary modal sentences as "A frog couldn't exist, and it never could have existed, without first there being a tadpole from which the frog developed". Now, I turn to seek some thoughts, similarly substantial, each naturally expressed with ordinary modal sentences much the same as may be found in the passage from Kripke cited so saliently. From that passage, we now recall this interrogative sentence: "Now could *this table* have been made from a completely *different* block of wood, or even of water cleverly hardened into ice—water taken from the Thames River?" Kripke suggests that the answer is "No".

Actually, there are many related questions in this semantic vicinity. Here are two. (1) Could that table have first been made from a completely *different* block of *matter*, which matter, at the time of the table's origin, happened to be so configured as to constitute a block of *wood*? (2) Could the table have first been made from matter that, at the time of the table's origin, was very different from any wood—as with brass, for example, or as with ice? As best I can tell, Kripke would prefer a negative answer to both of these neighboring questions. If so, then throughout this little neighborhood, he'll be wrong. However that may be, noting all his errors won't do much toward furthering our understanding, and even less toward widening our horizons.

Hoping to start our search along a promising line, I'll first focus on (2), the second of those two questions. Put perspicuously, that question is this: Could a certain wholly wooden table have first been made not from any wood, but only from matter that, at the time of the table's origin, was very different from wood? Moving away from that question just a tad, and adding some words that may help express an apt exploratory perspective, I'll next consider this closely neighboring question: What *concretely substantial* thoughts may be expressed, quite well and very naturally, with such an ordinary modal sentence as "A wooden table must first be made of wood, and can't first be made of ice"?

More or less instructively, each of very many thoughts will fill that bill. Among them all, I'll limit us to those that, first, *do depart significantly* from Scientiphicalism and that, second, *don't depart drastically* from that View. Well, here's a substantial idea that fills the bill: Each of a certain Eon's basic physical entities may be so propensitied that the "peculiarly powerful" particles will enter into various arrangements only in a sequentially selective manner. For example, should some particles *first* be arranged in such a way as to compose a *brass* complex, or any *brass* at all, then, even according to how it is propensitively with *those very particles*—and also according to how it is *propensitively* with *other* particles then, too—our considered particulate particulars *won't ever later* be arranged in such a (very different) way that they'll then serve to compose a *wooden* complex, or any *wood* at all. And, just as it is with brass and wood, so it will be, of course, with many other "ordinary sorts of stuff".

Generalizing straightforwardly, this may be said: If some particles are first arranged so as to compose a complex that's *not a wooden* complex, then, according to how it is *propensitively* with *those* very particles, the particulate individuals *won't ever later* be arranged in such a (very different) way that they'll then serve to compose a wooden complex, or any wood at all.

Now, for there to be any wooden complex, in the Eon I'm imagining, there must be a complex that's constituted from the Eon's basic physical particulars, which concrete particulars must be arranged in a way that's suited for there to be a complex, then constituted by them, of just that materially non-basic kind—the kind *wood*. Given that all the Eon's particulars are propensitied just as they *are* propensitied, that's the only way for there ever to be any wood, in this Eon, or for there then to be any wooden complex, as with a wooden table, for example. But, now, given the just previous paragraph's propensitive stipulations, what that means will then be nothing less than this: For a wooden complex to come into being, there must be available, for a suitably wood-constituting arrangement, many particles which *didn't previously serve* to constitute anything of some *other non-basic sort* of matter—*other than wood*, of course. Suppose that one of these other non-basic sorts is *ice*. Then, for us to have something made of wood, there must be many particles that never served to compose any ice.

When talking about the complex wooden particulars present during such an Eon, it won't be any empty idea naturally offered when saying that the Eon's present-day wooden individuals, or certain indicated ones among them, *couldn't (first) have been made* of some non-basic sort of matter *other than wood*, of ice, for example, before they were composed of wood, as now they are. Rather, and by marked contrast with the likes of Kripke, we'll then be offering a correct concretely substantial idea, a pretty novel thought that's no perfectly parochial proposition.

How interesting is all of this? For a pretty fair answer, I refer you to our Mantra, found near the close of the previous chapter. Given what's there, here's a good short answer: It's more than just to a terribly minute degree that it's interesting, but at least for now, it's not very interesting.

As is unsurprising, once again we find ourselves to be pretty pessimistic. But, much as I said near the prior chapter's close, even in the face of our pessimism, it may be moderately interesting, at least, to explore some still other mainstream offerings, thoughts that, to many, have seemed impressively deep ideas. Without further ado, that's what we'll next do.

5

THE PERSISTENCE OF MATERIAL INDIVIDUALS

Empty Issues and Self-Directed Propensity

When discussing Kripke's claims about the material origins of a certain material table, in the previous chapter, we focused on certain of the table's *origination conditions*, here using a term I coined in that chapter. But, while that was our focus there, we also considered some of the table's *persistence conditions*, now using a term that, in mainstream philosophy, has been common coin for many years. Now, by contrast with the prior chapter's focus, in this present chapter we'll focus on questions concerning the persistence conditions of a wide variety of material individuals, far wider than the group whose salient members are just the tables, the strables, the shmables and the lables.

1. Material Sculptures and Pieces of Matter

The persistence conditions of many concrete objects greatly interested philosophers long before Kripke lectured on origination conditions.[1] Generally, even

---

1. The *Stanford Encyclopedia of Philosophy*, for instance, has an entry, *Material Constitution*, which provides historical information as well as discussion of contemporary thoughts on the topic: Wasserman, Ryan, "Material Constitution," *The Stanford Encyclopedia of Philosophy* (Summer 2013 Edition), Edward N. Zalta (ed.), URL = <http://plato.stanford.edu/archives/sum2013/entries/material-constitution/>. In section 1 of *Material Constitution*, this entry's author, Ryan Wasserman, presents (at least) three puzzles about this matter as being ancient puzzles, while still interesting to mainstream philosophers: *The Debtor's Paradox, The Puzzle of Dion and Theon,* and *The Ship of Theseus Puzzle.* The last-mentioned of these is of very great interest to very many current and recent mainstream

if not universally, the objects whose persistence conditions exercised olden philosophers, and now fascinate very many current philosophers, too, are quite
ordinary spatial concreta, as with rocks, tables, ships, sculptures, and so on.

Now, as the particulate form of our shared Scientiphicalism has it, each of
these ordinary concreta, each sculpture, for example, will be a material complex, composed of many physically smaller and simpler material things, as with
an ordinary sculpture's many molecules, and yet more numerous atoms, and
still yet more numerous elementary particles. But, in this chapter, my discussion
won't turn on any such presumed features of ordinary material things. Indeed,
even if every sculpture should be composed entirely of perfectly continuous
and homogeneous matter, and each should be entirely surrounded by utterly
empty space, my remarks will be perfectly pertinent, as we'll soon see.

A certain artist, whom we may call "Art Garfinkel", often visits so-called
junkyards, in search of such scraps of metal as will not just catch his eye, but,
more than that, which will hold his attention quite enjoyably. On one of these
visits, as it happens, he finds most appealing a certain junky piece of copper,
shaped just like a lump, and nothing like, say, a disk. Purchasing the piece for just
a pittance, and naming his acquisition "Peter *Copperfield*," Art has it in mind to
use this newly named Peter in a certain moderately complex artistic endeavor, a
brief description of which I now provide.

Covering Copperfield with a suitable sort of wax, Garfinkel first uses the
purchased piece to make a suitably shaped mold, the mold being made not of
copper, of course, but of some quite different material, very well suited for
making a mold of just the sort Art knowledgeably aims to produce. What the
mold will be used for, once completed, is to make a sculpture, from molten
copper. For Garfinkel, the point of that is this: After that copper hardens, he
will have produced, in that way, a sculpture that, at least in all intrinsic regards
and respects, is very like Peter Copperfield, the purchased piece of coppery
junk. Using this mold, Art pours into it (at least very nearly) exactly as much
(molten) copper—at least down to the nearest one thousandth of a milligram—
as is contained in Copperfield. That copper hardens so as to form a piece of
copper, one that's always spatially distant from, and that's ever so separate
from, the purchased Copperfield. This newly hard piece of copper, it may be
noted, contains no matter that ever served to compose the piece bought in the
junkyard, Peter Copperfield. Amusingly, Garfinkel names the piece of copper
he intentionally produced "Peter *Copyfield*".

---

philosophical thinkers; when one plugs "ship" and "Theseus" into the "with all words" slot of
Google Scholar's Advanced Search, and when one requires, as well, that at least one of the three
words "puzzle", "paradox" and "problem" also be present, that Search returns a list running into
the thousands, with the first item in the long list, being Theodore "Ted" Sider's rather recent book
Four-Dimensionalism, Oxford University Press, 2001.

Having studied philosophy when in college, AG was quite uncertain that any *piece of* copper could ever *be* a copper *sculpture*; indeed, he was inclined to think not. In any case, he gave another name, "Untitled #42", to the sculpture he produced exactly when and where he produced Peter Copyfield. So it was that, entirely made of copper, there came to be *Untitled #42*, an artwork that, fairly rocking even the coolest of the cognoscenti, brought AG a cool $6,000,000, with an equal amount going, of course, to his very fashionable dealer.[2]

With that said, we're almost done with our little story. The rest is just this: After resting in a billionaire's penthouse for a while, perhaps about a month, the matter composing Untitled #42—matter also composing Peter Copyfield— is annihilated. In a moderately realistic case of that, the matter may be nuked. Perhaps better for our consideration, though not a great deal better, is a case where the matter is converted to energy. In this latter case, even the matter itself suddenly ceases to be.

In the story just told, a certain piece of copper and a certain copper sculpture are, from the first moment of their existence until their very last, always spatially perfectly coincident. And, throughout their history, each is composed of the same (copper) matter as the other. Still and all, it may well be that there are, indeed, those two distinct things I mentioned, Peter Copyfield being one of them, and Untitled #42 being the other notable thing. Just so, there will be only some quite confused thinking on the part of anyone who may think that, in our little story, we mentioned *just one most salient cuprous thing*, mentioning twice over just a single salient cuprous thing—with our sometimes using *one of its names*, "Peter Copyfield" and, with our using, at other times, *another of its names*, "Untitled #42". As the chapter progresses, how confused that is will become very clear.

Toward beginning to make that clearer, we may ask about what *could have been done to Untitled #42* with the result that it should *then continue to exist*, and also what could have been done to it with the opposite result, with the result that it should *then cease to exist*. Additionally, we may ask parallel questions concerning Peter Copyfield. In philosophically favored terminology, when asking those questions, what we're asking is this: What are the *persistence conditions of* Untitled #42, the expensive copper *sculpture*? And, of about equal interest, what are the *persistence conditions of* Peter Copyfield, the *piece* of copper composed of just the

2. As I said, it often may be best for us to think of the matter, in our cases, as being completely continuous and homogeneous. Now, some may think that, when doing this, they won't be able to think the matter in question is copper, as copper simply must come in the form of copper atoms. That is the standard Kripkean thought on such a question. Myself, I think the Kripkean thought to be just a failed attempt at proposing a strictly necessary truth, the upshot being no offered truth at all. But, to get on with a reasonable discussion of larger issues, let us grant that the Kripkean is a correct idea. That granted, the reader might then proceed like this: Wherever I write "copper", the reader may substitute the new word "capper As stipulated, when some matter is capper then, even though it's like copper in very many ways, it needn't come in the form of atoms.

very same copper that, throughout all the very same period of time, also serves
to compose the pricey copper sculpture, Untitled #42?

Let's see what we can do by way of answering these questions.

Here's a nice start on that: Quite independently of any intentions AG ever has
or had, we could feed the salient copper into, and through, a wire-forming
Extruder. The resulting piece of copper will be very long and very thin. What
would this mean for Untitled #42? Well, especially as the sculpture's involvement with the Extruder has nothing to do with Art G, after it would have been
fed through the Extruder, the copper that served to compose Untitled #42
wouldn't still compose that sculpture. (Indeed, it then wouldn't serve to compose any sculpture at all.) Just so, at that point in time *Untitled #42 wouldn't exist*
(whether or not, under certain conditions, it might still later exist). But, even at
that point in time, *Peter Copyfield, our piece of copper, would (still) exist*. It's just that
this piece of copper's shape would have changed remarkably, from a quite
lumpy shape to a shape that's very wiry.

Should we think, then, that copper sculptures are more special sorts of
things than are (mere) pieces of copper, perhaps somewhat as automobiles are
special sorts of vehicles, or children are especially young people? No; not really.
Let me explain.

As our little thought experiment helped to show, in *one* way, at least, the
persistence conditions of Untitled #42 are *stricter than* those of Peter Copyfield:
There are certain processes of change that *won't allow* Untitled #42 to *continue
to exist*, and will have it that the sculpture *then ceases* to exist (*whether or not* it may
still later exist). But, these processes *will allow* Peter Copyfield, the piece of
copper, to continue to exist.

While that may be perfectly true, this may also be true: In at least one *other*
way, the persistence conditions of Untitled #42 are *laxer than* Copyfield's persistence conditions; in *another* way, the persistence conditions of the *piece* are *stricter*
than those of the *sculpture*. In some instructive detail, I'll illustrate that point.

Even when it's serving to compose both Copyfield and #42, the *copper* in
question may be suddenly cut in half—whether by a vandal with a chisel, or
whether by naturally occurring bolts of lightning, or whatever. Putting things
piecewisely, what would then result is this: There would be two resultant (max-
imally continuous and free-standing) pieces of copper, as concerns both mass
and volume each (about) equal to the other. In this *Bisection Case*, as I'll call it,
neither of these pieces would be Peter Copyfield. Nor would anything else then
be PC. Rather, right at the Bisection's end, or once it should be done, Copyfield
wouldn't exist. Now, continuing to think about the composing copper's possible
Bisection, what would happen as regards our copper sculpture, *Untitled #42*?
As I'm pretty sure, even should its copper be bisected, our copper sculpture

would still exist. (This becomes especially clear, I think, when we bother to make certain further suppositions, all quite proper to do here. So, as we do well to suppose, the two (roughly equal-sized) copper pieces can be nicely rejoined, perhaps via a suitable metallurgical procedure. How nicely rejoined must that be? Well, it's at least nicely enough for the sculpture to be *restored*—perhaps not absolutely perfectly restored, but, still, restored all the same.) So, even while our *piece of copper can't* directly survive Bisection, our copper *sculpture can* directly survive Bisection. So, even while, in *certain* ways, the persistence conditions of a copper sculpture are *stricter than* those for a piece of copper, in *certain other* ways the reverse is true.

At least at first glance, that's quite certainly right. But, even while most mainstream thinkers would agree with this, many would disagree.[3] For the most part, those disagreeing will hold that, exactly occupying a given region of space at a certain particular time, and composed entirely of just some certain matter, there cannot possibly be more than just one material individual. So, as they see things, it can't possibly be that, where there's the material individual that's the copper sculpture Untitled #42 there's also another material individual right then and there, composed of just that very same copper. All this stuff about persistence conditions, they may say, is just so much fancy confusion.

Before passing beyond this terribly severe position, I'll say just three things about it. First, the thought they offer is just another analytically empty proposition. Second, and even as it goes against commonsense thinking, it's most likely an incorrect idea. Third, in the next chapter I'll consider some views that are far more severe than the position now just so quickly considered; by comparison with them, this quickly considered view looks to be an ontologically profligate position, hardly severe at all.

---

3. Among the very many for whom it's perfectly acceptable for more than one material thing to present, perhaps the philosopher presently promoting the position most prominently is Kit Fine, as with, for example, his "Coincidence and Form," *Proceedings of the Aristotelian Society Supplementary Volume* lxxxii, 2008, 101–18.

During somewhat less recent years, at least, another advocate of this commonsense "pluralist" position was Mark Johnston. In his "Constitution is Not Identity," *Mind*, Vol. 101, 1992, 89–105, Johnston identifies at least these four advocates of the opposing "monist" view: Allan Gibbard, as in "Contingent Identity," *Journal of Philosophical Logic*, Vol. 4, 187–221, Anil Gupta, as in *The Logic of Common Nouns*, Yale University Press, 1980, Dennis Robinson, as in "Re-Identifying Matter," *Philosophical Review*, Vol. 81, 1982, 317–42, and David Lewis, as in several cited works, including "Counterparts of Persons and their Bodies," *Journal of Philosophy*, Vol. 68, 1971, 203–11.

Another only moderately recent work advocating a sort of pluralism, perhaps a very different form from the sort Fine advocates, is Lynne Rudder Baker's "Why Constitution is Not Identity," *Journal of Philosophy*, Vol. XCIV, 1997, 599–621. As works advocating the opposing monist view, she cites the four just rehearsed from Johnston, as well as Stephen Yablo's "Identity, Essence and Indiscernibility" *Journal of Philosophy*, Vol. LXXXIV, 1987, 293–314.

For a recent monist work applying some of David Lewis's ideas, see John Divers' "Coincidence and Form," *Proceedings of the Aristotelian Society Supplementary Volume* lxxxii, 2008, 119–37.

In this present chapter, we'll next explore various issues suggested by the thought, apparently quite correct, that a copper sculpture and a piece of copper, though each numerically different from the other, may always be composed of just the same matter, and may always share just the same space, as well.[4]

2. Are There *Inconveniently* Persisting Material Individuals?

To move on with our business in a pretty rapid fashion, let's agree to use a lot of fashionable terminology, even if we may have many reservations about the trendy ways of talking. So, let's agree to be happy with our saying things like these: The two-word expression "copper sculpture" *expresses* the *concept (of a) copper sculpture.* Each of the copper sculptures *falls under* that very concept, and nothing that's not a copper sculpture falls under it. As well, each copper sculpture *satisfies* that concept, while nothing else satisfies it. Correlatively, the concept of a copper sculpture *is true of* each of the copper sculptures, and it's *not* true of anything *else*, not a copper sculpture.

In parallel with that, there's this: The three-word expression "piece of copper" *expresses* the *concept (of a) piece of copper.* Each of the pieces of copper *falls under* that very concept, and nothing not a piece of copper does that; and so on.

---

4. To a fair extent, at least, what I'm saying here, and throughout the chapter, agrees with (most of) what Kit Fine has said in his paper "The Non-Identity of a Material Thing and Its Matter," *Mind* 112 (2003): 195–234. As there is this fair amount of agreement, I do well to cite that work in echoing this point that Fine takes pains to make plain:

> Although the point is often ignored, it is not a *piece* of alloy but of the *alloy* itself that can properly be said to constitute or make up a statue. (page 206)

Indeed, I should go further and say that, first, it is not any *piece* of alloy but only the *alloy* itself that can constitute the piece of alloy; for one thing, nothing can constitute itself, no more than anything can cause itself, or create itself. And, in another way, too, I should go further, especially with the coincident sorts of cases that Fine often had, and that I now often have in mind. It is the very same alloy that constitutes the piece of alloy as that which constitutes the alloy—or, in my own example, it is the very same copper that constitutes the piece of copper and the copper sculpture.

Earlier in the paper, Fine appears, at least to be somewhat less careful

> Where a pluralist sees several things—a statue, the clay from which it is made, the piece of clay—the monist sees a single thing. We might call it a "mere" thing since it is not taken to be, in itself, one of the more specific things picked out be the pluralist. (page 198)

As this earlier passage at least suggests, the clay from which a certain statue is made is to be regarded as a thing, quite in the same sense as, and apparently on a par with, the statue itself and, as well, a certain piece of clay, presumably just that piece which, more carefully, that clay then composes, and constitutes, and so on. But the clay itself, which also composes the piece of clay just noted by fine, is not a thing, at least not in the same sense as, or on a par with, the (perhaps infinitely many) things it constitutes, and composes, and so on. Rather the clay is just some stuff and, more specifically, it is just some clay. To be a true master of perfectly ordinary emptiness may be, I suggest, no very easy thing to be—nor a very important one, I might add.

Now, here's another fashionable thing to say: Even as the persistence conditions of copper sculptures are very different from the persistence conditions of pieces of copper, so the concept of a copper sculpture is a quite different from the concept of a piece of copper.[5]

Indeed, so different is the concept of a piece of copper from the notion of a copper sculpture that, quite as we've lately observed, there are very many items (even actual, not to mention merely possible) which satisfy the former concept without any of them satisfying the latter. This happens not only as with copper wires produced by vandals from lumpy copper sculptures; as well, it happens with the many copper wires produced by industry. And, it happens with the many tiny pieces of copper, each smaller than a piece of sawdust, all produced as by-products of industrial copper grinding processes.

Whatever it is that concepts may be, exactly, there'll be an enormous number of the items, presumably a *very large infinite* number. At all events, there'll be far more concepts than just those ideas which are quite *conveniently expressed* in English, or any other earthly natural language. Almost at will, we may just monkey about and, willy nilly, we'll have latched onto one or another of these "inconvenient concepts", usually a notion nobody's ever latched onto before. In the previous chapter, that happened when I latched onto the concept of a shmable, and the notion of a strable, and the idea of a lable.[6]

When not being so perfectly provincial intellectually as to be almost out-rageously picayune thinkers, we'll acknowledge this next point, an idea central

5. This is a point that goes beyond the perfectly patent thought that the expression most standardly used, by English speakers, to express the concept of a piece of copper—the expression "piece of copper"—is very different from the expression that's so used, by most speakers, to most standardly express the concept of a copper sculpture—the expression "copper sculpture ". For one thing, the expression "piece of copper" comprises precisely three English words, while the other expression, "copper sculpture" comprises only two words. That's not even a close call. What's quite close to being the same as the point about the two concepts may be this idea: The semantic condi-tions of "piece of copper" are quite different from those of "copper sculpture".

6. Here's a reader-friendly observation: In the previous paragraph, I suggest an employment for the term "concept" on which it will apply, of course, to ever so many concepts that nobody's ever so much as even entertained or considered, let alone employed at all intentionally. There are, to be sure, other employments of the term, perhaps every bit as common or natural, on which its conditions of application will be more constrained. On such a stricter course, it will be more straightforwardly natural to speak of people inventing, and having invented, many concepts—as with saying that people in the twentieth century invented the concept of an email, and as with saying Nelson Goodman invented the concept of grue and the concept of bleen. For ease of ex-position, it is best for me to use concept in the very liberal way that, in the previous paragraph, I've already begun doing—a way in which it would certainly be more natural to say, and would probably be more correct to say, that Goodman didn't so much invent the concept of grue as he latched onto a certain previously unconsidered concept. See his *Fact, Fiction and Forecast*, The Athlone Press, 1954.

At all events, nothing in this chapter's main lines of argument depends upon this choice of mine, as one who has read through the chapter will be able to verify. Having made my friendly observation, I return to the main line of our discussion.

to this section's main line of thinking: As concerns anything of any great philosophical importance, (almost all) the concepts expressed by our short and convenient expressions aren't superior to each of very many *other* concepts that aren't so conveniently expressed, that is, to each of very many *inconvenient* ideas.[7]

Along with the point that none of our convenient concepts (or almost none) will be importantly superior to each of very many inconvenient notions, there'll be this companionable idea: There's *nothing any more realistic* about, and there's *nothing any more fundamental* about, the *sorts* of things satisfying the *more convenient concepts* than there is to (very many of) the *quite different sorts* of things that, not satisfying those readily expressed ideas, satisfy only some quite inconvenient idea, or ideas. And, along with *that* point, there's this *still further* thought: There's nothing any more realistic or more fundamental about the *things of* the first ("more *convenient*") sorts than there is to the *very different things* of the second ("more *inconvenient*") sorts.[8]

With the previous chapter's encounter with shmables, strables, and lables, we've already had a little taste of that: It should be readily recognized, of course, that there's nothing more realistic about a table, or anything more fundamental about such a commonplace thing, than will be found with a shmable, a strable, or a lable. But, in the present chapter, we'll go from just a little taste to a veritable feast. Let's start on that.

First, we do some stage-setting: As observed with Extrusion, the persistence conditions for a piece of copper are, in at least *one* way, laxer than the persistence conditions for a copper sculpture. But, as observed with Bisection, the persistence conditions of the piece are, in at least *one other* way, stricter than those for the sculpture. Now, it will be useful to represent these observations in a standard rectangular table, with (horizontal) rows for conceptions of concreta that we're considering, and with (vertical) columns for the potentially terminating processes we're contemplating. Here's such a table, with a question mark representing a concrete conception not yet considered, possibly an inconvenient idea for some material concreta:

---

7. That may be true even while this also is true: There are very many *still other inconvenient* ideas that, as concerns some matters of great philosophical import, are inferior to (almost all) our convenient ideas—and also worse than very many inconvenient ideas, as well. Thus, the concept of an *elementary particle* might be superior, in a philosophically significant way, to the concept of an *elementary particle that's more than seven kilometers from any pharmacy*.

8. As I'm pleased to relate, I am far from being the only philosopher who takes the view that, concerning concrete reality, there is little or nothing of philosophical moment to be found in the neighborhood of these questions. Other recent and current philosophers have advanced much the same position in recent years, with Eli Hirsch among the most salient of them. Hirsch offers his view in a series of papers that includes his "Ontology and Alternative Languages," in David Chalmers, David Manley and Ryan Wasserman, eds., *Metametaphysics*, Oxford University Press, 2009, pages 231–59.

	Extrusion	Bisection
?	Survives	Survives
Piece of Copper	Survives	Doesn't Survive
Copper Sculpture	Doesn't Survive	Survives
?	Doesn't Survive	Doesn't Survive

As this table makes vividly evident, in the territory we're investigating there are *two further* possibilities, beyond the two we've noted. One will be a concept whose satisfiers will be material concreta that *directly survive both Extrusion and also Bisection*. In the *respects currently considered*, this concept has *very lax* persistence conditions. Let's call it *the concept of a mank*, allowing that we've here indicated it only quite partially and also very vaguely. While it's possible that this concept is a convenient and ordinary notion, now just newly named, it's more likely that the concept's an inconvenient idea, not previously noticed, much less mentioned or named. At any rate, quite different from the notion of a mank, the other newly noted concept will be an idea whose satisfiers will *directly survive neither Extrusion nor Bisection*. In the *respects considered*, this other concept's persistence conditions are *very strict*. Possibly just an ordinary idea already named or expressed, and possibly only inconvenient, let's call this other notion *the concept of a bost*.

As I've been suggesting, none of the four concepts lately in play is better suited, than is any of the others, for conceiving how things actually are with concrete reality. In line with that, and as I'll also suggest, the kind *pieces of copper* is on a par, ontologically, with the kind *copper manks*, which is on a par, ontologically, with the kind *copper sculptures*, which is on a par, ontologically, with the kind *copper bosts*. And, just as it is with these kinds, so it is with individuals of the four kinds: A piece of copper is no more fundamental than is a copper mank, or a copper bost. Of course, none of that specially concerns copper: A piece of iron is no more basic than an iron mank, or an iron bost.

Anyway, these four sentences express four thoughts that, as concerns questions of analytical emptiness, are all perfectly on a par:

> *Pieces of* copper can survive Extrusion, but they can't survive Bisection.
> Copper *sculptures* can survive Bisection, but they can't survive Extrusion.
> Copper *manks* can survive both Bisection and also Extrusion.
> Copper *bosts* can't survive either Bisection or Extrusion.

(With the first of the four, the full thought expressed entails little more than, and maybe nothing more than, this quite obviously merely conditional idea: If something is a *piece of copper*, then, while it can survive Extrusion, it can't survive Bisection. And, with the other three thoughts, that's just as aptly noted.) Anyway, and equally, all four thoughts are analytically empty ideas.

3. Pieces, Lumps and Hunks: A Problematic Plethora of Persisting Individuals?

With some profit to the exercise, we may consider enormously many other processes, beyond Extrusion and Bisection, each differing from the others as notably as Extrusion and Bisection differ from each other. Right here, I'll discuss just one of them.

Consider the rarely-if-ever-previously pondered process of *Rectoration*: To some matter not yet in the shape of a rectangular solid, pressure is applied in just such a way as to gradually transform the matter shapewise, so that it goes *from* being shaped, say, ovoidally *to* being shaped precisely as befits a *typical rectangular solid*, the Rectoration culminating in a piece of matter with eight nicely rectilinear corners. When a proper *Rectoration* is done, we stipulate, there'll be a solidly rectangular piece of matter that's no more than twice as long as it's wide, and no more than twice as wide as it's high.

Now that we've three distinct processes in play, Extrusion, Bisection and also Rectoration, it's useful to present a new table, expanding on the one already displayed:

	Rectoration	Extrusion	Bisection
Type-A Mank	Survives	Survives	Survives
Piece of Copper	Survives	Survives	Doesn't Survive
?	Survives	Doesn't Survive	Survives
Type-A Bost (Hunk of Copper)	Survives	Doesn't Survive	Doesn't Survive
Type-B Mank	Doesn't Survive	Survives	Survives
?	Doesn't Survive	Survives	Doesn't Survive
Copper Sculpture	Doesn't Survive	Doesn't Survive	Survives
Type-B Bost (Lump of Copper)	Doesn't Survive	Doesn't Survive	Doesn't Survive

This table is six times the size of our previous table: While that had four cells, this has twenty-four. More importantly, while that had four rows, each representing a relevantly distinct *possibility*, this has eight, with twice as many such possibilities represented.[9]

Taking cues from the new table, we may notice some points about our copper sculpture, and about our piece of copper. For one thing, about our *piece*

9. Of course, this will generalize: Each time we add a newly distinct sort of process, we'll have twice as many relevantly reckoned possibilities. So, with *six* distinct sorts of process considered, the number of relevant possibilities will be two (survives vs. doesn't survive) to the *sixth* power, which is, of course, 64 relevant possibilities.

of copper, we may say that it *will survive a Rectoration* (unlike a typical copper sculpture, which *won't* survive that.) And, about our (lumpy) copper sculpture, we may say that it will survive a process of Bisection (unlike a piece of copper, which won't survive *that*.)

When looking at our table's left-hand side, you'll see that I've already categorized (the sort) *pieces*, at least as far as our three (sorts of) considered process go: pieces are (among the) persisting concreta that survive Rectoration and Extrusion, but not Bisection.

Well, now, what about *lumps* of copper, which might differ not only from (lumpy) copper *sculptures*, but also, perhaps, from *pieces* of copper? In the terms of our table, how shall *lumps* be categorized?

First, there's this to observe: For all I can readily say, while it might be true that any lump of copper is a piece of copper, it's *not* true, I can safely say, that all pieces of copper are lumps of copper. Just so, consider this point about *shape*: Many pieces of copper are each shaped in a way that's very far from being lumpy, and from being lumplike, and from anything even remotely like that. So, for its having such an inappropriate shape, each of *those* pieces *won't be a lump* of copper.

Before, we saw a clear example of that: Where there's a certain long thin copper wire, there may be a single continuous piece of copper, directly surrounded by no matter at all. Spatially coincident with the wire, there'll be a *piece* of copper, but *not any lump*.

Now, another clear example becomes salient: Where there's a copper rectangular solid, there may be a single continuous piece of copper, surrounded by nothing more than empty space. Occupying just the space occupied by the rectangular solid, itself surrounded by empty space, there will be a single *piece* of copper. But, there *won't* be, right then and there, any *lump* of copper. (So, pretty early and easily, we know that (the concept of) a lump of copper has some fairly strict persistence conditions. As we already saw, lumps can't survive Extrusion or Bisection. And, as we've just seen, lumps can't survive Rectoration.) Going by our new table's terminology, lumps will be type-B bosts. Just so, in the box where I've written "Type-B Bosts", we may write "Lumps of copper".

Well, now, in terms of our table, how will *hunks* be categorized? Well, consider Rectoration. When put through that process, the very same copper that originally composes both a lump of the stuff and also a hunk of the material will come to compose *only a hunk* of the metal and *not any lump*, at all. For, when some matter is in the shape of a rectangular solid, the matter's far too boxy, and far too rectilinear, for the stuff to compose a proper *lump* of anything. And, for some matter to compose a lump of matter, that matter must be relevantly freestanding, not surrounded by (more) matter.

Happily, we experts in emptiness have little trouble distinguishing between real *lumps* of copper and true *hunks* of copper. Happily, we may display these empty ideas:

Hunks of copper *can* survive a process of *Rectoration* – *even though* they can't survive Extrusion and Bisection.

Lumps of copper *can't* survive a process of *Rectoration* – *just as* they can't survive Extrusion and Bisection.

In the terminology of our table, while Lumps will be Type-B Bosts, Hunks will be Type-A Bosts. And, as our table makes clear, no Type-A Bost will be any Type-B Bost, and vice versa. So, when some lumpily shaped matter composes both a lump and a hunk, the lump will be one thing the matter composes, while the hunk will be another.

Just above, I placed two sentences in display. When used as mainstreamers typically employ them, such sentences express only just so many analytically empty ideas. For us here, that's the central point. Still and all, even when trafficking in emptiness, we should try to get things right. Unlike those who see no differences between pieces, lumps and hunks, we're getting the empty ideas right here. That said, we move on.

4. Is There a Plethora of *Extraordinary* Persisting Individuals?

A few readers may think the sentences lately displayed express certain philosophically profound propositions. Many mainstreamers appear to think that, including a philosopher no less astute, about ever so many matters, as Kit Fine:

> There is a strong intuitive case for thinking that the modal difference between the statue and the piece of alloy stands in need of explanation...

> For one thing, there are other differences between the statue and the piece of alloy which also appear to stand in need of explanation... The most obvious difference in this regard is the difference in *sort*. The statue is a *statue* though not a *piece of alloy*, while the piece of alloy is a *piece of alloy* though not a *statue*.

> Moreover, the sortal differences plausibly stand in need of explanation. It is perhaps not always true that sortal differences stand in need of explanation. It might be thought, for example, that the behavior of different particles is to be explained in terms of their belonging to different basic sorts or kinds, even though there is no explanation of what the difference in kind consists in. But the difference between the sorts *statue* and *piece of alloy* are not plausibly regarded as basic in this way. Surely, one wants to say, there must be some account of what is involved in being a statue or a piece of clay, from which it should then be apparent why a given object is the one rather than the other.[10]

How might I help those enamored of such ideas abandon them?

10. Kit Fine, "Coincidence and Form," *Proceedings of the Aristotelian Society Supplementary Volume* 82, Issue 1, June 2008, pp 101–18. The material cited is all on page 105. With this material, Fine

Well, in the previous section, I presented a twenty-four-celled table. First, consider just these four rows of that table, the row for a copper *sculpture*, the row for a *piece* of copper, the row for a *lump* of copper, and the row for a *hunk* of copper. As should now be apparent, however great or deep is the need for an explanation of what's so different about a copper sculpture and a piece of copper, it will be just as great or deep as the need for an account of what's so different about a hunk of copper and a lump of copper. And, it's no greater or deeper than the need for an explanation of what's so different between any one of these four apparently different items and any other one of them, between a piece and a hunk, for example. Is there, in any of these cases, any very great or deep need? Only if there is such a great and deep need in all of them, each being (at least about) on a par with all the others. I cannot believe that there is a very deep need for an explanation of what's so different about a hunk of copper and a lump of copper, or any explanation that may fill such a need. What am I missing here? Not much, I think.

In an open-minded manner, let's further ponder the protestation proffered by Fine. In such a happily fair spirit, we may well come to think that, almost wherever we can confront a difference in persistence conditions, we will confront, in the bargain, a need to explain that difference and, in all but the most unfortunate cases, a clearly nontrivial account that explains the difference confronted. Just so, we may now do well to consider just *these other four rows* of the table, the two rows for our two types of manks, and the two rows where, at the left, there's a cell with a question mark. Now, as it may very well be, to put the point mildly, at least one represents only a terribly inconvenient concept.

For present purposes, it doesn't much matter whether or not there's a short convenient expression, entrenched in English, for our newly named sorts of persisting material individuals, for type-A manks and for type-B manks. Either way, there'll be *plenty of* inconvenient concepts, *any one of which* serves to make our present points. Each will be a concept apt for a different sort of potentially persisting material item, with each of the sorts and their exemplars being just as realistic, or just as real, as are all the others. And, in every case, there's no nontrivial need to explain any differences among the sorts (of concreta) that these unfamiliar concepts serve to delineate.

---

has a footnote citing two contemporary pieces that agree with him on some of his central points here: Karen Bennett, "Spatio-temporal Coincidence and the Grounding Problem," *Philosophical Studies*, 2004, Volume, 111, Issue 3, pages 339–71, and Eric Olson, "Material Coincidence and the Indiscernibility Problem," *Philosophical Quarterly*, 2001, Volume 51, pages 337–55.

In the same Supplementary Volume as Fine's paper appears, there appears, right after it, a paper replying to his work, written along lines following David Lewis's approach to such matters. That is "Coincidence and Form" by John Divers. As this chapter should help make clear, except when they may be concerned with merely parochial matters, all four of these papers concern only just so many concretely empty issues, as also holds for Lewis's work on these topics, as well as ever so many other philosophical publications, by ever so many other authors writing during the past half-century, or more.

There are several ways to see that this must be so. For, we may readily con-template *very many more sorts of relevantly involving processes*, each very different from each of the others that we may aptly consider. For our vividly represent-ing tables, each newly named process will provide yet another column. In line with that, there'll be added two more rows, in each successive table—one row for the (sorts of) things that *do* directly survive this new process, the other for those that *don't*.

It's easy to come up with very many complementary processes. Each no-tably different from the three we've already highlighted, here are four further processes, each nicely suggested by the name I give it, and each notably differ-ent, as well, from each other: Trisection, Sphericalation, Meltation, and Donutization. With that added, we've highlighted seven processes. Well, with just these seven differentiating, we're up to 128 different sorts of persisting ma-terial particulars. While there may be short convenient English expressions for about 100, it's nearly certain that there *aren't convenient* concepts for all, or almost all. Of course, there's nothing to stop at just seven different sorts of process. But, as there's little point to going further now, I turn to other ideas.

5. Ordinary and Not So Ordinary Persisting Material Individuals

Every *ordinary kind* of (presumably) material thing is a kind whose members are items that semantically satisfy a short ordinary expression, often just a one-word expression, that's a *standard name for that kind*. Thus it is, for example, that the ordinary kind *stone* has, as its members, just concrete particulars that each semantically satisfies the ordinary word "stone"—in the very central sense of that very common word. And, thus it is, also, with the ordinary kind *rosebush* and the ordinary kind *sculpture*, and the ordinary kinds *pieces of copper, lumps of bronze* and *hunks of marble*.

For each ordinary kind of material things, its most standard name is what I've often called a *vague discriminative term*, as with the terms "chair" and "table," the terms "rock" and "stone," the terms "twig" and "log," and the terms "knife," "fork" and "spoon".[11] Reminiscent of what's in previous sections, "lump" and "hunk" are also vague discriminative terms, as will be shown in several upcoming passages.

11. I coined phrases in this family in my old paper "Why There Are No People," *Midwest Studies in Philosophy*, IV, (1979), which is reprinted in Volume 2 of my *Philosophical Papers*, Oxford University Press, 1996. For instance, the phrase *vague discriminative expression* occurs in emphatic ital-ics there, just as it does in this very sentence.

For a much more recent discussion of vague discriminative terms, see "Beyond Discrimina-tive Vagueness, Safe from Nihilistic Sorites," which is the brief Appendix to chapter 7 of my *All the Power in World*, comprising pages 465–69 of that work.

Here are a few points about many vague discriminative terms: As each of these vague terms significantly differs from the others, as regards meaning, so each directly expresses a concept differing from those that others express. For example, while the vague term "log" directly expresses the vague discriminative *concept of a log*, so the significantly different vague term "twig" directly expresses the distinctively different vague discriminative *concept of a twig*. And, even as the idea of a twig is quite different from the notion of a log, however interestingly the two "woodsy" concepts should be related, so twigs belong to *one ordinary kind* of things and logs belong to *another.*[12]

Let's consider a copper spoon, or a "capper" spoon, nicely shaped and happily free of holes. As we're supposing, of course, our spoon is constituted of relevantly homogeneous, absolutely elemental, perfectly continuous matter: Each "region" of this spoon is constituted of the very same sort of continuous elemental matter as constitutes any other region. Also useful, we suppose our spoon is surrounded by just empty space.

Let's involve our spoon in a very gradual *Rectoration*; with continuous matter supposed, it may be infinitely gradual. So, our spoon's Rectoration will happen in a perfectly smooth and cohesive fashion, without any sort of abruptness at all, much less anything like breaking, tearing, or shattering. *Extremely* gradually, our Rectoration "takes some matter" composing a spoon and "makes the matter" compose just a rectangular solid, and no spoon at all.

Quite felicitously, we may speak of *the first half* of our spoon's purely shape-transformative Rectoration, even if there should be nothing distinctively separating the end of our Rectoration's first half from the start of its second half. Similarly, we may talk of infinitely many other fractional parts of this Rectoration, as with its *third fifth*.

Now, in terms of millionths of our Rectoration, consider just as much of our envisioned process as will take our matter from composing our spoon to just barely failing to compose a spoon. With just this much of our Rectoration, the matter will compose an extremely *spoonlike* freestanding material persistent, and certainly no freestanding bricklike concretum. Let's say that this terribly *spoonlike* material persistent is a *spoon-and-an-alpha*; where it's laid down that the two kinds, *spoons* and *spoon-and-and-an-alphas*, *aren't mutually exclusive* kinds, but, rather, the *spoon-and-and-alphas will include all the spoons and then some*. So, while otherwise terribly like a spoon, with purely shape-transformative Rectorations,

---

12. The *vaguest of all* our ideas *aren't* any vague *discriminative* concepts. These very vaguest concepts, like the *concept of a thing*, and the concept of an *item*, are such utterly general notions that, insofar as they may be said to hold true of anything at all, they'll hold true of absolutely everything. As I now understand the notion of an *item*—quite rightly enough, I think—*anything at all* may be an item. So, the concept of an item won't (even purport to) discriminate any things, or any items, *from any other* things or items. Just so, the concept of an item *isn't* a vague *discriminative* notion.

Unlike the utterly general concept of an item, the far less general concept of a spoon discriminates the spoons from all other things, from all the nonspoons.

a spoon-and-an-alpha can directly survive *more of a change* than any spoon can do. With respect to *Rectorations,* the *persistence conditions* of spoons are a *little stricter than* those of spoon-and-an-alphas.

In line with the above, we may consider an enormous series of material persistents and, with continuous matter, an infinite series. The first member of our series will persist through not only all that a spoon-and-an-alpha survives, but then the *next half a millionth* of our Rectoration as well. The second member will persist through all that and also the *next quarter* of a millionth; and so on. Focusing on the first member, I'll call that persistent a *spoon-and-a-beta.*

While the concept of a spoon is, of course, a quite common and convenient concept, the slightly different concept of a spoon-and-an-alpha is an uncommon and inconvenient concept, as is also the concept of a spoon-and-a-beta. Just so, even as we say that spoons are ordinary things, so we may say that spoon-and-an-alphas are *nonordinary* persisting material particulars and, different from them, so also are spoon-and-a-betas. But, of course, just as there's nothing to favor hunks over manks, as objects worthy of serious consideration, so there's nothing to favor spoons over spoon-and-an-alphas or, for that matter, over spoon-and-a-betas.

With bricks and other such rectangular ordinary things, we won't use exactly this same reasoning. But, using a suitable process for them, as with Extrusion, in each case we may engage in parallel reasoning. Thus, we'll soon come to encompass all manner of ordinary material persistents. Whenever and wherever any of them is composed of some matter, that very matter will also compose extremely many other material persistents that are nonordinary persistents—with continuous matter, there'll be infinitely many of them.

For almost everything done in this section, we didn't need to assume continuous matter, though that assumption was useful for considering series with infinitely many material persistents. Finally, it's important not to miss the forest for the trees: For both the finite and for the infinite case, the central thoughts are concretely empty ideas and, pretty certainly, they're analytically empty, too.[13]

---

13. Lately, there has arisen a worry that women have not been cited enough in recent philosophy, perhaps most especially in what I've called recent mainstream philosophy. However important, or unimportant, that worry might be, I shall now do bit to cite some very able women who have been writing a good deal on the matters addressed in this chapter, and also on the pretty closely related questions the next chapter addresses.

There is an issue of *Philosophy Compass* which, under the heading METAPHYSICS, pairs together these two papers: "The Puzzles of Material Constitution," L. A. Paul, *Philosophy Compass*, Volume 5, Issue 7, (2010), pages 579–90 and "The Controversy over the Existence of Ordinary Objects," Amie L. Thomasson, *Philosophy Compass*, Volume 5, Issue 7, (2010), pages 591–601.

As may become clear when reading even just her paper's first four sentences, Paul is using "material constitution", and cognate terms, in a highly technical way, a way quite far removed from ordinary usage:

6. Using These Sentences Differently and Expressing Substantial Ideas

At least to all appearances, as far as our world's material realm is concerned, we live in a fundamentally fairly gradual world. Still, there are many abrupt phenomena, even among readily perceived phenomena.

For one example of that, there's this: A certain river-crossing bridge may be just barely able to bear a certain load near the center of its river-crossing

---

Consider a statue made of a piece of clay. Call the statue 'Statue' and the piece of clay 'Clay.' Clay materially constitutes statue. What is this relation? (page 579)

Toward making my comment clear, recall that, when discussing Fine's "The Non-Identity of a Material Thing and Its Matter," in note 4 of this chapter, I observed that it is not really ordinary usage to say "a statue is made of a piece of clay"; rather, much more in line with ordinary practice is to say "a statue is made of clay". (Also quite ordinary is to say, e.g., "that piece of clay is made of red clay and this piece of clay is made of grey clay". One almost longs for "the bad old days".) With that being so, it is apparent, I think, that the mentioned "relation of material constitution" isn't any very ordinary relation. And, with *that* being so, I can't say much, with any confidence, about the ins and outs of this paper. But, perhaps, one thing that I can say is this: In the paper's second half, Paul places on offer quite a lot by way of (often competing) philosophical explanations. Very possibly, I think, what Paul there offers is, at a very general level, the *sort of accounting* that Fine thinks is needed somewhere in this neck of woods, the sort of thing that, still reckoning things only very generally, he calls for in his "Coincidence and Form". At all events, beyond what may be some few quite parochial ideas, I can no more find any novel concretely substantial thoughts in Paul's paper than in either of, or both of, the papers by Fine that I have just recalled for our renewed attention.

By contrast with Paul's piece, Thomasson's paper is not nearly so heavily involved in technical philosophical matters. Insofar as it goes, I agree with most of its philosophical claims, as most seem almost as unremarkable as they are sensible. (On matters of philosophy's recent history, I am sure she largely misses the mark, however unimportant that lapse may be—probably quite unimportant, indeed.)

As regards this book's central thrust, however, both papers are perfectly on a par with each other, and they are on a par, as well, with the works I've discussed by such prominent male authors as Putnam, Davidson, Kripke, and Fine, to mention just four mainstream men. As with the works of these four males, and as with the paper by Paul just cited, beyond what may be some few quite parochial ideas, I cannot find any novel concretely substantial thoughts in Thomasson's cited paper, either. Apparently, it is not because almost all the most prominent mainstreamers are male philosophers that recent and current mainstream philosophy is so terribly replete with empty ideas, and so lacking in novel nonparochial concretely substantial ideas.

This note is already too long, I fear, and I still have some observations to make, which certainly should here be made, concerning the citations made in the three papers lately mostly in focus, that by Fine and, especially, those by Paul and by Thomasson. To that observational work I now turn.

First, in the two papers found in *Philosophy Compass*, neither author cites any work produced by the other. Second, each of them cites several of her own works. Third, each of them cites work produced by still other contemporary women philosophers, even though (when properly placing aside self-citation) each cites at least eight times as many male philosophers as females. Fourth, there is considerable overlap in the works by women cited by our two authors. Here are the works that both of them cite: Lynne Rudder Baker, "Why Constitution is Not Identity," *Journal of Philosophy*, Vol. XCIV, 1997, Karen Bennett, "Spatio-temporal Coincidence and the Grounding Problem," *Philosophical Studies*, 2004, and Judith Jarvis Thomson, "Parthood and Identity Across Time" *Journal of Philosophy*, 80, 1983. Notice that Kit Fine also cites the first two of these three papers, and so they have already appeared in previous notes to this very chapter. The citation of a work by Thomson, however, does have these notes feature yet another work by yet another female philosopher.

span. Just so, when a load even just a tad greater than that is placed near the bridge's center, the bridge will collapse. All of a sudden, much of what spanned the river will break apart from the rest of the bridge, and it will fall into the river.

For a second example, evidently much more extreme, there's this: An enormously powerful bomb may be dropped on the bridge, perhaps from a bomber-plane flying high above it. Upon impact with the bridge, the bomb will explode and the bridge will be blown "sky high". When that happens, all the matter that served to compose the bridge will suddenly come to compose nothing more cohesive than millions of tiny pieces of matter, each spatially distant from all the others.

Being pretty proficient in recognizing which empty ideas are correct thoughts, and which are incorrect, it's with some fairly considerable confidence that I'll endorse this next pair of analytically empty propositions: In the first case, with a bridge collapsing under a very heavy load, the bridge will still exist; it will just be that there's a badly broken bridge, a bridge in need of repair, where before there was a bridge in no need of repair. In the second case, the case of the pulverizing big bomb, an opposite empty idea will hold true. This bombed bridge will cease to exist (whether or not it ever later exists).

Let's focus on the second case, where our bridge doesn't survive the destructive effects of the powerful exploding bomb. Why did the bridge fail to survive that? In answer to this question, there are many things correctly to be said. Of course, each of them is consistent with all the others, even while some are very impressively detailed and, at another extreme, others are so very unspecific as to appear almost pointless.

For making much philosophical progress, it may be useful to ponder some of the very unspecific responses. With that in mind, consider this: Our bridge ceased to exist when it was so very destructively bombarded because, in our world's current Eon, *no ordinary material complex can survive* such a very destructive event as that extremely powerful explosion, as such an explosion will radically tear asunder the complex's matter.

With several of the sentences just lately placed on offer, I've adverted to some substantial thoughts about concrete reality, even if none of them should be any philosophically important idea. (Or, at the least, that will be so, providing that we grant—quite as I *am* now granting—that there *are* such things as river-crossing bridges, and very heavy loads, and very explosively destructive bombs, and so on.)

One such concretely substantial but currently uninteresting thought is this proposition, a thought that's as safe to assert as it's peculiarly specified:

> There are river-crossing bridges that, though they *won't collapse* under a load *of two tons*, placed at, or near, the center of their span, certainly *will collapse* under a load of *two million tons* placed there.

Now, if we all knew extremely little about the actual world, then the thought just so safely asserted might be, at least for us, a pretty interesting thought. But, of course, that's purely hypothetical. As things actually are, the contemplation of this safely proffered proposition isn't intellectually interesting.

Saliently related to the uninteresting substantial idea just encountered, there's this very different substantial thought, also quite uninteresting:

> There are bombs that are so very destructively explosive that, when one is dropped on a river-crossing bridge, and it explodes upon impact, the bomb will blow the bridge into very many mutually separate and distant tiny smithereens.

In fairly short order, I'd like to place on offer some still other happily substantial thoughts. By contrast with those just displayed, they may be more interesting.

In preparation for our encounter with the more interesting thoughts, it's useful to rehearse a couple of analytically empty ideas, both suggested by this section's opening passages. Here's the first of them, apparently a quite correct empty idea:

> If there's placed, near the center of the span of a river-crossing bridge, such a very great load that the bridge then and there collapses, and if, beyond this, nothing more momentous than that ever happens with the bridge, or with its constituting matter, then the bridge *will continue to exist* (though it will be, of course, a bridge in a state of collapse).

And, here's another analytically empty proposition, also quite correct, as far as I can tell:

> If there's dropped, near the center of the span of a river-crossing bridge, such a very powerfully destructive bomb as will cause the whole bridge to be blown into millions of tiny separate smithereens, and if, beyond this, nothing at all notable ever happens with the bridge, or with the resulting smithereens, or with their constituting matter, then the bridge *won't continue to exist*.

Very far from any such empty ideas, we're waiting to confront some substantial thoughts, advertised as being at least a little bit interesting.

To that end, we return to consider our much-discussed malleable lump of copper. And, for vivid impact, we'll now get real, as they say. So, we'll now consider not anything whose matter is perfectly continuous, but something made entirely of actual copper, comprising very many copper atoms. Though composed of just so many atoms, even such entirely realistic copper will be, under any ordinary conditions, very malleable stuff. Now, when this malleable matter undergoes one of our purely shape-transformative processes, as with, say, Rectoration, then, under ordinary conditions, there's *nothing radically distinctive* that ever takes place, as far as anything *fundamental to concrete reality* goes. As far as what's materially fundamental goes, there'll be nothing absolutely destructive, or completely annihilational, that occurs during a process of Rectoration, which will, on the contrary, proceed in such a gradual way as to be utterly boring. Whatever takes place at any one point, in such an actual process, it will be a very great deal like what goes on at neighboring points of the process. It's just this that happens with, for instance, the nicely smooth material change from the potato-like shape of a copper lump to the rectangular brick-like shape obtaining at a Rectoration's end.

By contrast with that, we may conceive concrete possible worlds very different from our own—and distantly past Eons of our actual world, possibly very different from our present Eon. In these very different situations, there may be *matter* that is, in certain ways, fundamentally propensitied very differently from how our currently actual matter's basically propensitied. One way for there to be such a materially salient propensitive difference is this: Peculiar matter may be so peculiarly propensitied that, while it *will continue to exist through certain* ranges of the shapes it might (be imagined to) assume, still, and in the very same bargain, *it won't continue to exist upon its (being on the verge of) assuming other shapes*, shapes that *aren't* within those ranges. In such an event as that, the matter will be absolutely annihilated. That matter will cease to exist.

A fairly specific example of that dovetails with our recent discussion of Rectoration: When some lumpily shaped matter is on the verge of forming something with corners, that matter suddenly ceases to exist, quite as it's propensitied to do, without it's ever assuming a shape even just rather like the shape of a truly rectangular solid. At least in my own idiolect, a nice way to describe such a terribly anti-rectilinear situation is to say that (with the far-fetched concrete reality currently considered) a *lump* of matter *can't survive* a process of Rectoration. Equally all right, we might indicate the *substantial* point at which we're now aiming by employing somewhat different words. Just so, we might say, to quite the same effect, that a lumpy *piece* of matter can't survive Rectoration. And, also equally all right, to that same effect we might use still different words: Freestanding *matter* that's shaped in a lumpy way *can't survive* Rectoration.

There are other possible concrete worlds where, at least in my idiolect, it will be fine to say each of the first two things just indicated, but wrong to say the third and last thing. But, then, what am I getting at, here? I will explain.

Worlds where matter suddenly ceases to exist, rather than coming to be shaped in any "propensitively forbidden form" are, we may say, worlds whose (previously) persisting material particulars fail to persist in *the most radical way for* such a particular so to fail. But, with certain *other* conceivable worlds, we may have *only fairly radical ways for* the material persistents to cease to exist. I will explain.

In some of these other worlds, this may happen: When some lumpily shaped matter is on the verge of forming something with corners, that matter suddenly breaks apart rather radically, forming millions of tiny descendant pieces all flying asunder, each quite distant from all the others. Here, *none of the matter* ceases to exist.

In this section, we've already managed to contemplate two very different sorts of concrete worlds, each with a sort of a material realm propensitively very different from the other's, and each very different, as well, from (what we suppose to be) the actual world's current material realm. In thinking about how things happen in these worlds, we entertain thoughts that are concretely substantial ideas. That much is crystal clear. What's not so clear is whether these concretely substantial thoughts are characteristically philosophical ideas. But, that may not be a terribly important question. For what's quite clear enough is at least this. Even as those thoughts concern how it is with certain material concreta quite fundamentally, they're certainly *not any parochial* thoughts.

As with the novel substantial philosophical ideas featured in the previous two chapters, one may well ask how interesting are those encountered here. For a pretty fair answer, I refer you to our Mantra, found near the third chapter's end. That supplies this good short answer: Though more impressive than quite trivial thoughts, still, at this present time, at least, they're not very interesting.

7. Fundamentals of Fundamental Material Persistents

Canvassing the concretely substantial persistence-thoughts this chapter's considered so far, I doubt that any of them is true of our actual world, at least during this current multi-billion-year Eon. In this section, by contrast, I'll try to articulate some substantial thoughts about material persistents that may well be true of our actual current reality. But, I will not begin so realistically.

Certain presumably basic physical particles may annihilate, or they may self-annihilate—with various results, in various cases. In a most extreme case of this sort, at the end there's no physical remains of the particle that annihilates. As well, nothing remains of *the matter* that, at our case's start, wholly constituted the basic concretum. As we may suppose, in at least some of these terribly extreme cases, what occurs isn't a purely random happening. Even given just that much, we do well to ask: *Why* did our imagined particle *cease to exist*? And, *why did our particle's matter cease to exist?*

Now, with purely random happenings, there's nothing to be understood. But, with other happenings, there *is* something that may be understood. In these more intelligible cases, the particle in question will have a *propensity to annihilate*. In cases of *this* sort, a particle will have ceased to exist *because*, first, it *had* a propensity for so ceasing and, second, the particle will have *manifested* that propensity. And, so it will be, too, for the propensitied *matter* serving to constitute the particle in question.

In some intelligible cases, a particle's propensity to cease may be perfectly deterministic: First, the propensity may be deterministically set to be manifested, in just a certain range of conditions and, second, the particular condition of its manifestation, within that range, may be deterministically set to obtain. As may have been fully determined, for example, the particle may always be propensitied so that it will continue to exist for as long there's at least one electron within a meter of its center and, on the other side of that propensitive profile, it may be always fully disposed to *cease to exist otherwise*, that is, in case there's *not* any electron that nearby. So, when it comes to pass that there's no longer even a single electron within a meter of the concretum's center, an event that may itself have been fully determined to occur, then, quite certainly, that basic particle self-annihilates and, in the event, it ceases to exist.

What's true for our particle may hold true, as well, for the matter of which it is composed. So, our particle's *matter* may always be propensitied in just the way we just specified for our deterministically annihilated particle. When the conditions for the propensity's manifestation obtain, as they presumably must do, then the matter itself ceases to exist, just as it was then destined to do.

Reflection on that brings up these complementary ideas, not yet explicitly articulated for our imagined particle: Just as holds true of its constituting matter, our basic material individual is *so propensitied* that, when *other* conditions obtain—other than those "triggering" its annihilation, of course—the particle will *continue to exist*. We *won't now* suppose that, until the time when its annihilation-conducive conditions obtained, it was just purely *random* that the basic particle *continued to exist*—there then having occurred, so to say, a series of happy accidents to just such a persistent effect! To the contrary, the substantial supposition here is that, just as our same considered concretum is deterministically propensitied to *cease* when *certain* conditions obtain, so it's deterministically propensitied to *continue to exist*—that is, it's just so propensitied *not to cease*—when *any other* conditions obtain. And, what may be said for the particle may also be said for its constituting matter: Even as *this matter* is deterministically propensitied simply to annihilate when *certain* conditions obtain, so *it's* deterministically propensitied to *continue to exist* when *any other* conditions obtain.

Though I don't fully understand what's what with (at least putative) matters of objective probability, I'm happy enough to allow that there really are, in basic concrete reality, irreducibly probabilistic phenomena—an idea that many very smart people think makes perfect sense to them and, what's more, an idea many take to be correct, as well.

In line with this, I'll happily allow that, in some possible worlds, at least—and maybe in this actual world, right now—various particles are propensitied probabilistically, with certain particles having certain probabilistic propensities, even while certain others have certain other probabilistic proclivities. Apparently, that may happen in a very wide variety of ways. One way for this to happen is for a particle to be thus propensitied to only a very, very low degree. For example, according to some grand theories, a proton has a probabilistic propensity to decay with an enormously long "half-life", about 10^{33} years. (By contrast, the so-called Big Bang is thought to have occurred only about 13.7×10^9 years ago; so, as many leading physicists still think the (so-called) *universe* has existed for only that many years.) On those assumptions, it's only to a very, very low degree that a given proton is probabilistically propensitied to cease to exist within the next day. Conversely, it's to a very, very high degree that it's probabilistically propensitied to exist for more than a day.[14]

Considering one of our protons, we may take it that the enormously low objective chance that it will decay within a day and the enormously high chance that it will continue for at least a day sum to exactly one. On that sensible supposition, it *won't be a purely random matter* whether the particle ceases to exist, within the next day, or whether it does not. Rather, this matter will be probabilistically determined by the manifestation of the particle's propensities—perhaps along with other factors.

Now, I'm well aware that, according to contemporary particle theory, neither protons nor neutrons are considered to be any truly elementary particles, unlike our still-exalted electrons. But, while this prevents my exposition's being, all at once, both highly dramatic and utterly realistic, it does little to detract from what's here the main point.[15] According to contemporary physics,

14. In striking contrast with protons, free neutrons have a short half-life: When a neutron isn't ("stabilized," by being) combined with protons in an atom's nucleus, a neutron will decay with a half-life of around 10.3 minutes! Given this *very different* proposition, (I'll say that) it's to quite a high degree that a given free neutron is probabilistically propensitied to cease to exist within the next day.

15. Even as the state of play, in particle theory, is almost spookily fascinating, I'll provide, in this note, an accessible description of it, penned by a leading physicist.

Though electrons are elementary particles, both protons and neutrons are composed of certain sorts of quarks, up-quarks and down-quarks, with each of the last two being a different sort of elementary particle. On page 52 of (the paperback edition of) his book *The Cosmic Landscape*, Leonard Susskind tells us this about that:

> Quarks are in some ways similar to electrons, although somewhat heavier, and they have peculiar electric charges. In order to have a basis for comparison, the charge of the proton is traditionally taken to be one (+1). The electron's charge is equally big but opposite in sigh (−1). Quarks, on the other hand, have charges that are fractions of the proton charge. In particular, the charges of the u-, c-, and t-quarks are positive, like the proton's, but only two-thirds as big (2/3). The d-, s-, and b-quarks have negative charges equal to one-third the electron charge (−1/3).

electrons *are* perfectly elementary particles and they're expected *never to decay,
never to self-annihilate*. Typically, they're all taken to last *forever*—well, for the
whole future of our so-called observable universe.

At all events, with particles just like our protons, we may expect that,
during any even moderately short period, only a very, very small fraction of
them will cease to exist, perhaps a fraction so small that beings anything much
like humans will never detect even so much as a single such particle's annihilation, and cessation.

Just for the sake of an argument both vivid and instructive, let's suppose
that, during the past century, only one of our planet's very many protons ceased
to exist. In way of a real explanation of this particular particle's cessation, is
there anything to be said? Yes; there is. Though it's neither very detailed nor
especially informative, what follows the next colon, and completes this very
paragraph, will be a real explanation of that: The particle was probabilistically
propensitied to cease, even if only to a very, very low degree. And, though its
cessation was very unlikely to happen, during the time period in question, its
propensity to cease actually was manifested. So, rather than there being any
purely random happening here, it was owing to (the manifestation of) its propensity to annihilate that our considered proton ceased to exist.

On the other side of the same logical coin, we may also give an explanation, at least as real and as good, of the continued existence of a certain proton,
over the course of a certain human's long lifetime, say, 100 years. As should be
clear, this explanation will be at least as good as the explanation of why it was
that our self-annihilating proton ceased to exist, during just such a relevantly
short period. Indeed, as we're now explaining only what's to be expected, this
may be, in salient ways, a better explanation. Just so this following account
complements the explanation offered in the previous paragraph: To a *very, very
high* degree, this (still-existing) proton was *probabilistically propensitied to persist*. No
surprise at all, what came to pass was this enormously likely manifestation of
how this particle was propensitied. So, far from any random happening, *that's
why* the proton *continued to exist*, and that's why, right now, *it (still) does exist*.

In this section, I've presented both several empty thoughts and also several
substantial ideas. As I hope, the empty ideas may provide some useful instruction

---

Both protons and neutrons have three quarks. In the case of the proton, there are two
u-quarks [up-quarks] and a single d-quark [down-quark]. Adding up the electric charges
of these three quarks, the result is the charge of the proton: $2/3 + 2/3 - 1/3 = 1$.

The neutron is very similar to the proton, the difference being that the up-and down-
quarks are interchanged. Thus, the neutron contains two d-quarks and one u-quark.
Again adding the three charges, we find the neutron has (as expected) no electric
charge: $2/3 - 1/3 - 1/3 = 0$.

My paperback, published by Little, Brown and Company, appeared a year after that same company first published, in 2005, the original hardcover edition.

or clarification. Complementing those empty ideas, there's this substantial thought that's suggested by them: At least in certain possible worlds, apparently including this actual world of ours, there *are basic physical concreta propensitied to continue to exist*, whether they're so disposed quite deterministically or whether they're so propensitied only probabilistically. And, in a perfect parallel with that, there'll also be this perfectly substantial proposition: Even as much of the world's matter serves to compose these basic physical concreta, so much of our world's matter is propensitied to persist, whether deterministically or whether only probabilistically. Unlike many of (the pretty novel philosophical) substantial thoughts I've previously offered in this book, these more recently proffered substantial claims aren't any very far-fetched propositions. To the contrary, these latest substantial ideas about material persistence are, as far as we can tell, perfectly true or, at least, very nearly true.

6

EMPTY DEBATES ABOUT
MATERIAL MATTERS

As we've been increasingly observing, for decades prominent analytic philosophers have accepted *Scientiphicalism*. Even if they should hold that there
are concrete worlds where this metaphysics fails to hold, as only a minute
minority may do, they take our actual world to be a Scientiphically Respectable world. Now, near the start of this book, I articulated, in a sketchy way, a
certain main form of our Scientiphical View, namely, a Particulate Form of
the View. On this Form, as you may recall, there are many perfectly fundamental concreta, each a completely insensate, absolutely elementary physical
particle, each disposed for dynamical interaction with many other such particles. As almost goes without saying, each of the particles is spatially (or spatiotemporally) related to all the others.[1] And, each *ordinary* physical individual,

1. On one version of this Particulate view, I take pains to notice, though the particles will all
have (at least relative) spatial location, they'll not have any spatial extension; rather, each will be a
dynamically powerful *point-particle*, in an utterly strict sense of that term. Famously, Roger Boscovitch upheld this view; apparently, Immanuel Kant also embraced it, during his pre-critical period.
A nice feature of this version is that, at least apparently, it doesn't allow for the particles to have any
parts, not even in a very lenient sense of the term. But, on any natural expression of it, this version
will suggest many debatable issues. Though they all prove to be empty issues, in this book's discussion they needn't be discussed.

On another version of a Particulate Scientiphicalism, substantially different from the Boscovitchian, the basic particles *will be spatially extended*, as Isaac Newton held, even as each will be composed of (the very same amount of) absolutely continuous and homogenous matter. Now, just for

like my refrigerator, will be a *complex physical entity* wholly composed, most fundamentally, of just so many of these basic physical particles. What's more, *all the powers of the physical complex* in question, here my old fridge, will be *physically derivative propensities*, deriving from the basic powers of that complex's fundamental constituents, along with how the particles are physically related, each to all the others, even while they're all freestanding enough from other physical concreta.

When framing a Scientiphical Metaphysic in the way just suggested, I use ordinary words for *certain physical complexes*, as when I refer to my *refrigerator*. But, nowadays, a fair number of mainstream philosophers would object to my natural and intuitive rendition of the Scientiphical Metaphysic—even while many others may rush to defend my rendition.

In terribly unspecific terms, I've adverted to some salient philosophical argumentation. Very briefly, I'll do a bit to specify the *first part* of such a dispute, as might be said. I do that through contriving an objector who expresses her stance with words like these: "As you've been presenting the View, Scientiphicalism holds that there are physical individuals other than all the simple basic physical entities. In addition to them, you've said, there will be numerous and various complex nonbasic material entities. But, that can't be right. At least near enough, the only actual physical individuals—or entities, or beings, are those that are basic and simple (or perhaps just a single simple and basic physical thing). So, either Scientiphicalism must be presented in a better way or you should forget about attempting to sketch any such allegedly widely shared worldview." Later in this chapter, I'll present this objection in more detail and, on the other side, I'll present a detailed defense of my rendition. Discussing it all, I'll conclude that, between the two sides, no substantial question is at issue.

Before encountering that, it may be instructive, I think, to notice some other ways of objecting to my readable rendition, ways that are both closely related to the one I've just indicated and also are peculiarly different from it. Let me explain or, better, let us explore.

---

being so wholly composed of just such matter, it's natural and comfortable to think that these Newtonian particles won't have any natural parts, or significantly substantial parts, or nonarbitrary parts. Placing aside (analytically empty) questions concerning what parts a Newtonian particle may or may not have, on this conception there'll be suggested, perhaps, fewer debatable issues than with the discomforting Boscovitchian conception. (But, a fair lot will be suggested here, too, it should be realized, with a Newtonian style of Particulate Scientiphicalism. As with the debatable issues suggested by the Boscovitchian ideas, those suggested by the correlative Newtonian ideas will also be analytically empty questions.) Largely to provide an exposition that's pretty reader-friendly, our discussion will proceed along a quasi-Newtonian path; even as we will assume that our world's elementary particles are both spatially (or spatiotemporally) located and also spatially (or spatiotemporally) extended. For historical background on Boscovitch, Kant, and Newton, see Thomas Holden, *The Architecture of Matter*, Oxford University Press, 2004.

1. Matter Distributed Particulately, but Not Even a Single Material Individual?

Though it's seldom noticed, here is another objection to my rendition of Sci-entiphicalism and, of course, to any idea that presumes the existence of ordi-nary spatial things, like my refrigerator. From at least certain perspectives—I don't say from all—this neighboring objection appears to be prior to, or more fundamental than, the fairly familiar one, briefly expressed in this chapter's preamble. To my mind, at least, here's an easily accessible rendering of this seldom seen objection: "As you've been presenting the View, Scientiphicalism holds that there are physical individuals (some simple and basic and others not). But, that can't be right. At least near enough, all that there is, in actual physical reality, is just so much *physical stuff*, or just so much *matter*, in a lenient sense of that time-honored term. So, either you must provide a much better presenta-tion of Scientiphicalism or you should forget about attempting to sketch any such allegedly widely shared worldview." Now, as it will be useful to have a memorable label for one who may make this objection, I'll call any such person a *Nihilist about Material Individuality*.

Central to the objection just noted, this Nihilism is meant to be an abso-lutely comprehensive and universal position, so far as physical reality is con-cerned. Just so, our Nihilist doesn't have in mind, and she doesn't want to rely on, anything at all peculiar, or particular, about how things are with our actual world's matter; she doesn't care about how it is spatially (or spatiotemporally) distributed, or about how any of it is propertied or modified, or about whether or not it's perfectly continuous, and so on. No matter how things stand with our world's matter, she holds, none of it will be the matter of any physical indi-vidual. Our Nihilist about Material Individuality means her view to be an *abso-lutely radical* position concerning physical reality.

To appreciate the terribly radical character of this Nihilism, it will be useful for us to contemplate a materially rich concrete world where all the matter is spatially distributed and happily modified in a most particulate manner or, in fewer words, it's all distributed *particulately*. In this world, most of the space will be entirely empty, utterly devoid of matter, with just a little of the world's matter occupying one small spherical spatial region and, quite far away from that, just a little more of the world's matter occupying another small spherical spatial region, and so on. Now, according to our newly noticed Nihilist, even in such a nicely particulate world as this, reminiscent of what Newton envisioned, there *aren't* any *material* individuals. While there's lots of matter all distributed particulately, still, there are no material individuals, ob-jects, entities, or beings that any of the matter ever serves to compose, not even any spherical material particles. Quite simply, there's only ever just the matter itself, distributed and modified in just a certain absolutely specific particulate way.[2]

According to my presentation of Scientiphicalism, a world with matter arranged particulately may well be a world wherein particles serve to compose complex physical objects, or quite ordinary physical spatial inhabitants, as with my actual fridge, composed of very many particles. So, my sketchy presentation conflicts with Nihilism about Material Individuality. But, what sort of issue, or issues, does the conflict concern? As I suggest, they're concretely empty questions.

2. Matter Distributed Particulately, but Only a Single Material Individual?

Concerning the material matters we've been discussing, however empty they may be, there's another seldom noticed position available, one that's nearly as radical as our newly noticed Nihilism. Moreover, quite readily and easily, this other position may be made as salient as that newly noted Nihilism. I'll call this potentially salient view *Monism about Material Individuality*.

On this Monism, no matter how things stand with a concrete world's matter—or however it is materially in a concrete world—there will always be, in the world, just one material individual.

In application to a world whose matter is distributed and modified in a most happily particulate way, the verdicts of this Monism will centrally include the following propositions: First, there will be, in such a happy world, all that particulately distributed matter; on this positive point, our Monism will agree with our Nihilism (and also with my sketchy presentation of Scientiphicalism).

---

2. To the best of my knowledge, few prominent mainstreamers even so much as consider the Nihilism just sketched. One who does consider it, or a view very like it, is Peter van Inwagen, as in his excellent textbook, *Metaphysics*, Third Edition, Westview Press, 2009, page 30ff. And, in that writing, he may also be just about the only salient mainstreamer who considers the Monism just sketched, or some view very like it. Unfortunately, to my mind, he takes a view of matter, or of (material) stuff, on which a world with material simples must be a world whose matter is all absolutely alike, as with perhaps a world with Newtonian particles. But, "matter," "material," and "stuff" are, I take it, rather flexible terms. So, a world may have as its material simples just protons and electrons and neutrons, pretty much as Neils Bohr and his contemporaries hypothesized. Where there are that world's electrons, the world's matter is charged negatively electrically; where there are its protons, the matter is charged positively, and where there are the neutrons, the matter isn't electrically charged at all. Myself, I can find nothing terribly untoward in the thought roughly expressed by the sentence directly preceding.

Though I won't discuss their views, at least a couple of other mainstreamers are exercised by something like the Nihilism I've roughly outlined. For salient examples, see the Introduction to Ted Sider's *Four-Dimensionalism*, Oxford University Press, 2001, especially pages xvii–xviii, and see the (at least apparently) radical "Towards Ontological Nihilism," *Philosophical Studies*, 79 (1995) by Andrew Cortens and John O'Leary-Hawthorne. (That last is John Hawthorne.)

But, second, and against that Nihilism, this Monism says that our particulately distributed matter does serve to compose at least one material entity. Third, finally and rather radically, our Monism will say that, even in such a world as this, there won't ever be more than just one material individual.

What sort of physical entity will it be that, on this Monism, is the only individual even in a world most of whose space is empty and all of whose matter is distributed particulately? At least near enough, it will be what many philosophers have called a *scattered object* or, spelled out more fully, a *(spatially) scattered (material) object*. Some of the material individual is here and, spatially quite distant from whatever of the individual is here, some of the very same material individual is way over there. (Talking in terms friendly to this Monism, various situations will have various things be rightly said. For example, if there's more matter right here than there is way over there, then *more of* the single scattered material thing is right here than is over there—and, conversely, *less of* the material thing is over there.)

But, of course, as far as the *number* of material individuals goes, we've already said all there'll ever be to say: No matter how a world's matter may be distributed and modified, the number of material individuals in that world will be exactly *one*.

3. Matter and Material Objects: Salient Positions on Empty Questions

As concerns the number of material individuals in a material world whose matter is all distributed particulately, we've observed three things to be said, each with at least some appeal.

First, and most appealing to almost everyone, it may be said that, in such a world, there'll be many perfectly distinct and numerically different physical individuals; at the very least, there'll be many quite simple and basic particles. Using an apt term, we may call those who say this first thing *Pluralists about Material Individuals*. No doubt, most mainstreamers are such Pluralists.

Second, and as our noted Nihilist does, it may be said that, even with a world whose matter is all distributed and modified in such a nicely particulate manner, as concerns how things stand materially with that world, there's only the world's matter that's ever present anywhere; in contrast to that, there never are any material individuals.

Third, and as our noted Monist does, it may be said that, even in such a nice world as we're currently considering, there's always just a single (spatially scattered) material entity that's ever anywhere in the world, an object whose matter is, at any time, all the matter of the world.

With a world with matter distributed particulately, do any of these mutually conflicting positions *differ substantially* from any of the others? Is there any concretely substantial difference among this Nihilism, this Monism, and this Pluralism? I don't think so. And, the analytic emptiness will prevail, as well, for any nonparticulate concrete material reality.

Happily, we're about to engage with the centerpiece of the chapter, the *Debate about Complex Material Individuals*. As I see things, it's been a useful exercise for us to have gone through, before that, the thoughts of the chapter's first three sections, which in an obvious sense may be considered prior questions, perhaps more basic empty issues. But, you may ask, in doing that, haven't I just conjured up all too many straw men? Far from it, in the literature, there are very many more such strange positions than those few I've considered and, to my mind, the big lot includes quite a few stranger than any we've here seen. Just look and see.[3]

4. The Debate about Complex Material Individuals

Wedded to commonsense, as they are, the vast majority of mainstream philosophers are Pluralists about Material Individuality, even as most accept the sketched Scientiphicalism. But a small minority has, in recent decades, been very vigorous in denying the ordinary objects of commonsense, denying the likes of tables, chairs, rocks, and stones. Though they are Pluralists about Material Individuality, they will also object to my rendition of Scientiphicalism.

More extreme than what any of these philosophers have held, as best I can tell, is the thought that, however things may be with material individuals that are basic and simple, there *never will be any complex physical entities*. This pretty extreme view may be called *Nihilism about Complex Material Individuals*. Even as there may never be anyone who holds this position—I myself never did so—it provides a useful point of reference for describing a debate that, during the past several decades, has figured quite prominently in mainstream philosophy, the *Debate about Complex Material Individuals*. Directly, I turn to explore this prominent debate.

Opposing our Nihilism about Complex Material Individuals, there are, in this debate, two main sorts of standard philosophical figures. One of them is *diametrically opposed* to this Nihilism, while the other is *less than diametrically* opposed. In turn, I'll introduce them.

Diametrically opposed to our noted Nihilism, there are philosophers whom we may call *Universalists about Complex Material Individuals*. According to these Universalists, whenever there are several (two or more) basic or simple material entities, those basic material objects will serve to compose another material entity,

3. In the most widely used of philosophical reference sources, see Mark Stern's "The Metaphysics of Mass Expressions," *The Stanford Encyclopedia of Philosophy (Winter 2012 Edition)*, Edward N. Zalta (ed.), URL = <http://plato.stanford.edu/archives/win2012/entries/metaphysics-massexpress/>.

more complex than the individuals composing it. Not to be conflated with any or all of its components, the complex is yet another material individual.

What's the central thrust of that pretty unpleasantly abstract verbiage? Consider an electron that's among the many trillions now "in your right big toe" (and, presumably, that's now serving, along with very many other elementary particles, to compose that toe). And, consider, as well, a certain up-quark that's somewhere in the planet Mars (and, presumably, that's serving to compose that planet). Naturally enough, let's suppose that our considered electron is a *basic* material individual (as are all its world's other electrons), and our considered up-quark is *also a basic* material entity (as are all its world's other up-quarks). Finally, let's suppose that these two considered basic particulars, the electron in your toe and the Martian quark, aren't related (to each other) in any even just apparently important way, as concerns anything like ordinary questions of how it is that simple material things might serve to compose more complex material things. Colloquially put, neither basic physical thing "has anything much to do with the other."

Along with our compositional Nihilists, most folks won't think that *these* two elementary particles serve to compose *anything at all*; much less will they suppose that there's a single material individual that's composed of just those two basic material objects. By contrast, our Universalists *do* hold that just those two indicated particulars, the electron on earth and the up-quark on Mars, serve to compose a further thing. (What's more, that further thing, which they together compose, is *also a physical individual*. As most of them may well hold, this composite object has a certain mass, which mass is the sum of the masses of its two [slightly] massive constituents. And, as they all should hold, this composed individual's matter will be widely scattered, as compared with the tiny spaces occupied by each constituent.)

Third, and finally, there are those participants, in this debate, who hold some sort of middle position, more generous than our perfectly niggardly Nihilism, but less generous than our perfectly profligate Universalism. These comparative moderates hold that, in *some* circumstances, there'll be basic material things that together wholly compose a complex material individual— presumably, at least partly in virtue of how it is that, in those very circumstances, the basic physical objects are physically related to each other. And, of course, the moderates will also hold that, in *some other* circumstances, there'll be *only* a plurality of basic physical things, and not any complex material entities. By contrast with both our Nihilists and our Universalists, those holding this position may be aptly called *Moderates about Complex Material Individuals*.[4]

4. The debate we're considering needn't be presented using the term "compose" or any cognate expression. So, even if the debate may be aptly characterized as semantic, first, that's not the only way for it to be properly considered and, second, the semantic debate we're considering doesn't turn on just some small semantic niceties. Here's one way to appreciate what's just been claimed and, with that, the scope of the debate in focus: Return to consider our envisioned electron

Provided the actual world has the complement of elementary particles that we usually take it to have, and that these particles really are our world's basic physical individuals, most typical Moderates will be *Commonsensical Moderates*. These typical Moderates hold that not only do sticks and stones actually exist, but that each stick is a complex material individual, a complex composed of very many much simpler and more basic physical concreta, and so is each stone. (Berkeley also held that sticks and stones do exist. By contrast with our typical Moderates, he *didn't* take them to be any *material* things.)

Others of our currently contemplated Moderates will be far more severe about these presently pondered matters. Indeed, the views of these *Anti-Commonsensical Moderates* may be quite close to our Nihilism about Complex Material Individuals. For example, in his *Material Beings*, Peter van Inwagen holds that material simples compose a complex material entity only when they are so related as to compose a *living* material complex, as with a live rosebush.[5]

Now, the Debate about Complex Material Individuals has been contested with great vigor and considerable ingenuity, over more years than just a few. A good testament to that may be found in this writing from Ted Sider, starting off his paper "Ontological Realism":

> In 1987, Peter van Inwagen asked a good question.…He asked: what do you have to do to some objects to get them to compose something—to bring into existence some further thing made up of those objects? Glue them together or what?
>
> Some said that you don't have to do anything. No matter what you do to the objects, they'll always compose something further, even if they're scattered. Thus we learned of the fusion of the coins in our pockets with the Eiffel tower.
>
> Others said that the objects have to be fastened together in some way, the way that the things we usually think about are. But van Inwagen taught us of people stuck or glued or sewn or fused to each other. Such entanglements, van Inwagen thought, create no new entities.
>
> Others said that nothing you could do to the objects would make them compose something further. According to these "Nihilists," tables, chairs, computers, molecules, people, and other composite objects, simply don't exist. All that exist are subatomic particles "arranged table-wise," arranged "chair-wise," and so on.[6]

---

on earth and our up-quark on Mars. Now, suppose that, all of a sudden, all the other basic physical individuals cease to exist. So, as we're supposing, now there are precisely two basic and simple material things, one of them our up-quark and the other our electron. Now, our Nihilist will hold, of course, that in this physically quite impoverished world, these two things are the only material entities. And, any even half-way sensible Moderate will agree. But, our Universalist will say that, in this case, there are three material individuals, the quark, the electron and a scattered thing that, in certain ways, is greater than either of them.

5. Peter van Inwagen, *Material Beings*, Cornell University Press, 1990.

6. Theodore Sider, "Ontological Realism," in David Chalmers, David Manley, and Ryan Wasserman, (eds.), *Metametaphysics*, Oxford University Press, 2009, pages 384–423. In the passage I've

Questions about what's alive placed well to the side, van Inwagen agrees with our Nihilist. In stark contrast with that, and following W. V. Quine and David Lewis, here Sider agrees with our Universalist (though it's not important for the cited paper that Universalism be favored).[7]

That said, it's well worth noticing that our Nihilist needn't be anyone's fool. A good testament to that may be found in this writing from van Inwagen:

> To make things as simple as possible, let us suppose that chairs—if there are any—are made entirely of wood and let us suppose (though nothing remotely like this is true) that any object that is "made entirely of wood" is composed of simples called "wood-particles." Now consider those regions of space that, according to those who believe in the existence of chairs, are occupied by chairs. Call them chair-receptacles. One of these chair-receptacles is beneath me as I write. Call it R. I concede the truth of this proposition:
>
> (A) The chair-receptacle R is filled with rigidly interlocking wood-particles; the regions immediately contiguous with R contain no wood-particles; the wood-particles at the boundary of R (that is the wood-particles in R that are not entirely surrounded by wood-particles) are bonded to nearby wood-particles much more strongly than they are bonded to the non-wood-particles immediately outside R; the strength of the mutual bondings of wood-particles within R is large in comparison with the forces produced by casual human muscular exertions.
>
> What [I endorse doesn't entail] the denial of . . . (A), but rather [it entails the denial of] the two following theses (and therefore the proposition that either of them is entailed by (A)):

---

quoted, Sider cites these following philosophical works. First, of course, there are some works by Peter van Inwagen; there's his 1987 paper "When Are Objects Parts?" in James Tomberlin (ed.), *Philosophical Perspectives 1: Metaphysics*, 21–47, Ridgeview; and there's his book *Material Beings*, cited in the first note for this present chapter. For what I've called the Universalist position—"you don't have to do anything special"—he cites W. V. O. Quine, "Whither Physical Objects," in R. S. Cohen, P. K. Feyerabend, and M. W. Wartofsky (eds.), *Essays in Memory of Imre Lakatos*, 497–504, Dordrecht, Holland: D. Reidel Publishing Company, 1976; and he cites David K. Lewis, *On the Plurality of Worlds*, Oxford: Basil Blackwell, 1986, pages 212–13. As for our currently considered Nihilism, Sider cites Cian Dorr, *The Simplicity of Everything*, Ph.D. thesis, Princeton University, 2002. (As well, Sider observes that locutions like "arranged table-wise" were coined by van Inwagen in his *Material Beings*.)

Directly after the paragraphs quoted in our text, Sider has this following short paragraph, about van Inwagen's own view on the currently fashionable question of (alleged) material composite objects, one that ends with a delightfully humorous (bracketed) sentence:

> Van Inwagen himself also dispensed with tables and chairs, but departed from the Universalists by admitting people and other living things into his ontology. (Why he spared the living few could tell.)

In our terminology, then, Van Inwagen was a peculiar sort of Moderate, one whose view, on this question, is decidedly closer to our Nihilist's position than it is to our Universalist's.

7. For Quine, a locus classicus is W. V. Quine, *Word and Object*, MIT Press, 1960, though Sider cites his "Whither Physical Objects," as indicated in note 5 to this chapter. For Lewis, a locus classicus is his *On the Plurality of Worlds*, cited by Sider, and indicated in that same note.

(B) There is something that fits exactly into R.

(C) There is something that the wood-particles within R compose.

Now if either (B) or (C) were true, there would be a chair. If either of them is false, then there are no chairs. (Or, at least, there is no chair in R.) Because it is (B) and (C) that I deny, and not (A), I am a metaphysician and not a madman.[8]

With the aid of that selection, this is tolerably clear: First, van Inwagen holds that, where we should ordinarily take a certain single chair to be, there is plenty enough by way of materiality.

Before I cite another passage from *Material Beings*, let me make this potentially clarifying suggestion: Between van Inwagen's Anti-Commonsensical Moderate View and the more generous view of most folk innocent of philosophy, there is a certain disagreement about the likes of tables and chairs. But, unlike the disagreement that these folks may have with a madman, this might not be a *concretely substantial* disagreement.

5. An Exploration of the Salient Debate: Popular Paraphrases, Problematic Parallels

Only a few pages after the passage I've just cited, van Inwagen starts his chapter on (what he calls) *paraphrase*. It's here that he coins some "adverbs of arrangement," saliently including the by now philosophically popular predicates "chairwise" and "tablewise." For exploring the Debate on which we're focusing, here's a most relevant selection from that writing:

> Let us consider the problem of how to paraphrase the sentence 'Some chairs are heavier than some tables' in language that does not appear to make reference to, and does not appear to presuppose the existence of, anything material besides simples. I shall help myself to three variably polyadic predicates: 'are arranged chairwise,' 'are arranged tablewise,' and 'are heavier than.' The Xs are arranged chair- (table-) wise if they fill a chair- (table-) receptacle and satisfy certain conditions that can be gleaned from an inspection of proposition (A) of the preceding section. For the Xs to be arranged chairwise is as much a matter of their contrast with their surroundings as it is of their distribution in space. Thus, the simples occupying a chair-shaped and chair-sized region of space that falls entirely within a certain tree are not arranged chairwise, though they would be if the rest of the tree were stripped away. Simples arranged chairwise do not, of course, compose a chair or anything else (unless there should be chair-shaped living things). The third predicate, which could

8. Peter van Inwagen, *Material Beings*, pp. 104–105. Where I've inserted the square-bracketed phrase, [I endorse], van Inwagen has "my answer to the Special Composition Question." I do that because, in this present context, discussion of that Question will be a distraction.

also be written as 'are collectively heavier than,' seems to me to be unprob-
lematical. There is nothing unclear about such sentences as 'The weights on
the left-hand balance are (collectively) heavier than the weights on the right'
and 'The pebbles in the jar are heavier than the jar and the lid.'

We are now ready to consider a paraphrase of 'Some chairs are heavier
than some tables':

> There are Xs that are arranged chairwise and there are Ys that are
> arranged tablewise and the Xs are heavier than the Ys.[9]

For the points of most interest to us here, we do well to consider, in the style of
van Inwagen, paraphrases of just the most simple and boring sentences in our
Debate's neighborhood, as with 'There is at least one chair' and 'There is at
least one table.' For the first, the paraphrase is 'There are Xs that are arranged
chairwise'; for the second, it's the obvious counterpart.

Toward reasoning instructively, let's suppose that each of the paraphrastic
predicates contained in these boring sentences is perfectly equivalent semantically
to the ordinary English predicate that's its counterpart. That will help to promote
what may be a happily illustrative debate between the (moderately) nihilistically
inclined likes of van Inwagen and, on the other side, the friends of tables and
chairs. Quite well enough, I'll suggest, this debate may be regarded as revolving
around what we should make of (the propositions expressed by) certain English
conditional sentences, including this one that, in chapter 1, was placed in display:

> COMPOSITE TABLES: If there are, at a certain time in a certain spatial
> region, very many particles arranged tablewise, there is, then and there, a
> composite *table*.[10]

As you may recall, when commenting on the proposition this sentence (at least
apparently) expresses, I made some remarks about several positions one may
take in the Debate about Complex Material Individuals. In the present context,
we do well to partition these positions like this: On one side of our partition,
there'll be the Nihilists about Complex Material Individuals as well as nihilistically inclined Anti-Commonsensical Moderates, like van Inwagen. On our
partition's other side, there'll be both our Universalists about Complex Material Individuals as well as the many Moderates who are commonsensical, not
nihilistically, inclined.

Anyway, those remarks of mine were to this effect: Thinkers on the more
nihilistic side of the present dispute can say this: No material simples can ever
be so related in a manner that's conducive *enough* toward there being tables *for*

9. *Material Beings*, p. 109.
10. In the present book, the displayed conditional first appeared in Chapter 1, section 3.

there ever to be any tables. Why so? Well, the putative tables in focus would have to be material *complexes* and, so, not any material simples. But, in truth, the only real material existents are just so many perfectly simple material things.

With all that said, we may take it that the debate concerns the truth of, or the untruth of, COMPOSITE TABLES. And, with that being so, we may take it that this debate concerns no concretely substantial issues. This will be so even if there may be an obviously correct answer to the empty question debated, presumably the table-friendly answer (and, just as well, it will be so even if there may be no correct answer).

I've just said the most important thing to say about the debated conditional proposition. Still, there may be further points worth noticing in connection with that conditional thought, points concerning how it may differ from certain other empty ideas. Let's give that a try.

6. Complex Material Individuals and Arrangements of Simple Material Individuals

Toward noticing some potentially interesting empty ideas, at least very modestly interesting, I'll begin by rehearsing a conditional sentence first displayed in our first chapter:

> TABLEWISE ARRANGEMENTS: If there are, at a certain time in a certain spatial region, very many particles arranged tablewise, there will be, then and there, a tablewise *arrangement* (of particles).

Now, let's juxtapose the sentence just displayed above, in the preceding section:

> COMPOSITE TABLES: If there are, at a certain time in a certain spatial region, very many particles arranged tablewise, there is, then and there, a composite *table*.

When we consider the thoughts expressed by these two juxtaposed sentences, this following question is almost bound to strike us: Supposing that some material simples *compose* a complex table, and supposing that these same material simples *are in* a tablewise arrangement, as they'll then quite certainly (have to) be, is that complex table *the very same thing as* this tablewise arrangement or, alternatively, is the complex table *one* thing while, perhaps always actually perfectly spatially coincident with the table, the tablewise arrangement is *something else?*[11]

---

11. We may do well to compare that question to this nicely parallel one: Supposing that some copper composes a table, and supposing that the very same copper is in a tablewise arrangement,

As I'll argue, the complex table is one thing and, even if always wholly co-incident with it, the tablewise arrangement is something else.

Here's one argument for that: A complex material table has many nonre-lational physical properties—saliently including (properties concerning) the mass of the object. So, a certain table may have a mass of 10 kilograms—if the mass isn't one of that table's properties, then, at the *very least*, one of its proper-ties is *having a mass of 10 kilograms*. By contrast with the comparatively robust likes of a table, an *arrangement*, even an arrangement of massive objects, doesn't have any mass, or the property of having mass. Suppose that you arrange some furniture in your study like this: You place two large lamps on a massive desk, and you slide a wheeled chair partly under that desk. Well, then, there's now this arrangement of that relevantly massive furniture. But, that mere arrange-ment, as with any arrangement, is not itself pretty heavy or massive. Nor are things relevantly different with tablewise arrangements. So, no complex mate-rial table is any arrangement, not even any tablewise arrangement of basic in-dividuals.

Here's a second argument for the diversity favored: Suppose that the matter of a complex material table is, indeed, in a tablewise arrangement. Then there will be the tablewise arrangement of the table's matter. Well, this material table may be happily bisected, with the result being two saliently dis-tinct material individuals (usually neither a table) each spatially very distant from the other. In such an event, there will no longer be a tablewise arrange-ment of the (bisected) table's matter, or a tablewise arrangement of its material constituents. Indeed, there won't be any tablewise arrangement (of anything) at all. But, there will still be the table; it will just be broken. So, again, no complex material table is ever any tablewise arrangement.

As I've argued twice over, a complex material table isn't ever any arrange-ment at all. Even without the arguments, I'd believe that to be true. Still, there are many other things I more strongly believe. One is this: Insofar as it's an intelligible issue, the question of whether a complex material table is ever a tablewise arrangement is an empty issue.

7. Mereological Sums of Simple Material Individuals: Fusions, Fusions Everywhere

In the last several sections, our discussion of the Debate about Complex Mate-rial Individuals has explored the Nihilistic position, and certain Moderate posi-tions, especially those that are nihilistically inclined. By contrast, I'll now move

---

is the copper table the very same thing as the tablewise arrangement of the copper or, alternatively, is the copper table one thing and the tablewise arrangement something else?

to focus mainly on Universalism about Complex Material Individuals. As we'll recall, according to this Universalist, whenever there are several (two or more) utterly basic material individuals, or perfectly simple material entities, those simply basic material individuals will serve to compose a complex material individual, which complex physical entity will be yet *another* material individual.[12]

Our Universalists are philosophers who, like Lewis, Quine, and quite a few lesser lights, give the "laziest" possible answer to van Inwagen's question: "What do you have to do to some objects to get them to compose something— to bring into existence some further thing made up of those objects?" These thinkers will say such relevantly "lazy" things as this: "You don't have to do anything at all. As long as you don't annihilate the simple material things, well, they'll *always* compose something. Indeed, they'll always compose something that's as fully and fairly a material thing as any of them. Thus, without anyone's taking pains to produce it, there'll be the fusion of the coins in your pockets and the Eiffel tower. Though it will be a quite widely scattered entity, this fusion will be as fully and fairly a material thing as is any of the coins."

What are we to make of these material fusions, of mereological sums of material individuals? For a good look at what a Universalist may have in mind, I'll cite Lewis:

> I claim that mereological composition is unrestricted: any old class of things has a mereological sum. Whenever there are some things no matter how disparate and unrelated, there is something composed of just those things. Even a class of things out of different worlds has a mereological sum. That sum is a trans-world individual. It overlaps each world that is a part of it, and so is partly in each of many worlds.
>
> We are happy enough with mereological sums of things that contrast with their surroundings more than they do with one another; and that are adjacent, stick together, and act jointly. We are more reluctant to affirm the existence of mereological sums that are disparate and scattered and go their separate ways. A typical problem case is a fleet: the ships contrast with their surroundings more than with one another, they act jointly, but they are not adjacent nor do they stick together. A class of things from different worlds may do well on the first desideratum, but it will fail miserably on the other three. Far from being adjacent, these things will not be spatiotemporally related in any way; they can exert no cohesive forces whatever on one another, nor can they have any joint effects. . . . So if composition could be restricted in accordance with our intuitions about this-worldly cases, then doubtless trans-world composition would fall under the ban.

12. With extreme caution, there may be Universalists who say just this: Whenever there are two or more simpler material things—and especially, perhaps, whenever there are two (or more) basic and simple material individuals, those material individuals will compose yet another thing, *whether or not* this other individual is a *material* thing. But, as such caution appears wholly unmotivated, I won't give any special attention to this extremely cautious proposition.

But composition cannot be restricted in accordance with our this-worldly cases, as I shall shortly argue.... The simple principle of absolutely unrestricted composition should be accepted as true.[13]

Appended to the last sentence displayed just above, Lewis has a striking footnote:

I really do mean *absolutely* unrestricted—for instance, I see no bar to composition of sets with individuals, or particulars with universals, or cats with numbers. But here it will be enough to consider the composition of particular individuals.[14]

Even as absolutely any items may be mereologically summed, all that's necessarily *material* about a material mereological sum is that the things fused are wholly material things. There's nothing material, or physical, about the fusing of these material things, or about how it is that the material things composing the sum should be related to each other.[15]

At all events, this much seems absolutely clear to me: Even as it's technically laid down that *mereologically summing* must occur providing only that there is more than one item anywhere or anywhen, it's an analytically empty truth that two material individuals will mereologically sum to mereologically compose yet another entity, more complex than either.

Sometimes the material individuals mereologically summed will be fairly well ordered, physically or otherwise, as with the sum comprising just the ships in a certain fleet. More interestingly, perhaps, sometimes the individuals summed will be very well ordered physically, and maybe otherwise, too, as with the sum of just those perfectly elementary particles wholly composing a certain fully material ship.[16] In this latter case, we may notice this: Occupying exactly the space precisely occupied by that single ship, and sharing with it exactly the same matter, there'll be the sum of all the basic material individuals, and only

---

13. Lewis, *On the Plurality of Worlds*, pp. 211–12.

14. *Loc cit.*, p. 212.

15. As with quite a few other areas that have exercised mainstream philosophers, there is a vast literature on mereology. For an overview, see Varzi, Achille, "Mereology," *The Stanford Encyclopedia of Philosophy (Winter 2012 Edition)*, Edward N. Zalta (ed.), URL = <http://plato.stanford.edu/archives/win2012/entries/mereology/>. The body of this entry runs to more than 17,000 words, and is followed by a very lengthy list of Cited Works, in turn followed by a list of Monographs and Collections devoted to the topic, comprising twenty-four volumes. For mainstream philosophers, the most salient author of any of these twenty-four books is, of course, David Lewis, there represented by his *Parts of Classes*, Oxford: Blackwell, 1991.

16. For those unacquainted with mereology, this perfectly good case of a sum, the sum of the particles composing a certain ship, well, it won't be any example that will helpfully introduce them to mereological thinking. But, as should be perfectly clear, that's not any metaphysically significant consideration.

them, that are the basic material constituents of that very vessel. That observation leads to related questions.

Is the ship just considered the very same thing as the mereological sum just contemplated or, alternatively, is the ship one material thing and, numerically different from it, the material mereological sum quite another material item? Let's explore the question.

8. Sums of Simple Physical Entities and Complex *Ordinary Material Individuals*

To see this question as reasonably challenging, we'll make some happy suppositions about the mereological sum we're considering. So, for one thing, we'll assume that the mereological sum is, at the time considered, exactly where there's the nice ship. Indeed, any region really occupied by the ship is, we'll assume, also occupied by the sum, and vice versa. And, as we'll also assume, any physically important feature of the table, such as its mass, is also a feature of the sum: Just as the mass of the table is equal to the sum of the masses of its constituent particles, so the mereological sum has a mass equal to the sum of the particles summed. I'll be charitable about all this, perhaps even to the point of absurdity. Even so, we'll be able to argue quite effectively.

By considering some thoughts as to persistence conditions, we'll have enough to show what's what. On the most standard way of thinking of fusions, they are what Kit Fine has called *aggregates*.[17] Now, it is laid down that an aggregative fusion, or an aggregative sum, will exist as long as even just one of the items fused to form it still exists. So, a composite table won't be one of these standard mereological fusions, or sums: For, first, when all but one of a composite table's many particles is absolutely annihilated, and nothing else relevant happens here, the table will no longer exist. But, second, the aggregative fusion with which the table once coincided, it will still exist. Again, the aggregative fusion, or sum, isn't a table.

There is another way of thinking about mereological fusions or sums that, insofar as one can have intuitions about such formal critters, seems more intuitive to me: Perhaps along with others, Fine suggested that there be recognized another sort of fusion, or sum, which he calls *compounds*. This time, it is laid down that a compound fusion, or a compound sum, will exist only as long as every single one of the items fused to form it, or summed to form it, still exists. So, a composite table won't be a compound fusion, or sum, either: For, first,

---

17. My main source on fusions is Kit Fine, "Compounds and Aggregates," *Noûs* 28:2 (1994), 137–58. Generally, when I talk about mereological sums, in this chapter, or about fusions, it will be about what Fine calls compounds, or compound fusions, that I am concerned.

when just a single one of a composite table's many particles is absolutely annihilated, and nothing else relevant changes, the table will still exist. But,
second, the compound fusion or sum won't still exist. As with an aggregative
fusion, a compound fusion isn't a table.

Some fast friends of compound fusions may respond with these words:
Perhaps a compound sum of particles might be a certain very peculiarly vulnerable sort of table, a table that must cease to exist should even a single one of
its parts, however miniscule and peripheral, cease to be. That response is pre-
posterous on its face. What else may we say against that poor response?

Return to consider our Extruder. When having the table's matter, and its
particles, put through the Extruder, the table will cease to be, at least for the
meanwhile. But, even during the meanwhile, there will still exist the mereological fusion or sum of those particles. So, once again, we may rightly conclude that the complex table is one thing and, quite unlike it in telling ways, the
compound fusion of its simple particles isn't the table, or any table, at all.

Here is a correlative consideration: When discussing complex tables and
correlative tablewise arrangements, we noted that only the former can directly
survive, or could directly survive, a standard bisection. As we may now notice,
as with our table, our mereological sum, whether it is compound or whether it
is aggregative, can also survive such a bisection process. But, again, that's not
so with our arrangement. Our tablewise arrangement of particles isn't a mereological sum of particles and, of course, vice versa.

Even without argument, I'd think the noted differences to hold true. Still,
there are many other things that I more strongly believe, including this: The
question of whether a complex material table is ever a mereological sum is a
concretely empty issue, as is the question of whether either of those is ever a
tablewise arrangement, or any arrangement at all.

9. Four Distinct Sorts of *Spatial Inhabitants:* Material Mereological Sums, Material Arrangements, Complex Material Objects, and (Complex) Ordinary Individuals

As aptly patient reflection suggests, there are several assumptions shared by
many participants in the Debate about Complex Material Individuals. Here
are three such assumptions, with some parenthetical commentary provided for
just the first of them, much of it applicable to the others:

> The First Assumption: Actual tables and chairs, if there really are any such things,
> *are all material objects* and, what's more, they're all *complex* material objects, each
> wholly composed, most fundamentally, of certain simple and basic material ob-
> jects (or, in the nonparticulate case, of just some of a single basic material object).

(This is not a strictly necessary truth, as thoughts of Berkeley, for example, suffice to show. But, even when Berkeley is placed aside, it's quite doubtful, really, whether this assumption is even true at all, even during the current eon of the actual world. Indeed, as I'll be arguing, even utterly materialist philosophers should think this Assumption is nowhere near being true. In presenting my arguments against the First Assumption, I'll choose pieces of reasoning that, with only minor variations or extensions, can be deployed, to an equally devastating effect, against the two other Assumptions, which I'll now list.)

> The Second Assumption: Nihilists about Tables and Chairs, if they're to have a consistently sustainable position, must all be Nihilists about Complex Material (Individuals and) Objects. And, conversely, the Nihilists about Complex Material (Individuals and) Objects, if *they're* to have a consistently sustainable position, must all be Nihilists about Tables and Chairs.

> The Third Assumption: Those who uphold unrestricted mereological composition, if they're to have a consistently sustainable position, must all also uphold the existence of many tables and many chairs. What's more, each of the many tables will be a certain mereological sum, distinct from all other such sums, as with also each of the many chairs.

Though they're widely accepted, none of these Assumptions is even close to being correct.

Here's an argument for the First Assumption's inadequacy: A typical table may be broken into two (roughly) equal pieces, equal as concerns both their mass and their volume. Hearkening back to the previous chapter, our typical table may be a purely *copper* table, even though, of course, in a nicely particulate world, a copper table won't be composed of continuous matter. Let's call it *Tab*. Now, at least temporarily spatially coincident with Tab—some would say at least temporarily identical with Tab—there's a certain single material something that, in our particulate actual world, is as good a candidate for being a complex *material object* as is anything in this world. Let's call this apparently existing material object *Milton Oscar* or, for short, *MO*. Imaginatively, let's perform a distancing bisection on the matter at hand, thus performing one, as well, on Tab and on MO. Well, when this bisection is complete, each of the two most salient "material resultants," one being *Melvin Richard* and the other *Martin Robert*, will be a complex material object, as well.

Now, as is very clear, when our considered table, Tab, was neatly broken in two, it *didn't cease to exist*, not even for a moment. (A table that's been neatly broken in two is, once that's done, a broken *table*—quite as a table that's been fully disassembled is, once *that's* done, a disassembled *table*. Just as broken mechanical clocks are clocks, and disassembled clocks are clocks, so broken tables are tables. In our example, the bisection just makes Tab be broken.)

By contrast with all that, when, in the very same process, our considered material object, MO, was neatly broken, it *did* cease to exist, at least temporarily. (Whether or not MO *may yet later* exist—as *perhaps* may happen should all its original matter come to be "arranged" as it was before the bisection, well, that's another question entirely, irrelevant to the present issue.)

Not very sensitive to the proper use of our fairly ordinary expression "material object," a few will balk at what I've just said. To heighten their sensitivity and to foster agreement, it will help to notice this contrast case. Alternatively, we may neatly break MO into two *terribly unequal* resultants, one *far greater* than the other, both as to volume and as to mass. One of the resultants has very nearly all of MO's original matter, while the other, a tiny object, has hardly any. Now, in this very different case, our original material object, MO, *won't* cease to exist, not even temporarily. Rather, precisely where there's the far larger resultant, that's where MO would be; now slightly smaller than it just was, MO still exists. With that appreciated, it will be agreed that, in our case of bisection, by contrast, MO *does cease* to exist, at least temporarily. But, then, and as I'll remind us, our table, Tab, *doesn't cease* to exist, at all. So, our complex table, Tab, is one thing and, numerically different from it, our complex material object, MO, is something else.

Here's another argument to the same effect, but one that, in an obvious way, runs oppositely: Again we consider our original copper table, Tab. This time we don't do any bisectional breaking. Rather, we put Tab through our Extruder. As agreed in an earlier section, once our process of Extrusion is complete, *Tab ceases to exist*, at least temporarily. Not noted earlier, we now ask this question: Once our Extrusion is complete, *does our material object, MO, cease to exist?* Pretty obviously, the answer is "No." MO still exists; it's merely that, owing to the Extrusion, its shape is now very different from before. So, by a different route, we again arrive at our conclusion: Our complex table, Tab, is one thing and, numerically different from it, our complex material object, MO, is something else.[18]

18. As may be easily confirmed, the foregoing arguments have *nothing to do with the complexity* of the items involved. The very same arguments, or perfect parallels of them, work just as effectively to further the thought that any material table at all is one thing and, numerically different from it, a spatially coincident material object composed of just that table's matter is something else, again. From the just previous chapter, recall the material individuals entirely composed of perfectly continuous and homogeneous matter, each of them surrounded by perfectly empty space. In certain concrete worlds, there will be tables entirely composed of such matter, with none of them being relevantly complex. Then, at least temporarily spatially coincident with those tables, these worlds will feature table-shaped material objects, with none of *them* being relevantly complex. As our arguments show, each of those (partless) tables will be numerically different from each of those (partless, table-shaped) material objects.

As also seems true, those arguments also have nothing to do with the materiality of the items involved. For, a follower of Berkeley may run perfectly parallel arguments, thereby distinguishing between the likes of tables and the likes of some apt idealist counterpart of whatever may best answer to our ordinary notion of a material object.

Now, there are some philosophers, aptly enough called *Nihilists about Material Ordinary Things*, who deny that there really are any tables, and any chairs. These philosophers need not deny, as far as I can tell, that there are material objects, or any other sort of material concreta. (Indeed, perhaps some of them may embrace the idea that there are complex material individuals.) In support of that claim, I'll reference, in the note appended to this very sentence, several of my early publications, wherein I provided arguments for Nihilism about Material Ordinary Things.[19] As I'm pretty sure, nowhere in those papers is there any argument for Nihilism about Complex Material Individuals. Anyway, that's enough about the First Assumption, extremely doubtful for even thoroughly materialistic philosophers.

When presenting our Three Assumptions, I said (parenthetically) that, when I'd argue against the First, I'd "choose pieces of reasoning that, with only minor variations or extensions, can be deployed, to an equally devastating effect, against the other Assumptions." As most readers can readily see, I've done just that. Accordingly, I won't bother to take up space here spelling out arguments against these other Assumptions.[20]

Instead of trying your patience with many words along those lines, I'll now move toward closing the section and, with it, the chapter. I'll begin this movement with some happily general thoughts about the philosophical neighborhood of the Debate about Complex Material Individuals, the linchpin of the chapter we're now closing: It has long been assumed, ever so widely, that those who go in for unrestricted mereological composition will have far more than enough, in their ontology, to satisfy our commonsense thoughts as to existing tables and chairs, and actually extant sticks and stones. Or, as we may put it artfully, they'll have far more than enough to satisfy our commonsense thoughts

---

Given what's in the preceding paragraph, it may well be doubted that, in our thought concerning various sorts of recognized *spatial inhabitants*, to use a fairly apt highly general term, there may be little coherence, and a great deal of incoherence. But, then, I am uncertain here.

19. I do this in "There Are No Ordinary Things," *Synthese*, 41, 1979:117–54; and in "I Do Not Exist," pages 235–51 in *Perception and Identity*, G. F. MacDonald (ed.), London: The Macmillan Press, 1979; and in "Why There Are No People," *Midwest Studies in Philosophy*, IV.1979, pages 177–222, all of which are reprinted in my *Philosophical Papers, Volume 2*, Oxford University Press, 2006. And, as its title indicates, I do it, as well, in "Skepticism and Nihilism," *Noûs*, 14 (1980): 517–45, which is reprinted in my *Philosophical Papers, Volume 1*, Oxford University Press, 2006.

20. Almost every mainstream philosopher who's written at length on any of this chapter's main topics promotes conflations regarding the sorts of spatial inhabitants that, in this chapter, I am highlighting, even while signaling some differences among them. For an overview of much of the more salient writing on these topics see Korman, Daniel Z., "Ordinary Objects," *The Stanford Encyclopedia of Philosophy (Winter 2012 Edition)*, Edward N. Zalta (ed.), URL = <http://plato.stanford.edu/archives/win2012/entries/ordinary-objects/>. As it seems to me, even while there is quite a lot of instructive material here, at the same time there is, as well, material that promotes conflations concerning what are actually various different sorts of spatial inhabitants. Of course, this last bit does nothing to distinguish this entry from almost every last one of the very many writings whose ideas it explores.

as to existing *ordinary things*.[21] In that same bargain, of course, it's been assumed that the only real worry about what's placed on offer by these unrestricted mereologists is just this following trouble: They may be asking us to embrace *too many (sorts of) material things*—including, most saliently, all sorts of gerrymander-ish material things. But, as I've been arguing, the actual dialectical situation is really far more complicated than that. Placing aside, for the moment, the ques-tion of whether or not any tables are ever complex material objects, it is quite clear, as we've seen, that *no table is ever any mereological sum*. Indeed, even such a table as may be wholly composed of basic material particles isn't ever the mereological sum of the particles that, at any given time, are precisely all the basic constituents of the table.

As I've been observing, tables are no more any mereological sums of any-thing than ever they are *tablewise arrangements* of anything—even assuming that there really are the tables themselves, the mereological sums, and the tablewise arrangements. And, as I've also observed, none of those three (sorts of) things is any material object, and vice versa.

Just so, and in particular, those who want to do well by an ontology endors-ing the existence of (what I've called) *ordinary things*—as with tables and chairs, and as with sticks and stones—well, they *won't* get all they need (and then some) from those who offer little more than (what can be gotten through) unrestricted mereological composition. Rather, even while they'll then have to embrace, as real wholes, what will look to them to be unpleasantly gerrymanderish what-nots, that won't help them at all.

Along with much else in this chapter, we can quite neatly sum up most of this section's material, I think, like this: Let us say that complex material objects are a certain sort of *spatial inhabitants*, as are material arrangements (of material individuals), and as are also mereological sums of material objects, and as are, still yet further, very many ordinary things, like our familiar tables and chairs. Then any spatial inhabitant of *any one* of these four sorts of spatial inhabitants *isn't* a spatial inhabitant of *any of the three others*. For example, anything that's a material arrangement isn't a mereological sum, and it isn't a complex material object, and it isn't a material ordinary thing, like a stick made of matter, or a material stone. (Of course, if we expand our discussion so that it *includes both compound sums and also aggregative sums*, then there will be, in such situations, *at*

---

21. Certainly quite conspicuously and, as I hope, pretty usefully, I first made heavy use of this expression, "ordinary things," over thirty years ago, in my paper, "There Are No Ordinary Things," *Synthese*, 41, (1979). (As I also hope has been pretty useful, the paper is reprinted in Volume 2 of my *Philosophical Papers*, Oxford University Press, 2006.) Even while I was there arguing against the existence of all putative sticks and stones—indeed, against all *ordinary things*—it's always been clear that I was *not* arguing against the existence of *material objects*. So even in those early days, I was clear that, whether or not such ordinary things as sticks and stones existed, none of them would be (strictly identical with) any material objects and, of course, vice versa.

least five sorts of spatial inhabitants that we'll be discussing, each quite different from all the others.) The idea of all this mutual exclusivity is a thought for which, by this point, we've argued amply.

With what's just been provided, I've finished with all the *first-order philosophical matters* treated in the chapter. As with most other such first-order thoughts I've offered in the book, I'm not very confident about those I've favored here.

But, happily for the book's main message, we can be a lot more confident that none of this chapter's first-order thoughts is a concretely substantial idea. And, though not quite as confident as that, we can be pretty confident, at least, that the reason they're all concretely empty is that, in our aptly useful sense of the terms, they're all analytically empty ideas.

Worldy Appendix

Are There *Any* Concrete Worlds, Including Even the Actual World?

Broadly characterized, much of our sixth chapter concerned questions of material composition. Yet more broadly, some concerned (at least certain views of) composition quite generally, as with the fusions "mereologically composed" of pretty much any old sorts of items, whether material, or nonmaterial, or both, or neither. With that being so, this is a good place for me to make some observations pertaining to certain remarks made earlier in this book, remarks that are similar to many made by many mainstreamers over the last several decades.

At the time of this writing, it is still true to say that, on work currently done in mainstream philosophy, the influence of David Lewis is greater than that of any other recent philosopher, even if it may be that most of his great influence comes in the form of vigorous disagreement with ideas he placed on offer. As all mainstreamers well know, among the philosophically famous thoughts Lewis offered, the very most famous is that which he called "The Thesis of Plurality of Worlds", and which I'll call, *The Plurality Thesis*. At least at the heart of this thesis, there's a quite novel and sweeping idea that's concretely substantial.

At the same time, and as I'd now like to notice, surrounding that heart, there may be just so much quite optional verbiage, potentially contested by those who might disagree with the thesis, as Lewis proposed it, but then only in ways that are concretely empty ways, not engaging with him in any substantial disagreement. Of course, that cryptic critique needs explanation, which I now try to provide.

Very sparsely, we may focus on just whatever are taken to be the most basic inhabitants of any given one of Lewis's proposed worlds and, as well, on what we may take to be the most basic inhabitants of another. Using quite simple worlds, we will consider, on the one hand, the three basic inhabitants of a certain putative world, Wade, and we'll consider, on the other hand, the three basic inhabitants of another putative world, Walter. Supposing that Wade exists, we may say that Wade's basic inhabitants are just the three electrons Ed and Eve and Earl. And, supposing Walter to exist, we may say that Walter's basic inhabitants are just the three other electrons Elliot and Esther and Evangeline.

As we may now clearly notice, the heart of the Plurality Thesis is a quite sparse and simple thought that does not advert to worlds or, indeed, to any entities at all, beyond just the six electrons we're considering. According to all those dogmatically slumbering before awakened by Lewis, it was assumed that, as needs must be, any electron must be physically related to any other electron and, so, of course, externally related, in the bargain. Once awakened by Lewis, we no longer must make any such apparently quite optional assumption. Rather, we may take the previous paragraph's proposal, or its heart, to be this completely coherent idea: Even though Ed and Eve and Earl are all physically, and so externally, related to each other, and also Elliot and Esther and Evangeline are all physically related to *each* other, still it may be that none of Ed and Eve and Earl is physically related, or is externally related in any way, at all, to any of Elliot and Esther and Evangeline.

With no adverting to worlds, indeed, with no reification at all, it's thoughts quite like that one—an enormous infinity of them–that are just exactly what's most directly sanctioned by *the heart of* the Plurality Thesis. So, in effect, Lewis's expression of his Thesis *combines the concretely substantial heart with something else.* What is that something else? It is a positive view on a certain issue that, as seems quite clear to me, is a concretely empty issue. Well, then, what issue is that? At least roughly, and quite minimally, it is the issue of whether, when there is this concrete particular spatially related to that other concrete particular—or temporally related, or spatiotemporally related, or somehow otherwise externally related—there is, in addition to the related particulars, something else of which they are parts, or of which they are inhabitants, and which itself isn't similarly related to some yet other thing of which it is a part, or an inhabitant.

Now, it must be admitted, I fear, that Lewis's most salient writing readily raises the thought that even this empty issue is one of considerable philosophical importance. With unnecessary verbiage deleted, here's the first paragraph of (the body of) *On the Plurality of Worlds*:

> The world we live in is a very inclusive thing. Every stick and every stone you have ever seen is part of it. And so are you and I.... Anything at any distance at all is to be included. Likewise the world is inclusive in time.... No... long-gone primordial clouds of plasma are too far in the past, nor are the dead

dark stars too far in the future, to be part of this same world. Maybe, as I myself
think, the world is a big physical object; or maybe some parts of it are entel-
echies or spirits or auras or deities or other things unknown to physics. But
nothing is so alien in kind as not to be part of our world, provided only that it
does exist at some distance and direction from here, or at some time before or
after or simultaneous with now.[1]

The book's second paragraph talks about various ways in which our world
might have been different, adding only a bit to what's relevant now. But, the
third paragraph adds a lot:

> ...There are countless other worlds, other very inclusive things....The
> worlds are like remote planets; except that most of them are much bigger
> than mere planets, and they are not remote. Neither are they nearby. They are
> not at any spatial distance whatever from here. They are not far in the past or
> future, nor for that matter near; they are not at any temporal distance from
> now. They are isolated: there are no spatiotemporal relations at all between
> things that belong to different worlds. Nor does anything that happens at any
> one world cause anything to happen at another. Nor do they overlap; they
> have no parts in common, ...[2]

As it may well seem, then, for Lewis it's important not only that there be enormously many concreta each mutually isolated from each other, but it's important that many of them each belong to a world, and that each of these worlds
is mutually isolated from all the others. But, I'm not sure that Lewis really believes this. For one thing, it seems crazy to burden him with anything like the
following thought: When a certain electron is utterly isolated from another
electron, that always obtains indirectly, via the first belonging to a certain
world, and the other belonging to another world, with these two worlds being
mutually isolated. It's better to forget about the middlemen, I think, and, as I'd
like to think, Lewis might come to agree.

However, and as must be admitted, Lewis's famous paragraphs certainly
suggest a certain concretely empty dispute, expressed by me using the word
"concrete", a word that Lewis himself might prefer not to use. Anyhow, I will
call the dispute the *Debate about Concrete Worlds*. On one side of the debate, there
are the *Nihilists about Concrete Worlds*: When some concrete particulars are externally related to each other, however numerous and various should be the particulars, and however variously they may be externally related, that's all there
is to it, period. It's not that, in addition to that (and maybe in virtue of that)

---

1. David Lewis, *On the Plurality of Worlds*, Blackwell, 1986, p. 1.
2. Lewis, *On the Plurality of Worlds*, p. 2.

there's a concrete *world* that includes all those nicely related particulars (and not any others, unrelated to them spatially, temporally, causally, and otherwise externally). On the other side of this debate, there's everyone else. There are, on this other side, both the very many commonsensical *Monists about Concrete Worlds*—there's only one such world, the actual world. And, as well, there are, on this other side, the very few *Pluralists about Concrete Worlds*. Though it's in *some sense a worldly* matter that's at issue in this Debate, that's just in a punning sense, of course. At all events, this Debate concerns only a concretely empty issue, or perhaps several such empty issues.

To more than a few, what I've just been saying may *seem* to be an utterly *contrived* affair, perhaps even just a *parody* of real mainstream philosophy. But that's not so; indeed, it's not even a close call.

A single example may sufficiently attest to that fact. Published just shortly before most of this chapter's sentences were first composed, and published in what's long been academic philosophy's most prestigious journal, here are some sentences from Jonathan Schaffer:

> In particular I will assume that there is a world and that it has proper parts. More precisely, I assume that there is a maximal actual concrete object—*the cosmos*—of which all actual concrete objects are parts. I should stress that I am only concerned with actual concrete objects. *Possibilia*, *abstracta*, and actual concreta in categories other than object are not my concern...
>
> The assumption that there is a world with proper parts may seem modest and plausible, but it is certainly controversial, in at least two respects. First, it is controversial to assume that there are parthood relations at all. The nihilist holds that there are no actual—and perhaps even no possible—instances of the proper parthood relation. * Second, it is controversial to assume that there is a world. For instance, the organicist holds that there are only particles and organisms, and presumably the actual cosmos is neither. ** [3]

Quite clearly, the issue between Schaffer and his noted nihilist is a concretely empty issue, as is also the issue between him and his noted organicist. And, though these issues may be argued arduously, the questions are, I submit, of precious little consequence.

---

3. Jonathan Schaffer, "Monism: The Priority of the Whole," *Philosophical Review*, Vol. 119, N. 1, 2010, pp. 33–34. Where I've put an asterisk, Schaffer cites, as relevant nihilists, Gideon Rosen and Cian Dorr, "Composition as a Fiction," *The Blackwell Guide to Metaphysics*, ed. Richard Gale, Blackwell, 2002. Where I've put a double asterisk, he cites, as a relevant organicist, Peter van Inwagen, "who embraces the consequence that there is no world, paraphrasing 'the world' as a plural term". That citation directs us to page 127 of the second edition of van Inwagen's *Metaphysics*, Westview Press, 2002.

7

INDIVIDUALS, PROPERTIES
AND TIME

A Few Substantial Thoughts and Many Empty Ideas

In the just previous chapter, all the main debates and ideas critiqued were concretely empty, with the exception of some few that were highly parochial, concerning little more than how it is that some humans use those languages they employ. In each of the book's first three chapters, we encountered more than that. By contrast, in each of the three chapters right before that one, chapter 3, 4 and 5, there was, in addition to just so much emptiness and parochiality, the consideration of some novel concretely substantial characteristically philosophical ideas. But, as it certainly seems, at least in this present era, there is little or no reason to believe any of those new ideas. And, so, it seems that, at this present time, we needn't pursue them earnestly.

In this present chapter, one thing I'll do is steer a certain middle course between our earlier trio and our just previous chapter: On the one hand, in some large topic areas not yet discussed, I'll relate how almost everything offered, by prominent mainstreamers, will fall under either of our two somewhat dispiriting heads: Either it will be concretely empty, at least usually for being analytically empty, or else it will be far more parochial than properly philosophical. On the other hand, when we discuss some topics in the philosophy of time, we shall notice an important divide between issues of those two sorts: There we'll again note ideas that are just either empty or parochial, it's true, but, we'll also note some (even ancient ideas) that, at least to all appearances, are both concretely substantial and properly philosophical.

This last-noted question concerns whether events that have not yet oc-curred, and are not yet occurring, in any ordinary senses of those terms, never-theless have some sort of reality, anyway. Equally, of course, it will concern whether there are concrete entities, any people, for example, that, while they have never existed, and while they do not now exist, nonetheless have some sort of reality, anyway. In a phrase, this substantial philosophical issue is the ques-tion of whether there is "an open future". In what may be less metaphorical terms, it is the question of whether there are alternative ways for our actual world to develop, or fail to develop. (As I'll observe, this apparently concretely philosophical issue may be of great interest not only to philosophers. For, as it certainly appears, on the view that there *isn't* any open future, it may well follow that none of us will ever have any real options from which to choose and, so, that nobody ever really chooses ([from among any real options].) Now, none of this will be any novel concretely substantial material, all of it going at least as far back as Aristotle.[1] While lacking novelty—and no surprise here—these sub-stantial thoughts are quite plausible ideas. For that reason, they may be, for many philosophers, far more interesting than the novel philosophical thoughts, all concretely substantial, too, presented in chapters 3, 4 and 5.

But before turning to questions mainly concerned with time, some of them quite substantial and others, I think, entirely empty, I will first address, in this chapter, a philosophically salient topic that's orthogonal to any of those ques-tions. Accordingly, I'll begin by considering some apparently large questions concerning (i) on the one hand, how things may be with various entities, sali-ently including various concrete individuals, or concrete particulars, and (ii) on the other hand, how things may be with various properties, if there really are any such items, that the entities may be thought to have.

Given the recent history of analytic philosophy, there's good reason to treat these two topics in the same single chapter, *the topic of properties*, as I'll call the one, and *the topic of time*, as I'll call the other: As devotees of the mainstream literature know, that's due, in largest measure, to the enormous and central place, in this literature, occupied by the towering figure of David Lewis. Not only did Lewis write very influentially about properties and about time, but, as well, he wrote famously on issues occurring at the intersection of these two large topic areas. What I have in mind is, of course, the argumentation he offers by

---

1. According to historians of ancient philosophy, as best I can tell, Aristotle had it that there was, indeed, an open future, and offered argumentation to that effect, as with his thought about a possibly imminent sea battle. On his view, I'm told, with at least quite a few matters regarding the future, there simply *is no fact of the matter*. By contrast, of course, his opponents thought otherwise, taking it that, in this central regard, there was no difference between the future and the past; for them, *concerning absolutely all temporal matters, whether past or present or future, there really is a fact of the matter*. Full disclosure: Providing I've gotten the ancient philosopher right here, on this concretely substan-tial issue, I stand with Aristotle.

way of presenting, and by way of resolving, what he calls "the problem of temporary intrinsics", a topic I'll address in the chapter.

Trying to provide a most readable rendition of all that, I'll first discuss just the topic of properties and then, while not abandoning that topic, I'll begin to treat, as well, the topic of time.

1. Are There Really Any Properties or Are There Only All the Propertied Individuals?

In the introduction to Volume I of his *Philosophical Papers*, Lewis provides a brief list of "recurring themes that unify the papers in this volume".[2] Right now, it will be best for us to go no further than what, with good reason, occurs first on that list:

> Extreme modal realism, according to which there are many unactualized possible individuals, and according to which the actual individuals do not differ in kind from the unactualized ones.[3]

Pretty obviously, I think, Lewis means very little here by "do not differ in kind from". Indeed, it's pretty obvious that about all he means to convey is something like this: Even as the actual individuals really are concrete individuals, so all the many unactualized possible individuals *also really are concrete individuals*. The unactualized individuals aren't just some abstract templates for how an individual should be, for example; nor are they any other abstracta, for that matter.[4]

Anyhow, it's perfectly obvious that Lewis holds that there are actual individuals. In holding this, Lewis disagrees with, among others, the Nihilist about Material Individuality, whom we encountered early in the previous chapter. And, he'll similarly disagree with a Nihilist about Immaterial Individuality, who may allow that there's immaterial spiritual stuff, but no immaterial entities at all. And, perhaps, there are still others with whom he'll disagree. (Now, as I'm inclined to think, in all these parallel disputes, Lewis will be right and

---

2. David Lewis, *Philosophical Papers, Volume I*, Oxford University Press, 1983, p. xi.

3. Lewis, *loc. cit.*

4. He can't mean anything with much more punch than that. For example, he can't mean that, even as all the actual individuals are material or physical individuals, so the unactualized individuals are also material or physical. For he wants to allow, of course, that among the unactualized individuals there are spirits, and deities, and even Berkeleyan minds, I suppose. And he doesn't want to say that these are all material or physical. (Indeed, he's quite prepared to agree that, in almost any other context, we should say that material individuals *differ in kind from* such spirits, deities, and immaterial Berkeleyan minds.)

these extreme nihilists will be wrong. As I'm more than just inclined to think, these disputes concern only empty issues.)

Whatever it amounts to, exactly, it's fair to say that, at a bare minimum, Lewis holds there are concrete individuals. In this, he agrees, of course, with almost all other prominent mainstream philosophers. Having settled on that, these complementary questions arise: Are the concrete individuals all there is to concrete reality? (Or, in addition to all the concrete individuals, does concrete reality *also include something else*, so to say, or, perhaps, some several other things?) Some answer "Yes" to our leading question here, saying there *are only all the individuals*. (They will then answer "No", of course, to our complementary parenthetical question.) Let's say that each of them is a *Concrete Individualist*. And, let's say that, in addition to holding that *all there is to concrete reality are the concrete individuals*, this Individualist also holds that, in anything much like the sense in which philosophers use the term "property", there simply *aren't any properties* at all, not even a single one, whether concrete or whether otherwise. Pretty perversely, perhaps, I'm unconfidently inclined to agree with these Concrete Individualists, even while I take this agreement to concern only some empty ideas.[5]

It's pretty clear that Lewis denies Concrete Individualism, upholding an opposing view, or maybe even several opposing views. Let's discuss that.

There are several standard ways to disagree with our Concrete Individualist, each paralleling the others, but each also differing from the others. First, here's the parallel: On each of these ways, one will say that, in addition to all the individuals, there are *properties*, which various individuals may *have*, or *possess*. With

---

5. As I certainly grant, there are quite a few thoughts that, while they at least suggest the existence of certain properties, are taken by us all to be correct ideas. And, as it may very well be, these apparently quite correct thoughts even strictly entail the existence of properties. One correct thought to that effect, for example, is this idea: Many metals have several properties that are usually found in combination, as with the property of being ductile and the property of being malleable. That thought is, of course, equivalent to this one: There are several properties usually found in combination that many metals have, as with the property of being ductile and the property of being malleable. Perfectly obvious in the case of the second of those two equivalent thoughts, it is equally true that they both entail this next one: There are several properties. And, as is also obvious, that entailed thought entails, in turn, this yet simpler idea: There are properties. And, if any more should be needed here, we may note, just as well, that all of the foregoing will then entail this briefly expressed thought: Properties exist.

As I'll unconfidently respond to this observation, all it may show is that, like other natural languages, our language is a harmlessly defective linguistic device, whose standard employment may involve us in the reification of properties and, more directly on point here, in our acceptance of a statement to the effect that properties exist. When being reflectively serious, however, we may deny, quite at will, any such ideas as our linguistic involvement has us accept, temporarily holding our involvement in abeyance, and moving to an aptly stricter way of talking and thinking about the matters in question.

But, at all events, for the main issues this chapter concerns, none of that much matters.

that noted, we move to notice the differences among standard views that oppose
our nihilistic Concrete Individualism.

On the first of them, quite salient for Lewis, what it is for an individual to
have a certain property is just for the individual to be a member of a certain set
of individuals, the set whose members are absolutely all the individuals having
the property:

> We have frequent need, in one connection or other, to quantify over proper-
> ties. If we believe in possible worlds and individuals, and if we believe in
> set-theoretic constructions out of things we believe in, then we have entities
> suited to play the role of properties.
>
> The simplest plan is to take something just as a set of all its instances – *all*
> of them, this- and other-worldly alike. Thus the property of being a donkey
> comes out as the set of all donkeys, the donkeys of other worlds along with the
> donkeys of ours.[6]

If we take this Lewisian view, then we'll disagree with our Concrete Individualist in a way that, as may appear, isn't all that radical. For sets are abstract and,
accordingly, they are not any concrete items at all. So, taking this view, we may
still say that all there is to *concrete reality* are all the *concrete individuals*. And, then,
the disagreement may be just this: While our Concrete Individualist holds that
all there is to reality is *concrete* reality, her Lewisian opponent holds that there's
more to reality than just concrete reality, an issue upon which the Concrete Individualist may be agnostic and silent. Amplifying, the Lewisian thought is that reality
includes, in addition to all that's concrete, more than that, as well. Following
tradition, what's more may be regarded as *abstract* items, or *abstracta*.

Having said that, in this present discussion the only important thing left to say
is this. As I understand things now, it is no part of this thought of Lewis's that there
should be many mutually isolated worlds, in addition to our actual world. Rather,
this latter idea, concretely substantial, serves as a mere presupposition for, or of,
the idea as to properties being certain sets. Without that presupposition, this idea
may still make some sense, but it will be wildly and obviously false; in that sense or
respect, it will then be an absurd idea. Well, that's enough for the first way.

On the second way, quite salient in the metaphysics of David Armstrong, and
perhaps even in Aristotle, we take it that there is *more to concrete reality than just its individuals*, however variously propertied, and variously related, they may be.[7] In
addition to all the propertied concrete individuals, there are the *concrete properties of*
these individuals.[8] Armstrong calls these posited concreta *universals*. Accordingly,

---

6. Lewis, *On the Plurality of Worlds*, p. 50.

7. See D. M. Armstrong, *Universals and Scientific Realism*, Cambridge University Press, 1978.

8. And, there are the relations in which, typically, each of many concreta stand, with respect
to each of many other concrete individuals.

I will call his view, perhaps Aristotle's view, as well, *Concrete Universalism*. When contrasting his own view with Armstrong's Concrete Universalism, Lewis reserves the word "property" for the sets of individuals he favors, and he uses "universal" as a term *contrasting with* "property". On that, here are his words:

> Universals and properties differ in two principal ways. The first difference concerns their instantiation. A universal is supposed to be wholly present wherever it is instantiated. It is a constituent part (though not a spatiotemporal part) of each particular that has it. A property, by contrast, is spread around. The property of being a donkey is partly present wherever there is a donkey, in this or any other world. Far from the property being part of the donkey, it is closer to the truth to say that the donkey is part of the property. But the precise truth, rather, is that the donkey is a member of the property.
>
> Thus universals would unify reality...in a way that properties do not. Things that share a universal have not just joined a certain class. They literally have something in common. They are not entirely distinct. They overlap.[9]

As it often appears to me, when Lewis tries to show how dramatically his position and Armstrong's differ, almost all that's advanced are some strangely suggestive metaphors.[10]

Nor do the standard treatments of these empty issues stop with the two positions just noted: In a somewhat roundabout way, I'll present a third apparent alternative to our Concrete Individualism, the so-called *theory of tropes*. To do that, in the context of a discussion of Lewis, it will be useful first to do a bit of stage setting. So, in the next couple of paragraphs, I do that.

Now, Lewis is concerned to focus on how it might be that certain things are *perfectly natural* with certain concrete individuals, or at least they're relevantly more natural than are some other things. And, when doing metaphysics most seriously, he would have us place to the side what's not so very natural with our concrete particulars. For example, we do well to focus on just how it is that a

---

9. David Lewis, "New Work for a Theory of Universals," *Australasian Journal of Philosophy* 61 (1983), pp. 343–77; reprinted in David Lewis, *Papers in Metaphysics and Epistemology, Volume 2*, Cambridge University Press, 1999, pp. 8–55. In the reprinted paper, the material cited is on pages 10–11.

10. As the quoted passage suggests, at least at certain times Lewis may *not* take sets, at least certain sets, to be any *abstract* entities—at least not on the usual understanding of the term. For, as usually understood, while the concrete members of certain sets may be spread around in space, the sets themselves, for being abstract, aren't spread around in space—nor are they, of course, all clustered together spatially, much less overlapping. But, going by this passage, not only are very many of Lewis's properties, those sets of his, spread around the space of the actual world—as will be true for those properties possessed by several spatially scattered actual-worldly concreta—but, what's far more, they'll be spread around the infinitely many space of infinitely many worlds. Perhaps, then, he is not simply pressing into service items already acknowledge by ever so many other philosophers. I don't know.

Anyhow, let's pass over this question, as it's of little importance for the present discussion.

certain basic particle is charged electrically—say, the particle is electrically negatively charged to such-and-such a perfectly specific degree, even as we do well
to place to the side the question of whether the particular particle has been
observed, perhaps ever so indirectly, by at least one scientist. (Though the example is far from perfect, I'm sure you get the point.) Now, with that being so,
Lewis is concerned to articulate, at least very moderately well, the distinction
between what it is that we focus on here when properly doing metaphysics most
seriously, and, by contrast, pretty much everything else. And, as he believes, his
conception of properties will figure very centrally in any such terribly basic and
serious articulation. With that said, the stage has been set, to consider some
other views of (what many philosophers call) properties.

Well, then, it should be noted that, while Lewis thinks his set-theoretic
conception is adequate to the serious task, he *doesn't* think it clear that his treatment of these issues is *to be preferred to all others*. Rather, he's prepared to give
high marks, as well, to two other positions. One is Armstrong's Concrete Universalism. What's the other? This is Lewis's answer:

> The other is a theory of tropes, more or less as in D. C. Williams' "On the
> Elements of Being," but made sparse in a way that imitates Armstrong's
> theory. In the contest between these three alternatives – primitive naturalness,
> universals, or tropes – I think the honors are roughly even, and I remain un-
> decided.
>
> The difference between universals and tropes comes when we consider two in-
> stances of the same perfectly natural property – for instance, two particles each
> having unit positive charge. Each one contains a non-spatiotemporal part cor-
> responding to charge. But if this non-spatiotemporal part is a universal, then it
> is the same universal for both particles. One and the same universal recurs; it is
> multiply located; it is wholly present in both particles, a shared common part
> whereby the two particles overlap. Being alike by sharing a universal is "having
> something in common" in an absolutely literal sense. If the non-spatiotemporal
> part whereby a charged particle is charged is a trope, on the other hand, then
> there are different tropes for different charged particles. There is no recurrence,
> no sharing of multiply-located part. (sic - it should be parts) Instead, we say that
> the charge-trope of one particle and the charge-trope of another are *duplicate*
> tropes, in a way that a charge-trope and a mass trope, say, are not.[11]

Now, Lewis is well aware that, just as the theory of universals may apply to
complex nonbasic individuals, each replete with many less than perfectly natural properties, so the theory of tropes may also apply ever so widely, and just
as nicely throughout all its application.

---

11. Lewis, *On the Plurality of Worlds*, p. 64. A fuller reference to Williams goes as follows: Donald
C. Williams, "On the Elements of Being," *Review of Metaphysics*, 7 (1953), pp. 3–18 and 171–92.

For quite a few, I imagine, a homey illustration will be helpful: Well, we've talked of donkeys, certainly not any basic individuals, and we've talked of the property of being a donkey, certainly not any perfectly natural property. Now, let's consider two particular donkeys, one *Don*, as we'll call him, and the other *Dan*. And, let's suppose that, as with most actual donkeys, Don is grey and Dan is grey. These grey donkeys will be happily illustrative.

Now, we've noticed three standard views on properties, and also the nihilistic position on properties, Concrete Individualism. Let's notice what they say about our donkeys.

First, there is Lewis's treatment of properties as aptly inclusive sets. Here it will be said that Don has the property of being grey, which property amounts to Don's being a member of the set of absolutely all grey individuals, and Dan also has the property of being grey, which amounts to *Dan's* being a *member of that very same set of* individuals.

Second, there is the Concrete Universalist, as with D.M. Armstrong, and perhaps also Aristotle. Here it will be said that, in his being grey, Don instantiates the immanent concrete universal of grayness, perhaps a certain non-spatiotemporal part of Don, even as in *his* being grey, *Dan instantiates this very same* immanent universal, perhaps a part of Dan that's the same as the just noticed part of Don. Just like that, this grayness is not only wholly present in Don, but, just as well, it's wholly present in Dan.

Third, there is the Trope Theorist, as with D. C. Williams, and perhaps also John Locke. This theorist will say that, in his being grey, Don has his very own particularized grayness, perhaps a certain part of Don, which is present nowhere else at all, nowhere, that is, where Don is not. And, she'll say that, in *his* being grey, *Dan will have his very own particularized* grayness, perfectly distinct from Don's grayness. Just so, Dan's grayness is only exactly where *Dan* is; it's certainly *not* over there, where Don is, and where Dan is not.

Fourth, and finally, there is the Nihilist here, our Concrete Individualist. He says that all that's there, really, are Don, who is grey, and also Dan, who is also grey, of course. There are no properties of these grey individuals, because there aren't, really, any properties at all.

Now, try as I might, I find no concretely substantial difference between any of the positions lately noted, including even between all the presumably quite various friends of properties and, on the other side, our nihilistic Concrete Individualists. Any difference among, or between, any of these views is a divergence that's only a concretely empty difference.[12] Don't you agree?

12. Even in relatively recent philosophy, say, that of the most recent hundred years, there are many other views as well, with all manner of philosophers exercised by the question of what view to prefer, and then why to prefer it. For a sense of how vast is the literature here, see Swoyer, Chris and Orilia, Francesco, "Properties," *The Stanford Encyclopedia of Philosophy (Winter 2011 Edition)*, Edward N. Zalta (ed.), URL = <*http://plato.stanford.edu/archives/win2011/entries/properties/*>,

It's perfectly possible, I suppose, that Lewis would agree that, in the whole topic area, the issues I've highlighted are concretely empty matters. Even in such an event, I imagine, he'd think that they're philosophically important issues, anyway. And, as I also imagine, Armstrong and Williams would concur, as might many others. At least apparently, they'll think something a lot like this: Intertwined with these questions, there are questions of which *philosophical accounts* may be secured, on one or another of the noted metaphysical views, for *relevantly fundamental phenomena*. What's more, there are questions about the (at least relative) value of the various available accounts and analyses. Yet again, here is Lewis:

> I would willingly accept the distinction [between natural and unnatural properties] as primitive, if that were the only way to gain the use of it elsewhere in our analyses. The contribution to unity and economy of theory would be well worth the cost. But I think there are two attractive alternatives: theories which, for some price both in ontology and in primitives, give us resources to analyze the distinction without foregoing any of its applications.[13]

About all that, I'm quite skeptical (though my skepticism certainly isn't written in stone). For one thing, and quite specifically, I see no reason to think that a more economical or more unified theory (of these concretely empty matters) is more likely to be *correct* than one that's less economical, or less unified, or both. For another, and more generally, I don't think that what we humans can accomplish with certain resources, as against certain other resources, is an accurate guide to how things are with nonhuman reality itself.

Apparently contravening the alleged desiderata, I'll notice a position, apparently ontologically generous, incorporating all the positive posits of the three views just noted, which I'll call *Property Ecumenicalism*. (As does Lewis's idea of properties being certain sets, a presupposition of this Ecumenicalism is that there is an ample plenitude of worlds, only one of which is the actual world.)

On this Ecumenical view, all this will hold true of Don and Dan: First, Don is a member of the set of absolutely all grey individuals, both all the many actual grey individuals and also all the very many more merely possible grey concrete particulars, and, of course, so is Dan. Second, Don instantiates the immanent concrete universal of grayness, perhaps a certain non-spatiotemporal part of Don, even as Dan also instantiates this universal, perhaps also a peculiar part of Dan. (Owing to that, perhaps it may be said that, in a quite peculiar non-spatiotemporal way, Dan and Don overlap.) Third, Don has his very own particularized grayness, perhaps another part of Don, which part is

---

including the lengthy bibliography near its end. If anyone can find a concretely substantial difference, between any two of these many views, I will be very surprised.

13. Lewis, *On the Plurality of Worlds*, pp. 63–64.

present just where Don is, and no place else at all. Likewise Dan has *his* very own particularized grayness, distinct from Don's grayness, and present just where *Dan* is. (So, if Dan and Don overlap, it *won't* be owing to this *last* fact that they do. Indeed, such an overlap will have nothing to do with any trope of Dan's, or any of Don's.)

As indicated, the differences between this Property Ecumenicalism and the other views lately encountered are concretely empty. But, though empty, might some be *important*?

According to Lewis, there is a *contest* among theories of properties (one that's closed, of course, to our Nihilist here). Just before, we saw him say this about that: "In the contest between these three alternatives—primitive naturalness, universals, or tropes—I think the honors are roughly even, and I remain undecided." If there is a contest here, then how important a contest is it? Apparently, Lewis considers it to be at least quite important.[14] But, I can't see that. For one thing, there's nothing that really favors any of Lewis's three noted views over Property Ecumenicalism, even as nothing favors it over any of them. Anyhow, by now we may be on the verge of beating a dead horse.[15]

So, we turn away from focusing so exclusively on properties, turning to focus on time.

---

14. And, Lewis is hardly alone here. For a salient example of much the same thing, we can turn to Armstrong's *A World of States of Affairs*, Cambridge University Press, 1997. On page 22 of that work, Armstrong writes:

In my view, the last battle between Nominalism and realism (the Grand Final) should be fought between trope theorists (of various sub-types) and Aristotelian realists (also of various sub-types).

When I note that Armstrong's Aristotelian realists are our Concrete Universalists, we readily realize that, first, his last battle is our noted contest and, second, he thinks it's a very important contest. (Unlike Lewis, Armstrong doesn't think that, in addition to all the grey donkeys of the actual world that simply walk, there are the purple donkeys of some other worlds, which both walk and also fly. So, like almost everyone else in mainstream philosophy, he doesn't give high marks to Lewis's properties-as-absolutely-inclusive-sets approach. But, excepting that, there's precious little difference between the two here.)

15. Would that this were so, I feel. Though I certainly don't want to be stultifying, there seems no danger of there soon becoming a paucity of work done along each of the various lines Lewis has highlighted, as well as other lines in much the same neighborhood. For one example, as recently as in 2011, there appeared at least one book not only devoted to tropes, but also having "Tropes" as its title. See Douglas Ehring, *Tropes: Properties, Objects and Mental Causation*, Oxford University Press, 2011. For another example, and this one co-edited by one of mainstream philosophy's leading figures, in 2006 there appeared a book largely devoted to discussing universals. See P. F. Strawson and Arindam Chakrabarti, eds., *Universals, Concepts and Qualities: New Essays on the Meaning of Predicates*, Ashgate, 2006. In line with those works, placing "tropes" into the search box of Philpapers, and doing that search, returns very many works published during the just previous decade, 2002–2011, as well as many published during the previous decade, 1992–2001. And, quite the same result is found, or a parallel result, when doing such a search by placing "universals" into that search box, and following through.

2. The Temporal, the Empty and the Substantial: First Part

Until about a century ago, almost all philosophers, along with almost everyone else, held that very many things that once existed, like Plato's hair and Plato's heart, don't exist. Unlike individual electrons from millions of years ago, each of which still does exist, those others simply don't exist—full stop, and that's that.[16] In a nutshell, the only concreta that exist, in absolutely any sense or way, are those that exist *now.*

In days of yore, that's what almost everyone thought. But, more recently, mainstream philosophers, along with quite a few scientists, have taken that once-ubiquitous way of thinking to be just a certain optional position, on matters concerning existence and time, competing with other views on those matters. Owing to some of these recent philosophers, that time-honored view has come to be called "Presentism", though it goes under other names as well. Or, at the least, its most closely allied positions do, as with what's called "Three-Dimensionalism". Even nowadays, Presentism and its allies have prominent proponents: Each of them influenced by the late A. N. Prior, prominent present-day Presentists include Kit Fine, John Bigelow, and Dean Zimmerman.[17]

Now, at least as far back as Bertrand Russell, this happily ordinary way of thinking about temporal matters began to fall out of favor among mainstream philosophers, until it became, in mainstream philosophy, only a minority view. Just so, Presentism has been opposed not only by Russell, but also by Hans Reichenbach, W. V. Quine, D.C. Williams, J. J. C. Smart, David M. Armstrong, Theodore Sider, and very many others.[18] Most pertinent for this chapter,

16. My source on this, historically reliable in the main, I think, is John Bigelow, "Presentism and Properties," *Noûs*, Vol. 30, *Supplement: Philosophical Perspectives*, 10, *Metaphysics*, 1996, pp. 35–52. Most of the historically most relevant stuff is on the first page of the paper.

17. Among A. N. Prior's writings on behalf of Presentism are his "Thank Goodness That's Over," *Philosophy*, Vol. 34, No. 128 (Jan., 1959) pages 12–17, his "The Notion of the Present," *Studium Generale*, 23 (New York: Springer-Verlag, Inc., 1970) pages 245–48, and his "Some Free Thinking about Time," in B. J. Copeland (ed.), *Logic and Reality: Essays on the Legacy of Arthur Prior*, Oxford University Press, 1996, pages 47–51. John Bigelow defends Presentism in his "Presentism and Properties," *Noûs*, Vol. 30, *Supplement: Philosophical Perspectives*, 10, *Metaphysics*, 1996, pages 35–52. Kit Fine defends this intuitive view in his "In Defense of Three-Dimensionalism" first published in the *Journal of Philosophy*, Vol. CIII, No. 12, December, 2006, pages 699–714. Dean Zimmerman defends Presentism in his "Temporary Intrinsics and Presentism," first published in Peter van Inwagen and Dean Zimmerman (eds.), *Metaphysics: The Big Questions*, (Oxford: Basil Blackwell Publishing, 1998) pages 206–19. In another way, and more recently, he does that in his "The Privileged Present: Defending an 'A-Theory' of Time," in Theodore Sider, John Hawthorne and Dean Zimmerman (eds.), *Contemporary Debates in Metaphysics*, (Oxford: Basil Blackwell Publishing, 2008) pages 211–25.

18. The first few of these Eternalist authors are cited as such in John Bigelow's "Presentism and Properties". On the paper's first page he writes: "Russell, Reichenbach, Smart, Quine, Lewis and many other anglophonic, analytic philosophers also denied Presentism..." For Bertrand Russell, the works cited are "On the Experience of Time," *The Monist*, 25 (1915) pages 212–23,

among those rejecting Presentism, David Lewis certainly may be counted. Even as these mainstreamers reject Presentism, so they embrace a competing view, often called "Eternalism".[19]

What is it, exactly, that all these Eternalists positively uphold? Well, according to them, Plato's hair and his heart (tenselessly?) *do exist*, though they *don't exist now*, and they *don't exist at present*. And, according to these same thinkers, many *future* things also (tenselessly?) *do exist*, like the hair of, and the hearts of, my students' grandchildren, though that hair and those hearts *don't exist now*, and they *don't exist yet*. While one can do a bit more toward articulating their view, even right now you should recognize the central thrust of their position. Though it's only a terminological point, it should be observed here that, while the view I'm calling "Eternalism" is now quite often so called, it also falls under various other names as well, as with "Four-Dimensionalism". Or, at the least, that is the name of a view most closely allied with Eternalism. Nowadays, within mainstream philosophy, this Eternalism, and its allied views, is the dominant approach to questions concerning existence and time.

Between Presentism and its allies, on one hand, and Eternalism and its allies, on the other, it often appears that several separable issues are disputed. Let's suppose that to be the case. Then we should ask this: Are all of these different issues concretely empty matters, and even analytically empty? Impressed by the

---

Human Knowledge: Its Scope and Limits, Simon and Schuster, New York, NY, 1948, and *Mysticism and Logic*, Unwin Books, London, UK, 1963. For Hans Reichenbach Bigelow cites, among his other works, *The Direction of Time*, M. Reichenbach (ed.), University of California, Press, Berkeley, CA, 1956 and *The Philosophy of Space and Time*, transl. M. Reichenbach and J. Freund, Dover, New York, NY, 1958. For J. J. C. Smart, Bigelow cites, among Smart's other works, "The River of Time," *Mind* 58 (1949), pages 483–94, "Spatialising Time," *Mind* 64 (1955), pages 239–41, *Philosophy and Scientific Realism*, Routledge and Kegan Paul, London, UK, 1963, and *Between Science and Philosophy*, Random House, New York, NY, 1968. For W. V. Quine, the works cited are *From a Logical Point of View*, Harvard University Press, Cambridge, MA, 1953 and *Word and Object*, MIT Press, Cambridge, MA, 1960. For David Lewis, Bigelow cites, among other works, his "The Paradoxes of Time Travel," *American Philosophical Quarterly*, 13 (1976), pages 145–52 and his *On the Plurality of Worlds*, the work I've been repeatedly citing in this chapter. Not there listed, I'll add a few more works, by a few more "anglophonic, analytic philosophers": Remembering our section on properties, I'll add a Trope Theorist whom we encountered there, namely, D. C. Williams, as with his Eternalist paper "The Myth of Passage," *Journal of Philosophy*, 48 (1951), pages 457–72. And, not to discriminate, I'll also add an encountered friend of Concrete Universals, D. M. Armstrong, as with his Eternalist paper "Identity through Time," in P. van Inwagen (ed.), *Time and Cause* (Dordrecht, Holland: D. Reidel, 1980), pages 67–78. Among those Eternalists just mentioned in the text, perhaps the most prominent relatively recent denier of Presentism is Theodore Sider, especially in his *Four-Dimensionalism*, Oxford University Press, 2002. Of course, still others have yet more recently have advocated Eternalism and, in the bargain, they've rejected Presentism.

19. Though the two positions just outlined are the major contenders nowadays, there are also other views championed, or at least discussed with some energy. For an overview of almost all these discussions, as well as a treatment of some historically central views on matters temporal, see Markosian, Ned, "Time," *The Stanford Encyclopedia of Philosophy (Winter 2010 Edition)*, Edward N. Zalta (ed.), URL = <http://plato.stanford.edu/archives/win2010/entries/time/>.

just previous section, many may think I'll answer "Yes" to that question. But, then they would be wrong. To be sure, I do think that *almost all* the disputed temporal issues are even as much as analytically empty. With that much admitted, it may well be asked: Even if not going quite all the way, why do I go that far, which is, of course, quite far indeed? The devil is in the details.

As with much else in this chapter, when doing our detailed business we look first to Lewis's work. Before arguing for Eternalism, or for a close ally of the view, Lewis says this:

> ...Let us say that something *persists* iff, somehow or other, it exists at various times; this is the neutral word. Something *perdures* iff it persists by having different temporal parts, or stages, at different times, though no one part of it is wholly present at one time; whereas it *endures* iff it persists by being wholly present at more than one time. Perdurance corresponds to the way a road persists through space; part of it is here and part of it is there, and no part is wholly present at two different places. Endurance corresponds to the way a universal, if there are such things, would be wholly present wherever and whenever it is instantiated. Endurance involves overlap: the content of two different times has the enduring thing as a common part. Perdurance does not.[20]

Of course, that's just the introduction of some technical terminology. It's not the favoring of any view, much less is it an argument in support of any position. But, now, couched in that terminology, I'll display an argument Lewis gives for the thought that persisting concreta always do that by perduring, and never by enduring. Here's his "argument from temporary intrinsics":

> The principal and decisive objection against endurance, as an account of the persistence of ordinary things such as people or puddles, is the problem of temporary intrinsics. Persisting things change their intrinsic properties. For instance shape: when I sit, I have a bent shape; when I stand, I have a straightened shape. Both shapes are temporary intrinsic properties; I have them only some of the time. How is such change possible? I know of only three solutions.

> First solution: contrary to what we might think, shapes are not genuine intrinsic properties. They are disguised relations, which an enduring thing may bear to times. One and the same enduring thing may bear the bent-shape relation to some times, and the straight-shape relation to others. In itself, considered apart from other things, it has no shape at all. And likewise for all other seeming temporary intrinsics; all of them must be reinterpreted as relations that something with an absolutely unchanging intrinsic nature bears to different times. The solution to the problem of temporary intrinsics is that there aren't any temporary intrinsics. This is simply incredible, if we are

---

20. Lewis, *On the Plurality of Worlds*, p. 202.

speaking of the persistence of ordinary things.... If we know what shape is, we know that it is a property, not a relation.

Second solution: the only intrinsic properties of a thing are those it has at the present moment. Other times are like false stories; they are abstract representations, composed out of materials of the present, which represent or misrepresent the way things are.... This is a solution that rejects endurance; because it rejects persistence altogether. And it is even less credible than the first solution.

Third solution: The different shapes and the different temporary intrinsics generally, belong to different things. Endurance is to be rejected in favor of perdurance. We perdure; we are made up of temporal parts, and our temporary intrinsics are properties of these parts, wherein they differ from one another. There is no problem at all about how different things can differ in their intrinsic properties.[21]

As he makes quite clear, Lewis greatly favors the third solution, taking that to be the kernel of "the decisive objection against endurance".

What are we to make of this? Well, in the first place, there's next to nothing here that's concretely substantial. As should be obvious, that's certainly true with the thought that a persisting object has temporal parts, which parts can help to explain how it is that the object exists at various times, some of the times being earlier than others, even as the others are later times.[22] Just so, almost everything involved here, including even the mere presuppositions of the passages, is quite certainly concretely empty. And, at least almost certainly, that's owing to so very much of it being analytically empty. But, in the second place, there's a little bit in what we've observed, or at least in some (others) of its presuppositions, that's concretely substantial.

What's that? Well, however dominant it may look as compared with its rival, or rivals, it's just one way for concrete reality to be that (it should include at least one world wherein) its concrete individuals, or at least some of them, ever should change. Indeed, within this apparently dominant way, it's just one way for concrete reality to be that (it should include at least one world wherein) its concrete individuals, or at least some of them, ever change

21. Lewis, *On the Plurality of Worlds*, pp. 203–204.

22. With Lewis the central figure here, as in so much else of recent mainstream philosophy, there's a vast literature, by now, on so-called temporal parts. For an overview of this vast literature, or much of it, see Hawley, Katherine, "Temporal Parts," *The Stanford Encyclopedia of Philosophy (Winter 2010 Edition)*, Edward N. Zalta (ed.), URL = <http://plato.stanford.edu/archives/win2010/entries/temporal-parts/>. As best as I can tell, all of it is—except where utterly parochial—concretely empty, and also analytically empty, too boot. What's more, while there's a fair bit of clever maneuvers to observe here, it's almost impossible, for me at least, to shake off the feeling that, in addition to being so empty, it's arid and sterile, much as one then might expect. Still, what do I know? If you can do so, judge the literature for yourself, a sufficient basis for so doing probably supplied by reading the encyclopedia entry just referenced.

qualitatively, or intrinsically, or nonrelationally. Well, then, we've observed some concretely substantial points, and not merely parochial propositions. What should we say about them?

In this context, perhaps the first thing to say is that these points are, at the very most, merely presupposed by Lewis, never articulated by him, much less advocated. More importantly, however, we should observe that these points are, by most relevant measures, very small points and, accordingly, they're not thoughts of any great philosophical import. With that said, we've properly observed these substantial ideas and, in the bargain, we've given them their just due, but not more than their just due. And, with *that* said, we may observe that, in the passages on time displayed just above, Lewis provides us with no concretely substantial material, but presents, instead, only some analytically empty ideas.

With the previous paragraph's last sentence, I've expressed this section's most important point. Still, there's more to be said. Here's some of it: As against Lewis, *I haven't any intuition at all that shape is an intrinsic property* of (shaped) concreta in a sense of "intrinsic" that precludes relations to all manner of whatnots, with the like of mere *times* included (whatever exactly a particular *time* might be). By contrast, if we restrict our allowed relata to be just so many quite separate concrete individuals, then, insofar as I have a handle on properties, I have the intuition that shape is an intrinsic property. It's intuitive, I'll agree, that how it is that I'm shaped, or how it is that *my body's shaped*, is strikingly independent of how things are shapewise with any other people, or with *the bodies of other people*, each a body spatially distinct from mine. But, with times, not bodies, I draw a blank. So should everyone, I think.[23]

Almost too good to be true, this sensible line of mine is more than borne out by recent work from a couple of sharp young analytic metaphysicians: First, and quite recently, Bradford Skow seriously questions whether shape is an intrinsic property, in any useful or sustainable sense of "intrinsic", offering arguments for his skepticism.[24] Next, and just as recently, Kris McDaniel positively holds that shape isn't an intrinsic property, offering arguments for that position.[25] Much as one would expect, with both authors the candidate relata featured, the featured candidates for a shaped individual to be related to,

23. By now, there is a vast literature concerning questions of which properties are intrinsic and, on the other hand, which extrinsic. As best as I can tell, all of it is—except where utterly parochial—concretely empty, and also analytically empty, too boot. What's more, while there's a fair bit of clever maneuvers to observe here, it's almost impossible, for me at least, to shake off the feeling that, in addition to being so empty, it's arid and sterile, much as one then might expect. Still, what do I know? If you can do so, judge the literature for yourself, a sufficient basis for so doing probably supplied by reading Weatherson, Brian and Marshall, Dan, "Intrinsic vs. Extrinsic Properties," *The Stanford Encyclopedia of Philosophy* (Spring 2013 Edition), Edward N. Zalta (ed.), forthcoming URL = <http://plato.stanford.edu/archives/spr2013/entries/intrinsic-extrinsic/>.

24. Bradford Skow, "Are Shapes Intrinsic?" *Philosophical Studies*, (2007) 133:111–30.

25. Kris McDaniel, "Extended Simples," *Philosophical Studies*, (2007) 133:131–41.

aren't anything like other shaped individuals. In the case of McDaniel, to get specific, it's something like spatial regions to which spatially shaped material objects are aptly related.

Recollection of the previous section's Ecumenical Propertyist leads to a final point of commentary on the Lewisian passages just cited. We start with some emphatic labeling: One who says that persisting objects persist by perduring will be called a *Perdurantist* (about persisting concrete particulars). And, one who says they do that by enduring will be called an *Endurantist*. Enter another philosopher, an *Ecumenical Persistentist*. On the *Standard Version of Ecumenical Peristentism*, each persisting concretum always persists *both by enduring and also by perduring*: A persisting table itself is wholly present at every time throughout which it persists, even while the table is composed of temporal parts each present at only an instant of, or each present during only a certain period of, the time throughout which the table persists, with different instants for, or with different periods for, each of the different temporal parts. So, on this Standard Ecumenical Persistentism, each persisting particular will be quite a "busy" persisting individual, always doing double duty, as it were, throughout its entire career.

By contrast with that, *another sort of Ecumenical Persistentist won't* have any persisting individual doing that much. Just so, on *Divergentist Ecumenical Persistentism*, what holds is this: Even while all persisting particulars must either perdure or else endure, some will do the one thing, say, they'll all be perduring, even while the others do otherwise, with these others all enduring. But, no persisting individual both endures and also perdures.

So, now we have, before us, four positions concerning a certain issue about how it is that ever so many concrete particulars persist: Perdurantism, Endurantism, and two types of Ecumenical Persistentism. On this issue, each position conflicts with the three others. But, what sort of issue can this be, really? Is it a concretely substantial issue? I don't think so.

3. The Temporal, the Empty and the Substantial: Second Part

If there is a concretely substantial difference between Presentism and Eternalism, or between Three-Dimensionalism and Four-Dimensionalism, it's not to be found in the issues debated by Endurantists and Perdurantists, or any other parties to that debate. But, mightn't such a substantial difference be found elsewhere? In this section, I'll argue that there is indeed a concretely substantial difference between Presentism and Eternalism, and that it is in their treatment of the future where that properly philosophical substantial difference may be found.

Before proceeding with the argument, I'll make a timely observation: In claiming that there is a properly philosophical substantial difference here, between the chief mainstream views regarding time, I am being friendly, in a certain obvious way, to mainstream philosophy. Specifically, I am trying to point to a place where different mainstreamers endorse properly philosophical views that differ concretely substantially. So, if my pointing goes awry, matters will be even more dreary for mainstream philosophy than if, in this claim of mine, I'm pointing in the right direction. On the other hand, if I am right, still, there won't here be any great point in favor of recent mainstream philosophy. For, in such a circumstance, there *still won't be any novel* substantial philosophy provided by recent mainstreamers. At least very much the same substantial difference is to be found between Aristotle and his allies, on one side, and the ancients who, on the other side, denied there was an open future. With that said, we proceed.

Well, with respect to past matters, and with respect to the present matters, too, it's quite doubtful that there's any substantial difference between the two views. Both parties agree, for example, that it is fully true that dinosaurs roamed the earth millions of years ago. To be sure, the Presentist will talk and think about this in a certain way, while the Eternalist will talk and think about it in another way. And, at first blush, it may appear that, with each of these different ways of talking and thinking, there's offered a view that's substantially different from what's offered with the other way. But, as I'll argue, any such appearance is illusory.

For her part, the Presentist may say such things as these: Though dinosaurs no longer exist, many used to exist and, when they existed, many roamed certain parts of our planet's surface while many others roamed other parts. And, she may go on to say such things as these: Right now, no dinosaurs exist and, in recent years, none have existed. So, of course, both currently and recently, there's not been any dinosaur roaming our planet.

For his part, the Eternalist may say such other things as these: Though dinosaurs don't exist now, they (tenselessly) exist at times each millions of years ago. To express just what's most relevant and most unquestionably real here, we may use a *tenseless sense of, or form of,* "exist", and of "be", along with dating and timing locutions that (tenselessly) let us say when it (tenselessly) is that certain concreta (tenselessly) exist, or when there (tenselessly) are those concreta. So, millions of years before this inscription is (tenselessly) produced, dinosaurs (tenselessly) exist, and they tenselessly) roam the earth then, when they (tenselessly) exist.

Responding to this, the Presentist says that there aren't any such tenseless senses of, or forms of, "exist" and "be", and any other naturally available constructions featuring verbs. Even when it comes to purely arithmetical statements, scarcely concerned with any concreta, that's how it is. Just so, when it is said that two and three make five, the only real sense of that is the same as the single sense of what's stated when it's said that two and three now make five. If we want properly to say that this arithmetical relationship, between the three numbers, will hold irrespective of what the time may be, or what temporal perspective is salient, then we use *all* of our tenses, *not none* of them. So, properly, we should say that two and three always *did* make five, *and* they now *do* make five, *and* they always *will* make five.

Of course, the Eternalist can forswear any attempt to coopt ordinary expressions. Instead, he can construct, completely from scratch, a tenseless way of talking and, with that, a tenseless way of thinking. But, for her part, the Presentist will be ready with replies. First, she may say that, even at best, there's no productive point in doing any such thing. Second, she may say that, rather worse than that, there's this to realize: Insofar as it's foisted on us, such a tenseless way of talking and thinking will have us (at least tend to) "spatialize time", thus (tending to make or) making obscure to us the *dynamic* aspect of concrete reality or, perhaps better, the dynamism of any concrete reality that, not being temporally utterly monotonous, features temporal change.

But, of course, the Eternalist will have his reply to that response from the Presentist. And, of course, she'll have her rejoinder to that response of his. And, so it will go—on and on and on. But, is there anything substantial in the interminable discussion? I doubt it. Let me amplify.

Though the typical Eternalist doesn't like to use tensed constructions, and he deplores our using expressions like "the past", "the present", and "the future", he'll agree with the Presentist about many metaphysical temporal matters. For one very large thing, here put pretty metaphorically, our Presentist and our Eternalist will agree that "what's past is already fixed and determined; it's a done deal which cannot possibly be undone". Of course, the Eternalist won't put his agreeing thought in such words as those. But, amounting to much the same, he may well say something like this: Anything that (tenselessly) happens before I'm (tenselessly) expressing this very thought of mine is (tenselessly) completely beyond any alteration, or modification, or prevention, or "postvention". As regards any matter concerning occasions before the time of this yet more newly expressed thought, there's a fact of the matter, one way or the other. So, for example, as regards the matter of whether, when he was a boy, Abe Lincoln was ever friends with a boy named "David" or, here much the same, the matter of whether, when a boy, Lincoln (tenselessly) has a young male friend named "David", there is a fact of that matter. Just so, either Abe then had or (tenselessly) has such a friend, or else he didn't or (tenselessly) doesn't. Perhaps, nobody will ever know which (and, indeed, let's suppose that to be so). But, that makes no difference. Either Abe was friends with a young "David" or else he wasn't. Either the one is a fact or else the other is. Whichever is the fact of the matter, it's a done deal, so to say, with no possibility of undoing it, or preventing it, or postventing it, either.

Just so, on all matters concerning what took place before their present brief discussion, the Presentist and the Eternalist will be, most deeply, in full agreement. At such-and-such a very early time, there were, or there (tenselessly) are, so-and-so beings doing this-and-that, as they both agree. And, at so-and-so only somewhat later time, there were, or there (tenselessly) are, those-and-these beings doing A-and-B, as they also both agree. And so on, for everything that ever took place, or ever (tenselessly) takes place, in what, as the Presentist has it, is in the past. Insofar as they dispute what's what about occurrences at any such earlier times, what can be going on with the debate they'll be having? Myself, I can see no concretely substantial difference between what the Presentist holds here and, supposedly opposed to it, what the Eternalist holds. Is that just an eccentric inability of mine? I don't think so.

Toward having you agree with me about that, and to further some related ends, as well, I'll move to a parallel debate, one that concerns not the past, but the future.

At the time these words are written, anyhow, it is a fact, I assure you, that I have a son, my one and only child. And, at this very same time, anyway, it is also a fact that my son has no children and, in consequence, I have no grandchildren, not even a single one. Now, just insofar as her Presentism goes, what must our Presentist hold about the question of, or the matter of, whether I will have at least one grandchild? Unlike what she must hold about matters regarding the past— and matters regarding the present, too—she may well hold that, concerning this matter, there *isn't any fact of the matter*. Putting much the same point in different words, she may well hold that it's not *true* that *either I will have at least one grandchild or I won't*. Rather than endorsing that incorrect idea, we should uphold, instead, these two complementary thoughts: First, *it's not true that I will* have at least one grandchild *and it's also not true that I won't*. And, second, what's here true is that *I might have* at least one grandchild *and I might not*. Just so, the matter in focus is an *open* question; the matter at hand is a factually *indeterminate* matter.[26]

Opposed to our Presentist, our typical Eternalist thinks oppositely. He holds that, as regards the matter of my coming to have a grandchild, there's a fact of the matter. Just as the past is factually fully determinate, and there is nothing even remotely like an open past, so the future is also factually fully determinate and there's nothing even remotely like an open future. Against the Presentist, the Eternalist holds that there are no alternative possibilities for the course of our actual world's development. Just as everything about the world before this current thought, or before right now, is fully fleshed out, quite absolutely specifically, so, also, everything about our world after this same thought, or after right now, is fully fleshed out, as well.

---

26. Now, along with their Presentism, some few Presentists may be *Strictly Complete Determinists*. These few Presentists will hold that, as regards every matter concerning the future, it's fully determined exactly how that matter will develop, or will "play out". *These* Presentists *won't* hold that matters regarding the future are open matters; they *won't* hold that they're factually indeterminate. So, on the matter so lately presented, they will hold this: Either, as has already been fully determined, I will have at least one grandchild or else, as has already been fully determined, I will not. But, please notice this: The "hard line" taken by these Presentist Determinists is *wholly due to their Strictly Complete Determinism*. It's *not owing to their Presentism* that they should take the hard line.

This difference between Presentism and Eternalism is a concretely substantial difference. As well, it's an important difference: According to Eternalism, even as there are no alternative possibilities for the course of our world's development, so there are no alternative courses of thought or action available to, or for, any actual individuals, none for you, and none for me. So, as Eternalism has things, we never choose *from among actually available alternatives for our thoughtful activity*. By contrast, Presentism has no such consequence.[27]

That said, we turn from focusing on the topic of time to focus on the topic of properties.[28]

4. Is There a Real Need That Properties (Alone) Suitably Serve? First Part

When quoting Lewis in this chapter, the first sentence I had us confront was this:

> We have frequent need, in one connection or other, to quantify over properties.[29]

27. In addition to Presentism and Eternalism, there's a third position that, for purposes of a more complete canvas, might be mentioned here, one that's been called *The Growing Block View*, and that's also been called *the Growing Universe View*. Though not nearly as popular with mainstream philosophers as Eternalism or even Presentism, it is the only other "grand view" that, in the recent literature, is discussed with any prominence at all. (In analytic philosophy's early days, it was vigorously upheld by C. D. Broad, as in in his *Scientific Thought* (London: Routledge and Kegan Paul, 1923. Much more recently the view has been upheld in Michael Tooley's *Tense, Time and Causation*, *Time, Tense and Causation*, Oxford University Press, 1997. But, that's about it for anything like prominent proffering of this quite unpopular view.

Very recently, the view is labeled "growing block" in Berit Brogaard, "Sea Battle Semantics" *Philosophical Quarterly*, Vol. 58, no. 23, 2008, 326–35 and in Theodore Sider "Quantifiers and Temporal Ontology," *Mind*, Vol. 115, no. 457, 2006, 75–97. In his *Stanford Encyclopedia of Philosophy* entry on *Time*, Ned Markosian has called it "the Growing Universe Theory".

Using very vague and largely gestural language, we may express the main thrust of this view and how it differs from the two main competitors in these terms: The Presentist holds that only the present is real, while the past and the future are not. Almost oppositely, the Eternalist holds that the past, the present and the future are all real, without giving even the slightest favoritism to any one of the three. Between those almost wholly opposite views, the Growing Universe Theorist holds that, while both the past and the present are real, the future is not.

Apparently, there may be a damning glitch in this view: Though perfectly real, people in the past will be wrong when saying things like this: "The time of this very utterance of mine is the present time". Very recently, this apparent glitch has received discussion in at least four papers in the journal *Analysis*. Whether or not the view has such a defect, I judge that, for the questions our central to this book, it is not important for us to discuss the view. So, I make mention of it only in this mere note. That said, we return to the text, where we will leave the topic of time behind us, and return to focus exclusively on the topic of properties.

28. Not that there aren't other matters to discuss on the former topic. But, as I think you may now agree, except insofar as questions of time are heavily infused with thoughts from actual science, those questions will be either empty issues or, if not that, then quite parochial.

29. Of course, in that cited sentence, Lewis was using "property" in a way that is common coin among many philosophers, and not in the restrictive way he employed the term, shorty after that, in connection with just certain absolutely inclusive sets of "propertied" individuals.

Myself, I doubt I've ever had any need even remotely like that, nor do I think I've ever met anyone else who was, in that way, so needy, Lewis included.[30] Being very generous, we place aside the gratuitous reference Lewis makes to *quantifying*, just a quaint distraction here, as the *present matters don't require any technical* treatment at all, much less any featuring so-called quantification. That done, we may more clearly focus on what's here meant to be the main question: What needs are there, really, that putative properties will meet and, indeed, that they will meet so surpassingly well? As I'll argue, this question will never receive any answer that's notably informative, or happily illuminating, or even pretty modestly impressive or useful.

Without trying to be anything like exhaustive, in our discussion of the matter, let's look at three initially (somewhat) promising candidates, first a couple taken from a rather recent essay, and then one going back to some historical figures, eventually even to ancient times.

Treating first the relatively recent couple, I start by citing sentences from C. B. Martin, a thinker who, while *not very widely* influential in mainstream philosophy, was pretty deeply influential on Lewis, and on Armstrong and, perhaps least as well as last, on me, too:

> Predicates are linguistic and mind-dependent entities, whereas many properties of objects are not. Linguisticism is silly... [it] suggests that it is the object *simpliciter holus bolus* that makes each of many statements about it true or false. But, when the statements:

30. If someone thinks that certain activities are absolutely required of him, then he may well think that he needs to quantify over properties. Apparently, Lewis is one such person. And, as it appears, at times so is Hilary Putnam. Here is a paragraph to that effect from Putnam's "On Properties" in N. Rescher et al. (eds.) *Essays in Honor of Carl G. Hempel* (Dordrecht, Holland, D. Reidel, 1970), and reprinted as chapter 19 of his *Mathematics, Matter and Method: Philosophical Papers, Volume 1*, Cambridge University Press, 1979, pages 305–22:

VIII. Are properties dispensable?

That there are many assertions that scientists make that we do not know how to render in a formalized notation without something tantamount to quantification over properties is easily seen. First, consider the question we have mentioned several times: whether there are any fundamental magnitudes not yet discovered. Second, consider the scientist who utters a conjecture of the form 'I think that there is a single property, not yet discovered, which is responsible for such-and-such'. Thirdly, consider the assertion that two things have an unspecified observable property in common.

When writing that, which in the reprinting appears on page 316, Putnam has it that a certain "we" must render many scientific thoughts in a formalized notation of a certain sort. And, apparently, Lewis thinks much the same thing. Myself, I've never met any scientist who, beyond adverting to her equations, felt she needed to render her work in any such notation. Rather, surrounding her equations, she uses a natural language, most typically, the English language. By contrast with such happily productive scientists, it is only some philosophers who even think they see a need, on anyone's part, to have scientific papers rendered in a formalized notation. As I'll suggest, there's little substance to that thought of those philosophers.

(A) The passion fruit is round

and

(B) The passion fruit is purple

Are true of one and the same object, in each case it is something in particular *and* different *about* the object that makes each statement true. The predicates are built to pick these out.

Furthermore, different things (properties) about (or of) the same object are causally operative in different ways (or inoperative) for different effects. The object is causally operative in some event for particular effects only in virtue of *some* of its properties *rather* than others. It is not operative *holus bolus* for each and every effect. Therefore, properties are needing for causality.[31]

Well, we have two items just put on the agenda here, one done in the first paragraph, and the other in the second. Let's take them in turn.

In the first paragraph, Martin says that for (A) to be (made) true it's just a *certain* property of the passion fruit that's needed—maybe it's the fruit's *roundness* that's needed, or maybe it's the fruit's *being round*, or maybe it's some yet other thing, doubtless a close cousin of what's just been emphatically mentioned. And, by contrast, for (B) to be (made) true, it's just a *certain other* property of the fruit that's needed—not it's roundness, of course, or anything of that ilk—but it's the fruit's *purple color* that's needed, perhaps, or maybe what's needed is the fruit's *being purple*, or some such. What are we to think of this?

Well, right off the bat, we may well doubt that there is anything sensible to be made of this talk of a given statement's being made true by anything. But, if we allow that to make much sense, why do we need more than just the fruit itself to have both (A) and (B) made true? Not at all far afield, we can say that it's just this very fruit that here does the truth-making. First, we can say this: Just *because the fruit is round*, and it's not some quite different shape, the statement (A) *is true*. Beyond that, and if we want to get heavy-duty about all this making business, we can happily describe that fruit as being ever so relevantly productive in just the presumably wanted way. As we might then say, it is *by being round* that this passion fruit *makes (A) true*. And, as we can also say, correlatively and contrastingly, it is *by being purple* that, just so differently, this very same fruit *makes (B) true*. To be sure, this poor little fruit can't walk and chew gum at the same time. But, it certainly can be round and be purple at the same time. So much, and maybe too much, for the first of our two most recently cited paragraphs.[32]

31. C. B. Martin, "On the Need for Properties: The Road to Pythagoreanism and Back," *Synthese*, 112: 193–231, 1997.

32. There is a vast literature, I assure you, treating the concretely empty issues we have just discussed. But, rather than simply taking my word for it, you may see MacBride, Fraser, "Truthmakers," *The Stanford Encyclopedia of Philosophy* (Spring 2013 Edition), Edward N. Zalta (ed.),

In the second paragraph, Martin makes some remarks about causality. As it certainly seems, he wants us to have in mind something much like this: A hard and massive rock—as it may happen, a rock that's also grey—crashes into a fairly fragile stained glass window—as it may happen, a window that's also blue, as well—with the causal upshot being that the window then breaks. What caused what here? Or, more generously and less contentiously, what were causally relevant factors, at least, in the window's breaking? As it appears, on the rock's side, so to speak, we should say that the rock's hardness, or the rock's being hard, was a causally relevant factor, as was also its massiveness, or its being massive. By contrast, certain of the rock's other properties played no causal role, notably the rock's greyness, or its being grey. And, as it also appears, on the window's side, similarly so to speak, correlative things should be said. Even while the window's (property of) being fairly fragile was causally relevant to its breaking, the window's (property of) being blue had nothing to do with that salient upshot. We need there to be the proper properties here, to have there here be what's really causally relevant!

Or, do we? Myself, I think it's all just quite optional, not really needed at all. For, in patently plainer terms, we may place on offer a less rarified story: *Because the rock was hard and the rock was massive*, and because of certain other things, when the rock crashed into the window, it broke the window. But, even while the rock *was grey*, *that had nothing to do with* the window's breaking. And, equally, we can plainly say this: *Because the window was fragile*, and because of yet other factors, when the rock crashed into the window, it broke the window. And, while the window *was blue*, that had *nothing to do with* the window's breaking.

For undermining the cited paragraphs, we've provided just so much over-kill. What do I mean here? Well, suppose that, contrary to fact, I didn't have available a language able to provide the happy alternative glosses just enjoyed. In that case, you wouldn't have been supplied with the nice alternative glosses provided, with no mention of properties. But, that would make no difference. Most of it nonhuman, the world is what it is. And, what we should take the world itself to be has little to do with what we should take to be our human capacities.

5. Is There a Real Need That Properties (Alone) Suitably Serve? Second Part

As advertised, I turn to consider a historically salient idea meant to favor the thought that properties are greatly needed. Writing more than a century ago,

---

forthcoming URL = <http://plato.stanford.edu/archives/spr2013/entries/truthmakers/>. In particular, see the long bibliography at, or near, the entry's end, which lists, along with very much else, works by all the thinkers that this chapter cites.

Bertrand Russell holds that we must get involved with abstract properties, with none of these abstracta being (nothing more than a mere) set. They're *transcendent universals*, a sort of abstract universal that, at least for Russell, figured centrally in Plato's philosophy. To make good on that, I'll cite several passages from Russell, starting here:

> The problem with which we are now concerned is a very old one, since it was brought into philosophy by Plato.... Let us consider, say, such a notion as *justice*. If we ask ourselves what justice is, it is natural to proceed by considering this, that, and the other just act, with a view to discovering what they have in common. They must all, in some sense, partake of a common nature, which will be found in whatever is just and in nothing else. This common nature, in virtue of which they are all just, will be justice itself, the pure essence the admixture of which with facts of ordinary life produces the multiplicity of just acts.... The 'idea' *justice* is not identical with anything that is just: it is something other than particular things, which particular things partake of.... [the 'idea' justice] is eternally itself, immutable and indestructible.[33]

Endorsing Plato, Russell holds that it is (only) by our understanding each of many particular things as "partaking of" the single universal *justice* that we may truly understand how it is that each of the many particular things is something that's just.

Well, I don't know about you, but I am doing nothing so much as drawing blanks here. The writing is easy enough to track, for sure, but what's the thought, really, that's expressed with the reasonably simple sentences? Alas, I am at a loss.

Shortly after that passage, in the same work Russell appears to get into higher gear, and more elaborate sentences befall his reader. But, as best I can see, the elaboration does nothing of any utility or import. Anyway, here's what meant to be more richly argumentative material:

> As a matter of fact, if anyone were anxious to deny altogether that there are such things as universals, we should find that we cannot strictly prove that there are such entities as *qualities*, i.e., the universals represented by adjectives and substantives, whereas we can prove that there must be *relations*, i.e. the sort of universals generally represented by verbs and prepositions. Let us take in illustration the universal *whiteness*. If we believe that there is such a universal, we shall say that things are white because they have the quality of whiteness. This view, however, was strenuously denied by Berkeley and Hume,... The

---

33. Bertrand Russell, "Universals," in *The Problems of Philosophy*, Oxford University Press, 1912, pp. 88–100. This is reprinted in Peter van Inwagen and Dean Zimmerman, eds, *Metaphysics: The Big Questions*, Second Edition, Blackwell Publishing, 2008. In that anthology, the material just cited appears on page 55.

form that their denial took was to deny that there are such things as 'abstract ideas'. When we want to think of whiteness, they said, we form an image of some particular white thing, and reason concerning this particular, taking care not to deduce anything concerning it which we cannot see to be equally true of any other white thing...But a difficulty emerges as soon as we ask ourselves how we know that a thing is white or a triangle. If we wish to avoid the universals *whiteness* and *triangularity*, we shall choose some particular patch of white or some particular triangle, and say that anything is white or a triangle if it has the right sort of resemblance to our chosen particular. But then the resemblance required will have to be a universal. Since there are many white things, this resemblance must hold between many pairs of white things, and this is the characteristic of a universal...the relation of resemblance, therefore, must be a true universal. And, having been forced to admit this universal, we find that it is no longer worthwhile to...avoid the admission of such universals as whiteness and triangularity.[34]

Though able thinkers have praised this passage, I find no argumentation here that's at all compelling, much less any that's fertile, or even just apparently fertile. Let me amplify.

As he has made known, Derek Parfit hasn't any visual imagination. Anyway, we may certainly suppose, at least, that this is so. And, as we may also suppose, Scientiphicalism holds true and, so, there may come to be, even quite suddenly, a perfect duplicate of Parfit. For an easy exposition, let's make the quite un-controversial assumption that this duplicate person is at a pretty considerable distance, but not more than that, from both an opaque black cube and white sphere. All of that makes it easy and comfortable for us to imagine that this duplicate may be visually experiencing both the cube and the sphere, experi-encing both of them quite clearly, quite accurately, and quite vividly. Quite easily, as we'll be thinking, he may see that the black cube is considerably fur-ther from him than is the white sphere. Now, except insofar as some genuine empirical science may apply to the matter, what explaining needs be done, in respect of the matter of this person's seeing that the cube is further from him than is the sphere? Is there any problem or puzzle attending this situation, crying out for some nonscientific explanation of how it should possibly obtain? I don't think so. Where does there enter here, in any important way, any thought about the cube resembling, quite notably, or to some impressively sig-nificant degree, the white sphere? There is no place to be found. Where must there be, regarding this situation, some thought to an *opposite* effect, say, the thought that, in various qualitative ways, the black cube differs from the white sphere? All positive suggestions are as ad hoc as they're irrelevant.

34. *Op. cit.*, page 57.

When matters turn closer to home, why can't our subject simply think that one of the items is black but the other is not? What is added to understanding by adding that, in respect of color, at least, the two objects are related by a universal of nonresemblance, or a universal of unlikeness?

At least to my 21st century mind, the thoughts Russell attributes to Berkeley and to Hume seem quite as absurd as they are unrealistic. Perhaps, they may be concretely substantial ideas. But, then, so is the thought that white cows produce white milk and brown cows produce chocolate milk. At best, these attributed ideas comprise only a pretty silly just-so story. And, when moving from that to what Russell attributes to Plato, and to what he puts forth as his own Quasi-Platonic offering, we appear to go from the possibly concretely substantial but certainly ridiculous to the utterly empty and most confusedly sublime.

However any of that may be, it is clear that, from days of old up through the present time, many prominent philosophers have each adopted a favorite quite general sort of property—some favoring transcendent abstract universals, others immanent concrete universals, and still others still other candidates, as with the so-called *abstract particulars* preferred by the trope theorists. And, most of these many philosophers—most by far—have claimed for their favored items that, when properly put to proper use, they can afford us some quite significant explanation and understanding, all of it sorely needed and not so available without their preferred properties.

With that said, I'll close this section by first citing another passage from Russell, and then remarking on that passage. In its entirety, I will cite the last full paragraph from the section of his book, *The Problems of Philosophy*, that I've lately cited a couple of times before:

> We shall find it convenient only to speak of things existing when they are in time, that is to say, when we can point to some time *at* which they exist (not excluding the possibility of their existing at all times). Thus, thoughts and feelings, minds and physical objects *exist*. But universals do not exist in this sense; we shall say that they *subsist* or *have being*, where 'being' is opposed to 'existence' as being timeless. The world of universals, therefore, may also be described as the world of being. The world of being is unchangeable, rigid, exact, delightful to the mathematician, the logician, the builder of metaphysical systems, and all who love perfection more than life. The world of existence is fleeting, vague, without sharp boundaries, without any clear plan or arrangement, but it contains all thoughts and feelings, all the data of sense, and all physical objects, everything that can do either good or harm, everything that makes any difference to the value of life and the world. According to our temperaments, we shall prefer the contemplation of the one or of the other. The one we do not prefer will probably seem to us a pale shadow of the one we prefer, and hardly worthy to be regarded as in any sense real. But the truth is that both have the same claim on our impartial attention, both are real, and both are important

to the metaphysician. Indeed, no sooner have we distinguished the two worlds
than it becomes necessary to consider their relations.[35]

Well, I don't know about you, but I don't think much progress will be made by
thinking about subsisting, or about having being, where that's taken to contrast
importantly with existing. As well, and also in opposition to Russell, it's my view
that, by contrast with mathematicians and logicians, most philosophers should
spend far more time and effort thinking about concrete reality—or about whatever it is that makes some "difference to the value of life and the world"—than
about anything else or, indeed, everything else combined. What is more, and
what may have forever escaped Russell's attention, I think we should try to offer
concretely substantial thoughts about concrete reality, the "realm to which
we'll be forever necessarily confined", and not only, or even mainly, such substantial thoughts as are just quite parochial ideas. As is all too likely, we may
have little success with any of that and, very possibly, none at all that should be
taken terribly seriously. But, then, it may well be almost impossibly difficult for
beings much like us to offer, at this stage of human history, any very novel philosophy that's anything like adequate, especially as regards the only realm of
reality—perhaps reality's only realm, after all—in which we exist and, in what
may really amount to the same, in which we have being.[36]

35. *Op. cit.*, page 59.

36. This chapter was written during 2011 and 2012, a period when I did not (yet) have any
grandchildren. However, in January of the year of the book's publication, 2014, my daughter-in-law, Nishi, gave birth to Cole Unger. So, at the time this book came forth from the press, in
the middle of 2014, there *was* a fact of the matter as to whether or not I have any grandchildren,
the fact being that I *do*. Rather than rewriting the chapter, I decided to trust my readers to aptly use
their imaginations.

8

WHAT WILL BECOME OF US

Empty Issues and Substantial Speculations

Up to this point, I have not discussed, at any significant length, matters or issues that are of any great interest to more than a few people—mostly just professional philosophers, a rather small group, and their acolytes, a group that may well be even smaller. On the other hand, I have addressed, quite concisely, two widely interesting questions.

Put briefly, one of the two is the question of whether, in the actual world, we really do choose, at least from time to time, from among actually available alternatives for our thoughtful activity.[1] Having said little about this, in what remains of the book I will continue to say little.

---

[1] Why are many interested in that? Here's a brief answer: When people are confronted by certain considerations, most of them quite philosophical, to be sure, but some not so philosophical, they can readily become distressed about the matter, even if, perhaps, only rather fleetingly.

As you may recall, my less than certain belief is that we do really choose from among actually available options. Now, it may well be that this commonsense belief our mine, and of yours, too, I imagine, is incompatible with many a deterministic view that's a concretely substantial proposition. And, this may be incompatible with (at least almost) any materialist view of ourselves. And, our choosing may be incompatible with any Scientiphical Metaphysic, whether materialist, or whether epiphenomenalist, or whether some third sort of Scientiphical proposition(s). But, then, as our commonsense belief is most likely correct, it's most likely that the conflict will mean bad news only for all those propositions incompatible with it. At considerable length, I argue for that commonsense belief in *All the Power in the World*, especially in chapter 6 of that work, "Is Free Will Compatible with Scientiphicalism?" but also in chapter 7 of the book, "Why We Really May Be Immaterial Souls".

The other widely interesting issue on which I've touched is the conflict between entity materialism and entity dualism (and entity idealism). (As best I can
tell, nowadays hardly anyone subscribes to idealism, or even takes the view seriously. Accordingly, I've said little about idealism and that will continue.)

Unlike entity idealism, both entity materialism and entity dualism are,
even nowadays, at least somewhat live options for many educated people.
Accordingly, I've said a fair bit about both of those contending positions and,
in this chapter, I'll say a lot more. Focusing on various views of those two sorts,
in the chapter's later sections, I'll address an issue that's of great concern to
almost everybody—*the question of what will become of us.* Let me briefly amplify.

Why are so very many people—most them innocent of philosophy, of
course—so greatly interested in the question of whether it's materialism or
whether it's substantial dualism that's (more likely to be) the correct view?
A happily brief and rough answer is almost directly at hand. At least for the
most part, it's this: Almost everyone is greatly concerned about what will become
of him, or of her, after biological death or, as I should prefer to say, after the
death of their (living biological) bodies. To almost all of these very many people,
it appears that, if materialism should be correct, and if their biological death
should occur within the next several decades, then their prospects are, as a
matter of actual fact, very bleak, indeed. As it ever so strongly appears, if entity
materialism should be true, and if your biological death should occur at no
very distant time, then, once it has occurred, you won't ever again experience.

By contrast, it appears, to almost everybody, that their prospects may be
much better if materialism should be false and, instead, what should hold true is
a familiar form of substantial dualism, a dualism on which each of us *is an immaterial soul*—or, much the same, each of us now *has, as her only truly essential part,
an immaterial soul.*

Why do people take it that, in such a dualistic circumstance, their prospects will be better? Well, almost everyone continues this line of thinking in a
way that runs a lot like this: Even though my body and my brain may die, and
deteriorate, and disintegrate, still my immaterial soul will continue to exist or,
at least, it might well continue. And, along with that, many also think this:
Even when my body and brain will be dead, and they will be entirely disinte-
grated, I will experience, at least from time to time. And, at least for the most
part, I will experience in ways that are happily enough all right for me, and very
rarely, if ever, will I experience in a terribly painful way, or in a fearfully terrible
way, and so on. And, after my biological death and destruction, this will go on
for an enormously long time, perhaps, as may be hoped, even forever after.

Focusing on a very bright aspect or side of the matter, I've made salient a
certain issue that, as should be obvious now, very greatly concerns very many
people, including many highly educated people. It is this issue that I have
called, and I'll continue to call, *the question of what will become of us.*

About this issue of such widespread and heartfelt concern, what, if any-thing, have mainstream philosophers newly placed on offer, during the last six decades. Well, for more than the last half century, many prominent mainstream philosophers have discussed, with considerable ingenuity and at great length, a topic that, following their usage, I will call the topic of *personal identity over time* or, more briefly, *personal identity*. Now, as I feel sure, insofar as those discussions may hold much interest for folks largely innocent of philosophy, that will be owing, in largest measure, to just these two factors: First, these innocents are greatly interested in the question of what will become of us. And, second, they may take that mainstream discussion, on the topic of personal identity, to bear very importantly on that question.

At least for the most part, as I'll be arguing, these innocent folks will then have been badly mislead by, or anyhow badly distracted by, the mainstreamers who've been discussing the topic of personal identity. For, at the least, it may be very unclear, or even worse, that each of us people is, quite essentially, a person—so that, if one of us ceased to be a person, then, as must needs be, he or she would cease to be. Indeed, and as I'll argue, there is no clear and useful sense of "person" on which any us is essentially a person.

But that's hardly all of what I'll be doing in this chapter.

Also quite negatively, but now concerned with this book's central theme, I'll be arguing that, in the recent literature on personal identity, as it's called, almost all prominent writers have offered just so many empty ideas, excepting when they've offered some perfectly parochial thoughts. (Whether or not I've been a prominent writer on this topic, anything distinctively novel in my ex-tensive writing on the subject is, in this same sense of the term, the offering of just so many *empty* ideas.) Or, the same thought put differently: Hardly ever have any mainstreamers offered, in what's by now well over half a century of pretty prolific production, some new concretely substantial philosophical propositions on the question of what will become of us. Instead, what's been offered has been, in largest measure, a great number of thoughts, all con-cretely empty ideas, as to the persistence conditions of people, or persons. Put roughly, that's the negative side of what's to be encountered in much of this chapter.

On the positive side, and mostly occurring after our having observed most of what's on the negative side, I'll offer various concretely substantial thoughts that aren't just some very parochial propositions. Some of these will be recogniz-ably philosophical ideas, some pretty plausible, and others utterly wild. Here's a wild one: You are one utterly basic physical thing, and I am another. (Assuming that electrons are utterly basic physical things, you may be one electron and I then will be another.)

Apparently backed by strong evidence, other substantial ideas to be en-countered will be neither parochial thoughts nor characteristically philosophical propositions. Rather, they will be concretely substantial thoughts of a third sort, in an obvious way a sort intermediate between the two just mentioned. Here is an example of this third sort of substantial proposition: Unless you and I each have a brain that works in certain ways, we won't enjoy any visual experiencing; that will be true whether we are wholly material beings, or whether we are immaterial souls, or whether some third thing is true.

The example just given is importantly typical of these apparently perfectly correct thoughts of which I'll be reminding us. That being so, and especially when they are all taken together, we will have much cause for great pessimism regarding our actual prospects, at least as they'll be during the next several decades. This will be entirely unsurprising. Indeed, that is what most educated secular thinkers believe, at least in our wide Western culture circle, in any case, whether steeped in philosophy or whether quite innocent of it all. This leads me to make, somewhat tentatively, a very broad suggestion: On any matter of great, wide and deep human concern, very few, indeed, will learn anything both new and substantial from philosophy, whether mainstream or otherwise.

All that having been said, let's begin to explore some of the issues that, in this preamble, I've been highlighting.

1. Locke's Proposed Persons

Among the canonical philosophers, John Locke is, I think, one of the worst guides to follow for thoughts about what it is that, at least by our own deepest and brightest lights, each of us takes himself, or herself, most centrally to be. For example, even as each of us takes it that he once was an infant with only quite meager mental manifestation—or perhaps was a soul intimately related only to an infantile brain, or body—Locke would have us deny that. And, one may fall victim to Alzheimer's disease, even in a most advanced and acute form, as happened with President Ronald Reagan, a long time after he was last a mere infant. Following Locke, we should say that when Reagan's disease was most acute, there wasn't any person lying in Reagan's old bed. For Locke would have us accept the idea that each of us is, most centrally or essentially, a *person* and, what's more, being a person is a very big deal, far beyond anything that, both at and near the start of his life and, as well, at and near its end, Reagan was.

Why do I say that? Well, let's look at the first words of the section of the *Essay* that Locke labels *Personal Identity*:

This being premised, to find wherein personal identity consists, we must consider what person stands for; which, I think, is a thinking being, that has

reason and reflection, and that can consider itself as itself, the same thinking
thing, in different times and places[2]

Being charitable to Locke, we do better to take this as (an attempt at) *some* sort
of mere definition than as a perfectly gratuitous stab at a correct concretely substantial idea. Now, if this is a try at a *standard* sort of definition, it is a very bad
attempt, providing only that Locke's ordinary word "person" was even remotely
like our ordinary word. Messy though it is, still, according to the semantics of
our ordinary word "person", from his birth until his death, at least, President
Reagan was a person. That is so even though both when he was a newborn
infant and when he was ravaged with Alzheimer's disease, he lacked such reason
and reflection. So, if we take Locke as attempting to define the ordinary word
"person", as used in our time or even in his, I suspect, he fails miserably.

As seems clear enough, Locke was engaged in what, centuries later, would
be taken as attempting *another sort of definition*, as with what's been called a *high
definition*, or a *stipulative definition*. This becomes clear, I think, some 17 sections
later in the *Essay*, in the section "Of Identity":

> 26. Person a Forensic Term—Person, as I take it, is the name for this self.
> Whatever a man finds what he calls himself there, I think, another may say is
> the same person. It is a forensic term, appropriating actions and their merit;
> and so belongs only to intelligent agents capable of a law and happiness, and
> misery. This personality extends itself beyond present existence to what is
> past, only by consciousness, whereby it becomes concerned and accountable,
> owns and imputes to itself past actions. . . .[3]

It's not much of a stretch to conclude that, as Locke would have us take things,
to be a person one must be competent to stand trial in a just court of law,
maybe even to assist, at least fairly well, in one's own defense. Clear as a crystal,
this has little to do with a question like: After our biological deaths, what will
become of *you*, and of *me*?

Apparently not realizing that sufficiently clearly, most of the mainstream
discussion of the last sixty years—and there has been a vast amount of it—
revolves around thoughts Locke proposed. In only moderate detail, I'll soon
show that to be so. Anyway, when observing that material, we'll see it to be as
empty of import for concrete reality as were Locke's own empty ideas on such
matters.

---

2. John Locke, *An Essay concerning Human Understanding*, 1694 edition. For our present topic, all
the most relevant material is reprinted in *Personal Identity*, ed., John Perry, University of California
Press, 1975. In this reprinting, the cited words appear on page 39.

3. John Locke, *An Essay concerning Human Understanding*. In the Perry anthology, mentioned in
the note just above, the cited words appear on pages 59–61.

Before exploring that, I should say a bit about how my discussion may be somewhat limited, so that it is in keeping with my aim, stated early in the book, to avoid much discussion of heavily normative matters. Well, it may be that several mainstreamers have, in recent decades, meant their characterization of the persistence conditions for persons to have a significant normative aspect. Insofar as that is so, it *isn't those* mainstreamers whose characterizations I'll address in the upcoming pages. Rather, I am concerned to discuss those *Quasi-Lockeans*, as I'll call them, who proffer one or another so-called *psychological* view of personal persistence, where psychology is taken to be separate from normative matters, at least in largest measure. According to this type of psychological approach, there are two main things now to bear in mind: First, there is no concern to comport with Locke's dictum that "person" is a forensic term, applicable to all and only those beings who may be properly held accountable for their actions. Nor is there, in any other way, a concern to capture anything heavily moral or normative. But, second, and on the other hand, there is a concern to follow Locke in this respect: The persistence conditions for persons, or for people, will be at least very nearly the same as those for what I most standardly refer to with my usual use of "I" and "me", and similarly for what goes on with you. On this view, the persistence conditions for you and me centrally concern the continuation of quite impressive psychological states on our part, including capacities, proclivities, and so on. It is these Quasi-Lockeans that have dominated this topic's literature for well over a half-century. Exploring some of the most salient writers in that dominant group, representative of the lot, I'll observe that none offered concretely substantial philosophical ideas. Beyond that, I'll argue that these mainstreamers did poorly when saying what's strictly required for us to exist at various times, especially at times yet to come.

2. Locke's Lame Legacy

Largely owing to Sydney Shoemaker's work on these topics, variants of John Locke's views on "personal identity" have dominated the vast literature on that subject for well over fifty years now, and with no end in sight.[4] Before observing his own view, let's look at Shoemaker's summary of Locke's position:

---

4. Shoemaker's Lockean work on these matters goes back at least as far as his "Personal Identity and Memory," *Journal of Philosophy* Vol. 56, no. 2, (October 22, 1959).

Even while most recent discussion centers more on Derek Parfit than on Shoemaker, the views Parfit favors—giving pride of place to what he calls psychological connectedness and psychological continuity—were made available for all the rest of us, I think, by Sydney Shoemaker. While admiring both philosophers, I somewhat humorously single out Sydney as the one most to blame for the unfortunate influence of Locke's ideas on contemporary discussions in this topic area.

Locke's central thesis was that personal identity consists, not in sameness of substance, but in "sameness of consciousness"....it is clear enough that "consciousness" for Locke includes memory, and that it is primarily memory he has in mind when he speaks of consciousness in his discussion of personal identity...He seems, in fact, to have held a fairly extreme version of that view: that a person A existing at a time t_2 is the same as a person B existing at an earlier time t_1 if and only if A remembers, or "can remember", at t_2 actions or experiences of B occurring at t_1.[5]

After observing several objections to this account, and replying to most of them, Shoemaker offers his own view, a liberalization of the view he attributes to Locke, which we may call a *Quasi-Lockean* view:

The memory continuity account of personal identity thus gives way to a more general psychological continuity account. Memory continuity is now seen as a special case of psychological continuity, and it is in psychological continuity that personal identity is now held to consist. Reverting to the "person-stage" terminology, two person-stages will be directly connected, psychologically, if the later of them contains a psychological state (a memory impression, a personality trait, etc.) which stands in the appropriate relation of causal dependence to a state contained in the earlier one; and two stages belong to the same person if and only if (1) they are connected by a series of stages such that each member of the series is directly connected, psychologically, to the immediately preceding member, and (2) no such series of stages which connects them "branches" at any point, i.e., contains a member which is directly connected, psychologically, to two different stages occurring at the same time.[6]

Even though Shoemaker's expression of his view features some evidently metaphorical usage, as with his talk of "containment", and even though it appears awfully ad hoc, as with his clause (2), the clause ruling out "branching", it is clear enough for us to know that the view expressed must be a quite clearly incorrect position, failing, indeed, in *both of the main ways* in which it is possible for any such view to fail. Presently, and pretty directly, we'll see that to be so. But, first, I'll make an observation that, for our main purposes, is far more important than whether or not any Quasi-Lockean is correct.

As should be obvious, and hardly needs argument, the main thought Shoemaker offers is a concretely empty idea: If it holds true at all, it will hold

5. The passage just cited is from Shoemaker's "Personal Identity: A Materialist Account," which is his main contribution to a book he wrote with Richard Swinburne, *Personal Identity*, Oxford: Blackwell, 1984. Several sections of that are reprinted in the anthology used for metaphysics courses I've taught: Peter van Inwagen and Dean Zimmerman, eds., *Metaphysics: The Big Questions*, Second Edition, Blackwell Publishing, 2008. In that anthology, the passage just cited is on page 338.

6. Shoemaker, *op. cit.*, Page 346.

true in all concrete possible worlds, never delineating any one way for concrete reality to be from any other way. As should be obvious, that's why even extremely far-fetched cases might prove to be effective counter-examples to Shoemaker's offering. In this crucial respect, as we will have occasion to observe, Shoemaker's thoughts here are quite like other prominent mainstream writers on the topic: Except when parochial, their ideas are empty ideas.[7]

With that central claim before us, let's look at passages from Derek Parfit that, to my mind, show Shoemaker's view to be clearly incorrect. Rather than citing Parfit's very influential and lengthy book *Reasons and Persons*, I'll cite two related passages from a succinct paper[8]:

> ...consider certain imaginary cases, often drawn from science fiction. One such case is *teletransportation*. Suppose that you enter a cubicle in which, when you press a button, a scanner records the states of all the cells in your brain and body, destroying both while doing so. This information is then transmitted at the speed of light to some other planet, where a replicator produces a perfect organic copy of you. Since the brain of your replica is exactly like yours, it will seem to remember living your life up to the moment when you pressed the button, its character will be just like yours, and it will be in every other way psychologically continuous with you. This psychological continuity will not have its normal cause, the continued existence of your brain, since the causal chain will run through the transmission by radio of your "blueprint".
>
> There seem good grounds for believing that, in the case of teletransportation, your Replica would not be you. In a slight variant of this case, your Replica might be created while you are still alive, so that you could talk to one another. This seems to show that, if 100 percent of your cells were replaced [not at all gradually, as Parfit's essay elsewhere makes evident], the result would merely be a Replica of you.

As is evident from these passages, Parfit subscribes to a Scientiphical metaphysic, as does Shoemaker, of course, along with virtually all other prominent

---

7. Later in the chapter, I'll notice a quite novel idea from Shoemaker that is, indeed, a concretely substantial philosophical proposition. (To the best of my knowledge, anyway, he was the first to propose this idea.) At least from the present perspective of most of us, the idea is highly implausible, and Shoemaker himself doesn't believe it to hold true. Still, being a novel concretely substantial philosophical idea, it is one of the terribly few such thoughts that, as far as I can tell, appeared in the mainstream literature of the last sixty years or so. I'll sketch this idea in a later note for this chapter, note 24.

8. As all the world knows, *Reasons and Persons* was first published by Oxford University Press in 1984. As is less well known, the paper I cite, "Divided Minds and the Nature of Persons," was first published in Colin Blakemore and Susan A. Greenfield (eds.), *Mindwaves*, (Oxford: Blackwell Publishing) which appeared three years later, in 1987. That paper is reprinted in the Second Edition of Peter van Inwagen and Dean Zimmerman's anthology, *Metaphysics: The Big Questions*, Blackwell Publishing, 2008, where the material I cited, and I placed in display, occurs on pages 364 and 365.

mainstreamers of the last sixty years, including, as noted, Lewis, Kripke, Putnam, Davidson, along with others, less influential, but otherwise alike as peas in a pod.

As should also be evident, Parfit offers nothing novel here that's any concretely substantial idea, (except, perhaps, insofar as he's perfectly parochial).

With the key point just noted, we turn to ideas that, though less important, may be aimed at Shoemaker's Quasi-Lockean view. So, now, let's consider Parfit's variant case, the case featuring a time when there are two people extant, each terribly similar to the other, with one having walked into the near booth and with the other, in the distant booth, having only recently arrived in the world. As is evident, in this case there is the "branching" that, according to Shoemaker's thesis, means the cessation of the person in the near booth, who recently walked into it. But, the person who walked into the near booth *hasn't* ceased to exist. So, about this, Shoemaker is wrong: While he aims to do so, he fails to provide a strictly necessary condition for a person's persistence.

Shoemaker has failed, then, to provide a necessary condition for what he is after. But, might he have only *barely* failed here? Might it be that his total preclusion of branching was just a bit too much, and too crude? Perhaps, it may be thought, we need only tweak the thesis a bit, either by making the branching clause more complicated, or, much the same, by adding other clauses, or, perhaps, by making some other maneuver. No; that will not do. Rather, for addressing the persistence conditions for you, and for me, Lockeanism is thoroughly misguided.

Let us see, quite clearly, that this harsh judgment of Lockeanism holds true.

To start our search for insight into this matter, I cite Roderick Chisholm, elaborating on ideas from C. S. Pierce[9]:

> Let us assume that you are about to undergo an operation and that you still have a decision to make. The utilities involved are, first, financial—you wish to avoid any needless expense—and, secondly, the avoidance of pain, the avoidance, however, just of *your* pain, for pain that is other than yours, let us assume, is of no concern whatever to you. The doctor proposes two operating procedures—one a very expensive procedure in which you will be subjected to total anesthesia and no pain will be felt at all, and the other of a rather different sort. The second operation will be very inexpensive indeed; there will be no anesthesia at all and therefore there will be excruciating pain. But the doctor will give you two drugs; first, a drug just before the operations which

---

9. Roderick Chisholm, "Identity through Time," in H. Keifer and M. Munitz, eds. *Language, Belief and Metaphysics*, State University of New York Press, 1970. The paper is reprinted in the First Edition of Peter van Inwagen and Dean Zimmerman's anthology, *Metaphysics: The Big Questions*, Blackwell Publishing, 1998. In that anthology, the essay appears on pages 173–85.

will induce complete amnesia, so that while you are on the table you will have no memory whatever of your present life; and secondly, just after the agony is over, a drug that will make you completely forget everything that happened on the table. Given the utilities involved, namely the avoidance of needless expense and the avoidance of pain that *you* will feel, other pains not mattering, is it reasonable for you to opt for the less expensive operation?

My own belief is that it would not be reasonable, even if you could be completely certain that both amnesia injections would be successful. I think that it is you who would undergo the pain, even though you, Jones, would not know at the time that it is Jones who is undergoing it, and even though you would never remember it.[10]

Almost everyone will agree, I think, with Chisholm's choice here, showing that, as we most deeply believe, memory is not required for your continued existence, and likely has little or nothing to do with the matter. So, the old Lockean view is badly wrong.

And, Shoemaker's liberalization of matters provides no help, at all. Should the first injection remove all your personality traits, preferences, and so on, it would still be foolish to undergo the extremely painful procedure. And, this remains true even if the second injection restored all of your mentality, as it was prior to the first injection, as well as insuring complete forgetting of the protracted pain suffered on the table. As it appears, psychological continuity has nothing to do with the matter. Or, perhaps better, there's no relevance of continuity of any psychology that's at all peculiar to just you.

So, it's not just by a little slip that Shoemaker's thesis fails. Rather, any view that's even remotely like a Lockean position, that is, any view placing much weight on continuity of even very modestly distinctive psychology, must miss its mark completely.

Before closing this section, let me notice that, even at the very peak of mainstream philosophy, we find Quasi-Lockean ideas prominently in play (even though the ideas are as incorrect as they're empty). To begin this notice, I'll relate what Parfit takes to be the most important point in this topic's neighborhood: In a wide variety of cases, even if (almost) all are hypothetical cases, the question of whether or not one survives in the case comes apart from "what matters in survival".[11]

---

10. Roderick Chisholm, "Identity through Time," a paper referenced in the just previous note. In its reprinted version, the cited passage appears on pages 182–83.

11. At considerable length, and from several directions, I've argued that Parfit was badly confused in his use of the expression "what matters in survival," and, following his confused lead, so were many other mainstream thinkers. In my *Identity, Consciousness and Value,* Oxford University Press, 1990, that is done on pages 92–97. For present purposes, it's best to be generous, and to pass over that unfortunate entanglement.

With our observation of Parfit's influential thoughts about what he calls "what matters in survival", we set the stage for an entrance, into the discussion of our currently salient topics, of mainstream philosophy's most influential recent thinker: Disagreeing with Parfit, David Lewis ingeniously argues that the two never do come apart, arguing that what matters in someone's survival is always the strict survival of that selfsame someone. As is made clear by these following sentences, when arguing for this tight connection, Lewis's view of what it takes for there to be the strict persistence of someone differs only slightly from Shoemaker's seminally influential Quasi-Lockean position:

> What is it that matters in survival?...
>
> I answer, along with many others, that *what matters in survival is mental continuity and connectedness*..... My present experiences, thoughts, beliefs, desires and traits of character should have appropriate future successors. The successive states should be interconnected in two ways. First, by bonds of similarity. Change should be gradual rather than sudden. Second, by bonds of lawful causal dependence. Such change as there is should conform, for the most part, to lawful regularities concerning the succession of mental states— regularities, moreover, that are exemplified in everyday cases of survival. And this should not be so by accident...but rather because each succeeding mental state causally depends for its character on the states immediately before it.[12]

As previous discussion makes clear enough, here Lewis is as badly off the mark as is Shoemaker. As with all such Quasi-Lockeans, the empty idea Lewis offers won't help spell out anything of much help in gaining clarity on the persistence conditions for you, and for me. And, thus, it won't be at all helpful, really, in any apt discussion of our central question, the question of what will become of us.

3. Beyond Locke, but Not beyond Philosophical Thoughts Both Incorrect and Empty

Over a period of many years, but not including recent years, I contributed many words to the vast literature concerning (the conditions of) our existence, and our persistence.

Early on, I wrote quite a lot about (what may appear to be) the most fundamental question in this whole neighborhood, namely, the question of (the

---

12. David Lewis, "Survival and Identity" a paper first appearing in *The Identities of Persons*, Amelie Rorty, ed., University of California Press, 1976, where the cited words appear on page 17. The paper is reprinted in David Lewis, *Philosophical Papers, Volume I*, Oxford University Press, 1983, on pages 55–72.

conditions of) our existence at any given time, however brief the period, and however lacking in change that brief time might be. All that was in my early "nihilistic period". In some of this work, which occurred to me first to compose, I needed to rely on our Scientiphical metaphysic (not yet recognized by me and, thus, just tacitly assumed).[13] And, I also assumed certain other characteristically philosophical thoughts that, while comporting well with Scientiphicalism, clearly went beyond even any extended version of such a view. Quite centrally, I assumed thoughts to this effect: All those physical processes most crucially underlying our capacity to experience, for example, or anything else we take to be most fundamental to ourselves, proceeded in a quite remarkably gradual way, with no point in the process meaning any abrupt breakdown; no minute change, in any fundamentally underlying physical reality would mean the sudden and complete loss of any of our most central features, or capacities. Perhaps, in assuming that, which I did quite explicitly, I was offering a then-novel philosophical idea; I don't know. But, in any case, I never had any strong reason for thinking that assumption to be correct, a situation still holding true, even as I write these very sentences.

In the rest of this nihilistic work, which I first composed a bit later, I offered no new concretely substantial new philosophical ideas, but just new thoughts that were all either empty ideas or else quite trifling parochial propositions.[14]

Years later, at much greater length, and with more direct relevance to the questions made salient in this chapter, I wrote a pretty long book mainly concerned to address, as I thought, questions concerning (the conditions of) *our own* strict survival over time, from earlier times to later times. In retrospect, and (only somewhat) more accurately, it may be said that this book, *Identity, Consciousness and Value*, mainly concerned (the conditions of) a *person's* strictly surviving from earlier to later times.[15] In this book, I assumed not only a pretty commonsense form of materialism, shared by most mainstreamers, but, as well, I assumed the Scientiphical Metaphysic shared by almost all mainstream philosophers. In line with all that, and I now see quite clearly, the book offered nothing, or next to nothing, in the way of any even pretty novel concretely substantial philosophical ideas.

Even though all that may be so, as I fear, it still may be quite worthwhile rehearsing, rather briefly, some main lines of that book. Quite interestingly

---

13. The work just mentioned is "I Do Not Exist," which first appeared in the *festschrift* for my teacher Sir Alfred Jules Ayer, *Perception and Identity*, G. F. MacDonald ed., London: The Macmillan Press, 1979, at pages 235–51. This paper is reprinted in, among other places, Volume 2 of my *Philosophical Papers*, Oxford University Press, 2006. In that much more recent volume, the essay appears on pages 36–52.

14. This work, empty except where parochial, is "Why There Are No People," originally appearing in *Midwest Studies in Philosophy*, IV, (1979): 177–222. It is also reprinted in Volume 2 of my *Philosophical Papers*, where it is on pages 53–109.

15. *Op. cit.*

enough, perhaps, the concretely empty thoughts I there offer, concerning the conditions of persistence for people, or for persons, conflict with anything even moderately much like any Lockean idea. And, to make some progress on this chapter's main topic, the conflict may be pretty important. (Just so, and as we'll soon see, my offering conflicts, on some pretty important counts, with the Lockean thoughts from Shoemaker, and his Quasi-Lockean allies, lately noted and briefly discussed.) Framed in somewhat technical terms, but none of them very daunting, I trust, here's my concretely empty proposal:

> The person X is one and the same as the person Y at some time in the future if, and only if, (1) there is sufficiently continuous physical realization of a core psychology between the physical realizer of X's core psychology and the physical realizer of Y's core psychology, and [probably] (2) (some clause suitable for ruling out unwanted cases of branching).[16]

Now, toward grasping this proposal pretty quickly and fully, here is some helpful commentary: Return to consider Chisholm's example of the operating procedure with two total amnesia injections. Then, recall my expansion on that example, where not just memory, but where absolutely all of a person's distinctive psychology is removed with the first injection. What still remains there is what I'm calling the person's core psychology, a psychology that she will share with even completely amnesiac utter morons, devoid of any even mildly distinctive personality traits, and so on.

Assuming a materialistic metaphysic, my old proposal does better than any Lockean thoughts, or any Quasi-Lockean ideas, on very many examples relevant to their common topic. And, as best I can tell, it does worse on no such example. Quite surely, that's how things transpire when the most relevant tests are used to elicit reactions, as with my "avoidance of future great pain test", a test much like Chisholm's Peircean procedure.[17] Still and all, in (at least) two ways, (even) my proposal is badly deficient.

First, my proposal assumes that a materialistic metaphysic holds true. Or, at the very least, it assumes that what holds true is a metaphysic where all of a being's mentality supervenes on how things are physically with that same being (most plausibly, with how things are just intrinsically, I imagine, but, in any case, how things are both intrinsically and otherwise). Even as that is assumed, it may very well be false. Indeed, I myself have argued, in more recent work, that

---

16. In *Identity, Consciousness and Value*, this appears on page 109.

17. This test was first employed in my *Identity, Consciousness and Value* on pages 27–34. Its application was extended in a more recent work, my paper "The Survival of the Sentient," which originally appeared in *Philosophical Perspectives*, 14 (2000): 325–48, and which is reprinted in Volume 2 of my *Philosophical Papers* on pages 265–92. In that reprinting, the most relevant material appears on pages 272–78.

an Interactionist Substantial Dualism may be preferred over anything that's even remotely like any materialistic view.[18]

Now, this defect may be readily remedied. All we need do is replace "physical" by "concrete", throughout, obtaining this improved idea:

> The person X is one and the same as the person Y at some time in the future if, and only if, (1) there is sufficiently continuous concrete realization of a core psychology between the concrete realizer of X's core psychology and the concrete realizer of Y's core psychology, and [probably] (2) (some clause suitable for ruling out unwanted cases of branching).

Even bracketing (2), the apparently ad hoc bracketed clause, the improved idea is, in a way not yet made salient, still quite badly deficient. For, as reflection reveals, it may give us little direction, perhaps even none, toward making progress on what's presently and properly our central question, the question of what may become of *us*, that is of *you*, and of *me*.

The deep deficiency that's still with us owes its presence to the fact that, even with our recent improvement of it, my proposal still shares a deeply unfortunate presupposition with the likes of Lockean thoughts on the questions to be confronted. And, that will have things be terribly stifling. But, what is it, exactly, that I mean here?

Well, as with Locke and his legion of recent and current followers, our proposal presumes that, not only are we people, you and I, but, what's far yet more, we are people most centrally, and importantly, and essentially. This presumption is manifest, of course, with our crucial use of "the person x" and "the person y". Now, as is at least somewhat plausible, for a being to be a person, that being must have a mentality that, at least at some times in its history, includes very much more than, say, just the capacity to feel extremely intense pain and, in marked contrast, to feel without feeling pain.[19] Or so it is both with

---

18. First, and in happily brief compass, I did that in "The Mental Problems of the Many," a paper appearing originally in *Oxford Studies in Metaphysics*, Volume 1, Oxford: Clarendon Press, 2004, where it appears on pages 195–222. The paper is reprinted in Volume 2 of my *Philosophical Papers*, Oxford University Press, 2006, where it appears on pages 183–208. At far greater length, and in greater depth, I did it in *All the Power in the World*, Oxford University Press, 2006, especially in chapter 7 of the book.

19. Here is why we need the phrase "at least at some times in its history": Return to consider Reagan. On almost any view, when very near his very end, and ravaged with Alzheimer's disease, he had very meager mentality. But, *at earlier times he had considerable mentality*. So, he counts as a person. Now, what about when he was a newborn infant? Very near his very beginning, he also had very meager mentality. And, in this case, at earlier times he had even less mentality previously. So, here we need to take another tack. One way to do that is to say this: When an infant, and not ravaged with Alzheimer's, Reagan had, as part of his mentality, *the potential to develop various mental capacities* (something he lacked, as we firmly believe, when very near his very end, and when ravaged with Alzheimer's). With that on board, the newborn also get counted as people, along with us, and along with the hopelessly senile, too.

Lockean notions of a person and, as well, those other notions of a person that have, in fact, exercised the interest of one or another prominent mainstream philosopher.

(In ordinary discourse, the conditions governing "person" are a motley crew, and they may even be a great mess. Of course, going by such a messy ordinary notion won't help us with our central question here, the question of what will become of us.)

As we've been observing, to address our main question, we must recognize facts like these: Even while surviving the whole process quite entirely, and perfectly strictly, you could come to have a mentality that comprises no more mental capacity than that of a normal *dog*, or a normal *cat*, and, in *all sorts* of ways, *ever so much more impoverished than that of even a remotely* typical human amnesiac moron. That would still be you, right there in our terribly detrimental situation, even if you should prefer death to this clearly nonfatal process.

So, there is no clear and helpful sense of the term "person" in which any of *us* is *essentially* a person. Even if what we now lack is mostly just a usefully clear label, what are we to do now, by way of providing this very small remedy?

As best I can tell, just about the shortest expression available, to label the kind of being we take ourselves most centrally to be, is "sentient being". No single word, already commonly used, will do the job. (Fiddling about a bit, we may take the first letter of that, the letter "s" and place that where the "p" in person is found, while removing the latter letter, and thus obtaining "serson". Indeed, while I didn't realize how centrally that term should figure, in the expression of our most central idea as to what we most centrally are, I've already employed that contrived word, *serson*.[20] Just as long as an entity can feel, at all, it is a serson.) Anyhow, for analytical guidance on answering our central question—what will become of *us*—this may be the most relevant empty idea:

> The sentient being (or serson) X is one and the same as the sentient being (or serson) Y at some time in the future if, and only if, (1) there is sufficiently continuous concrete realization of a capacity to feel between the concrete realizer of X's capacity and the concrete realizer of Y's capacity, and [probably] (2) (some clause suitable for ruling out unwanted cases of branching).

Having just completed a fair bit of merely analytical thinking, let's try to encounter, with an eye to our central question, some happily relevant concretely substantial ideas.[21]

---

20. This single-word term was coined in my paper "The Survival of the Sentient".

21. Place to the side the widely interesting question of what will become of us, an almost urgent concretely substantial issue. Then, usually with Scientiphical propositions supposed, there has been, during the last half-century, a vast literature on the topic, or topics, we've just been discussing. For an overview of much of that, see Olson, Eric T., "Personal Identity," *The Stanford*

4. So-Called Commonsensical Materialism

For several decades now, and with no end in sight, most mainstream philosophers have held to what might be called a *Commonsensical Materialistic View of
Ourselves* (even while most of the remainder have held to views of ourselves that,
as will develop, differ only rather slightly from that materialist view). As I plan
to show that this view flies in the face of our commonsense thinking, I prefer to
label it the *So-Called Commonsensical Materialistic View of Ourselves*, though, for
brevity, I'll here usually refer to it as just *Commonsensical Materialism*. Put roughly,
the view is this: Each one of us is a very complex physical sentient being, quite
distinct from all other sentient beings, and each a being entirely composed of
very many much simpler physical things. What's more each one of us has a
very complex brain, a very complex physical part of him or her, which complex
part most directly serves to instantiate, or to realize, all of his or her mental
capacities, propensities and powers. True enough, each of us has many quite
vital salient complex biological parts in addition to our brains, as with our
hearts, for example. But, among them all these vital parts, it is only one's brain
that is, from a *philosophical* perspective, one's *most central and essential* part, most
central to, and most essential for, *one's continued existence.*

What's the import of that? Well, at least roughly, it's this: If your brain
should be annihilated, while the rest of you should remain alive, and it should
even continue to function quite normally, then *you will cease to exist.* By contrast, if
the rest of you should be annihilated, while your brain should remain alive and,
it should even continue to function quite normally, then *you will continue to exist.*

With that said, we may complete a statement of our Commonsensical
Materialism, quite well enough for present purposes, by simply saying that eve-
rything about you, and your brain, and the rest of you, is to be understood
Scientiphically. So, absolutely all your powers physically derived from the

---

Encyclopedia of Philosophy (Winter 2010 Edition), Edward N. Zalta (ed.), URL= <http://plato.stanford.
edu/archives/win2010/entries/identity-personal/>. In that entry's long bibliography, all the
philosophers lately cited are listed, most multiply so. Quite rightly, there are six works of Shoemaker's cited, a number equaled only by that of the author, which is perfectly understandable,
and no to discredit to Olson.

Overlapping with any overview of these topics in a way that's fairly said to be extremely
strong, there is this other entry: Shoemaker, David, "Personal Identity and Ethics," *The Stanford
Encyclopedia of Philosophy (Spring 2012 Edition)*, Edward N. Zalta (ed.), URL= <http://plato.stanford.
edu/archives/spr2012/entries/identity-ethics/>. Overlapping not quite that strongly, but still very
strongly, there's this entry, as well: Gallois, Andre, "Identity Over Time," *The Stanford Encyclopedia
of Philosophy (Summer 2012 Edition)*, Edward N. Zalta (ed.), URL= <http://plato.stanford.edu/
archives/sum2012/entries/identity-time/>. As best I can tell, none of these entries offers any new
philosophical thought that's concretely substantial, which is to be expected, no doubt, as that also
seems true of all the even moderately recent work listed in their lengthy bibliographies. Admittedly,
that holds true of all those of my own works listed in these entries, as much so as with other recent
writers.

simple propensities of your basic physical constituents—perhaps from your constituent quarks and electrons—the derivation flowing from how it is that these constituents are physically related to each other (and from how that differs, physically, from how they are related to other quarks and electrons, then not constituents of you, or of your brain). These powers include not only what are obviously physical propensities of yours, as with your gravitational power weakly to attract massive objects, and what are just somewhat less obviously physical propensities as with your power to digest bread, meat and potatoes. These physically derived powers also include powers that may appear, at first blush, not to be physical, at all, as with, quite certainly, your power to experience, and as with, presumably, your power to choose from actually available options for your activity.

To almost all mainstream philosophers, and to many other folks, as well, the view just sketched should seem so familiar as to be nothing less than terribly boring. And, at least to most mainstreamers, it should seem to be, even with just the very rough presentation of it just provided, the correct view of ourselves, and by far the most credible view of us. Indeed, to most, it may seem the *only even remotely credible* view.

According to this Commonsense Materialism—along with a few facts, all widely known—it's pretty clear what will become of me and all my contemporaries: In just a few decades or less, each of us will come to an absolute end. For one thing, there will occur the biological death of our brains and bodies. And, perhaps after those biological deaths, there will occur the destruction, the decay, or the deterioration of our brains and bodies. Now, once that happens, none of us will ever again, in fact, experience at all. Most importantly, for us, we may sum this up in just these few words: If Commonsensical Materialism should be even just roughly right, then that is, in fact, what will become of us; in no very great time, our experiencing will come to an absolute end.[22]

Given that Commonsensical Materialism is at least roughly right, that's the most important thing to be said on the question of what will become of us. But, of course, very many people deny that materialism. By contrast with that materialist view, very many believe that each of us is an immaterial soul, or that each of us has an immaterial soul. Just so, there are very many Substantial Dualists. And, as almost all of these Dualists believe, even as your soul may continue to exist long after the death and destruction of your brain and body,

---

22. To be sure, even on these views, there may be brighter prospects for some of our very distant descendants. This may occur if there should come to pass, perhaps just a few centuries from now, certain astonishingly enormous advances in science that may very greatly prolong the lives of human people, or greatly postpone their demise in some rather more far-fetched way, not well categorized using terms like "life" and "death". However that may be, it will not change matters for those alive when these sentences are written. On our Commonsensical Materialism, it's nearly certain that my own prospects, at least, are those just stated in the text.

so you yourself may continue to exist long after that happens. On such a Substantial Dualistic view, might we really have brighter prospects for an extremely long and rather pleasant future?

In due course, we will discuss that question. But, first, I sketch some deep difficulties for So-Called Commonsensical Materialism.

5. So-Called Commonsensical Materialism and the Mental Problems of the Many

In a couple of publications, I've argued, each time in the same novel way, that Commonsensical Materialism is not even remotely close to what may be a correct view of ourselves.[23] Briefly, I'll recapitulate the main thrust of that argumentation, perhaps adding a little something new near this section's end.

As science certainly seems to deliver, in "the situation of each of us", there are billions upon billions of complex physical systems, each fully realizing a whole host of mental powers, including a power to experience quite fully and consciously, and a power really to choose from among options actually available to the chooser. Or, at least, just such a great multiplicity will obtain if, in "the situation of each of us", there is ever *any quite complex properly physical entity* ever doing any such thing, at all. Let me amplify.

Consider the neurons serving to compose your brain. Or, perhaps more accurately, as you really have billions of overlapping brains, consider the neurons serving to compose an arbitrarily selected one of these billions of brains of yours, a brain we'll call *Brian*. Now, among the billions of neurons serving to compose the selected brain, focus on just two of them, one to be called *Ned* and the other *Neil*. Both Ned and Neil serve to compose Brian and, with respect to Brian's functioning, neither is a more important component than the other (or, really, than are each of millions of other neurons, each similarly serving to compose Brian.) Now, with aptly imaginative grouping, first consider an aptly brainy System—doubtless also a brain—that's just slightly smaller than, and slightly less complex than, Brian, which System I'll call *Sid*. Now, unlike Brian, who has both Ned and Neil as neural constituents, Sid has only Ned as a component, lacking Neil, which is no part of Sid, at all. Now, very largely overlapping Sid, and Brian, too, for that matter, consider another brainy System—doubtless yet another brain—which I'll call *Sal*. No surprise, Sal *has Neil* as a component—just like Brian, but unlike with Sid—while *lacking Ned*—unlike both Sid and also Brian, too. Well now, as science has certainly

---

23. Published first, there is a happily short paper, "The Mental Problems of the Many," referenced in note 19. Published second, there is the very thorough, but still overly long book, *All the Power in the World*, Oxford University Press, 2006.

shown, and as many have known anyway, you certainly don't need every last one of your cranial neurons for the manifestation of your main mental powers. Not by a long shot. Rather, there is enormous causal over-determination of any mental functioning promoted on your part, at least any that's at all notable, as with the promotion of any of your experiencing, for example. Quite crudely, but also quite helpfully, this may be likened to having 100 firemen holding a safety net that may be upheld, quite perfectly well, by just any 60 of the full 100.

With that being so, we may be clear that, even though it lacks any contribution from Neil, which is no part of it, still Sid may serve to promote the experiencing of pain, should you experience painfully, quite wholly and fully. And, equally, even though *it* lacks any contribution from *Ned*, so may *Sal also* serve to promote, quite fully and wholly, just such experiencing of pain. As that's so, Commonsensical Materialism will have it that, in this very commonplace situation, there are at least three different experiencers of pain. One of them is Brian, of course, and only a bit less obviously, at this happily peculiar point in our right reasoning, another is Sid, and yet another is Sal. Of course, what we just did in a small way can be done, quite as effectively, in a much larger way. Just so, and with the mathematics of combinations in mind, we now notice this to be so: If there is, in your situation right now, any quite complex material thing that's experiencing, then there will be very, very many material complexes, each relevantly similar to the others, that, in your situation right now, are all experiencing.

In the simple case just considered, we could assume a very short and quite unremarkable period of experiencing or, for that matter, of any mental activity. In cases much like that, it may be best to assume that, for our complex Sid, for our complex Sal, and for all of their complex brethren, there is very little difference in the quality of, or in the character of, the experiencing that each of the overlapping experiencers undergoes. If any one of the many experienced just painfully and greenly, then, as commonsensical materialism has it, so did all the others.

Even with such great similarity of experiencing among ever so many different experiencers all in the same commonplace situation, perhaps even perfect similarity, there is already a great problem with being sanguine about our noted materialism. Still, I have found there to be a few mainstreamers—if only just a very few, indeed—who seem quite willing to bite the bullet here, accepting our anti-commonsensical multitudinous result, so that they may continue to accept their pretty popular sort of materialism. Though I take the rare response to be patently poor, I'll now be concessive.

Even if one is willing to deny common sense quite greatly, as these very few most certainly do, still and all, their now-eccentric stance can't be long sustained: With slightly longer time periods considered, matters become more complex in just such a way, I'll suggest, as may undermine that eccentric stance. Twice over, I'll amplify.

Little doubt but that, quite correctly indeed, you believe that, from time to time, you choose from among real alternatives for your own activity. And, even when not exercising it, you (almost always) have the power to so choose, as you also correctly believe. In parallel with that, we may suppose that, also quite correctly, *Brian* believes that *he* has this nice power and, at times, *he exercises it*, choosing from among alternatives available to *him*. And, so it is, too, with *Sal*, who sometimes chooses from among options really open to *him*, that is, to *Sal*. And, similarly, so it is with Sid, too, as with billions of others of our considered brainy Systems. Or, at least, thus it will be given our commonsense belief on choice, along with poor old commonsensical materialism.

Now, to make things most vivid to you, make the supposition that, here and now, *you are Sid*. As well, make the supposition that, right now, you are experiencing just as you were at this time yesterday, before ever having read any sentences even remotely like those in this section. In that ordinary context, I may ask you to imagine just one of the three standard colors used with traffic lights: either imagine just green, or else imagine just yellow, or else imagine just red. This I may do, perhaps, after having determined that you have no great favorite among these three colors, and you dislike none, too.

Perhaps closing your eyes, in order to help make your imagining quite vivid, you imagine just one of the three colors. After a few seconds, I ask you to perform this little exercise again, instructing you that you may choose the same color as just before or, if you so wish, you may imagine one of the other two colors. We'll suppose that, in an aptly bland way, you go through five "trials" of this simple choice procedure, in fairly rapid succession. As we may imagine, being a very aptly cooperative Sid, you chose to imagine, in order, this sequence of those colors: green, green, red, yellow, green. Now, as this was real choosing, with the character of each imagining event having been truly up to you, you could have chosen, at each of the five choice points, either of your two other options. Had you done something along those lines, that would have yielded, on your part, a different sequence of imagined colors. For example, you could have chosen to imagine, in order, green, red, yellow, green, and red, in which case that is what, with your eyes closed, you'd then have visually experienced.

Now, as we strongly believe, you often choose in a way that is quite independent of how anyone else chooses, which is also true, of course, with regard to (almost all) other human choosers. Thus, we should now suppose as much not *just for you*, our supposed Sid, but *also for Sal*, who is not Sid, and whose choices are, thus, independent of Sid's choices. And, so we should suppose, too, for each of billions of other of overlapping experiencers, other than Brian, and other than Sid, and other than Sal, too, but also, during the time interval noted, right there "in your situation". Given this, we should think that, on the first of our five trials, where both Sid and Sal chose to imagine green, *at least ten of these independent billions* chose to imagine *just red*, not green (and not yellow) at all, and so each of them then imagined only redly, not greenly (and not yellowy). And, for parallel reasons, we should think that *at least another ten* chose to imagine *just yellow*, not green (and not red) at all, and so each of *them* then imagined only yellowly, not greenly (and not redly). So, if Commonsensical Materialism is correct, and each of us does choose from among available real alternatives, then this following proposition will almost certainly be true: During the first of our five trials, even if a great majority of our presumed complex material experiencers may have been experiencing just green, and not red or yellow, others were experiencing only red, not green or yellow, and yet others were experiencing only yellow, not green or red at all.

What we have just run through is, in the most relevant regards, perfectly typical of ever so many cases where thoughtful experiencers choose among real options for the experiencing thinkers. So, on the idea that each of us is a highly complex physical experiencer, there will be, in ever so many everyday cases, *not only an astonishingly great number of experiencers* experiencing—but, quite as well, there will be a *marked variety as to the character of the experiences enjoyed.* Few, indeed, are the Commonsensical Materialists who, upon confronting this consequence, will continue to hold that view with great confidence. As I'll suggest, none should do so.

Perhaps wrongly enamored of Spinozistic themes, there are some who will say that none of us ever does choose from any options for her thoughtful activity, as there never really are any such options for any of us at all. (Some will *say* that, even if nobody most *deeply believes* it.) So, from argumentation based on thoughts of choosing, they might not face, just perhaps, a problem of marked experiential variety—even while they must still face, of course, a problem of great experiential multiplicity, or a problem of great plurality of experiencers, each experiencing so similarly to all the rest. But, then, there are these two things to be said to these possible philosophers: First, the latter problem is, all by itself, a quite serious difficulty. And, second, there may be another route to a problem of marked experiential variety. What might be this other route?

While I will be well out of my depth here, as I know next to nothing of modern physics, I will try to provide a helpful sketch. Now, as I have been given to understand, *basic physical propensities* are best regarded as *probabilistic* propensities, owing to quantum-mechanical considerations. If that is right, then a terribly complex material being, like our supposed Brian, and our Sid, and our Sal, will all have, on a Scientiphical view of the matter, physically derivative propensities that are themselves all merely probabilistic. Well, then, consider Sid at a certain moment when both (1) he *is not then* experiencing green and also (2) just as Sid's experience-fostering propensities have it, there is an enormous chance that, in the very *next* moment, Sid *will be* experiencing green. Even while all that is so, still, there is a tiny chance that, in that next moment, though Sid still will be experiencing, he will *not be experiencing green*, but he will experience only in some *contrary way*, as with experiencing only white or, perhaps, only red. Just as that may be true of Sid, it may also be true of Sal, and of each of the other very many billions of other material complexes, each ever so much like both Sid and Sal. Now, the mathematics of combinations will have there be a truly enormous number of overlapping complex material systems each fit to foster its own experiencing—if any complex material entity ever really does that. Indeed, as it appears, there is *such a very great number* of these material systems, all with merely probabilistic propensities, as to have this following thought be a pretty likely proposition: At least at some moments in your situation, there will be at least one complex experiencer experiencing quite differently from how at least one of the others is experiencing. If that is right, then, it may be *very likely*, indeed, perhaps even all but certain, that *once in a very great while, at least*, there arises a case of that peculiarly perplexing sort. That is very bad news, I think, for Commonsensical Materialism.

With that being so, and much else bad, as well, we should explore positions quite different from Commonsensical Materialism. Though I'm most happy to explore various versions of Substantial Dualism, I'll next consider a *very strange Materialist* view.

6. Might You Be a Quite Simple Physical Thing? If So, What Will Become of You?

There are, of course, an extremely great variety of materialist views of ourselves. Among the most incredible of them, there's the view that each of us sentient beings is, in fact, a basic physical entity without any substantial parts at all. Assuming current physics is correct, a certain specification of this view is that *you are a certain electron*, for example, and I am certain *other electron*. In an obvious way, this utterly incredible idea is a *terribly extreme* view. No doubt, that's why the view is so terribly incredible. Still, there are several reasons it's instructive to consider this view, aptly called *Extremely Simple Entity Materialism* or, for short, *Extreme Materialism*.

Here is one reason: This Extreme Materialism is the closest materialist analogue of, or parallel to, the most traditional sort of Substantial Dualist View of Ourselves: On a most traditional sort of Substantial Dualism, each of us is a *simple immaterial* entity, a simple immaterial *soul* without any substantial parts at all.

On this traditional Dualism, each of us souls will have, of course, quite significant mental powers and propensities. But, as none of us will have any immaterial parts, none of us will have, in any strict or literal sense, any immaterial structure, or any concrete structure at all. Indeed, rather than being derived, at least in part, from how you are structured, how it is that you're propensitied mentally will be utterly irreducible.

In a nicely noted parallel, on our Extreme Materialist View, each of us is a simple *material* entity, utterly devoid of any substantial parts at all: On this Extreme Materialism, each of us will have, of course, quite significant mental powers and propensities. But, as none of us will have any material parts, none of us will have, in any strict or literal sense, any material structure, or any concrete structure at all. Indeed, rather than being derived, at least in part, from how you are structured, how it is that you're propensitied mentally will be utterly irreducible.[24]

Here is another reason: With our Extreme Materialism, we have the clearest case of a materialistic view that avoids our mental problems of the many. As may be obvious, on this extreme view, there will be, in "your situation", just a single mentally powerful physical individual who's ever experiencing, or thinking, or choosing. Unlike all the other elementary particles serving to compose your bodies and your brains, there will be just a certain single one that is mentally powerful. It's just this peculiar electron that's you. Just a bit, I'll amplify: While similar to all other electrons in all basic physical respects, as with mass, electric charge, and so on, you will be the only electron, among all those serving to compose your brains and bodies, that has, in addition to those physical propensities, the power to experience, and the power to choose, and so on. So, even while you qualify as a physical thing, by having all your fully physical features, you'll be a very *special* basic physical entity, unlike the others composing your brains and bodies.[25]

24. It is worth noting that, going against the mainstream grain, one prominent mainstream thinker, Sydney Shoemaker, has floated a most nontraditional idea about how some immaterial souls might be: Even as many material bodies are composed of simple material parts, there may be immaterial souls each composed of simple immaterial parts. Moreover, while the simple immaterial parts each lack any power to think, or to experience, the soul that they together compose may have these powers, which powers may often be manifested in the soul's thinking and in its experiencing. Whatever else one may think of it, one should note, I think, that this idea has the virtue of being a novel concretely substantial characteristically philosophical thought. In the mainstream literature of the past sixty years, at least, that is very rare.

See Sydney Shoemaker, "Immortality and Dualism," which may be found in his *Identity, Cause and Mind: Philosophical Essays*, Expanded Edition, Oxford University Press, 2003. First presented as a lecture to the Royal Institute of Philosophy in 1975, the book in which "Immortality and Dualism" first appeared is *Reason and Religion*, Stuart C. Brown, ed., Cornell University Press, 1977.

25. As far as I know, the Extreme Materialism just floated is a quite novel concretely substantial characteristically philosophical idea. But, as may be well worth noting, Roderick Chisholm has floated a somewhat similar idea, though his thought is not as extreme as the one just placed on offer. Just so, after arguing that he must retain all of his parts in order to persist, Chisholm proposed the view that he was small enough and simple enough always to have retained all his atomic components,

By this point, you should have quite a clear idea of the Extreme Materialist View I've highlighted, and of the specific form of it on which each of us is a mentally powerful electron, each numerically different from all the (relatively few) other mentally potent electrons. With that being so, it's high time we began to address our two questions.

Recall the first of these questions: Why is it that this Extreme Materialist View is so utterly incredible, more so than Substantial Dualism? Of course, this utter incredibility is over-determined; there is ever so much to be said here. But, it may be worth trying to locate just a most poignant part of what may be said. What might that be?

By my lights, it's this: All the Dualist's simple souls have mental powers, saliently including a power to experience. It's *not* the case that, while there are lots of souls with this power, there are more souls without it. By contrast, on our Extreme Materialism, it *is* the case that only a minute fraction of the relevant simples will have the power to experience. But, then, of *any one of these* very few we may ask: Why does *it* have mental powers, *utterly unlike the vast majority of elementary* electrons, each of which has none? With little for anyone to say now, that's enough for our first question.

Now, recall our second question: On our Extreme Materialism, what are our prospects for continuing to exist for a terribly long time, far longer than however long it is—a few more decades, perhaps—that there will still exist our relevantly healthy brains and bodies? Given that each of us is an electron, our prospects may seem very good. As physics tells us, each and every electron lasts forever or, at the least, each lasts for billions and billions of years.

But, by itself, such great future persistence will mean little for you. For as regards most of what you value, there must be, at a minimum, for yourself and for quite a few others, tolerably good experiencing during whatever future each of you may have.[26] So, even given that every last one of us is an extraordinarily

---

each having served toward composing him for some several decades, even all the elementary particles ever serving to compose him. (Anything like a single nerve cell loses many of its small parts every day, and so it is much too big, much too complex and much too dynamic—it is far too big a loser—to last for even an hour, let alone for many years.) Chisholm is clear on this, saying that his offered thought "is the hypothesis that I am such a microscopic entity".

The view that he is a microscopic physical thing appears in Roderick Chisholm, "Which Physical Thing Am I?" an Excerpt from 'Is There a Mind-Body Problem?'." Composed of material from a couple of earlier pieces by Chisholm, this excerpt appears in *Metaphysics: The Big Questions*, eds, Peter van Inwagen and Dean Zimmerman, Second Edition, Blackwell Publishing, 2008, 328–33. The phrase quoted, in this note's previous paragraph, appears there on page 331.

26. I put in the part about various others having future experience, at least reasonably all right for each of them, for pretty obvious reasons, as almost everyone has at least one person, beyond herself, whom she loves, or at least cares for pretty considerably. There is yet more to be said in the neighborhood, as is quite well done, I think, in Samuel Scheffler's *Death and the Afterlife*, ed., Niko Kolodny, Oxford University Press, 2013. But, that won't matter for what matters most here: Should there be many people living a thousand years from now, but none of them experi-

enduring mentally powerful electron, what are our prospects concerning this crucial experiential question? To learn most about that, we'll do well, I think, to postpone an attempt to answer the question.

With that held in abeyance, let's first consider what may be our actual prospects, just for our future existence, on certain Substantial Dualistic Views. And, before that's done, let's rehearse our reasoning, or make more explicit our reasoning, for taking a serious interest in *that* question: the question of what may be our actual prospects, just for our future existence, on certain Substantial Dualistic Views.

7. Articulating Our Argument for a Substantial Dualist View of Ourselves

As is worth a brief mention, in the two preceding sections, we have confronted an argument against the idea that any of us is any material entity, leaving Substantial Dualistic Views as the only positions that are, at once, both at least pretty plausible positions and also the views that, among what's at all plausible, depart least radically from our widely accepted, but unacceptable Scientiphicalism.[27] Given what has already been done, this can now proceed very quickly.

First, we may note that any form of materialism that has us be less than quite complex purely material beings will be a highly implausible view. That is true not only of a view that will have you be a certain electron; it is also true of a view that will have you be a neural network comprising just three neurons. So, we may have as a very plausible premise, quite compelling for virtually any materialist, this thought, an idea that, quite rightly, has us already supposing that we exist; we are some sort of beings:

First Premise: If any of us is a material being, then he or she is a quite complex purely material being.

---

encing—or even just one or two conscious individuals—there'll then be little fulfillment, indeed, of the values on which Scheffler effectively focuses.

27. There are, it may be noted, panpsychist forms of materialism, which may be passed over now, for a variety of sufficient reasons: For one thing, they are not very plausible views. For another thing, and more important in the present context, they depart very greatly and radically from our accepted Scientiphicalism. On our Scientiphical Metaphysic, a great deal of actual concrete reality is only material reality, and it is not also any mental reality. But, a Panpsychist Materialist will hold, of course, that absolutely all of actual concrete reality is mental reality. So, even if only in the interests of trying to stay somewhat conservative, Scientiphical thinkers should not move to this very greatly different view. In the next chapter, I will say a bit more about Panpsychist Materialism, though none of it will be anything very unobvious, or anything terribly interesting. At all events, here and now, we do well to pass over any such view.

But, as we have observed in this chapter's fifth section, and as I have argued in other places, the thought that any of us is a complex material being will be undercut by the mental problems of the many, even in several ways, at least some of which are quite devastating. So, that allows us to employ this next thought, too, as a premise now:

Second Premise: None of us is any complex material being.

From just those two premises, we may readily deduce our wanted conclusion:

Negative Conclusion: None of us is a material being.

That's our argument against materialism. As far as I can tell, it is more compelling than any of Descartes's arguments—at least for people now alive—even as it's utterly different from them.

What's more, it's only a short trip to get from what we've just seen to the conclusion that each of us is an immaterial thinking being. First, from the conclusion just displayed, we may trivially derive this equivalent thought:

Equivalent Immaterial Conclusion: Each of us is an immaterial being.

Now, we add to that this relevantly unobjectionable premise:

Thoughtful Premise: Each of us is a thinking being.

Finally, we conjoin our Equivalent Immaterial Conclusion with that premise, to yield:

Dualistic Conclusion: Each of us is an immaterial thinking being.

So, there you have it, an argument for Substantial Dualism that is utterly different from any Cartesian argument.[28] (As far as I am aware, it is the only argument,

---

28. As appears to be widely thought among mainstreamers, there are three main (sorts of) argument newly offered against materialism, in recent years, each having some deep affinity with Descartes' dualistic argumentation, even while each differs importantly from what Descartes offered just as each also differs importantly from the two others. One of the three arguments, as I take it, is (at least thought to be) found in Saul Kripke's *Naming and Necessity* (1980). In this present note, I will say something about only this (sort of) argument, reserving for another note some brief commentary on the other two.

Now, it is very unclear, at least to my mind, what it may be that really is Kripke's argument here—or even what it is that he wished to conclude from what argumentation he might have placed on offer. One thing that is clear, however, is that Kripke hasn't any idea as to what Descartes offered as his first, and his main, argument for his Substantial Dualism. Mistakenly, Kripke writes: "Descartes, and others following him, argued that a person or mind is distinct from his body, since the

since Descartes wrote, that is terribly different from his argumentation, though that may be of little importance.) Anyway, because our argument is so utterly different from any Cartesian reasoning for Dualism, it is, at the least, quite

---

mind could exist with the body." (page 144). Whatever else one might think of the idea just claimed to be Descartes route to his Dualism, it is most certainly not reasoning Descartes offers of behalf of his Dualistic metaphysics. Not much like what occurs early in the Meditations, and what impresses Kripke in the wrong way, here is Descartes, much later in the Mediations, offering his main reason for being a dualist:

> It is true that I may have (or, to anticipate, that I certainly have) a body that is very closely joined to me. But, nevertheless, on the one hand, I have a clear and distinct idea of myself, in so far as I am simply a thinking nonextended thing; and on the other hand I have a distinct idea of body, in so far as this is simply an extended, nonthinking thing. And, accordingly, it is certain that I am really distinct from my body, and can exist without it.

(The passage just cited is written in English, whereas none of Descartes's writing is in that language. My source for the translated passage is *The Philosophical Writings of Descartes*, trans. J. Cottingham, R. Stoothoff, and D. Murdoch, Volume II, Cambridge University Press, 1984, page 54.)

Now, as it stands, what Descartes actually offers is terribly far from being a compelling argument. But, perhaps taking only a few liberties, and none of them undue, one may read that passage so that a pretty appealing case can be made for Descartes's view: First, we may have Descartes hold that the idea of a spatially *extended entity* is the idea of an entity such that *there is only ever one thing that is ever essential to such an entity, and that is (its) being spatially extended*. All of this is, I think, all very plausible—both the attribution of that thought to Descartes and, more importantly, the great plausibility of the thought just attributed to him. And, equally, we may have Descartes hold that the idea of a *consciously thinking being*, a being just like he himself, is the idea of a being such that *there is only ever one (other) thing that is essential to **such** a being, and that is (its) engaging in consciously thinking*. All of this too is, I think, all very plausible.

Now, anyone who has these conceptions, and who can tell that he or she does have them—most certainly including Descartes himself, of course—can tell, just by reflection upon them, that, even as being spatially extended is not the same thing as engaging in consciously thinking, so nothing satisfying either one of these ideas can ever satisfy the other and, of course, conversely. By my reckoning, though that might not be a great argument, it is, at least, a pretty good argument. That is true even while it's also true that the argument is rather ambitious, providing a quite positively robust conclusion about what it is that we are, and not just something about what we aren't.

It is a far better argument, at any rate, than anything Kripke ever offered, even just negatively, and, so, quite unambitiously, against the view all actual concrete reality is material reality. What, after all, did Kripke ever offer to any such large effect as that, even if it be only in the negative? Was it anything much more than just some thoughts about how certain people got confused as regards what was going on with certain terms they used, and how it should be that, once freed from those confusions, they should then see that (even panpsychist) materialism cannot hold true of conscious beings, like ourselves? If that was all, or pretty much all, then he offers us hardly anything at all here, certainly nothing anywhere nearly as interesting, or as compelling, as what Descartes provided. So, one well might think that there must be a lot more than that going on in Kripke's text, by way of undermining materialist views of ourselves. Being charitable about the matter, I have found a few hints as to there being some such more robust and more worldly argumentation in the neighborhood, mostly from what's to be found Eli Hirsh's useful but still pretty nebulous paper, "Kripke's Argument Against Materialism" in *The Waning of Materialism*, Robert C. Koons and George Bealer, eds. Oxford University Press, 2010, pages 115–136. Even after that, however, one is very hard put to find anything, even so much as suggested by Kripke's text, that's clearly an argument directed against (even panpsychist) materialism, much less even moderately convincing argumentation to any such wide or broad effect.

But, except perhaps on a very few quite parochial matters, one shouldn't expect to find much from Kripke, as has already been indicated in chapter 4 of this book.

possible for this argument to be more compelling than anything Descartes himself ever offered.[29]

Now, I do not say that my argument is any very compelling argument. Indeed, it does not strike me with such force that I actually believe its conclusion.

29. In the just previous note, I said that, as appears widely thought, there are three main sorts of argument that, in recent years, were newly offered against materialism. One is thought to be found in Kripke's *Naming and Necessity*, and that I addressed in the note just referenced. In this present note, I turn to address, briefly, the other two.

Well, a second imagined highlight of recent anti-materialist argumentation is (widely thought to be) Frank Jackson's so-called "knowledge argument", first proposed in his "Epiphenomenal Qualia" *Philosophical Quarterly*, Vol. 32, No. 127 (Apr., 1982), pp. 127–136. Unless it may be taken to be nearly a non-starter, or close to an absolute howler, it is very unclear what one is to make of anything argumentative that Jackson offers. To a pretty fair extent, that's shown by Hirsch, in subsection B of his paper "Kripke's Argument Against Materialism" aptly called "Jackson's Knowledge Argument", which appears on pages 129-130 of the essay. Rather than add fuel to the flames, I note that, as far as anything positive may be concerned, Jackson takes his argument to favor an *epiphenomenal* sort of dualism. Not only does that run afoul of commonsense, of course, but, as well, it is just a nonmaterialist sort of *Scientiphicalism*. So, even if he should have the means to do so—and he quite certainly *doesn't* have anything like that—Jackson doesn't so much as try to move more than the least little bit away from mainstream orthodoxy. At any rate, just as with Kripke, Jackson offers no new philosophical thought that's a concretely substantial idea.

This brings us to the third and last sort of much-discussed recent anti-materialist argumentation. This is what, in his cited paper, Jackson calls "The Modal Argument". The earliest work he cites as offering such a modal argument is Keith Campbell's book *Body and Mind*, New York, 1970. On pages 130–131 of the paper, here is Jackson:

> Sceptics about other minds are not making a mistake in deductive logic, whatever else may be wrong with their position. No amount of physical information about another logically entails that he or she is conscious or feels anything at all. Consequently there is a possible world with organisms exactly like us in every physical respect (and remember that includes functional states), physical history, et al. but which differ from us profoundly in that they have no conscious mental life at all. But, then, what is it that we have that they lack? Not anything physical ex hypothesi. In all physical regards we and they are exactly alike. Consequently there is more to us than the purely physical. Thus Physicalism is false.

Now, Jackson does not consider this sort of argument to be very compelling. Neither do I, of course. Better to be back there with Descartes. Or, if we allow a lot of empirical input, better still, I think, to go with our argument from the mental problems of the many.

In his book *The Conscious Mind*, Oxford University Press, 1996, David Chalmers greatly elaborates on this modal argument, disarming many objections to it and, at least in that small regard, offering supporting considerations for it. At the end of the day, however, it's still what it is and, so, it's still not very convincing. And, what of the view, on these matters, that Chalmers' favors in this book of his? Calling it "Naturalistic Dualism", his view is, so far as I can tell, the same as Jackson's more happily labeled epiphenomenal dualism. So, as with Jackson, and as with the quieter Kripke, Chalmers is happy to stay within the confines of our academically orthodox Scientiphicalism.

As is clear, the three (sorts of) main sorts of arguments recently leveled against materialism are all fully compatible with Scientiphicalism, none offering so much as a single new philosophical thought that's concretely substantial. Yet, in the recent mainstream literature, they have engendered an enormous amount of discussion. As some might now ask, "But, how can so much have been written about what's really so little?" They should, I suspect, reread this book's earlier chapters, being more thoughtful the second time around.

Rather, I really do not know what to think about this large and deep issue. With that being so, and with my being no slave to fashion, I am agnostic on the question of whether or not some Substantial Dualism is the correct view of ourselves, and of the rest of concrete reality.

8. How an Immaterial Soul May, or May Not, Survive the Death of Its Body

In *All the Power of the World*, I discussed, at length, several highly speculative sorts of Interactionist Substantial Dualism. Right now, I'll just briefly sketch two types of such a Substantial Dualism, each substantially different from the other.

On one of these two types of Interactionist Dualism, each elementary particle that's ever fit for serving to compose an aptly functioning brain—to put things in reasonably convenient terms—will always be propensitied in an aptly soulful generative way: Each such particle is propensitied to help generate an immaterial soul, it's then always helping along with ever so many other particles, of course, whenever it may be that enough such particles should be most aptly physically related for this generative propensity to be manifested. In such a happy event, the nice brain-constituting particles will, all together, generate a soul, which soul will be propensitied to interact with them, or enough of them, so as to promote mental activity on the soul's part, even as they will be reciprocally propensitied, also individualistically, with respect to that soul.

On this *Generational View of Souls*, it's most appealing to think that, once a soul comes to lose all apt physical partners, as will happen with the utter destruction of all its most happily partnering brains and bodies, the soul will cease to exist. Just so, while it may be possible to maintain that the generated souls each come endowed with a propensity to continue to exist under (virtually) all conditions concerning any physical things, for most that's not a very appealing view. Why so? Well, a large part of the reason may be this: For such generated souls that may continue without end, there will be an uncomfortable asymmetry between their depending on some physical things for their starting to exist, but their being independent of all physical things as concerns their continuing to exist. However that may be, I'll not go further into the Generational View. Instead, I'll sketch another substantial dualism, one without the noted asymmetry.

On this other dualism, we may suppose that, before a relevantly comprehensive cosmic event, say, a Super Big Bang, all of our world's concrete reality was, to put the point simply, just a single object, propensitied in an enormously rich manner, and extending not only through some space (or space-time) but also through some spacelike analogue of space itself (or such an analogue of space-time). Upon going into a certain state, this extremely rich object exploded variously. Most important here, the enormously rich single cosmic object exploded into, on the one hand, a spatial object, or many spatial objects, and, on the other hand, a merely spacelike nonspatial object, or many such merely spacelike objects. If the explosion first resulted in just two objects, one spatial and the other spacelike though nonspatial, then there would have be a second stage in which, in both the spatial and in the spacelike realms, there was a great shattering into very many apt objects. Either way, there came to be, on the one hand, a spatial realm inhabited, perhaps most fundamentally, by ever so many perfectly partless elementary particles; even as there also came to be, on the other hand, a spacelike realm inhabited, most fundamentally, by ever so many perfectly partless immaterial souls.

On this *Quasi-Platonic View*, each soul begins its existence without being interestingly partnered with anything physical. Indeed, for the first several billion years that a soul exists, there simply aren't, in the world's physical realm, any brains or organisms. But all souls may be *propensitied to* partner with a happily active brain, should some particles in the world's physical realm come to compose any such happily nice physical complex (or, here the same, should some such particles come to be mutually physically related in a happily active brainy way).[30]

As this View may have it, even as each soul *exists for billions of years before* ever "becoming embodied"—while many others may never become embodied—it's quite appealing to think that, after an embodied soul's brainy body ceases to exist, that soul itself will still continue to exist, for billions of years yet to come. By contrast with the Generational View, here symmetry is best served by having each soul's persistence be quite independent of how anything may develop in the world's physical realm. Just so, on this Quasi-Platonic View, it may be most plausible to think that, even after an embodied soul comes to lose all apt physical partners, as may happen with the destruction of its partnering brains and bodies, the soul will continue to exist, for billions of years.

9. If We Should Become Disembodied Souls, Will We Be Experiencing Souls?

When a human person's brain is functioning appropriately, the person is not only alive, but she's consciously experiencing. (Taking it to be merely emphatic,

---

30. What determines which of the many souls first comes to be aptly partnered with the first brain, or the first overlapping brains? Just perhaps, I'll suggest, that may be a random matter. More satisfying to most, and as I'll also suggest, there may have been differential features in the formation of the souls, and these may place an ordering on which soul gets the first dibs on a brainy body, which gets the millionth dibs, and so on. I shall not bother detailing any of the many ways in which, through an apt formation process, an ordering may be placed on the souls, as candidates for "becoming embodied".

from now on I'll not write "consciously".) By contrast, sometimes her healthy brain will not be undergoing processes appropriate for her to experience. Even in the ordinary course of events, this may happen, as may perhaps occur during deepest sleep, when nothing even remotely like dreaming occurs. More certainly, it will happen when a human person—and, perhaps, especially when her brain—is (temporarily but) very strongly influenced by a powerful general anesthetic. And, when a human person's brain(s) (and bodies) suffer not only biological death, but also quite complete deterioration, it is even yet more certain that none of the world's experiencing will then be that person's experiencing.

That is the deliverance of sensible common observation. Complementing and deepening that observation, there is our developed and developing scientific understanding. Quite certainly true on the assumption of So-Called Commonsense Materialism, or on any Scientiphical View, it will also be true on the assumption of those other metaphysical positions that, just lately, we've considered. Just so, it will be true if our Extreme Materialism should hold true. And, just as well, it will hold true should the correct view be, instead of any materialism, an aptly coherent form of Dualism, as with, for salient examples, the Generational View and the Quasi-Platonic view.

Partly because it will be helpful to our upcoming discussion of substantial dualistic views, I'll say something about how our Extreme Materialism should be most aptly detailed: Most aptly, we may understand the experiential propensities of a mentally powerful elementary particle, say, a certain special electron, to be propensities that will be manifested—with the experiencing of the electron—just when, in fact, that electron is aptly physically related to many suitable not-so-special elementary physical things. Of course, all those more ordinary physical elementary particles will then be aptly physically related to each other, which is required for the special particle to be aptly related to them, and so required for that particle to experience.

There is nothing exotic about what will be suitable here: Typically, even if not universally, the special electron must be aptly spatially related to just such an aptly impressive complement of elementary particles as are suitable to compose an aptly functioning human brain. In such an event, quite common, of course, there may be, in fact, ever so many "brainy groups of composing particles" each group sufficient to have the special electron undergo some experiencing. But, then, while our sentient electron may have many apt interaction partners sufficient for its experiential power to be manifested, still there will only ever be, in our electron's situation, just one experiencer.

With that said, let's turn from the thought that each of us may be a numerically different *material* simple, to the thought that each of us may be a numerically different *immaterial* simple. Now, it was worth observing, as we did, that different Interactionist Substantial Dualist views might give different most appealing answers to questions of continued existence. But, as I'll emphasize, none

of that may matter much for how good, even just for us, will be our likely prospects. For, if your continued existence is to be of any substantial value to you,
then, (even going by just your own deepest desires for yourself) your future existence must feature, first, at least a goodly run of future experiencing—not just a
few seconds of experiencing and experienceless coma for billions of years—
and, second, much of that goodly run must feature experiencing of a sort that
you value, and not prolonged excruciating boredom, loneliness, or pain.

First, I'll address the question of the first of these desired minima, the question of whether, on the available evidence, we will become souls, even *immaterial
simples*, undergoing much future experiencing. Well, given the available evidence, the most plausible answer is the same as what was given, just above, to the
relevantly parallel question regarding *mentally special material simples*. As we there
observed, even if we each should be just such a special particle, with each special
particle persisting for billions of years yet to come, still, and as the available evidence indicates, our situation will be this: Lacking apt relations to apt physical
interaction partners, none of us will ever again experience at all. That same
evidence also indicates that, should each of us be a metaphysically simple soul,
perhaps persisting for billions of years to come, still, for lacking apt relations to
apt physical interaction partners, we then won't experience at all.

10. If We Become Experiencing Disembodied Souls, Will We Be Fortunate Souls?

For a few moments, let's suppose that, somehow or other, we are mislead by all
the evidence supporting the idea that, for one of us to experience, he or she
must have aptly functioning physical interaction partners. But, let's also suppose that, such evidence as we have on *other* facets of our question—what will
become of us—is *not* misleading. Given that, what should we think of our likely
future prospects? From the perspective of our present values, at least, will they
be promising or, instead, might they be dreadful?

As it seems to me, it's more likely that they'll be dreadful. Let me amplify.

Return to consider a Quasi-Lockean view, much like the views favored by
Shoemaker, Parfit, Lewis and others. But, now, do not take this as a view about
what's necessarily involved in your existing at various times. Rather, fastening on
the psychological features it emphasizes, think about how good for you things
would be, or how bad, if you came to lose those features, even while assuming,
against what the View says, that you still exist. Taking historically first things
first, we focus on memory.

If an unerring authority told me that, in a couple of days from now, I should
lose all memories of my life, and virtually all other memories, besides, I would
take that as dreadful news. Such thoroughgoing *retrospective amnesia* would be, for

someone with my values, a very bad thing. But, of course, without having a brain that's in relatively good shape, so to say, much as my brain(s) now is, I would be just so badly off, in just that dreadful way. Or, so the available evidence strongly indicates.

Because I have such a well-functioning brain, the evidence indicates, I can form new memories, as new experiences befall me. Some very unfortunate people, whose brains were irreversibly ravaged by certain viruses, cannot do that. Not only do they have retrospective amnesia, but also, in addition, they have what may be called *prospective amnesia*. That is a dreadful condition. Fortunately, as my brain is in aptly good shape, I do not suffer from it. But, as the evidence strongly indicates, were I not to have such an apt brain, I would suffer not only retrospective amnesia, but also prospective amnesia. Taking stock, my likely prospects go from very bad to far worse.

Moving from matters of memory to other features favored by a liberalized Quasi-Lockean view, my likely prospects get bleaker still. It is very largely because my brain is configured as it is, the evidence indicates, and it functions as it does, that I have the interests, desires, convictions and all else constituting my personality and character. For me, it would be very bad to lose all that, or even almost all.

For present purposes, we've done quite enough by way of exploiting features of ourselves that figure centrally in Quasi-Lockean views on personal identity.

With that done, let's turn to consider what prospects we may have, most likely, as regards the sorts of experiencing we might undergo when no longer aptly related to apt physical interaction partners. Now, as stated at this section's outset, in addressing this question, we'll assume—against the available evidence—that we'll continue to experience, at least in *some* ways—even without apt relations with any physical entities. But, then, going by what available evidence indicates, what sort of experiencing is it, most likely, that we'll undergo, should we be so totally disembodied? Let's discuss this.

Well, as all sorts of evidence strongly indicates, without (partnering with) a brain that's functioning normally in a certain way—we may call it *the visual way*—you *won't suffer or enjoy any visual* experiencing. Not only will you be utterly blind, but, as well, you'll have *no visual imagining*, as well. In short, you won't experience visually, at all.

So far, that's some bad news for how things are likely to be for those of us who become disembodied souls, even should we not just continue to exist, but continue to experience. But, how bad is it? Given anything like our own present desires and values, these enduring soulful simples won't have anything like an optimally good time of things. On the other hand, even going by our own wishes and values, many of them may yet have a pretty good time, perhaps for billions of years, even while never experiencing visually. As with the best aspects of Ray Charles and Stevie Wonder, for example, they may enjoy a great deal of auditory experiencing, including a great deal of musical experiencing, even while all their auditory experiencing would greatly outrun, of course, their enormously vast musical auditory experiencing.[31]

Now, just as all sorts of evidence strongly indicates that your *visual experiencing* requires, in fact, that you be happily related to a *visually stimulating physical interaction* partner, so all sorts of evidence indicates, just as strongly, that your *auditory experiencing* requires, in fact, that you be nicely related to an *auditorally stimulating physical* partner: If your brain is deficient in a *certain one way*, you won't any longer have any *visual* experiencing; if it is deficient in a *certain other way*, you won't have any *auditory* experiencing at all, not even any auditory imagining.[32]

As almost goes without saying, if your brain is deficient in both of those ways, as very well may happen, then you will no longer enjoy experiencing of either sort. If you are an immaterial soul that lacks a visually stimulating partner and lacks an auditorally stimulating partner, then, as all sorts of evidence indicates, you'll never undergo either visual experiencing or auditory experiencing, much less both.

Even for obvious reasons, much time spent in darkness beyond darkness and also in silence beyond silence, that's not what you want to befall you. And, for a somewhat less obvious reason, too, it may be, for most of us, a condition rather worse than simply ceasing to be. What is this less obvious reason? Well, without seeing or hearing anyone, or any signs or signals from anyone, each of us will be, in fact, utterly without any personal communication. Each of us will be, in fact, just so utterly alone. To be sure, with some very young people, as with the young Helen Keller, the lack of all visual and auditory experience need not be quite so detrimental. Even without benefit of sight or sound, she learned to communicate with others. But, as I am rather old and inflexible, I cannot learn so much. So, I would prefer utter cessation to continuing on without any visual or auditory experiencing and, in the bargain, without any personal communication.

As can hardly help go unnoticed, the young Helen Keller enjoyed other sorts of experiencing, as with tactile and kinesthetic experiencing. Why did she

31. Of course, and as we've already rightly concluded, when disembodied you will come to lose almost all your desires and almost all your values regarding auditory experiencing. So, in a certain way, what is a blessing for Stevie Wonder will not, in that eventuality, mean anything much for you. But, for us now, that is not very important. What's much more relevant, to our present discussion, is what matters from the perspective of your present desires and values. This is simple stuff, really, which *should be* obvious.

32. When he was deaf, Beethoven could no longer enjoy auditory experience provided by sources beyond himself, or beyond his brain, so to say. But, he still could, through apt imaginative power, enjoy auditory experiencing. As we are here supposing things to be, by contrast, our poor experiencers will be nothing relevantly like Beethoven, as their brains won't be anything relevantly like his was. Rather, for them, there won't be any auditory experiencing at all.

enjoy that? Well, even while she lacked stimulating physical interaction partners apt for fostering visual and auditory experiencing, she *did have physical partners apt for fostering tactile and kinesthetic experiencing*. But, when your brain and body
are no more, you won't be like Helen was when a healthy young girl. Rather,
along with lacking apt physical partners for fostering visual and auditory experiencing, you'll also lack apt partners for fostering tactile, and kinesthetic, and
all other sorts of "sensory" experiencing. So, even if when disembodied, you
should somehow experience, it will be very drab experiencing that will befall
you and, in fact, terribly lonely experiencing, too.

Going by our own current desires and values, how worthwhile an existence
would there be for a disembodied soul, utterly alone and experiencing always
so terribly drably? Even if such an existence should not be so bad as ceaseless
severe torture, it would be worse than simply ceasing to exist. This is especially
clear if these experiential futures should last for billions of years, perhaps even
forever, *with no way out*.

Of course, we may hypothesize fantastically to opposite effect. For example, one might conjecture that, before embodiment, each Quasi-Platonic
soul experienced in 1001 ways, each as different from the other as typical visual
experiencing is from typical auditory experiencing. When first partnered with
a normal human brain, or within about a year of that first partnering, the soul
may experience, in say, just 11 of those diverse ways. On this hypothesis, then,
embodiment is always something that diminishes the diversity of a soul's experiencing, which full diversity may, perhaps, be restored, even quite fully, only
when the soul becomes disembodied, freed from physical partnering, so to say,
once again. In some sense, that is a possibility. But, given our available evidence, most will agree, I think, that such a possibility is very far-fetched, and
that it is not any likely possibility, not even pretty moderately likely.

In closing, I'll say just this about the question of what will become of us:
Unless almost all available evidence is badly misleading, what will become of us
is nothing that any of us really wants and, beyond that, it will be something—
whether of one sort or whether of another—that many of us may well dread.

Perhaps that is unduly pessimistic. If it is, then that's because I've offered,
in the last several sections, material that is deficient in either, or in both, of two
main ways. First, it's certainly possible that I've badly misjudged the bearing of
available evidence on the speculative propositions I've being discussing. Second,
and a more serious possibility, as it now seems to me, there is this: Perhaps the
available evidence, even that of which I am aware, may favor a speculative
proposition that, even while it's highly relevant to our main question, I have
not considered, or not addressed sufficiently. As it might just be, the propositions needing more thought may be nothing new, as should be the case if they
amount to, say, the likes of Berkeleyan idealism. Or, perhaps they may amount
to something very new, far beyond my quite meager understanding.

However all that may be, there are two things, at least, that won't be very helpful here. One is for us to consider ever so many concretely empty ideas—even along with such speculations as those lately entertained. And, the other is for us to consider, perhaps along with such empty ideas, ever so many quite parochial thoughts, as with which words we happen to employ, and which concepts, and how it is that we happen to employ them. What I think that means is, of course, nothing less than this: In making progress with the question of what will become of us, including any optimistic progress, we will get precious little help from anything very like recent and current mainstream philosophy. But, of course, that was only to be expected. Even when highly imaginative quite novel concrete speculative thoughts are added to the mix, as I have just done with you, we encounter no strong reason, of course, to be anything but quite pessimistic concerning the question of what will become of us.[33]

33. Mostly due to my irreligious upbringing, I feel sure, belief in a divine creator and savior has never been a fully available option for me. Perhaps if I believed in a God, one rather like, at least, the God of the Abrahamic religions, I would see things differently, in which case, most likely, I would not be so pessimistic as regards the question of what will become of us. But, that is not something over which I have even as much as a smidgeon of control or, as best I can tell, I ever did. So, writing from my own present perspective, as almost everyone almost always has similarly done, I have presented, in this chapter's latter sections, just what you find on those pages.

9

WHEN WILL THERE BE SOME SERIOUS NEW SUBSTANTIAL PHILOSOPHY?

There is little hope that, anytime soon, mainstream philosophers will offer much by way of novel concretely substantial ideas that are more than just so many parochial propositions. And, there is almost no hope, I fear, that any will offer much that merits serious and sustained consideration, let alone the hard labor needed for extensive development. (And, with almost absolute certainty, I think, the same may be said should we include, in addition to its mainstream core, the rest of analytic philosophy, as well.)

Let me jar you with a couple of sentences, the first appearing to puff me up a lot, with the second undoing the work of the first, perhaps even quite entirely: First, what's already presented in this book, much of it first proposed in my earlier *All the Power in the World*, probably comprises more in the way of novel substantial philosophical ideas than everything published by prominent mainstreamers, all taken together, during the last 70 years or so. But, second, precious little of it—maybe none at all—is worth significant or sustained consideration.

To get a good grip on that, it will be useful to recapitulate some salient steps in my parade of new concretely substantial philosophical thoughts, all just so many nicely illustrative flights of fancy. As we'll recall, then, in chapter 3 of this book we encountered the idea of *individualistically directed propensities*, both those that a certain concrete entity may have to a certain other such individual, or to some certain others, and those that a concrete individual may have with respect to itself.[1] So, that's one large-scale substantial idea, or one big cluster of them. And, not far removed from it, or from them, here's another, which we'll next recall: Almost always found along with individualistically-directed powers, but not invariably so, in chapter 4 we encountered the idea of *time-sensitive propensities*—as with basic particles propensitied in such a way that, roughly speaking, they would only ever be arranged frogwise after they'd been arranged tadpolewise. Moving right along, in our parade of impressively substantial but sadly just-fanciful propositions, in chapter 5 we encountered matter that was so propensitied that, while it would assume certain spatial configurations, would cease to exist should there be any force, or any whatnot at all, aiming to have it assume any other spatial configurations. Should some such spherically shaped matter be taken and transformed toward constituting a cube, for example, the matter would annihilate before any cube ever formed. And, in the just previous chapter, of course, we encountered a couple of forms of Interactionist Substantial Dualism, the so-called *Generational* Form and the so-called *Quasi-Platonic* Form, the quite novel forms of this time-honored Dualism discussed in my tome, *All the Power in the World*.

With that refreshing recapitulation, you should now be vividly entertaining the gist of what I've been doing and, to boot, a fair bit of that peculiarly imaginative activity's upshot: For guidance as to how things really are with concrete reality, or even for how things might very well be, what I've placed on offer is just some terribly gestural material and, at that, the gestures provided aren't likely to point along lines where, concerning much of concrete reality, any substantial discoveries will be found. (And, if, perhaps in the distant future, any of it ever should be so useful or fruitful, that will owe far more to good fortune than any prescient insight on my part.) Taking little for granted, however, it is best that I make it perfectly clear—or as clear as I can do—how little should be expected from a human philosopher, unless she should be, quite as well, a terribly impressive scientist. That might not always have been so. But, as I reckon, it has been true for at least a century by now, and it will continue to hold true going forward, with no end ever in sight. Indeed, at least for those who have read this book's earlier chapters, nothing else should seem even the least bit plausible. And, further exploration will serve only to confirm that assessment. (A few little object lessons of just that sort will occupy most of this final chapter.)

I do not make those statements lightly, or from out of the blue. More than a few times, I have asked leading philosophers of physics whether they know of any philosophers who have offered, in the last century or so, some novel large-scale concretely substantial ideas, at least pretty large-scale, concerning how

---

1. And, in addition to that, we encountered the pretty closely related idea of real-kind directed propensities, each of these being always historically based powers, rather than any merely generalistically directed dispositions. Anyhow, at this juncture, I mention them only in a mere note.

things are with concrete reality, presumably concerning, at least for the most part, quite clearly physical aspects of this reality. As I made clear, in each instance, I was *not* looking for any such ideas placed on offer by philosophically inclined *physicists*, or philosophically inclined *scientists of any other sort*. (Nor was I looking for new concretely robust hypotheses from scientists not so philosophically inclined, as I also made clear to my friendly informants.) Always, their answers were rather negative; indeed, the more terrifyingly intelligent and knowledgeable my informants, the more clearly negative were the replies. That was quite disappointing, as you may imagine.

Though, for obvious reasons, my hopes there were not as high at the outset, I have been disappointed, as well, even if not so deeply, when asking for relevantly similar positive input from philosophers of psychology, and from philosophers of biology. Placing aside many quite parochial propositions, and numerous empty ideas, of course, nobody had anything much to report and, as best I could tell, nothing at all clearly relevant to my query.

Anyhow, at least for the meanwhile, that's enough truthful gloom and doom. So, sometimes standing on the shoulders of some brilliant predecessors, and other times just lurching about, in most of the relatively few pages remaining in this book, I will conduct a few more philosophical exercises. To the more open-minded among us, I think these exercises may prove to be instructively convincing: Unless deeply informed by scientific thinking, little of moment will be gained from philosophy anymore, at least as concerns how things are with concrete reality, or all but the most parochial aspects of concrete reality. Of course, the more close-minded will still find it hard to see things in that painfully truthful way. But, even for the most dogmatic and complacent of readers, I trust that the material upcoming will provide some enjoyably entertaining philosophical exercises. That may be quite enough reason, I think, for them to be given a bit of my space and a bit of your time.

1. Concretely Substantial Ideas about Mutually Isolated Concrete Worlds: First Part

To this point in our exploration, I've mostly focused on just two main ways to confront notably novel and characteristically philosophical ideas. Both concern our widely shared Scientiphicalism. As you'll recall, one concerns how we might variously and substantially specify Scientiphicalism, with each such specification differing substantially from the others. And, as you'll also recall, the other concerns how we might variously and substantially depart from the Scientiphical Metaphysic, with each such departure differing substantially from the others. In this section, I'll consider a third way to confront some novel philosophical ideas.

As I said, this third way doesn't much concern our shared Scientiphicalism, but proceeds in a way quite unrelated to any of that. But, more positively, what is this third way?

Toward getting a good start on a nicely instructive answer, we will recall, from the first chapter, our own discussion of the most distinctively Lewisian of all the many novel thoughts placed on offer by David Lewis and, perhaps, the only new truly philosophical thought—the polar opposite of any parochial idea—that he ever proposed for serious consideration. As we'll now recall, then, one way for absolutely all concrete reality to be is for it to comprise, include, or contain, in addition to the concrete world that we ourselves inhabit, infinitely many other concrete worlds, each absolutely isolated from all the others, even as each and all are absolutely isolated from our own world, that is, from the actual world.[2] And, though Lewis himself never proposed anything much more than that, along the lines we're currently pursuing, still, our own earlier discussion happily did just that. As we there proposed, quite intuitively and correctly, I feel sure, this "relevantly plenitudinous" way for concrete reality to be is only one (far from absolutely specific) way for all concrete reality to be. By contrast with it, there are infinitely many other ways for it to be, including infinitely many ways each less plenitudinous than the way Lewis favored and, less obviously so, but just as well, infinitely many each more plenitudinous than any he ever wished seriously to consider, as well as infinitely many exactly as plenitudinous. Among the former ways—ways where all concrete reality isn't so terribly vast or so terribly varied—is the way in which there is always just one single concrete world. Of course, this is the way almost everyone takes all concrete reality to be, or almost all my own world-mates do. But, for our discussion, that may not matter, at least not at the discussion's start. Right now, what may matter most is for me simply to notice that, in terms of my most favored distinction, all the ideas just introduced are concretely substantial ideas. And, what's more, none is any mere parochial proposition, nor anything even remotely likely any mere definition.

But, with this last remark, I may be getting ahead of myself, or too far ahead of my readers, at any rate. So, let's slow down now, pausing to reflect on what's now been, for decades, some philosophical common coin. Trying to be helpful, I'll rehearse the bare bones of Lewis's favored conception of how everything is with all that's concrete.

On the central Lewisian idea, concrete reality is far more extensive than on our commonsensical ideas of things. As common sense has it, *absolutely every* spatially located object is spatially related to *absolutely all* other spatially located

---

2. See David Lewis, *On the Plurality of Worlds*, Blackwell Publishers, 1986, pages 1–3. This is the classic version of Lewis's many-worlds metaphysics: many of the ideas treated here were previously espoused, years earlier, in other publications.

objects. Here the same, absolutely all spatial objects are in a single spatial world, the only concrete world that ever there is. On the Lewisian idea, by contrast, there are many spatially located objects that are not spatially related, at all, to many other spatially located objects. Just so, those objects spatially related to other spatial things will be in the same world as them, while other spatial objects, not spatially related to the aforesaid concreta, will be in another concrete world or, taking them all together, in many other concrete worlds. As I feel sure, you've now gotten the hang of it all, and quite well, at that.

On the Lewisian idea, and against commonsense thinking, not only is concrete reality far more extensive than ordinarily thought, but it's far more varied, as well. Indeed, for Lewis himself, the importance of the thought that reality is so extensive is that, only in that way, can concrete reality comprise an extraordinarily great infinite variety of concreta. Just so, it's only in this way that concrete reality will include naturally purple elephants and singing chipmunks. And, more fundamentally, it's only in this way, too, that there will be, in absolutely all of what's concretely real, all manner of relevantly basic electrons (or electron-like particles): It's only thus that, for each value of n, where n may be any real number, there will be a world whose basic particles include all its electrons (or its electron-like particles), with every last one of that world's electrons having a mass exactly n times that of each of the electrons in our actual world (even as, we may suppose, electron's are basic in our own world.)

For decades, that's been much discussed in mainstream philosophical literature. Related to it, the issues next upcoming have received rather little discussion, though Lewis said something about them and, though I'd forgotten it, so did I. Two related passages from Lewis show that, one a paragraph from his masterwork's text, the other a note appended to that paragraph. Here's the text's (most relevant) paragraph itself, happily quite concise:

> For all I know, there are many indiscernible worlds, so that the worlds are even more abundant than we would otherwise think. I see no theoretical benefits to be gained by supposing that there are or that there are not, so on this question I advise that we remain agnostic.[3]

And, here's the note Lewis appends to that, complete with its typo, and not so concise:

> I am inclined to agree with Unger (Minimizing Arbitrariness, page 47) that we have reason to reject hypotheses that involve gratuitous arbitrariness, and thereby suggest – unacceptably – that the geography of space is a contingent matter. For instance, we may reject the obnoxiously arbitrary hypothesis that each world has exactly seventeen, or exactly aleph-seventeen, indiscernible

3. *On the Plurality of Worlds*, page 224.

duplicates; or the hypothesis that nice worlds have more duplicates than nasty ones. But the hypothesis that there is no duplication at all is not obnoxiously arbitrary; and neither is the hypothesis that all worlds alike are infinitely reduplicated to the same extent, provided we do not specify some obnoxiously arbitrary cardinal. So the principle of rejecting arbitrariness does not tell us whether or not there are indiscernible worlds.[4]

As Lewis appears to think, it's unacceptable to think that "the geography of space" is a contingent matter. Myself, I'm inclined to favor the idea. At all events, what's now most relevant for us is "the geography of logical space", so to put it. Let me amplify and clarify.

Though it's *not a plausible* thought and *not an elegant idea*, still, this following thought is a concretely substantial idea: There are always exactly fifty-two mutually isolated concrete worlds. Now, in one respect, that's a perfectly specific idea, by contrast with, say, the idea that there are *quite a few* mutually isolated concrete worlds. But, in virtually all other respects, it specifies hardly anything. Roughly, what are any of the fifty-two worlds like? Are some of the worlds substantially different from others? Our bald thought doesn't specify.

Even as it's highly unspecific, we can tell that our thought that there are exactly fifty-two concrete worlds is consistent with infinitely many more specific ideas, including these two:

(1)   There are always exactly fifty-two mutually isolated concrete worlds. At every moment of their existence, fifty of the worlds are exactly like each other, with one of these precisely similar worlds being our actual world; at every moment of its existence another world, far poorer than any of those fifty, comprises exactly two electrons, and no other concretum at all; and, at every moment of its existence, yet another world, poorer still, comprises just a single electron, and never any other concretum at all.

(2)   There are always exactly fifty-two mutually isolated concrete worlds. At every moment of their existence, each of the fifty-two worlds is pretty similar to all the others, with one of these pretty similar worlds being our actual world; one of the worlds that's not ours is as like ours as can possibly be, for a world that, unlike ours, never has any turnips; another world is also very much like our own, while slightly differing from ours in a somewhat different way—it's as much like ours as a

4. *On the Plurality of Worlds*, page 224. The paper of mine that Lewis refers to, "Minimizing Arbitrariness," was first published in *Midwest Studies in Philosophy*, IX (1984): 29–51. It's reprinted on pages 180–208 in Volume 1 of my *Philosophical Papers*, Oxford University Press, 2006. Not only did I forget about Lewis's passages, but I also forgot my own early work. Such is the lot of this sorry senior citizen. For directing me to the relevant section of Lewis's brilliant book, I thank Alan Sidelle, whose memory is far better than mine now is.

world can possibly be, for a world that, unlike ours, never has any *tulips*; still another world is also very much like our own, while slightly differing from ours in another somewhat different way..., and so on.

Just as our thought as to precisely fifty-two isolated worlds leaves ever so much completely unspecified and utterly open, so Lewis's idea also leaves a lot open. Let me explain.

Familiar to metaphysicians, Lewis has there be an infinite number of mutually isolated worlds. And, as he has it, some such slogan as this will hold good, or true: "For each utterly precise and specific way for a world to be, there's a world that is just that very way."[5] Never mind, at least for now, the difficulty in making this slogan into anything even remotely close to an adequate expression of Lewis's central idea here. That same idea may be otherwise expressed, also rather roughly and also not very badly: "Every possible combination of quality instances is realized, each wholly in, and with, its own isolated world."

Quite beyond all the hodge-podge in that, there's all the hodge-podge in this, too: On one concretely substantial idea, there's exactly one world that's precisely like the actual world; of course, it is the actual world—so, on this idea, the actual world has no precise twin. On a conflicting substantial idea, the actual world does have a precise twin, just precisely one world just like it. On a third conflicting idea, the actual world is one of three precisely similar mutually isolated triplets. And so it goes. Myself, I'm partial to a substantial idea along this much more generous line: "For each utterly precise and specific way for a world to be, there's an infinity of worlds each of which is just that very way."[6] Of course, what I happen to like here isn't anything of general philosophical interest. What's more interesting is, of course, the infinity of the presently salient substantial competitors.

---

5. In *On the Plurality of Worlds*, Lewis begins his section called "Plenitude" with these sentences, on page 86:

> At the outset, I mentioned several ways that a world might be; and then I made it part of my modal realism that
>
> > (1) absolutely every way that a world could possibly be is a way that some world is, and
> > (2) absolutely every way that a part of a world could possibly be is a way that some part of some world is.
>
> But what does that mean? It seems to mean that the worlds are abundant, and logical space is somehow complete. There are no gaps in logical space; no vacancies where a world might have been, but isn't. It seems to be a principle of plenitude. But is it really?

In the text I try to do a little something to put some flesh on these bare bones, but only a little.

6. If there's a certain infinity of worlds that's greater than another, then put me down for the greater of the two. If there's a greatest infinity in this pluriversal ballpark, then put me down for biggest batch of worlds. If there isn't any greatest, then there'll be nothing I'll favor greatly. At all events, I'm for Abundance here: As long as an item's fully concrete, or really real, let it in!

In recent mainstream philosophy, Lewis is not the only greatly talented philosopher to contemplate seriously the concretely substantial matters on which this present section focuses. Another is Derek Parfit. Though they have drawbacks, here are useful passages from him:

> It will help to distinguish two kinds of possibilities. *Cosmic* possibilities cover everything that ever exists, and are the different ways that the whole of reality might be. Only one such possibility can be actual, or be the one that *obtains*. *Local* possibilities are the different ways that some part of reality, or *local world*, might be. If some local world exists, that leaves it open whether other worlds exist.
>
> One cosmic possibility is, roughly, that every possible local world exists. This we can call the *All Worlds Hypothesis*. Another possibility, which might have obtained, is that nothing ever exists. This we can call the *Null Possibility*. In each of the remaining possibilities, the number of local worlds that exist is between none and all. There are countless of these possibilities, since there are countless combinations of local worlds.
>
> Of these possibilities, one must obtain, and only one can obtain.[7]

Here the great drawback is this: Parfit makes no provision for how many local worlds, of any absolutely precise sort for such worlds, there may be. Will each absolutely precise sort of local world be instanced only once, or will it be twice, or thrice, or what? It is all left open.

Be that as it may, the line of thinking Parfit hopes to convey is, in general, the line I mean, right here and now, to propose and even to highlight. While he may be quite unclear and confused, we may readily do much better: Even as there are infinitely many ways for concrete reality to exhibit variety or, on the other hand, to exhibit monotony, so there are, for each of those infinitely many ways, an infinity of ways in which it may be more or less numerously instanced, exemplified, or fulfilled. Along either of these lines for specifying how things are concretely, so to put it, there will be a vast infinity of concretely substantial thoughts as to how things are with concrete reality, each differing from all the others. With both lines together, the impressive infinity of ways is yet more impressive still.

---

7. See Derek Parfit, "Why Anything? Why This?" originally published in *London Review of Books*, 22 January and 5 February 1998; reprinted in Peter van Inwagen and Dean Zimmerman (eds.) *Metaphysics: The Big Questions*, Second Edition, Blackwell Publishing, 2008, on pages 576–94. In the reprinted paper, the cited passage is on page 581.

For Parfit scholars, I note that the first appendix to Volume Two of Parfit's *On What Matters*, Oxford University Press, 2011, has the very same title and, at least very nearly, the same substance, as well. That is Appendix D, which appears, in that volume, on pages 623–48.

2. Concretely Substantial Ideas about Mutually Isolated Concrete Worlds: Second Part

With that properly appreciated, let's reflect on a very different sort of question concerning all the ways that things may be with absolutely all of concrete reality.

What I now have in mind is this big idea: One possible way for all concrete reality to be is that it comprise (even infinitely many) concrete worlds that fulfill a thought, or some thoughts, represented by our displayed Entity Materialism—in all these worlds every entity is a material entity—*and that it comprise* (even infinitely many) worlds that fulfill a thought, or some thoughts, represented by our *Entity Idealism*—in all these *other* worlds every entity is mental and none is material—*and also that it comprise* (even infinitely many) worlds that fulfill a thought, or some thoughts, represented by our *Entity Dualism*—in all these *still other* worlds some entities are mental, and some are material, even while none at all are both mental and material. In at least a certain sense or way, then, with a nicely apt application of, or specification of, our substantial Lewisian idea, we may be (at least somewhat) ecumenical.

I shall not go on at any very great length about the variety of ways for all concrete reality to be that, with various specifications of our Lewisian idea, we may clearly enough contemplate. But along the lines we've just been discussing—indeed, quite a lot further along them—it's worth noting, I think, a certain variety that, in terms of this idea, may obtain in concrete reality. Let me amplify.

Somewhat interestingly related to all the concrete worlds representing our Entity Materialism, and those representing our Entity Idealism, and those representing our Entity Dualism, there may be, in addition to worlds of those three sorts, worlds of six other sorts of concrete worlds. This is pretty easy to contemplate, though I don't know of anyone who, before me, did consider the notion. Anyhow, I myself became aware of the matter after, at long last, realizing the following two things about our by-now-oft-noted trio: First, each member of the trio features just two salient properties that a concrete entity might be alleged to have, or that it might be said to lack, one (the property of being) mental and the other (the property of being) material. And, second, with respect to how a world's entities might realize each of these two properties, or exemplify them, and with how such entities might fail to do so, there are three (at least formal) possibilities to consider. With regard to each of the two properties, being material and being mental, a concrete world may be such that (i) all its entities have the property, or (ii) some but not all have it, or (iii) none of the world's concreta has the characteristic in question.[8]

8. Descartes held, of course, that it was absolutely impossible for any concretum that was spatially extended—for him the same as material—to be a thinking concretum—for him the same as a mental concretum, even as it was impossible for a mental concretum to be a material concretum. Why? Well, as he thought, he could tell this just from fully appreciating his idea of spatial

With that in mind, I will make it vivid by providing this combinatorial table:

Nine Sorts of Concrete World

	Material Entities	Mental Entities
1	All	All
2	All	Only Some
3	All	None
4	Only Some	All
5	Only Some	Only Some
6	Only Some	None
7	None	All
8	None	Only Some
9	None	None

(If only with a few parenthetical paragraphs, I'll provide instructions helpful, at least to some, for interpreting and using this table.)

(To use the table in a way that should satisfy even the silliest of irrelevant objectors—you may substitute for "material" a word that's more to your liking, though a word, of course, to much the same effect—perhaps choosing "physical" or, more adventurously, perhaps choosing "spatial", or "spatiotemporal". And, a similar instruction should satisfy other presently irrelevant objectors—as

---

extension and, as well, his idea of thinking—even as you and I can tell that it is impossible for something to be a perfect sphere and be something with corners, and impossible to be a clearly cornered thing and also be a perfect sphere. It is in his Sixth Meditation that Descartes assertively argues for his Dualism, when he offers the bold words of which this is an apt English translation:

> It is true that I may have (or, to anticipate, that I certainly have) a body that is very closely joined to me. But, nevertheless, on the one hand, I have a clear and distinct idea of myself, in so far as I am simply a thinking nonextended thing; and on the other hand I have a distinct idea of body, in so far as this is simply an extended, nonthinking thing. And, accordingly, it is certain that I am really distinct from my body, and can exist without it.

I lift that passage from *The Philosophical Writings of Descartes*, trans. J. Cottingham, R. Stoothoff, and D. Murdoch, Volume II, Cambridge University Press, 1984, page 54. Quite clearly, just that is Descartes' first and most central argument for his dualism. Despite what almost all most prominent mainstreamers appear to think, Descartes's (talking about his) being able to clearly conceive himself existing without anything spatial (or material) existing, and his suggesting that the same holds for you and for me, well, all that played no such central role in, what, even by his own lights, is the (strongest) reason for embracing his Substantial Dualism.

At all events, I take it that, at least more likely than not, Descartes is just wrong in thinking that its absolutely impossible for a concretum to be, at once, both a thinking thing and also a thing that is spatially extended. As it seems to me, he confuses *one's not clearly conceiving how it may be that something is so*—here our not clearly conceiving how it may be that a spatial thing is a conscious thinker—with one's clearly conceiving how it must be that something is not so. But, whatever the reason for it, it certainly seems, at least, that Descartes is wrong here. Assuming that, to put things more gently, I return to the text and proceed.

with those who don't like my choice of "mental"—they may choose, instead of that, "experiential", or "conscious", or some other cognate term.)

(As I have assumed almost everywhere in this book, and I am assuming in this exercise, there is nothing about the semantics of the main terms in play that renders them deeply deficient—unsatisfiable by any object whatever, or even any concrete individual that may be most useful for us here to consider. On the other side of the coin, I assume that nothing about the semantics of these terms, or anything of the like, has it that absolutely everything must satisfy either one of the terms, let alone both of them. Just so, we shall not allow any merely semantic issues, or anything of that ilk, to stop us from considering, well enough, relevantly wide varieties of philosophical thoughts that are concretely substantial ideas, a fair number of them novel and many more not so novel.)

With this table before us, and with it being used appropriately, we may almost mechanically specify a philosophically salient variety of ways for all of concrete reality to be. In one way for all concrete reality to be, concrete reality will comprise only worlds of the first of the nine sorts, including none of the other eight. In a second way, it will comprise only worlds of the second sort, and so on.

But, of course, with that we were just warming up for the bulk of our present mechanically imaginative exercise. So, on still another way, concrete reality will comprise worlds of just the first sort and the second sort, but none of the third through ninth sort. On still yet another way, it will comprise worlds of just the first sort and the third sort, and so on, and so forth. Finally, and *in one way* most fully, I suppose, concrete reality may comprise worlds of all nine of these sorts. (Of course, we may combine these current considerations with those explored in the previous section, seeing, with a bit of specificity, at least, infinitely many ways for concrete reality to be: On one of them, there will be 9 worlds of the first of our nine sorts, 53 of the second, 111 of the third sort, and you may fill in the rest. On another, perhaps here the way that's the fullest of the full, there will be infinitely many worlds of each of the nine sorts.)

Though the thought of such a nicely various infinity of possibilities is at least a bit more interesting than almost anything to be found in the philosophical literature of the last fifty to seventy years, it is, for all that, not very interesting, at least not to almost all suitably serious people. One important reason for that is this: There will never be any strong reason to think that any of these ways for how all concrete reality should be is the one that obtains, nor any strong reason to eliminate any of an infinity of possibilities. Another reason, perhaps yet more important is this: As nothing concrete beyond our actual world will ever bear any external relations at all to what's actual, including all actual sentient beings, nothing but actual concreta will ever have any effect, or influence, on any of us—even as none of us will ever have any influence on anything but that. And, along correlative or complementary lines, there are many other reasons for serious and sensible folks to find precious little interest, or none at all, in the fanciful thought, or thoughts, that I've brought to our notice in this section soon closing.[9]

With that said, let's turn to discuss (nothing more far-reaching than some questions concerning only what's our) actual concrete reality.[10]

3. Some Substantial Philosophical Thoughts about Actual Concrete Reality

To come by some ideas that are a bit more interesting than those contemplated in the just previous section, we can take that section's table and, changing only

9. Even while we'll never have any strong reason to believe that there is more to concrete reality than just what's in, or what's of, the actual world, it's also true, I feel sure, that we'll never have any strong reason to think the opposite, either. As far as our reasons for belief go, it's left open whether there are very many concrete worlds or whether there is only ever one. Little doubt but that almost everyone will continue to believe, even as almost everyone has long believed, that every spatial object is spatially related to all other spatial objects and, in all other ways relevant to the matter, as well, all there ever is to concrete reality is whatever there is to our actual world. That may well be right, of course, but, as far as our reasons for believing anything go, it also may well be wrong. Thinking all that to be so, I myself am agnostic on this issue.

10. Not that it's any big deal, I'll be the first to admit, but, especially at this juncture, there are some matters of formulation worth at least a very little bit of attention. As you'll recall from chapter 2, I presented three saliently competing metaphysical views, Entity Materialism, Entity Dualism and Entity Idealism. Not wanting to distract us with thoughts about anything remotely like a plurality of concrete worlds, I presented Entity Materialism just like this:

> Entity Materialism: There's at least one concrete entity. Any concrete entity is a purely material entity; that is, it's fully physical. (So, if there are any minds or souls, then each will be something material.)

Well, just because there are all these far-fetched possibilities for how things may be with concrete reality, it is somewhat worth noting that, for a most apt expression of quite typical philosophical views, more complex formulations may be wanted than those usually presented. For example, the view of a typical materialist philosopher is not meant to concern anything more than the actual world. And, indeed, except for Lewis himself, (almost) every materialist thinker has held the view that all there is to concrete reality is actual concrete reality. So, for a formulation fit to express the position of a typical materialist philosopher, we may turn from the Entity Materialism displayed to the more specific thesis:

> Explicitly All-Encompassing Entity Materialism: In all of concrete reality, there is only ever exactly one concrete world, the actual world. In this world, there's at least one concrete entity. And, any concrete entity is a purely material entity; that is, it's fully physical. (So, if there are any minds or souls, then each will be something material.)

Using that as a template, it's easy to formulate correlative Idealist and Dualist positions. As I feel sure, it is such tighter versions, or such more explicit versions of these views that have been endorsed by virtually all philosophers who've ever endorsed them, and have been rejected by virtually all who've ever rejected them. With that said, when discussing concretely substantial metaphysical views aimed at only our actual world, I won't bother to be so explicitly specific.

its heading, we may confront a most happily suggestive schedule to consider. Here it is:

Nine Ideas about Actual Concrete Reality

	Material Entities	Mental Entities
1	All	All
2	All	Only Some
3	All	None
4	Only Some	All
5	Only Some	Only Some
6	Only Some	None
7	None	All
8	None	Only Some
9	None	None

While I must give some instructions on how to read this table, they'll be pretty obvious, I should think. Anyway, they'll be very easy to grasp and to follow.

In this table, the number on the left is the number assigned, quite arbitrarily, to a certain view as to the nature and variety of entities—or maybe just a single entity—that are the entities of the actual world (or, in Lewis's jargon, that are the inhabitants of the actual world). So, the view that has "1" as its number is the concretely substantial thought that the actual world comprises entities—or a single entity—all of which are material and all of which are mental.

On the intended interpretation of the table, which is just the most obvious interpretation, each of the nine numbered views conflicts with each of the others. Moreover, as I've set things up, of course, the logical situation is this: While no more than one of the views can be true, at least one of these nine views must be true. (Indeed, even if there should never be any actual concreta at all, that will be so. In such a case, evidently absurd, view number 9 will hold true—as there will be no concreta at all, there will be none that are material and there will be none that are mental.[11])

11. Among earlier work of which I'm aware, none is terribly like what I'll next be doing. Perhaps what's closest may be some largely taxonomic work by C. D. Broad, in *The Mind and Its Place in Nature*, London Kegan Paul, Trench, Trubner & Co., 1925. On page 607 of the big book, there begins a section called *The Seventeen Types of Theory*. As it appears, the main factor for dividing theories into types is how a theory fares as regards its allowing, or its disallowing, things that might be material and, on the other side, things that might be mental. Within this framework, Broad is concerned with (1) what a theory says about whether being material is (what Broad calls) a *differentiating characteristic*, and similarly with whether being mental is that, and (2) whether being material is (what Broad calls) a *delusive characteristic*, and similarly with whether being mental is that, and (3) whether being material is (what Broad calls) an *emergent characteristic*, and similarly with whether being mental is that. Broad rings changes on these factors, sometimes in a way that seems idiosyncratic, rather than driven by a need for comprehensiveness. To my mind, this happens even with the first two of his seventeen types, as with this passage:

With our newest table as our guide, let's briefly consider the nine sorts of metaphysical position that, regarding actual concrete reality, we may now do well to notice.

As we know that we ourselves think and experience, we can immediately rule out, as false, all three of these views that say that none of the actual concreta are mental concreta. So, beyond this short paragraph, we need not discuss View 3, View 6 and View 9. This leaves only six broad views to consider as possibly true of actual concrete reality.

Contemplating only such views as are not conceptually impossible, or analytically false, we may say that a panpsychist view is a view according to which all of concrete reality is mental, whatever else the view might hold as to concrete reality. Concerning actual concrete reality, any view, in our schedule, that has an "All" in its right-hand column, the column for what it takes to be mental, is a panpsychist view. In our schedule, View 1, View 4 and View 7 are the panpsychist views. (For no very good reason, in recent decades, at least, that label has been applied only to versions of View 1, and not to versions of the other two sorts of views that, just as aptly, I call versions of Panpsychism.)

On View 1, all of concrete reality is material and all of concrete reality is mental. As many will agree, Spinoza held a version of View 1. In the recent literature, perhaps Galen Strawson has championed (a version of) View 1.[12] At the least, he has championed something rather like a version of View 1, even if perhaps rather more limited than what's most properly called (a version of) *pan*psychism.

On View 7, all of concrete reality is mental reality—so it is certainly a panpsychist view—though *none* of concrete reality is ever any material reality. As I understand him, Berkeley is the paradigmatic proponent of this view, often called *idealism*. In the recent literature, it has been endorsed by very few, but their small number does include at least one quite astute philosopher, John Foster.[13]

(1,1)   Mentality and Materiality are both differentiating attributes which can belong to the same substance. This I will call "Dualism of Incompatibles".

(1,2)   Mentality and Materiality are both differentiating attributes, but they cannot both belong to the same substance. This I will call "Pure Materialism". (page 607)

12. Among his more salient writings of this sort, there is his "Realistic Monism", appearing as the Target Paper of *Consciousness and its place in nature: does physicalism entail Panpsychism?* Anthony Freeman, ed., Imprint Academic, 2006. Strawson's paper appears on pages 3–31 of the volume. This volume contains many replies to Strawson, some of which strike me as quite devastating to his position or, for that matter, to any view remotely like it. In particular, see Philip Goff "Experiences Don't Sum" on pages 53 through 61 and Frank Jackson "Galen Strawson on Panpsychism", on pages 62 through 64.

13. See John Foster, *The Case for Idealism*, Routledge & Kegan Paul, London, 1982.

There remains only one sort of panpsychist view to consider, View 4. According this view, while all of actual concrete reality is mental, only some of that reality, and not all of it, is material. As I understand them, many theists have held, and many still hold, this view. But, as concerns secular thinkers, including the vast majority of mainstream philosophers, I know of nobody who has held this view. Why that is so may well be an interesting question, though I won't, in this book, discuss the question.

As best I can tell, for all any of us know, any of these panpsychist views might be true. At the very least, I have never seen any strong reason for denying any of them, even while I can't find any strong reason, either, for accepting any of them, or for favoring any one of the views over the two others. With that said, we turn to discuss, if only briefly, the three remaining views in this section's salient table.

Taking these three positions in numerical order, we first consider View 2. According to this view, while all of actual concrete reality is material, only some of it is mental. So, mental entities are, on this view, just a *special sort* of material beings. One version of this view is what I have called So-Called Commonsense Materialism. While no basic physical entity is mental, quite a few very complex physical entities have mental powers and, so, they are mental entities, as well. For the last half-century or so, this version of View 2, which we may also call *Selective Materialism*, has been the dominant view among mainstream philosophers, and by quite a wide margin. Among those discussed a lot in this book, David Lewis is, perhaps, the very most prominent of these Selective Materialist philosophers, some others being Hilary Putnam, Donald Davidson, David Armstrong, and Sydney Shoemaker. In the previous chapter, I offered an argument against Selective Materialism, or So-Called Commonsense Materialism. So, I am inclined to reject this view, though I haven't seen enough for me to reject the view.

View 5 comes in various versions, some of which are salient and time-honored, and others of which may have never been held by anyone, or at least not by anyone of whom I'm aware. The most famous view of this sort is, of course, mind-body dualism, upheld by Descartes and, in times long past, by other very brilliant philosophers, too. On this Cartesian view, there must be accepted, in addition to what is represented in our schedule, two further propositions. One of them is this: In all actual concrete reality, every entity is either a material entity or a mental entity. And, the other is this: In actual concrete reality, whatever is a material entity is not any mental entity, and whatever is a mental entity is not any material entity. As far as I can tell, there is nobody of any philosophical prominence who held a version of View 5 who did not also accept these two propositions. It may well be an interesting question as to why that is so. But, in this book, I shall not discuss that question.

While I prefer a Substantial Dualist position to any of its competitors, I can't see any reason in favor of the view that's so terribly strong as to compel belief in the position and, in fact, I don't go so far as to believe the view.[14] (Thinking that I have no terribly good reason to reject it, I don't reject it, either.)

As I'm pretty sure, it is a view of this sort that is believed by, for example, the vast majority of the United States electorate, at this present time, early in the 21st century. And, it is also true of the majority of various elite subgroups of that vast population, as with most of the top 5% by education, or by measured intelligence, or by income, or by measured happiness. None of these very many people, I am sure, neither those in the vast masses nor those in the elite classes, have any strong reason to believe the view. But, unlike me, who just likes the position, believe it they do. Little doubt, their belief in this dualism comports well with their religious views, or, at least, it comports *as well* with their belief in a Savior as can be expected from them. In the context of the present volume, that fact may be a quite notable fact. By contrast with those in these elites, not to mention those in the masses, the vast majority of mainstream philosophers— a miniscule group compared with even the smallest of the latterly mentioned others—won't so much as give a Cartesian view the time of day. Concerning large-scale questions of concrete reality, materiality and mentality, what do these philosophers know that makes them so different from the others, in this presently salient way? As I feel sure, it is nothing or, at the very most, it is not much at all.

It is now only View 8 that remains for us to address. This is the view according to which, while *only some* of the actual world's concreta are mental, none at all are material, or spatial, or physical. As with some other views noted just above, I know of nobody who holds this sort of view. As I feel sure, if it has been upheld, its advocates have not been any very prominent philosophical thinkers. Why should that be so? Perhaps it is an interesting question, and perhaps not. At any rate, I pass over the issue now.

Even if only with very broad brushstrokes, we have treated all the main positions, concerning the mental and the physical, as they pertain to all actual concrete reality. As we observed, there is strong reason to rule out some, and pretty strong reason to reject some others. But, there is no good reason, nor even anything close to it, to believe any of these views, as against a fair number of competitors, all of which remain in contention.

In this section, I have observed several novel concretely substantial philosophical ideas concerning the most central considerations regarding the mental

---

14. At the time of this writing, hardly any prominent mainstream philosophers have had much good to say, in their philosophical publications, in favor of any really robust sort of Dualism, or what I have called Entity Dualism. An exception to that is, I think, Dean Zimmerman in his "From Property Dualism to Substance Dualism", *Aristotelian Society Proceedings Supplement* LXXXIV (2010), pp.119–150. I hope that my reluctance to embrace Entity Dualism, or Substance Dualism, is not due, in any great measure, the fact that the View is so terribly unpopular, even so widely and deeply disdained, among almost all those in my professional culture-circle.

and the material as regards all actual concrete reality. Or, if not utterly novel, then at least views proposed, or upheld, by nobody of whom I'm aware. (The exact number of proposals depends, of course, on the level of abstraction used in categorizing the views: From View 5 alone, for example, we can detail several versions of the view that, so far as I know, nobody of any philosophical prominence has ever held.) While a few of these apparently novel views may be somewhat interesting, none strike me as very interesting. If I were to encounter even just a pretty strong reason to believe one of these newly proposed views, then that would be another matter. Indeed, and now placing normatively loaded language aside, if I were to encounter *anything that seemed to favor any of these views in a way that was, to me, quite strikingly appealing, then that* would be another matter. But, as things are, none of them strike me as being a very interesting view.

As well as observing some novel sorts of view, regarding the mental, the physical, and all actual concrete reality, I have also just considered some old views. At least at this point in time, anyway, even if they should be worth more attention than the more obscure views just newly noted here, none of these older positions does much, either, to excite the inquiring mind.

4. Scientific Philosophers and Serious New Substantial Philosophy

As almost any open-minded reader will now agree, the prospects are dim for there being proposed, at any time in the not very distant future, any novel concretely substantial philosophical thoughts that, both shortly after their being proposed and for some considerable time beyond that, are worth much serious consideration, investigation, or exploration. And, with that, most will agree that, from philosophical quarters, there will be little to be learned about the world in which we all live except, perhaps, for just so many quite parochial propositions. Is there any hope for matters to improve here, perhaps even before any very great time passes?

Myself, I think that there may be some significant hope, even if not a great deal of hope.

For there to be any significant hope as regards philosophy's prospects, at least two things must come to pass, making for a happy convergence even if, perhaps, no very likely convergence: On the one hand, and at the very least, some of the most intelligent and philosophically talented young people must become serious scientists, contributing a great deal to the science in which they are involved and, what's more, contributing *at least about* as much to science as they contribute to philosophy. To astute readers, at first blush that should seem all but impossible. But, I have not yet said anything about what's on the other hand. So, on the other hand, this must also happen: We must not require so very much of a proposed idea, by way of depth, or breath, or whatever other standard we have been employing, for the idea to count as a properly philosophical thought. This is not to say, of course, that the relevant standards—whatever they may be, exactly—must be lowered very greatly. To do that would be, of course, to give up on philosophy, at least as concerns its being a potential source for our learning anything much about the actual world. But, a little leeway can be, I think, happily tolerated. Putting the matter roughly, perhaps this much may suffice: As regards matters of depth, breadth, and the like, there will still be a significant difference between what will be allowed to count as a philosophical idea and, on the other side, very nearly all other concretely substantial ideas, including very nearly all scientific substantial propositions.

In such a circumstance, it will not be all but impossible for the very most intelligent and philosophically talented young thinkers to propose novel concretely substantial philosophical thoughts that, both shortly after their being proposed and for some considerable time beyond that, are worth much serious consideration, investigation, or exploration. Though it won't be all but impossible, it will be extremely difficult and, perhaps, it may be very unlikely. But, short of that, there is no realistic chance, at all, for there being offered, during the next century or so, any new concretely substantial philosophical ideas that amount to anything much more than idle speculation or—what may be worse—not so idle speculation. And, also short of that, beyond such rather baseless speculation, about all that will happen is almost certain to be just so much more of what, for the last century or more, has been happening.

With that said, there may be some significantly less grand work that, quite likely, at least a few philosophers can do and, indeed, perhaps some few have recently been doing. Even if less paradigmatically philosophical than what I've just been discussing, perhaps some of this less grand thinking may be philosophical *enough*, or *close enough* to what is (or has been) paradigmatically philosophical, that it may be properly regarded as being *more than just very marginally* philosophical.

5. Philosophy May Mine and Refine What Even the Most Ambitious Sciences Produce

The previous section's main message is, at least in its central thrust, I think, perfectly correct, or very nearly so. All too easily, I fear, the section suggests, even if it does not claim, that there is hardly anything worthwhile for "normal" mainstream philosophers to do now. But, that is not perfectly correct, nor even very nearly so. In the little that remains of this book, I shall try to say something along a more positive line. First, very briefly, and in just this short section, I'll relate worthwhile work that may be very available for a few present-day philosophers to do, even if it should not be available to the majority of present-day mainstream philosophers. Then, not quite so briefly, and in just the next section, I'll comment on work that may be very available to many more mainstream philosophers, very likely a clear majority of them. With that said, I proceed in the order just indicated.

In this present section, I will do little more than reproduce an e-mail exchange between me an one of my departmental colleagues, Tim Maudlin, whom, largely on the basis of all sorts of indirect evidence, I take to be at least as able a philosopher of science as anyone else currently active in that part of philosophy and, in particular, probably the philosophically most penetrating established philosopher of physics currently contributing to that more specific philosophical enterprise.[15]

After thoughtfully reading all the material in this chapter that precedes what is in this present section, but without his having read the book's earlier chapters, Tim e-mailed me some comments on what he there read. Here, I will reproduce most of that e-mail, comprising those comments most relevant to my present task, as well as a bit of verbiage that has the reproduced passages be most readable:

> I looked over your chapter, and have a few comments and some typos.

> Of course, I am doing a fair amount of guessing about what comes earlier in the manuscript, but I think I have some sense of the general thesis. You seem to have a rather jaundiced view of the accomplishments of "mainstream" philosophy. As you can imagine, I agree with the particular cases you discuss. But I think that the final conclusion is a bit too bleak. More specifically, I think that philosophers can make useful contributions to understanding the world even if they do not come up with large-scale, novel, fertile accounts of the world.

> In particular, philosophers are (at least sometimes) well trained in demanding some precision in concepts and argumentation. Many scientists are not, and the result is that there are arguments made in the sciences that are really quite dreadful. Furthermore, the explication of scientific theories is often rather poor. (For example, the so-called "twins paradox" is almost universally misexplained in the literature.) Philosophers have generally done a better job explicating the measurement problem in quantum mechanics than physicists. This sort of clarification would not, as far as I can tell, count as a novel

15. Much evidence for this remark may be found in these four books by Maudlin: *Quantum Non-Locality and Relativity: Metaphysical Intimations of Modern Physics*. Oxford: Basil Blackwell, 1994; Second Edition, 2002; Third Edition, 2011, *The Metaphysics Within Physics*, Oxford University Press, 2007, *Philosophy of Physics: Space and Time*, Princeton University Press, 2012, and *New Foundations for Physical Geometry: The Theory of Linear Structures*, Oxford University Press, 2014.

contribution from philosophy, but it is really quite valuable. So maybe you have set the bar too high in evaluating what philosophy can contribute.

. . . .

I also think that focusing on the various possible solutions to the mind/body (or consciousness/physical state) problem can be somewhat misleading. This is just (in my opinion) the hardest problem there is, and so it does not speak badly of philosophy that no solution commands rational assent. One might as well say that it is a failure of physics or of cognitive psychology. At least philosophers have kept the problematic alive.

I would also say that many scientists, especially physicists, rely on outmoded and unreliable views about semantics. That is, they often retreat to a very primitive form of behaviorism or instrumentalism, and act as if that is the only possible way to understand how language gets any content. Philosophers tend to have thought more about the relationship between language and the world, and what the "meaning" of a term may be. This can be salutary.

So all in all, I would give a larger scope for useful work done by philosophers than the long shot of the development of a revolutionary new ontological view that fits well with scientific research. Maybe you acknowledge all this earlier in the manuscript, but if so it does not come across in the chapter you sent.[16]

In using these comments to clarify this book's positions, I should begin, and I will begin, by saying that, in all that precedes this present chapter, in the body of the book, I don't go so far as positively to acknowledge that there may well be quite a lot of opportunity "for useful work done by philosophers than the long-shot of the development of a revolutionary new ontological view that fits well with scientific research." I do take great pains not to deny that that there is such opportunity, and to allow that, to a fair extent, at least, it is being met. And, by implication, I may do something like suggest as much. But, in response to Tim's words, I shall now go a bit further. As I assert right here and now, there is quite a large scope for useful work done by philosophers than the long-shot of the development of a revolutionary new ontological view that fits well with scientific research. At the same time, I will add that precious little of that scope will include attempts to advance thoughts concerning the general character of concrete reality, or anything of the like, that are not aptly informed by a deep knowledge of science, quite in the manner that I sketched in the just previous section. Though this does not do very much to make clear my views about mainstream philosophy's prospects, it is at least a clear start on diminishing the most daunting of the discouraging inferences that readers may make, upon encountering this book's material.

16. E-mail from Tim Maudlin to Peter Unger of June 6, 2013 at 2:16 p.m.

Even in this section, mostly focusing on some suggestions from Maudlin, I may go further toward making matters clearly less discouraging as concerns the prospects for analytic philosophy: Left to themselves, it appears, even the most philosophical of working scientists will often place on offer only something that is so badly confused that it is difficult to extract any interesting concretely substantial proposition from what they provide—from their provided strings of symbols, whether verbal or whether mathematical or whether otherwise. A few philosophers, both very knowledgeable scientifically and also very talented philosophically, can take whatever it is that these scientists provide and, through thinking about it suitably, they can provide reasonably clear concretely substantial ideas that may be, at once, both scientific and also philosophical.

At this present time, however, and in the not very distant future, that sort of worthwhile work will be done by only a very few professional philosophers—if the past, including the very recent past, is any indication. But, then, what might be done by the vast majority of those populating (even) the most reputable and respected philosophy departments? In the next section, which will be the very last in the book, I'll try to provide a reasonably realistic answer to this pretty daunting question.

6. Concrete Reality and Modest Philosophy

As I'm inclined to believe, most of any most realistic answer will center on thoughts like those expressed by the words that will quite directly follow this impending colon: In the near future, at any rate, mainstream philosophers may place on offer, in addition to ever so many quite credible *perfectly parochial* propositions, quite a few credible thoughts that are at least a bit more ambitious than that, even if, perhaps, not much more that a bit. In a phrase, they may do something pretty worthwhile by placing on offer quite a few *pretty parochial* (concretely substantial) propositions. Well, I've just vaguely indicated, twice over, what I take to be a very real possibility. Trusting that things may become a little less vague as we proceed, I'll briefly explore the possibility.

Quite as with many *perfectly* parochial ideas, many of these *pretty* parochial propositions will involve, quite centrally, points about which are the words ordinary human beings most ordinarily employ and how it is that, at least by their own lights, they employ the words most central to their working vocabularies. Beyond that, most of the rest will concern what we might call the specification of, or the articulation of, the more central of our common sense beliefs and, in the bargain, the more central of various others of the so-called *propositional attitudes*, saliently including our more central desires and values. (For my part, at least, I don't think we can get very far with either of these relevantly quite modest projects without, in the process, making some significant progress with

the other. Now, if that should be so, then, if they are to be quite reflective inquirers, most mainstream philosophers should be aware that it's no more than
this they'll be doing, or, perhaps, only a very little bit more.)

With only a few moments reflection, that should not seem very surprising.
As I said near the outset of the book, it is not any radical idea that, without
much infusion from the natural sciences, philosophy won't provide much, at all,
by way of credible concretely substantial ideas that are far from being just some
perfectly parochial propositions.

Look, I'm certainly not someone who seeks to stifle any intellectual crea-
tivity, or even much in the way of perfectly baseless speculation, a lot of which
might be, at least, pretty entertaining. (Indeed, I'm happy to place on offer very
many new baseless speculative ideas, none of them the least bit parochial, and
all quite concretely substantial, perhaps more than all other recent philosophers combined.) But, when doing this, we should be well aware, I'll suggest,
that it is only this that we are doing.

With that said, I'll return to the central thrust of this section's starting
paragraphs: When investigating our use of our ordinary language, or languages, it may well be a good idea for analytic philosophers to be, at once, increasingly systematic and increasingly skeptical. To a fair extent, at least, a
drive toward systematic inquiry has already gathered quite a bit of steam, with
the best young philosophers of language learning about as much linguistics as
philosophy. That must, I think, have been a helpful development, and it may be
hoped that lots more will occur, even as linguistics itself becomes more scientifically serious and fruitful.

That leads me to say a few things on behalf of some skepticism here.

In the first place, in those areas of linguistics most closely akin to philosophy—or of most interest to mainstream philosophers—what is taken as data is
often worse than terribly shaky. In both semantics and syntax, there are few
experiments done. Usually, scholarly linguistic work proceeds more like this:
What the linguist herself *feels is* acceptable—as this, or as that—is taken as *being*
acceptable—as this, or as that. Better to have sample sentences presented to
experimental subjects, with apt questions presented to the cooperative people,
and with hard statistical analysis done on what comes back from them. And,
equally important, it should be recognized—even emphasized—that often
there may be more variation, from one subject's idiolect to the idiolect of another, than there is commonality among the experimental subjects.

In the second place, and for now perhaps the last place, it should be recognized that there is a fair degree of play—and even arbitrariness—involved in
quite a few (at least) of the distinctions upon which linguists have relied, and
still rely. As I am confident, that is true for the distinction between what is a
semantic feature and, in supposed contrast, to that, what is a (merely) pragmatic feature. And, as I at least suspect, it is also true for the distinction between

what is a semantic feature and what is a syntactic feature. Let me amplify, as well as tantalize.

It has often occurred to me that, in unobvious ways, our language or, at least, our linguistically involved dispositions, allow us—indeed, they may even enjoin us—to go from a quite straightforward sentence we take to be plainly true to its opposite, which we take to be plainly false. Here is an instance of that, one among indefinitely many, with most of the others varying, in many ways, from this one that I display:

> There is no gold made from lead.
> Gold made from lead does not exist.
> There is something that does not exist that is gold made from lead.
> There is something that is gold made from lead that does not exist.
> There is something that is gold made from lead.
> There is gold made from lead.

Taken by itself, each move in this sequence seems quite appealing, and none much less so than most of the others. Of course, nobody is going to believe, as a result of going through this sequence, that there is gold made from lead. Certainly, there won't be any rush to resume alchemy. Nor will real trouble arise for at least almost anyone, with the possible exception of some tricky problems for those who would attempt an adequate understanding of how it is that we use the language we do, doing that in a way in which, almost always, has it be far more useful than frustrating.

I don't know quite what to make of this at least apparently paradoxical sequence, or of many others each also at least apparently paradoxical. Others may be better able than I to understand adequately these very many strange linguistic phenomena. Among them, some may wish to treat the moves along our noted sequence as moves rooted in semantics—or rooted in mistakes I've made about semantics. Others may wish to treat the moves as rooted in syntactic considerations—or in mistakes I've made regarding just so many syntactic matters. Still others, I should guess, may wish to treat everything here as turning on just some pragmatic considerations—or on some mistakes I've made about pragmatic matters.

Speaking for myself, I don't see anything to favor any one of these positions over any of the others. For that matter, I don't see anything, or anything much, to favor any one of them over the view that our progress may be rooted, all at once, in semantics, and in syntax, and in pragmatics, too. Or, at the least, so it seems to me.[17]

---

17. In my *Philosophical Relativity*, University of Minnesota Press, 1994 and Oxford University Press, 2002, I give reasons for being extremely skeptical that, in most of this, there is even any fact of the matter at all.

But, perhaps I may be wrong about that. For example, perhaps the 'semantic' position will emerge as being the most reasonable to adopt, or the closest to being true, or, in some other way, the position to be preferred. Or, as may also be, perhaps the 'pragmatic' position will emerge as being the best treatment of the matters in question. However any of that might turn out, one thing does seem, to my mind at least, to be quite clear. Whatever the outcome, there is nothing deep that is going on here, nor anything very substantial, in any apt sense of that word I've so often been using: Nothing of much importance will hinge on which of these categorizations is correct (assuming one of them is, which I'm happy to do for the sake of argument).

Even if I'm right in absolutely all of the foregoing commentary, I doubt that it will mean any great trouble. Of course, it won't lead to a troubling stampede into alchemy. But, more seriously, I doubt that it will mean any great trouble even for the likes of philosophy, or for any (other) rarified intellectual activity, e.g., for the scope and success of linguistic inquiry.

Certainly, it is not my aim to cause much long-lasting consternation. Rather, my thought is that, along with imaginative intellectual inquiry, we philosophers should assume, or maintain, a deeply held attitude of intellectual modesty. Indeed, as I see things, that thought is quite undeniable. For, even if there is very little for us to be ashamed of, there is an enormous amount—almost everything—about which we should be most modest.

BIBLIOGRAPHY

Armstrong, D. M. *Universals and Scientific Realism*, Cambridge University Press, 1978.

Armstrong, D. M. "Identity through Time," in P. van Inwagen (ed.), *Time and Cause*, (Dordrecht, Holland: D. Reidel, 1980.

Armstrong, D. M. *A World of States of Affairs*, Cambridge University Press, 1997.

Baker, Lynn Rudder. "Why Constitution is Not Identity," *Journal of Philosophy*, XCIV, 1997.

Baker, Lynn Rudder. *The Metaphysics of Everyday Life*, Cambridge University Press, 2007.

Barnett, David. "Is Water Necessarily Identical to H_2O?" *Philosophical Studies*, 98, 2000.

Barnett, David. "The Problem of Material Origins," *Noûs*, 39, 2005.

Bennett, Karen. "Spatio-temporal Coincidence and the Grounding Problem," *Philosophical Studies*, 111, 2004.

Berto, Francesco. "Impossible Worlds," *The Stanford Encyclopedia of Philosophy* (Winter 2012 Edition), Edward N. Zalta (ed.), URL = <http://plato.stanford.edu/archives/win2012/entries/impossible-worlds/>.

Bigelow, John. "Presentism and Properties," *Noûs*, Vol. 30, *Supplement: Philosophical Perspectives*, 10, *Metaphysics*, 1996.

Brogaard, Berit. "Sea Battle Semantics," *Philosophical Quarterly*, 58, 2008.

Broad, C. D. *Scientific Thought*, London: Routledge and Kegan Paul, 1923.

Broad, C. D. *The Mind and Its Place in Nature*, London, Kegan Paul, Trench, Trubner & Co., 1925.

Brown, Curtis. "Narrow Mental Content," *The Stanford Encyclopedia of Philosophy (Fall 2011 Edition)*, Edward N. Zalta (ed.), URL = <http://plato.stanford.edu/archives/fall2011/entries/content-narrow/>.

Burge, Tyler. "Individualism and the Mental," *Midwest Studies in Philosophy*, IV, 1979.

Burge, Tyler. "Other Bodies," in Andrew Woodfield (ed.), *Thought and Object*. Oxford University Press, 1982.

Campbell, Keith. *Body and Mind*, New York, 1970.

Caston, Victor. "Epiphenomenalisms, Ancient and Modern," *Philosophical Review*, Vol. 106, No. 3 (July 1997).

Chalmers, David J. *The Conscious Mind*, Oxford University Press, 1996.

Chalmers, David J. "Consciousness and Its Place in Nature," in Stephen P. Stich and Ted A. Warfield, eds. *The Blackwell Guide to the Philosophy of Mind*, Blackwell, 2003.

Chalmers, David J. *Constructing the World*, Oxford University Press, 2012.

Chalmers, David, David Manley, and Ryan Wasserman, eds. *Metametaphysics*, Oxford University Press, 2009.

Chisholm, Roderick. "Identity through Time," in H. Keifer and M. Munitz, eds. *Language, Belief and Metaphysics*, State University of New York Press, 1970.

Chisholm, Roderick. "Which Physical Thing Am I?" in *Metaphysics: The Big Questions*, eds, Peter van Inwagen and Dean Zimmerman, Second Edition, Blackwell Publishing, 2008.

Copeland, B. J., ed. *Logic and Reality: Essays on the Legacy of Arthur Prior*, Oxford University Press, 1996.

Coppock, Paul. "Review of Nathan Salmon, *Reference and Essence*," *Journal of Philosophy*, 81, 1984.

Cortens, Andrew and John O'Leary-Hawthorne. "Towards Ontological Nihilism," *Philosophical Studies*, 79, 1995.

Cottingham, J., R. Stoothoff, and D. Murdoch, trans. *The Philosophical Writings of Descartes*, Cambridge University Press, 1984.

Davidson, Donald. "Knowing One's Own Mind," *Proceedings and Addresses of the American Philosophical Association* (1987).

Davidson, Donald. *Subjective, Intersubjective, Objective,* Oxford University Press, 2001.

Davidson, D. and G. Harman, eds. *Semantics of Natural Language*, Dordrecht, Holland: D. Reidel, 1972.

Dennett, Daniel C. "Beyond Belief," in Andrew Woodfield (ed.), *Thought and Object*. Oxford University Press, 1983.

Descartes, Rene. *The Philosophical Writings of Descartes*, trans. J. Cottingham, R. Stoothoff, and D. Murdoch, Cambridge University Press, 1984.

Divers, John. "Coincidence and Form," *Proceedings of the Aristotelian Society Supplementary Volume* LXXXII, 2008.

Dorr, Cian. *The Simplicity of Everything*, Ph.D. dissertation for Princeton University, 2002.

Ehring, Douglas. *Tropes: Properties, Objects and Mental Causation*, Oxford University Press, 2011.

Fine, Kit. "Compounds and Aggregates," *Noûs*, 28, 1994.

Fine, Kit. "The Non-Identity of a Material Thing and Its Matter," *Mind*, 112, 2003.

Fine, Kit. "In Defense of Three-Dimensionalism," *Journal of Philosophy*, CIII, 2006.

Fine, Kit. "Coincidence and Form," *Proceedings of the Aristotelian Society Supplementary Volume* LXXXII, 2008.

Fodor, Jerry A. *Psychosemantics: The Problem of Meaning in the Philosophy of Mind*, MIT Press, 1987.

Foster, John. *The Case for Idealism*, Routledge & Kegan Paul, London, 1982.

Foster, John. *The Immaterial Self,* Routledge, 1991.

Freeman, Anthony, ed. *Consciousness and its place in nature: does physicalism entail Panpsychism?* Imprint Academic, 2006.

Gale, Richard, ed. *The Blackwell Guide to Metaphysics*, Blackwell, 2002.

Gallois, Andre. "Identity Over Time," *The Stanford Encyclopedia of Philosophy (Summer 2012 Edition)*, Edward N. Zalta (ed.), URL = <http://plato.stanford.edu/archives/sum2012/entries/identity-time/>.

Gibbard, Allan. "Contingent Identity," *Journal of Philosophical Logic*, 4, 1975.

Goff, Philip. "Experiences Don't Sum" in *Consciousness and its place in nature: does physicalism entail Panpsychism?* Anthony Freeman, (ed.), Imprint Academic, 2006.

Goodman, Nelson. *Fact, Fiction and Forecast,* The Athlone Press, England, 1954.

Grimm, Robert H., and D. D. Merrill (eds.), *Contents of Thought.* University of Arizona Press, 1988.

Gunderson, Keith, ed. *Language, Mind and Knowledge: Minnesota Studies in the Philosophy of Science,* vol. 7, Minneapolis: University of Minnesota Press, 1975.

Gupta, Anil. *The Logic of Common Nouns,* Yale University Press, 1980.

Hawley, Katherine. "Temporal Parts," *The Stanford Encyclopedia of Philosophy (Winter 2010 Edition),* Edward N. Zalta (ed.), URL = <http://plato.stanford.edu/archives/win2010/entries/temporal-parts/>.

Hill, Christopher. *Consciousness,* Cambridge University Press, 2009.

Hirsch, Eli. *Dividing Reality,* Oxford University Press, 1993.

Hirsch, Eli. "Against Revisionary Ontology," *Philosophical Topics,* 2002, 30 (1).

Hirsch, Eli. "Ontology and Alternative Languages," in David Chalmers, David Manley and Ryan Wasserman, eds. *Metametaphysics,* Oxford University Press, 2009.

Hirsch, Eli. "Kripke's Argument Against Materialism" in *The Waning of Materialism,* Robert C. Koons and George Bealer, eds. Oxford University Press, 2010.

Hobbes, Thomas. *De Corpore* II.11.7, *The English Works of Thomas Hobbes of Malmsbury,* William Molesworth, ed. London: John Bohn 1839, Volume 1.

Holden, Thomas. *The Architecture of Matter,* Oxford University Press, 2004.

Hughes, Christopher. *Kripke,* Oxford University Press, 2004.

Jackson, Frank. "Epiphenomenal Qualia," *Philosophical Quarterly,* 32, 1982.

Jackson, Frank. "Galen Strawson on Panpsychism" in *Consciousness and its place in nature: does physicalism entail Panpsychism?* Anthony Freeman, ed., Imprint Academic, 2006.

Jackson, Frank and Philip Pettit. "Functionalism and Broad Content," *Mind,* 97, 1988.

Johnston, Mark. "Constitution is Not Identity," *Mind,* 101, 1992.

Keifer, H. and M. Munitz, eds. *Language, Belief and Metaphysics,* State University of New York Press, 1970.

Koons, Robert C. and George Bealer, eds. *The Waning of Materialism,* Oxford University Press, 2010.

Korman, Daniel Z. "Ordinary Objects," *The Stanford Encyclopedia of Philosophy (Winter 2012 Edition),* Edward N. Zalta (ed.), URL = <http://plato.stanford.edu/archives/win2012/entries/ordinary-objects/>.

Kripke, Saul. "Identity and Necessity" in *Identity and Individuation,* M. Munitz, ed., New York University Press, 1971.

Kripke, Saul. "Naming and Necessity" in D. Davidson and G. Harman (eds.), *Semantics of Natural Language* (Dordrecht, Holland: D. Reidel, 1972), pages 254–355.

Kripke, Saul. *Naming and Necessity,* Harvard University Press, 1980.

Kripke, Saul. *Reference and Existence,* Oxford University Press, 2013.

Lau, Joe and Deutsch, Max. "Externalism About Mental Content," *The Stanford Encyclopedia of Philosophy (Winter 2012 Edition),* Edward N. Zalta (ed.), URL = <http://plato.stanford.edu/archives/win2012/entries/content-externalism/>.

Lewis, David. "Counterparts of Persons and their Bodies," *Journal of Philosophy,* 68, 1971.

Lewis, David. "The Paradoxes of Time Travel," *American Philosophical Quarterly,* 13, 1976.

Lewis, David. "Survival and Identity" in *The Identities of Persons*, Amelie Rorty, ed., University of California Press, 1976, pp. 17–40.

Lewis, David. "New Work for a Theory of Universals," *Australasian Journal of Philosophy*, 61, 1983, pp. 343–377.

Lewis, David. *Philosophical Papers, Volume I*, Oxford University Press, 1983.

Lewis, David. *On the Plurality of Worlds*, Blackwell, 1986.

Lewis, David. *Parts of Classes*, Oxford: Blackwell, 1991.

Lewis, David. *Papers in Metaphysics and Epistemology, Volume 2*, Cambridge University Press, 1999.

Locke, John. *An Essay Concerning Human Understanding*, P. H. Nidditch, (ed.), Oxford University Press, 1975.

MacBride, Fraser. "Truthmakers," *The Stanford Encyclopedia of Philosophy* (Spring 2013 Edition), Edward N. Zalta (ed.), forthcoming URL = <http://plato.stanford. edu/archives/spr2013/entries/truthmakers/>.

MacDonald, G. F., ed. *Perception and Identity*, London: The Macmillan Press, 1979.

Markosian, Ned. "Time," *The Stanford Encyclopedia of Philosophy (Winter 2010 Edition)*, Edward N. Zalta (ed.), URL = <http://plato.stanford.edu/archives/win2010/ entries/time/>.

Martin, C. B., "On the Need for Properties: The Road to Pythagoreanism and Back," *Synthese*, 112, 1997.

Martin, C. B., and K. Pfeifer. "Intentionality and the Non-Psychological" *Philosophy and Phenomenological Research*, 46, 1986.

Maudlin, Tim. *Quantum Non-Locality and Relativity: Metaphysical Intimations of Modern Physics*. Oxford: Basil Blackwell, 1994; Second Edition, 2002; Third Edition, 2011.

Maudlin, Tim. *The Metaphysics Within Physics*, Oxford University Press, 2007.

Maudlin, Tim. *Philosophy of Physics: Space and Time*. Princeton University Press, 2012.

Maudlin, Tim. E-mail from Tim Maudlin to Peter Unger of June 6, 2013 at 2:16pm.

Maudlin, Tim. *New Foundations for Physical Geometry: The Theory of Linear Structures*, Oxford University Press, 2014.

McDaniel, Kris. "Extended Simples," *Philosophical Studies*, 133, 2007.

McDowell, John. "Putnam on Mind and Meaning," *Philosophical Topics*, 20, 1992.

McGinn, Colin. "Charity, Interpretation, and Belief," *Journal of Philosophy*, 74, 1977.

Merricks, Trenton. *Objects and Persons*, Oxford University Press, 2001.

Molesworth, William, ed. *The English Works of Thomas Hobbes of Malmsbury*, Volume 1, London: John Bohn, 1839.

Molnar, George. *Powers: A Study in Metaphysics*, Oxford University Press, 2003.

Munitz, M., ed. *Identity and Individuation*, New York University Press, 1971.

Olson, Eric. "Material Coincidence and the Indiscernibility Problem," *Philosophical Quarterly*, 51, 2001.

Olson, Eric. "Personal Identity," *The Stanford Encyclopedia of Philosophy (Winter 2010 Edition)*, Edward N. Zalta (ed.), URL = <http://plato.stanford.edu/archives/ win2010/entries/identity-personal/>.

Papineau, David. *Thinking about Consciousness*, Oxford University Press, 2004.

Parfit, Derek. *Reasons and Persons*, Oxford University Press, 1984.

Parfit, Derek. "Divided Minds and the Nature of Persons," in Colin Blakemore and Susan A. Greenfield (eds.), *Mindwaves*, Oxford: Blackwell Publishing, 1987.

Parfit, Derek. "Why Anything? Why This?" *London Review of Books*, 22 January and 5 February 1998.

Parfit, Derek. *On What Matters*, Oxford University Press, 2011.

Paul, L. A. "The Puzzles of Material Constitution," *Philosophy Compass*, 5, 2010.

Pessin, Andrew, and Sanford Goldberg, eds. *The Twin Earth Chronicles*, M. E. Sharpe, Armonk, New York and London, England, 1996.

Pinker, Stephen. *The Stuff of Thought*, Viking, 2007.

Place, U. T. "Is Consciousness a Brain Process?" *British Journal of Psychology*, Volume 47, 1956.

Prior, A. N. "Thank Goodness That's Over," *Philosophy*, 34, 1959.

Prior, A. N. "The Notion of the Present," *Studium Generale, 23* (New York: Springer-Verlag, Inc.), 1970.

Prior, A. N. "Some Free Thinking about Time," in B. J. Copeland (ed.), *Logic and Reality: Essays on the Legacy of Arthur Prior*, Oxford University Press, 1996.

Putnam, Hilary. "On Properties" in N. Rescher et al. (eds.) *Essays in Honor of Carl G. Hempel*, Dordrecht, Holland, D. Reidel, 1970.

Putnam, Hilary. "Meaning and Reference," *Journal of Philosophy*, 70, 1973.

Putnam, Hilary. "The Meaning of 'Meaning,'" in Hilary Putnam, *Mind, Language and Reality: Philosophical Papers, Volume 2*, Cambridge University Press, 1975.

Putnam, Hilary. *Mind, Language and Reality: Philosophical Papers, Volume 2*, Cambridge University Press, 1975.

Putnam, Hilary. *Mathematics, Matter and Method: Philosophical Papers, Volume 1*, Cambridge University Press, 1979.

Putnam, Hilary. *Reason, Truth and History*, Cambridge University Press, 1981.

Putnam, Hilary. Introduction in *The Twin Earth Chronicles*, Andrew Pessin and Sanford Goldberg eds., M. E. Sharpe, Armonk, New York and London, England, 1996.

Quine, W. V. O. *From a Logical Point of View*, Harvard University Press, 1953.

Quine, W. V. O. *Word and Object*, MIT Press, 1960.

Quine, W. V. O. "Whither Physical Objects," in R. S. Cohen, P. K. Feyerabend and M. W. Wartofsky (eds.), *Essays in Memory of Imre Lakatos*, Dordrecht, Holland: D. Reidel Publishing Company, 1976.

Ramsey, William. "Eliminative Materialism," *The Stanford Encyclopedia of Philosophy (Fall 2012 Edition)*, Edward N. Zalta (ed.), URL = <http://plato.stanford.edu/archives/fall2012/entries/materialism-eliminative/>.

Rescher, N. ed. *Essays in Honor of Carl G. Hempel*, Dordrecht, Holland, D. Reidel, 1970.

Rey, Georges. "The Analytic/Synthetic Distinction," *The Stanford Encyclopedia of Philosophy (Summer 2012 Edition)*, Edward N. Zalta (ed.), URL = <http://plato.stanford.edu/archives/sum2012/entries/analytic-synthetic/>.

Reichenbach, Hans. *The Direction of Time*, M. Reichenbach (ed.), University of California, Press, Berkeley, CA, 1956.

Reichenbach, Hans. *The Philosophy of Space and Time*, transl. M. Reichenbach and J. Freund, Dover, New York, NY, 1958.

Robinson, Dennis. "Re-Identifying Matter," *Philosophical Review*, 81, 1982.

Rorty, Amelie. ed. *The Identities of Persons*, University of California Press, 1976.

Rosen, Gideon. "Abstract Objects," *The Stanford Encyclopedia of Philosophy (Spring 2012 Edition)*, Edward N. Zalta (ed.), URL = <http://plato.stanford.edu/archives/spr2012/entries/abstract-objects/>.

Rosen, Gideon and Cian Dorr. "Composition as a Fiction," *The Blackwell Guide to Metaphysics*, ed. Richard Gale, Blackwell, 2002.

Russell, Bertrand. *The Problems of Philosophy*, Oxford University Press, 1912.

Russell, Bertrand. "On the Experience of Time," *Monist*, 25, 1915.

Russell, Bertrand. *The Analysis of Mind*, G. Allen & Unwin, 1921.

Russell, Bertrand. *Human Knowledge: Its Scope and Limits*, Simon and Schuster, New York, NY, 1948.

Russell, Bertrand. *Mysticism and Logic*, Unwin Books, London, UK, 1963.

Russell, Gillian. "The Analytic/Synthetic Distinction," *Philosophy Compass*, 2/5 (2007).

Russell, Gillian. *Truth in Virtue of Meaning: A Defense of the Analytic/Synthetic Distinction*, Oxford University Press, 2008.

Salmon, Nathan. *Reference and Essence*, Princeton University Press, 1981.

Salmon, Nathan. *Reference and Essence*, Second Edition, Prometheus Books, Amherst, NY, 2005.

Schaffer, Jonathan. "Monism: The Priority of the Whole," *Philosophical Review*, Vol. 119, 2010.

Scheffler, Samuel. *Death and the Afterlife*, Niko Kolodny, ed., Oxford University Press, 2013.

Searle, John R. *Intentionality: An Essay in the Philosophy of Mind*, Cambridge University Press, 1983.

Shoemaker, David. "Personal Identity and Ethics," *The Stanford Encyclopedia of Philosophy (Spring 2012 Edition)*, Edward N. Zalta (ed.), URL = <http://plato.stanford.edu/archives/spr2012/entries/identity-ethics/>.

Shoemaker, Sydney. "Personal Identity and Memory," *Journal of Philosophy*, 56, 1959.

Shoemaker, Sydney. "Immortality and Dualism," in *Reason and Religion*, Stuart C. Brown, ed., Cornell University Press, 1977.

Shoemaker, Sydney. "Personal Identity: A Materialist Account," in Sydney Shoemaker and Richard Swinburne, *Personal Identity*, Oxford: Blackwell, 1984.

Shoemaker, Sydney. *Identity, Cause and Mind: Philosophical Essays*, Expanded Edition, Oxford University Press, 2003.

Shoemaker, Sydney and Richard Swinburne. *Personal Identity*, Oxford: Blackwell, 1984.

Sidelle, Alan. *Necessity, Essence, and Individuation*, Cornell University Press, 1989.

Sidelle, Alan. "Identity and the Identity-like," *Philosophical Topics*, 20, 1992.

Sidelle, Alan. "Rigidity, Ontology and Semantic Structure," *Journal of Philosophy*, 89, 1992.

Sidelle, Alan. "Conventionalism and the Contingency of Conventions," *Noûs*, 43, 2009.

Sidelle, Alan. "Modality and Objects," *Philosophical Quarterly*, 60, 2010.

Sider, Theodore. *Four-Dimensionalism*, Oxford University Press, 2001.

Sider, Theodore. "Quantifiers and Temporal Ontology," *Mind*, 115, 2006.

Sider, Theodore. "Ontological Realism," in David Chalmers, David Manley, and Ryan Wasserman, eds. *Metametaphysics*, Oxford University Press, 2009.

Sider, Theodore, John Hawthorne, and Dean Zimmerman (eds.), *Contemporary Debates in Metaphysics*, Oxford: Basil Blackwell Publishing, 2008.

Skow, Bradford. "Are Shapes Intrinsic?" *Philosophical Studies*, 133, 2007.

Smart, J. J. C. "The River of Time," *Mind*, 58, 1949.

Smart, J. J. C. "Spatialising Time," *Mind*, 64, 1955.

Smart, J. J. C. "Sensations and Brain Processes," *Philosophical Review*, 68, 1958.

Smart, J. J. C. *Philosophy and Scientific Realism*, Routledge and Kegan Paul, London, UK, 1963.

Smart, J. J. C. *Between Science and Philosophy*, Random House, New York, NY, 1968.

Stalnaker, Robert. "On What's in the Head," *Philosophical Perspectives*, 3, 1989.

Steen, Mark. "The Metaphysics of Mass Expressions," *The Stanford Encyclopedia of Philosophy (Winter 2012 Edition)*, Edward N. Zalta (ed.), URL = <http://plato. stanford.edu/archives/win2012/entries/metaphysics-massexpress/>.

Stich, Stephen P., and Ted A. Warfield, eds. *The Blackwell Guide to the Philosophy of Mind*, Blackwell, 2003.

Strawson, Galen. "Realistic Monism," in *Consciousness and its place in nature: does physicalism entail Panpsychism?*, Anthony Freeman, ed., Imprint Academic, 2006.

Strawson, P. F. and Arindam Chakrabarti, eds. *Universals, Concepts and Qualities: New Essays on the Meaning of Predicates*, Ashgate, 2006.

Susskind, Leonard. *The Cosmic Landscape*, Little, Brown and Company, 2005.

Swoyer, Chris and Orilia, Francesco. "Properties," *The Stanford Encyclopedia of Philosophy (Winter 2011 Edition)*, Edward N. Zalta (ed.), URL = <http://plato.stanford.edu/ archives/win2011/entries/properties/>

Thomasson, Amie L. *Fiction and Metaphysics*, Cambridge University Press, 1999.

Thomasson, Amie L. *Ordinary Objects*, Oxford University Press, 2007.

Thomasson, Amie L. "The Controversy over the Existence of Ordinary Objects," *Philosophy Compass*, 5, 2010.

Thomson, Judith Jarvis. "Parthood and Identity Across Time" *Journal of Philosophy*, 80, 1983.

Tienson, John. "Review of Nathan Salmon, *Reference and Essence*," *Journal of Symbolic Logic*, 49, 1984.

Tooley, Michael. *Tense, Time and Causation*, Oxford University Press, 1997.

Unger, Peter. "On Experience and The Development of the Understanding," *American Philosophical Quarterly*, 3, 1966.

Unger, Peter. *Ignorance: A Case for Scepticism*, Oxford University Press, 1975.

Unger, Peter. "I Do Not Exist," in *Perception and Identity*, G. F. MacDonald ed., London: The Macmillan Press, 1979.

Unger, Peter. "There Are No Ordinary Things," *Synthese*, 41, 1979.

Unger, Peter. "Why There Are No People," *Midwest Studies in Philosophy*, IV, 1979.

Unger, Peter. "Skepticism and Nihilism," Noûs, 14, 1980.

Unger, Peter. *Philosophical Relativity*, University of Minnesota Press, 1984, Oxford University Press, 2002.

Unger, Peter. "Minimizing Arbitrariness," *Midwest Studies in Philosophy*, IX, 1984.

Unger, Peter. *Identity, Consciousness and Value*, Oxford University Press, 1990.

Unger, Peter. "The Survival of the Sentient," *Philosophical Perspectives*, 14, 2000.

Unger, Peter. "The Mental Problems of the Many," *Oxford Studies in Metaphysics*, Volume 1, Oxford: Clarendon Press, 2004.

Unger, Peter. *All the Power in the World*, Oxford University Press, 2006.

Unger, Peter. *Philosophical Papers, Volume 1*, Oxford University Press, 2006.

Unger, Peter. *Philosophical Papers, Volume 2*, Oxford University Press, 2006.

Unger, Peter. "Reply to James Van Cleve," *Philosophy and Phenomenological Research*, Volume 80: 2, 2010.

Van Inwagen, Peter. "When Are Objects Parts?" in James Tomberlin (ed.), *Philosophical Perspectives 1: Metaphysics*, Ridgeview, 1987.

Van Inwagen, Peter. *Material Beings*, Cornell University Press, 1990.

Van Inwagen, Peter. *Metaphysics*, Second Edition, Westview Press, 2002.

Van Inwagen, Peter. *Metaphysics*, Third Edition, Westview Press, 2009.

van Inwagen, Peter, ed. *Time and Cause*, Dordrecht, Holland, D. Reidel, 1980.

van Inwagen, Peter and Dean Zimmerman, eds. *Metaphysics: The Big Questions*, Basil Blackwell Publishing, 1998.

van Inwagen, Peter and Dean Zimmerman, eds. *Metaphysics: The Big Questions*, Second Edition, Blackwell Publishing, 2008.

Varzi, Achille. "Mereology," *The Stanford Encyclopedia of Philosophy (Winter 2012 Edition)*, Edward N. Zalta (ed.), URL = <http://plato.stanford.edu/archives/win2012/entries/mereology/>.

Yablo, Stephen. "Identity, Essence and Indiscernibility" *Journal of Philosophy*, LXXXIV, 1987.

Wasserman, Ryan. "Material Constitution," *The Stanford Encyclopedia of Philosophy* (Summer 2013 Edition), Edward N. Zalta (ed.), URL = <http://plato.stanford.edu/archives/sum2013/entries/material-constitution/>.

Weatherson, Brian and Marshall, Dan. "Intrinsic vs. Extrinsic Properties," *The Stanford Encyclopedia of Philosophy* (Spring 2013 Edition), Edward N. Zalta (ed.), forthcoming URL = <http://plato.stanford.edu/archives/spr2013/entries/intrinsic-extrinsic/>.

Williams, Donald C. "The Myth of Passage," *Journal of Philosophy*, 48, 1951.

Williams, Donald C. "On the Elements of Being," *Review of Metaphysics*, 7, 1953.

Woodfield, Andrew, ed. *Thought and Object*. Oxford University Press, 1982.

Yagisawa, Takashi. "Possible Objects," *The Stanford Encyclopedia of Philosophy (Winter 2009 Edition)*, Edward N. Zalta (ed.), URL = <http://plato.stanford.edu/archives/win2009/entries/possible-objects/>.

Zimmerman, Dean. "Temporary Intrinsics and Presentism," in Peter van Inwagen and Dean Zimmerman (eds.), *Metaphysics: The Big Questions*, (Oxford: Basil Blackwell Publishing, 1998.

Zimmerman, Dean. "The Privileged Present: Defending an 'A-Theory' of Time," in Theodore Sider, John Hawthorne and Dean Zimmerman (eds.), *Contemporary Debates in Metaphysics*, Oxford: Basil Blackwell Publishing, 2008.

Zimmerman, Dean. "From Property Dualism to Substance Dualism," *Proceedings of the Aristotelian Society, Supplementary Volume*, LXXXIV, 2010.

INDEX

CPSIA information can be obtained
at www.ICGtesting.com
Printed in the USA
BVOW09s0251150817
492074BV00002B/7/P